D1049824

Command and Persuade

Command and Persuade

Crime, Law, and the State across History

Peter Baldwin

The MIT Press
Cambridge, Massachusetts
London, England

The MIT Press would like to thank the anonymous peer reviewers who provided comments on drafts of this book. The generous work of academic experts is essential for establishing the authority and quality of our publications. We acknowledge with gratitude the contributions of these otherwise uncredited readers.

This book was set in ITC Stone Serif and ITC Stone Sans by Westchester Publishing Services. Printed and bound in the United States of America

Library of Congress Cataloging-in-Publication Data

Names: Baldwin, Peter, 1956- author.
Title: Command and persuade : crime, law, and the state across history / Peter Baldwin.
Description: Cambridge, Massachusetts : The MIT Press, [2021] | Includes bibliographical references and index.
Identifiers: LCCN 2020017932 | ISBN 9780262045629 (hardcover)
Subjects: LCSH: Crime—History. | Punishment—History. | Criminal law—History. | Criminal justice, Administration of—History.
Classification: LCC HV6251 .B4273 2021 | DDC 364.9—dc23
LC record available at https://lccn.loc.gov/2020017932

10 9 8 7 6 5 4 3 2 1

For Lisbet,
love of my life

Contents

Introduction: Crime and the State through the Ages

Of the state's many tasks, none is more crucial than security. To protect us against foreign enemies, we have the military. Against domestic unrest, violence, and crime, the police and judicial system are the first line of defense. Despite declining rates of offending, fear of crime dominates modern politics—egged on by sensationalist media and politicians of all stripes hoping to appear tough-minded. Under President Bill Clinton and Prime Minister Tony Blair, even the center-Left parties in the United States and Britain joined the hard-on-crime bandwagon.[1] The last two US presidential campaigns have rung out with dog-whistle appeals to law and order. Public surveys routinely identify crime as among citizens' most pressing concerns. Yet at the same time we live in a world that is by any measure better ordered, less violent, and more peaceful than any in human history. Even accounting for the carnage of the twentieth century's world wars, violence has nosedived over the past two millennia.[2] Compared to the bloodthirsty sacrifices of prehistoric states or the unthrottled savagery of absolutist executions, modern democratic regimes police us with a velvet glove—with more subtlety and ever less force. They discipline us into adopting civilized behavior through the institutions that shape our psyches and instincts to become model citizens—kindergartens, schools, armies, hospitals, workplaces, and, only as a last resort, prisons. Despite the attention lavished on prisons, fines—a mere slap on the wallet—have become the most common sanction in most nations outside the United States and the former East Bloc.

Most of us pass our lives avoiding serious contact with the law. Even today, with prisons bursting, less than 5 percent of Americans on average will ever spend time there. In other nations, far fewer do. The chances of dying of either cancer or heart disease—the kinds of eventualities we all reckon with—are together eight times greater. For the average middle-class, mainstream citizen, years pass without meeting uniformed officers face-to-face, and policing is something that happens at society's margins: to minorities, the disenfranchised, addicted, poor, and outcast. Nevertheless, the sense that crime is serious and growing hangs heavy in the air.

Punishment may have been moderated since the days of absolutist excess, but has crime really diminished? With the birth of criminology in the late nineteenth century, social science developed a stake in sounding the alarm over inexorably advancing criminality, thus buffing its own sheen. Not only now-forgotten alarmists such as Cesare Lombroso and Max Nordau but even the great sociologist Émile Durkheim assumed that crime advanced in tandem with civilization.[3] We are heirs to this cultural pessimism. Whether it is true that crime has grown over time depends on how the question is framed. In some respects, crime has indeed increased. Using the penal code to help regulate the new technology of motor vehicles created the now single-broadest interface between citizen and police—indeed, the large majority of all contacts.[4] The decision to criminalize inebriants has likely occasioned the second-largest source of prosecutions, with the prohibition of first alcohol and then other substances. American drug arrests climbed twelvefold from 1965 to the end of the century.[5]

These are, however, crimes we inflict on ourselves. They are acts that society has decided to consider and treat as penal transgressions but that could equally well have been dealt with by other means—or not at all. Smuggling was widespread in eighteenth-century England because high tariffs, imposed by a state with few other sources of tax revenue, made it a lucrative enterprise. And it was hard to combat because smugglers were popular, offering the average person cut-rate goods. When England made primary schooling compulsory in 1870, almost one hundred thousand parents of truants were hauled before courts in the law's first year.[6] Had crime really increased? Or had it merely been redefined upwards? To lament today that criminality is skyrocketing because prisons are crammed with pushers and users says less about our narcotics problem than about how we have dealt with it. It is rather like worrying that Armageddon must be nigh because the executioner is busy hanging more infidels and apostates than ever.

For other offenses, ones that are indisputably the sort intended for the penal code, reliable statistical answers are hard to come by. Definitions of crime have varied, as has victims' willingness to report. Not every transgression exists objectively out there as an evident offense, even though all crimes are obviously defined in and by the penal code. Novel technologies have created new crimes where once there were none—phishing, say. The most commonly committed crime today is the robocall—180 million daily in the US, half of all phone calls.[7] Awash, as we are, in a cornucopia of pilferable objects, little wonder that theft is up. Yet stealing an unguarded cell phone in a metropolitan bus terminal is a different act than larceny of a firearm or other prized singular possession from a home in a seventeenth-century village—especially considering how buffered we are from the consequences of theft by our hypertrophied insurance industry. Whether victims of rapes are willing to report them and whether such violations are legally actionable have varied dramatically. Acts once illegal (adultery) are no longer, whereas formerly tolerated behaviors (spousal abuse) have become prosecutable. Whether such shape-shifting offenses have increased or diminished is hard to track.

Homicide—indisputable and hard to conceal—is therefore the most studied crime. Here we see a dramatic decline. In Europe, where the data over long periods are available, killings plummeted from one hundred per one hundred thousand inhabitants in the Middle

Ages to one per one hundred thousand by the early twentieth century.[8] This bears restating: over the past five centuries, average rates of homicide have declined a hundredfold. Today's English are one percent as likely to be killed as Chaucer's contemporaries. During the early period of frontier violence, the American colonies of the Northeast had rates as bad as those in medieval Europe, which then declined starting in the early seventeenth century. In the mid-eighteenth and again in the early nineteenth century, US homicide rates were comparable to the rest of the Western world. In the nineteenth century, they then rose again. The slave-holding South and the frontier West suffered much higher levels, though the West was long so sparsely populated that its statistics may be misleading.[9]

This happy decline of killings holds over the long run. But in the long term, as Keynes famously lamented, we are all dead. Political debates are not framed against centuries-long secular oscillations but against what happened last year. Crime and then imprisonment did rise during the final decades of the twentieth century as a blip on these larger and longer downward trends. Such temporary reversals of the overall decline have occurred before—for example, in Sweden between the 1790s and the 1840s and in England from the 1580s to the 1610s.[10] The larger trend eventually reasserted itself, as it has again today in the United States. By the early 1990s, crime rates had levelled off and once again began to decline. In the United States, the numbers not only of murder but also of almost all other offenses have drifted downward over the past three decades, with a small uptick for some crimes again starting in 2016.[11] The cost of massive incarceration has made itself felt, and Americans now debate how to reverse three-strikes rules and other avenues of overfilling prisons.

Paradoxically, we feel beleaguered by crime at the very moment in history when mainstream citizens objectively have the least to fear. Why? If we take a long historical approach to how the state has dealt with crime, a few conclusions emerge. First, the state took its own sweet time accepting as its task what we now count among its primary functions—fighting crime and adjudicating disputes. For most of recorded history, crime was left to civil society's members to sort among themselves. If lucky, they did so via informal mechanisms of mediation, paying or accepting restitution for harm done. But if they arrived at no understanding, the disputants took vengeance and fought blood feuds—sometimes stretching over centuries. The Greeks and Romans had the rudiments of a judicial and policing system, but it had to be rebuilt after each of these empires fell. An ancient and continuous empire, China had law and courts, but even it outsourced most legwork to civil society—holding kin and village communities responsible for their members' conduct rather than intervening directly. By the European Middle Ages, administering justice had gradually become the state's remit again. The law codes of the sixteenth century bristled with regulations of urban citizens' behavior, conduct, and deportment, but they were enforced haphazardly by whatever muscle the administrations of the day could muster. Policing, in the modern sense of a uniformed state authority seeking to apprehend and punish misdeeds, had to await the nineteenth century.

The state came late to this crucial function. But once it had accepted its mandate, it never looked back. Dealing with crime became and has remained one of its core tasks. By the sixteenth century, absolutist monarchs tortured their errant subjects in orgies of agony to frighten and thus deter the crowd in the town square. Yet such brutality could not continue. Moralists worried about its coarsening effect on the audience, realists questioned its effectiveness. When first built, prisons were intended as an admittedly costly but also merciful and potentially reformatory alternative to the noose and the blade.

A second conclusion is that the state eventually moderated its punishments—not because it pulled its punches but because it no longer had to be brutal. It was not the state's humanitarian inclinations that prompted a softening of sanctions but its ever-growing power. Dismembering criminals in the town square was the equivalent of smoke signals in the era before the telegraph: the best the authorities could do. The state had to shout loudly to convey its deterrent threat. As executions were eventually hidden behind walls starting in the eighteenth century, they remained a deterrent. The public did not have to witness them to fear them. The modern state no longer had to swagger in all its grisly brutality. It governed ever more subtly—detecting, prosecuting, punishing, and eventually even preventing crime, all without rattling sabers.

Multiplying its capabilities, the state grew better able to detect and punish transgression. Now that it was more reliably able to punish, its sanctions no longer had to be severe. The Enlightenment philosophes rightly argued that predictability deterred more than ferocity. During the early modern era, the death penalty was reserved for violent crimes and in most nations eventually abolished. Starting in the eighteenth century, torture was officially banned. Offenders were imprisoned rather than banished, executed, or otherwise directly pained. Even prison was eventually regarded as harsh, and alternatives found for misdemeanants and juveniles. Today, the most common punishment is the fine. That marks just how little overtly violent policing and punishing are required of the modern state. Most citizens are law-abiding and prosperous enough to atone through property and not their bodies.

The state moderated punishment from a position of strength. The more it knew about us, the more lenient it could be. The better its information, the stronger and more pervasive its forces, the more effectively and therefore benignly it could police. But the state's growing power was only half the story. Civil society also increasingly policed itself, leaving the state with fewer overt duties. This is the other half of the equation and the third conclusion. Kin, family, community, and church have long been the forces most immediately molding our behavior, especially in the millennia before the state, too, piled into the act. Civil society's role in controlling its members' conduct is obvious. But this function has expanded. The civilizing process, to use Norbert Elias's term, means we have gradually internalized the behavioral restrictions that were once impressed on us from the outside by social and governmental institutions.[12] The reward for self-control has been to be spared the state's impositions. Democracy rests on self-discipline.

Elias myopically saw this self-discipline as a process that began in fifteenth-century Europe, not one that was more ancient, ongoing, and widespread. And it was a bitter irony that he published a theory of cultural self-discipline in 1939, on the eve of Europe's descent into barbarism. Nonetheless, Elias identified a crucial motor force in history's *longue durée*. Largely ignoring the dark sides of repressing instinct, he sociologized Freud's theory of sublimation, examining on the level of society as a whole how dark and primal impulses that otherwise mar human interaction were channeled into acceptable behaviors. Even allowing for the twentieth century's genocidal barbarities and the persistence of assault, rape, and murder, a broad scholarly consensus concurs that our lives today are far less blighted by interpersonal violence than ever before. The state has largely disarmed us and it polices our interactions. But it would be farfetched to explain this pacification solely in terms of our fear of legal sanction were we to act on our untamed aggressive impulses. A more plausible explanation is that we have curbed our propensity to violence by elevating our thresholds of arousal and anger.

We have learned to control ourselves in ways that would have surprised even our recent forebears. Instead of the burping, belching, farting, spitting, sneezing, snorting, indiscriminately defecating creatures of the early modern era, we are now a people who fastidiously control and suppress our bodily eruptions—more Vulcan than Viking. Consider venereal disease as an example of how we have learned to master our bodies in ways now considered second nature. Strictly speaking, there is no such thing as a solely sexually transmitted disease. Illnesses spread through sexual contact can equally well be passed along via other blood or mucous-membrane interactions. In the eighteenth-century European countryside, syphilis propagated via daily interactions that today are rare: sharing the use of filthy household implements, spitting in or licking the eye to remove sties, sleeping many to a bed, and following earthy child-minding practices such as sucking babies' penises to calm them, licking clean their runny noses, and prechewing their food.[13] It is because of our changed habits that syphilis now spreads primarily via sex. Sex is the only infectious route that remains.

In sexual terms, too, we control ourselves better. The sexual stimuli surrounding us today, whether from advertising, styles of dress and deportment, or easy access to pornography, would have strained our ancestors' self-control. In the 1840s, with the first trains, etiquette manuals advised young female travelers to hold pins between their lips as coaches entered tunnels and darkness descended, thus preventing stolen kisses from men in the carriages. It was customary for bedroom doors to be locked. A common trope of novels was the sexual signal of leaving them unfastened.[14] Trying the door to find out was considered normal. Today, stolen kisses are actionable behavior, building codes frown on bedroom locks for safety reasons, and a houseguest rattling door handles might well not be invited back.

Modern society sees itself as sexually less tight-laced than the Victorians, but in fact we have adopted thresholds of male arousal higher than just a century ago. We are insouciant with respect to sex because we mutually agree not to act on stimuli that people earlier would have found difficult to resist. A sense of how things have changed can be had from observing the uncomfortable juxtaposition of differing thresholds of sexual arousal in the multicultural metropolis. While the local males in Scandinavian or German parks resist tumescence as efficiently as hard-baked nudists, tourists from abroad eagerly gawk at and photograph the seminude female sunbathers there. The mixed saunas and nudist beaches, riverbanks, and parks of central and northern Europe mark an unusual degree of self-mastery.[15]

Or consider the automobile. We tolerate untold slaughter on the roads—as many deaths every year in the United States as during the entire Vietnam War. And yet, if anything, it is a miracle that the figure is not many times that. Our everyday assumption that we will arrive safely at our destination is based in part on the road infrastructure provided by government and on regulated automotive safety—brakes, seatbelts, lights. It is the outcome, too, of policing errant transportation behavior such as speeding, tailgating, and road rage. But, above all, thanks is due to the average driver's extraordinary self-control. We navigate pathways plied by what might otherwise be assumed to be inconsiderate, intemperate, distracted, and inattentive fellow voyagers who are maneuvering two tons of steel at high speeds within inches of our vital organs but who are also, in fact, almost as good as we are at reining in their animal spirits behind the wheel and remaining focused, attentive, and alert.

To govern self-mastering citizens is a different task than reigning over short-tempered, choleric, irritable, dyspeptic, impulsive early modern humans. Much of the behavioral control needed for dense urban life has in effect been shifted from the state to civil society. What remains in statutory hands requires less violence and force. Indeed, the modern state trains its powers largely on those citizens least likely to rein themselves in—the marginal, the poor, and other outsiders. The rest of us are policed only gently. Institutions have shaped our psyches and instincts to become model citizens.

Even so, the state has not stepped down. The behaviors considered offenses have changed dramatically over the past millennium. Many actions that once were illegal are now either private matters (such as most sexual behavior, what we wear, where we live, what we imbibe) or regulated by codes other than the penal (employment, public health, zoning, etc.). Yet many other acts have now become illegal. New crimes respond to new technologies (securities fraud, insider trading), but we have also invented novel transgressions. Inchoate offenses, for example, make conspiring, planning, and intending to commit an offense in themselves crimes. The total sum of the prohibited has grown continuously. More laws now govern our behavior than ever before. And they encompass a broader variety of acts. Indeed, they go beyond acts to criminalize our intentions, thoughts, and proclivities.

In other words, and this is the book's final conclusion, at the same time as we have become more civilized, the state has extended its formal reach, multiplying law and punishing us for transgressions. We have learned to delay gratification, moderate our impulses, resist our instincts, and act with a restraint, forbearance, and self-abnegation unknown in the early modern era. Yet the more we discipline ourselves, the more law the state trains on us. One might have expected a trade-off between self-restraint and the law's impositions. We now master ourselves. So why do we need more formal proscription? Should not the state's legal apparatus be withering away?

On the contrary, seen over a long historical sweep, law and self-discipline have run in tandem: not only more discipline and socialization into correct conduct but also more law forbidding more behaviors and probing further into our minds and intentions. We undergo an increasingly insistent process of socialization to become functioning members of a specialized, sophisticated, dense, complex, metropolitan civilization. Yet we also have an ever-growing law that governs our actions from above. We are caught more and more in an unforgiving forcefield between expanding formal prohibitions and stricter requirements for personal mastery. The law plays a growing role in socializing us into the conduct required by modern society. Although most of us still keep up with this behavioral arms race, those who cannot fall further behind. Our jails are filled with the dispossessed and the marginal. The stark inequalities of modern society are becoming behavioral, not just economic.

The state seems to have no intention of relinquishing its power to forbid and punish, relying instead on informal social control. We may now be socialized into proper behavior, but the realm of the illegal continues to grow. The state not only trains on us the institutions of social discipline but also maintains and expands the law as a powerful tool of socialization. Our prisons are full of social outcasts. But for the rest of us, too, the law hovers ever present. As more acts are forbidden, as the state also delves into our thoughts, law continuously defines the parameters of allowable behavior. It restricts the scope of other arenas of socialization where we learn to rein ourselves in. The state is the socializer of last resort for the dispossessed and defines the terrain on which the rest of us are schooled into acceptable behavior, narrowing evermore the turf on which we are expected to control ourselves.

Chapter 1
Crime's Ever-Expanding Universe

Who has prosecuted crime and what they were pursuing have changed dramatically over the course of human history. Gods and kin groups were the first enforcers; religious edict and customary precepts preceded statute and law. But the state eventually took up crime and its suppression as important tasks. The behaviors outlawed have also changed. Acts once forbidden are no longer, but others that were once legally indifferent are now pursued. Whether the total number of offenses has increased is harder to discern. Nonetheless, it seems that even though different acts are now illegal, there are more crimes on the books today than ever.

Crime and authority are joined at the hip. Without official stricture, no crime. As dirt is matter out of place, weeds unwanted plants, and deviance behavior we disapprove of, so crime is action at odds with the law. Yet it took most of human development for this to become true. Of course, law is more than statute. Long before legal codes, custom and religious precept wove fabrics of regulation. Law, as Durkheim pointed out, was formulated only when custom began to lose its hold.[1] Custom had no badges, truncheons, or penitentiaries, but it unleashed collective violence against those who snubbed its strictures. Norms were enforced communally long before laws formalized such obligations.[2]

At first, the supernatural policed this world, whether as mere sorcery or the divine itself. Gods punished offenses before kings did. Four thousand years ago, Egypt's Middle Kingdom brought forth a concept of hell peopled by sinners. Individuals faced judgment, and punishment became a matter for both this and the next life.[3] Justice in this world is rare. No wonder humanity's longing for a fair shake demanded immortality of the soul and an afterlife. If death were but extinction, or if postmortem life were a morally neutral twilight zone, then evil would rarely be punished, or virtue rewarded.[4] As Socrates says in Plato's *Phaedo*, if death were a separation from everything, it would be a godsend for the wicked.[5] But postmortem punishment could be only retributive, at its worst an eternal suffering for a momentary lapse in the mortal world. If punishment after death were to be just, much less be able to reform or deter, it needed reincarnation or at least some sort of ascendable hierarchy of life after death.[6]

The ancient Chinese did not see law as connected to the divine, though this view may have been as due to polytheism's inherent morcellization of divine power as to any lack of feeling for the supernatural.[7] Conversely, Egyptian pharaohs were powerful enough to feel no need for a source of law beyond themselves. Yet most other major ancient civilizations did connect law and the supernatural: Mesopotamians, Jews, Indians, Greeks, Romans, Muslims, Incas, Aztecs, and, of course, Christians.[8] Their earliest injunctions were religious, or at least supernatural, enforced by higher powers. Taboos were rules imposed by transcendent forces, sins their violation.[9] When there were identifiable gods, sometimes they did the enforcing. In Greece and Rome, those struck by lightning were denied regular burials because they were assumed to have been punished directly by Zeus as perjurers. Since he handled matters, there was no need for human law on the subject.[10]

Yet it remained unclear why Greek gods bothered to punish mortals. They did enforce order and balance, especially curbing our excesses of vengeance. But they acted for the same reason as their human subjects: anger at being wronged, not enforcement of code or principle. Why any specific offenders were punished, for what, and even that they had been brought to heel—all that was unclear. In early societies, everything happened for a reason—spirits or gods offended, witchcraft invoked, magic gone wrong—nothing by chance.[11] Offenders whom something ill befell therefore presumed they were being chastised.[12] Gods' favorite tool for punishing humans was the weather, which could often be hard to divine.[13] Sin and crime were largely fused since both violated divine will. In the deep past, humans thus found themselves transgressing against norms nowhere spelled out, only vaguely apprehended, and often violated by the gods themselves. Punishments were meted out by (or on behalf of) higher forces. Before the state existed, sacrilege and heresy were the primal trespasses, the defying of transcendent powers. But all crimes, whether an attack on God, such as blasphemy, or on humans, such as murder, ultimately wronged the divinity by violating its commandments or wishes. All crimes were public wrongs, and all were sins.

Yahweh was a lawgiver and enforcer, laying waste to followers who disobeyed him, threatening them with misery sevenfold their transgressions.[14] Violating his covenant with his tribe was sin. Hebrew law was divine because it was God's word. When Cain slew Abel, God, in the absence of any other humans than their parents, was judge, jury, and prosecutor, and the ground where blood had spilled was the only witness.[15] Among the ancient Greeks, law was ultimately given by the gods, with codes submitted to the oracle at Delphi for approval.[16] Yet divine law was also seen, as among the Romans too, as distinct from the gods, an abstract realm of rationality and natural order. Though formulated by the gods, it was also independent of them, not merely an expression of their will.[17] Christianity, in turn, was equally abstract and universal but more magnanimous. It regarded sin in terms of mortal weakness and divine forgiveness, Christ having died to save humans from their own evil. Penitence, not punishment, brought the sinner back into the fold.[18]

Supernatural edicts did not govern all human action in antiquity. Worldly law regulated much everyday behavior even as the divinities watched over what concerned them. But the overlap between edict and law was far greater than it later became. Secular and religious offenses were eventually distinguished, enforced respectively by state and church—though some cultures, notably Islam, continued to conflate the two.[19] The state came to punish acts that violated secular law, which—as the gods were pushed aside—began to define the only enforceable public sanctions. Human law forbade many previously religious offenses: incest, slander, libel, usury, and perjury.[20] Of 119 offenses punished by execution in Sussex in the early seventeenth century, all but two were transgressions of the Ten Commandments.[21] Outside a few theocracies, purely religious offenses were eventually relegated to the private sphere, punished not at all or only within voluntary communities of faith. Yet even the most secular modern societies keep blasphemy and sacrilege on the books as exceptions to this rule—though mainly to ensure public order, not to enforce theology.

The state thus came late to enforcing law and chastising offenders. Even law formulated in statute was in place before the state did any punishing, whether among the ancient Jews or on ninth-century Iceland. Replacing the gods, the state eventually got to decide what crime was and what transgressions were punishable. Yet if the state is five thousand years old, assuming this power took it more than four millennia.

Except for the transgressions that affected it directly—treason, sacrilege—the state lacked until recently the will or ability to keep order and enforce norms. For most of history, disputes were resolved communally among the directly interested parties. Self-help was how conflict was dealt with, as it remains today among sovereign nations. When people harmed each other, kin groups righted the balance, shedding blood as vengeance or transferring value as compensation. Such private justice only gradually fell under the state's remit. A judicial system, with the state punishing violations of collective norms, was achieved incipiently by the ancient Greeks, Romans, and Chinese, but not again in the West until the Middle Ages. The state eventually defined crime by laying down the law, and it provided the means to deal with it: surveilling, policing, trying, sentencing, and punishing. As the state took on such tasks, broad changes followed. Punishing shifted from resolving conflicts between kin groups to publicly imposing generalized norms whose violation offended the whole collectivity. Rather than relying on civil society's self-help, with families resolving disputes, the state enforced the communal interest by facing down transgression itself. Crimes became public concerns. Victims were no longer allowed to ignore an offense, much less settle it themselves. Since the state represented society as the ultimate victim, whether and how to prosecute became its decision.

Even then, the road stretched out ahead. Echoes of private justice from the deep past could long be heard. In the 1790s, 80 percent of criminal cases in England were still initiated by the victims, who also bore the costs. In the latter half of the eighteenth century, courts finally began paying the expenses of bringing successful felony prosecutions.[22] Not until 1879 did the English establish a national system of public prosecutors, and it took another century for it to be made effective. Even today, prosecutions are sometimes handled privately in Britain. Shoplifters, for example, are often left to retailers to pursue.[23] Authorities elsewhere enjoy a wide range of discretion whether to prosecute or not, ranging from extensive in Japan to almost nonexistent in Finland.[24] In Japan and Germany, some crimes remain prosecutable only if the victim asks for it. Such *Antragsdelikte* in Germany include breach of the peace, domestic theft, exhibitionism, and poaching fish.[25] Islamic law allows the families of murder victims to forgive killers—often for payment—and thus spare them death. And the role of the family, once the main enforcer, still shines through in contemporary disputes over how publicly to prosecute spousal violence, marital rape, and child abuse. But, on the whole, the state now leads in dealing with crime.

As the state came to monopolize punishment, it resented private parties poaching on its turf. Having once been the only means of redress, self-help was eventually forbidden, though vigilantism and other informal means of victims enforcing justice on their own have not vanished even today. Few developments in the history of the law and the state have been more important than the emerging concept of public offenses—the idea that crimes harm not just their immediate victims but also society as a whole. Torts (private damages) were gradually distinguished from crimes (public offenses). Criminal law, or punishable offenses against society, emerged as distinct from civil law, where private parties restituted harms. The oldest mention of this distinction dates perhaps from Roman law in 194 CE, though the Greeks were familiar with it.[26]

As the state came to dominate law's enforcement, punishments grew more moderate and subtle. Two major changes were at work. With emergence of representative government—initially republicanism and eventually democracy—laws no longer needed to be enforced by drastic means. Only despotic governments required severe punishments, Montesquieu observed. In republics (he included also monarchies), citizens were impelled to behave as much by honor, virtue, and fear of disapproval as by punishment.[27] Subjects had to be coerced, but citizens motivated themselves to obey. He might have added that the nature of law also changed, making it less burdensome to follow. Laws emerged from decisions taken ultimately by citizens who, obeying them, conformed to what they had mandated their representatives to pass. Breaking the law now came closer to the self-inflicted harm that Immanuel Kant and G. W. F. Hegel discussed: thieves whose own right to property was undermined by their refusal to respect that of others.[28] Described most generally, laws came to be self-imposed, and obedience was self-will. Legitimate law was voluntarily obeyed.[29] Those regimes that most deviated from this participatory ideal—autocracies and totalitarianisms—also imposed the harshest punishments.[30]

Yet the lesser need for force when there is a political consensus was not the whole story. Yes, the state and society grew evermore symbiotic as political participation widened into democracy. But the state also grew increasingly able to enforce the measures resulting from this participatory process. The more powerful the state became, the less it had to flex its muscles.

In this process, the tools at the state's disposal changed dramatically. The savage brutality of early punishments gave way to a subtler but also more regularized and broader enforcement. Spectacular inflictions of pain in public were less needed to deter as the authorities developed new means of anticipating and preventing crime. Torture was no longer necessary to extract testimony once the burden of proof imposed by Roman law loosened in the late seventeenth century to allow conviction without two eyewitnesses or a confession. Subjects could now be punished on less evidence, as they were in those countries that did not insist on such a high standard in the first place, such as England. Banishment, mutilation, death, and other cheap, cruel punishments were less urgently required once society marshaled the resources to afford the comparative mildness of incarceration. Capital punishment was less pressing once the state successfully suppressed private vengeance. The state, in sum, no longer needed to show who was boss.

A state able to assert its might only intermittently had to hope for powerful deterrent effects from spectacular public demonstrations of it. At 1800, Britain's criminal code was startlingly savage. Well more than two hundred capital offenses were enforced, mainly for forms of theft and often for trivial acts. Yet most violations were without consequence. Offenders went uncaught; if caught, unprosecuted; if prosecuted, unconvicted; if convicted, unhanged. In sixteenth-century England, only 10 percent of those convicted of capital crimes were actually hanged. Even in the first half of the twentieth century, 45 percent of men and 90 percent of women condemned to die had their sentences reduced to life in prison.[31]

Harsh punishments could be imposed only sporadically on anything other than abject subjects without provoking resistance.[32] In any case, such severity absorbed resources otherwise available for other forms of enforcement.[33] The harsher the punishment, the less it served an everyday function.

In contrast, the powerful omnipresent modern state hums away in the background, ensuring compliance less through manifest displays than by regular, predictable, moderate sanctions that it reinforces by a spectrum of behavioral encouragements—all rendered more effective by its subjects' voluntary compliance. The stronger the state, the less draconian it needs to be. The law makes clear what transgressors can expect, and the judiciary metes it out.[34] Moderate, foreseeable law enforcement was a core demand of the Enlightenment philosophes, seeking to reform the early modern state's grisly, sporadic flailing about. The English Reform Act of 1835 illustrates the point: it abolished the death penalty for many of the two hundred existing capital offenses and simultaneously extended to all municipal boroughs the system of policing that London had introduced in 1829.[35] The law became both more lenient and better enforced. As the English state reduced the number of capital crimes in the nineteenth century, its conviction rates rose. Juries no longer resisted condemning defendants to their deserts when the balance between offense and sanction seemed just.[36] Appearing merciful, the state in fact punished more citizens. It was nicer and yet more effective.

Yet more than rationality and humanitarianism were at stake here. Michel Foucault's mantra was certainly true: the point was to punish better, not less.[37] But better also meant less or at least less savagely. The contemporary state's ability to relinquish much of the armamentarium of sanctions demonstrated its growing effectiveness. It once brandished a panoply of pain: branding, flogging, mutilation, banishment, shame, death. Today it relies largely on prison and fines. That fines are the most common sanction shows how moderate punishments have become. In earlier eras, almost no defendant pled guilty, most were acquitted, and the convicted sometimes were hanged. The law's grasp was intermittent, localized, and sanguinary. Today it is constant, broad gauged, and comparatively low key. In early nineteenth-century England, a quarter of defendants were acquitted.[38] Today, many fewer are. Since prosecutors have done their homework, because offenders are no longer threatened with disproportionately harsh punishments, and because plea bargains grease the rails of justice, most accused plead guilty.[39] Almost 80 percent of defendants before British magistrates' courts enter guilty pleas, as do more than 90 percent of felony offenders in the United States.[40] And of those tried, the vast majority are convicted. The 92 percent conviction rate achieved in the United States compares favorably with the 95 percent under Joseph Stalin's trials in the late 1930s.[41]

Yet It Continues

And yet, for all the state's subtlety, for all the cooperation between the penal code and other means the state uses to modify citizens' conduct (school, market, workplace, family), the number and reach of its laws, the range of the formal and explicit codex of behavioral prescription, continue to expand. The state has not withered away. Quite the contrary, it has grown. It is often noted that were every law punctiliously enforced, all citizens would be criminals.[42] The Kinsey report in 1948 argued that laws criminalizing sexual acts then considered deviant made 95 percent of the (male) population potential criminals.[43] According to a police rule of thumb, a motorist followed for three blocks will end up committing a violation. Already in the 1930s, it was estimated that traffic laws—strictly observed—were violated 2.5 million times daily in the United States.[44] Assuming no recidivism, every single man, woman, and child thus crossed the law seven times annually. Few actions do not trespass one law or another.[45]

Whether the range of criminalized behavior has narrowed or widened is hard to say, but it certainly has changed. As actions once outlawed have been removed from the penal code, new ones have been added. The number of laws in the penal code has massively increased. True, many statutes duplicate or add only nuance to prohibitions already on the books. And many earlier laws accrete, rarely being removed. But even as some acts have been decriminalized, the range of offenses has also expanded. The US republic enforced half-a-dozen federal crimes at its birth, a couple hundred in the late nineteenth century, and more than four thousand today. The federal penal code has expanded massively, from eight pages in the 1875 version to almost nine hundred in the 2018 edition.[46] Illinois has ten types of kidnapping offenses, thirty sex offenses, and forty-eight assault crimes. Virginia has twelve forms of arson and attempted arson, sixteen kinds of larceny and receiving of stolen goods, and seventeen types of trespass crimes.[47] Including regulations, not just penal statute, would add another ten thousand crimes. Perhaps some three hundred thousand US regulations are criminally enforceable.[48]

At first, all manner of actions were punished—crimes, torts, sins, and immorality, not to mention acts that today fall under health, labor, safety, zoning, economic, housing, and many other regulations. Crimes punishable by death in early colonial America included idolatry, witchcraft, blasphemy, bestiality, sodomy, and adultery, most of which are no longer even offenses. Usury was once considered a sin, violating natural and religious law and punishable by death.[49] Today it underpins banking—though only covertly in the Islamic world. Apostacy was once a capital crime in many religions, including Christianity, but is so today only in Islam, where it is not decreed in the Quran.[50] Only gradually were things sorted out. Sin, as violation of God's commands, was left to the church as religion separated from the state. It retains a sense of a collective, enduring transgression rather than of an individual moral lapse, as when slavery is described as a stain that needs cleansing.[51] Penal law once governed ideological and theological beliefs as well as countless behaviors that we now consider personal choices but that once were the province of sartorial, sexual, sumptuary, or consumption codes. With the Enlightenment, however, authority's role was understood as preserving order, not morality. Only acts that directly harmed others were to be banned. Matters of conscience and private belief ceased being the state's concern. Moral wrongs fell to individuals and their conscience, only rarely did they remain the remit of the penal code. Disputes over individual harms were now sorted by the interested parties within the civil law.

The state also spawned other regulatory instruments to police many activities that were once covered by the penal code: workplace and food safety, public health, labor relations, unemployment, zoning, competition and monopolies, construction, trade, opening hours, and so forth. What we regard as social problems today were earlier handled by criminal law. Vagabonds, vagrants, beggars, Roma, prostitutes, demobilized soldiers, and other marginals, if away from the local community responsible for their upkeep, were shooed off elsewhere by penal sanctions.[52] Credit markets were policed by debt slavery and debtor's prison.[53] The law allowed creditors to target debtors' bodies, not their property. Debtors used to outnumber conventional criminals by far in prison, threefold in early nineteenth-century America. In Islamic jurisprudence, wherein corporal punishments were the primary coercive mechanism, unpaid debt was the predominant basis for imprisonment.[54] The aim was coercive—forcing debtors to pay what they owed. Sentences were indeterminate—until payment or creditors were otherwise satisfied.[55] Modern bankruptcy—with a proper discharge of debt—emerged from reform of this self-contradictory system in the early eighteenth century. Ultimately, it was back-stopped by jail, but—barring fraud—most cases came to be resolved without resort to prison.[56] The problem was moved out of the penal code and into economic regulation.

The actions left behind in the penal code are what we now think of as crimes—murder, theft, fraud, and the like. Offenses in this narrow modern sense have become the province of the state alone: they are acts that not only leave behind victims but also are seen to harm society as a whole. As crime's focus narrowed, many public concerns were relegated to the private sphere. Sartorial rules once punished Romans who wore clothes in imperial purple, Aztec commoners in sandals, and Elizabethan Englishmen sporting felt hats on Sundays.[57] Working on the Sabbath was forbidden, as was sacrilege and drunkenness. With a few exceptions, owning more than one loom was a penal offense in Tudor England.[58] Medieval Iceland and England punished parents who failed to baptize their infants; Austria sanctioned mothers who took babies into their beds at night.[59] Being out and about at night without pressing reason was once illegal, as was sleeping during the day.[60]

The ancient Greeks made stealing the clothes off a person in public (*lōpodusia*) a crime for which one could justly be killed on the spot.[61] In early modern Holland, undressing a child was singled out as a crime—not for the reasons we might imagine, but because the cost of clothing made it worth stealing.[62] Once a broad variety of sexual behaviors was forbidden, including homosexuality, sodomy, fornication, and adultery. Today, only necrophilia, bestiality (with exceptions), and pedophilia are uniformly illegal. Incest was once defined expansively, criminalizing marriage with a broad range of family relations, including in-laws. Until 1907, British widowers could not marry their former wives' sisters. For another fourteen years, deceased brothers' widows remained forbidden fruit. Adultery was once a capital crime, one of the three inviolable sins in the Bible, along with idolatry and murder. By the early nineteenth century, though, Bavaria punished it only if the harmed party insisted.[63] Today adultery has largely vanished from the penal code—outside the remaining theocracies and eighteen US states.[64]

Once illegal and immoral, suicide is now considered a mental-health issue. Abortion, once punished as a variant of homicide, is increasingly treated as a regulatory problem. Euthanasia may be moving in this direction, too. Formerly a pressing public concern, blasphemy has been privatized. The initiative to prosecute it must come from a private party, claiming offense—if, indeed, the act can be pursued at all.[65]

Witchcraft these days is at most a public nuisance (Santería and other practices that include animal slaughter). As a crime, it has fallen victim not only to the general removal of religion from the state's purview but also to a widespread skepticism of its efficacy.[66] Sorcerers are no longer charged with attempted murder however intensely they incant their spells and curses.[67] Indeed, in India, where village witches are still persecuted in their communities, accusations of witchcraft have been criminalized.[68] But the Catholic Church continues to fear the dark arts and trains priests in exorcism.[69] The Bavarian police code had special provisions against occult activities. And in Canada, hucksters who prey on the psychologically vulnerable can still be convicted for practicing dark arts.[70] Cursing, once an invocation of occult powers and thus a serious affront, is now just a harmless annoyance. Scolding, which used to be a major disturbance of the peace, no longer counts as a transgression.[71] Public drunkenness has moved from being the reason for a majority of arrests in the United States in the 1940s and 1950s to causing a small fraction of that today.[72] Public disorders that earlier led to arrest (begging, public sleeping, vagrancy) have been (partly) decriminalized.[73] Slander, libel, and defamation became harder to commit as our ancient honor cultures, with their easily raised insults, faded.[74] (Digital technologies, however, facilitate such offenses, and the rates of their commission appear to be rising, but at the same time they are making slander increasingly archaic.[75])

Crime Expands

Yet this narrowing of offenses has not freed us of the state's impositions. Quite the contrary. Durkheim rightly pointed to how countless behaviors had been shifted from the penal law's purview, but his anticipation that this move signaled the decline and obsolescence of the criminal code and repressive law in modern, complex societies was wide of the mark.[76] In other respects, crimes defined in the law have massively expanded. They have enlarged in response to the growing complexity of human activity, giving us many more ways of harming each other, as well as in response to how the law itself has become increasingly sophisticated and elaborate. In the autocracies and totalitarianisms, this relationship was painfully obvious. Not only did these systems multiply law in response to industrialized technologies, as in all political systems, but also many behaviors that in liberal democracies were transferred to the private realm here remained public and actionable. Fragile and paranoid, illegitimate regimes inherently expanded the opportunities to offend. But even liberal states, with their robust private spheres, have enlarged what is illegal and punishable. States have expanded illegality explicitly and consciously when faced with states of exception, feeling especially beleaguered. From Henry VIII's massive inflation of treasonable prosecutions to the English suspension of habeas corpus during the French Revolution to the Weimar Republic's raft of emergency laws and on to current terrorism-inspired legislation extending the state's surveillance and powers—regimes anticipating crisis have amplified the law's reach.[77]

Liberal democracies, even in their everyday, peacetime functioning, have extended the law's compass, criminalizing ever wider swaths of behavior. Assault and larceny made up 85 percent of all ordinary crimes reported in preindustrial Europe. In seventeenth- and eighteenth-century Massachusetts, fornication was the single most commonly punished offense.[78] Since then, the number and variety of crimes prosecuted, or the ways of contravening the law, have increased dramatically.

Start with the simplest. New technologies have created behaviors just waiting to be punished. Counterfeiting was not actionable before currency came into widespread use, or check bouncing before banks, not to mention money laundering. And of course the crimes associated with money have changed in tune with technologies of value transfer, from shaving the edges off coins to holding up customers at ATMs and committing digital bank fraud. Public urination could not be actionable before indoor plumbing. Shoplifting became more common as the goods were no longer hidden behind the merchant's counter. Mail fraud attended on the post. Towns policed who could inhabit them in the Middle Ages, but violations of immigration law awaited the development of the nation-state. Before locks became widespread, everyone carried their valuables with them, and theft was largely petty larceny of consumables.[79] Pickpocketing increased with urbanization.[80] The invention of anesthesia brought great blessing, but it also created a class of drugs whose misuse was then made actionable. Traffic policing started as early as the seventeenth century. Furious driving of horse-drawn carriages and even driving without reins were infractions in the nineteenth century, but that today's police would spend much of its time regulating cars was not foreseeable.[81] A large section of the Virginia criminal code covers railroad crimes, which may not be much enforced any longer. But the offenses associated with automobiles (carjacking, joyriding, auto theft) have mushroomed. Driving back and forth in the same area (cruising or "repetitive unnecessary driving") has gone from an innocent pleasure to a crime.[82] Indeed, traffic policing has become a gateway for authority's continued ingress into everyday life. Exercising their regulatory powers over automobiles—stopping cars for moving violations, expired registration stickers, or broken running lights or at inebriation checkpoints—police have assumed expansive abilities to detain and investigate any member of the motorized public.[83]

New business models have led to new crimes: forgery, insider trading, mail-order peculation, breach of trust, wire fraud. The emergence of corporations created new legal personae, which, at least in the Anglo-American realm, could be held liable for infractions of the law. More laws criminalize business behavior, with fewer due-process restrictions, than target the poor.[84] The growth of bureaucracy spawned the vast field of white-collar crime. As a total of federal criminal prosecutions in the United States, such offenses rose from 8 percent in 1970 to 24 percent in 1983. Fraud has continued to evolve and expand, chasing the possibilities for deception permitted by ever new and more sophisticated business practices.[85] The administrative complexity of modern polities allowed opportunities for leverage, corruption, and blackmail that had to be recognized before they could be outlawed. Only in 1863 did the French forbid extorting hush money.[86] Price fixing and other abuses of monopolies, tax and securities fraud, and foreign bribery all eventually were attended by possible prison sentences.[87] Because the United States developed an equities market earlier than most nations, insider trading became a crime there by the 1930s, but not until later elsewhere. To regulate potentially dangerous consumer products, whether baby blankets, ski slopes, or airplanes, liability law mushroomed in the late twentieth century with an orgy of lawsuits forcing manufacturers to internalize the costs of safety.[88]

Formerly private relations have been made public and actionable. We smirk at the minute behavioral regulation of the early modern codes—forbidding sloth and adultery, for example. Yet though sexual relations have been largely turned over to the private sphere, the modern state has again begun poaching on the same turf. The Mann Act, passed in the United States in 1910, allowed federal prosecutors to track down extramarital sex throughout the nation.[89] Although that ability was reined in by the 1980s, sexual relationships with and among the young have become increasingly policed. Raising the legal age of consent expanded the scope of statutory rape.[90] Sexual relations in the workplace have come to be regulated by law, not by custom. Even among equals—students at university, say—relations are a matter of statute. No longer regarded as a *Kavaliersdelikt*, a petty offense, rape has been prosecuted more frequently and seriously.[91] Its scope has expanded, too. What used to require force and was widely regarded as properly a crime only if a demonstrably virtuous woman was hurt became an offense no matter who the victim. It also became premised on lack of consent, a much wider definition that did not necessarily involve violence. Acts that once would have been considered sexual coercion or assault, such as oral or anal penetration, came to be classified as rape proper.[92] Even wives—long regarded as their husband's property—eventually could be considered to have been raped. Other acts of forced sex were specified in evermore painstaking detail. Oral copulation, for example, was finely parsed and considered a crime if achieved by immediate threats of violence, threats for the future, or threats against others than the victim; if perpetrated on an unconscious or intoxicated person; if presented fraudulently as serving a professional purpose; if initiated and achieved by someone pretending to be known to the victim or by other artifice; or if ordered by someone pretending to be a or invoking public authority.[93]

Behaviors once relegated to the private sphere as part of personal morality have remerged as public concerns. Rather than being outlawed as immoral, they are now punished as harmful. Once considered immoral, pornography is pursued because it objectifies women, encourages rape, and helps spread venereal disease.[94] Where prostitution has been outlawed, similar arguments apply to it. In the 1960s and 1970s, Sweden not only tolerated prostitution but also actively encouraged sex workers to organize, pay taxes, and service the handicapped, old, and others who could not otherwise find erotic satisfaction on their own. In recent years, however, it has clamped down once again on commercial sex as exploiting women and encouraging trafficking. Zero-tolerance policing has used neighborhood blight as the motive to turn once barely actionable behaviors (loitering, public urination, graffiti, panhandling) into offenses. Public drunkenness has been a long-standing problem, but not until 1873 did it become a crime in France.[95] The wave of drug legislation that swept the twentieth century rendered illegal behaviors that were otherwise widespread and popular. Homelessness may not precisely have been criminalized, but its effects have often been left to the police to deal with.[96]

The paterfamilias's remit has narrowed, with the state extending its wing over many functions that were once the family's purview. Women and children were emancipated into full legal status directly subject to the state, not to the husband and father. Domestic violence against children and spouses became a crime, no longer acceptable or considered somehow natural patriarchal conduct.[97] Tolerated by the Romans, infanticide became prosecuted by the Christian Church for moral reasons, then later by states as they expanded their claims to define who merited legal protection as subjects.[98] Already in the sixteenth century, births in England were registered, signaling official interest in the infant citizen.[99] Schooling was eventually made compulsory, and parents were punished for their children's truancy. Vaccinating children, too, was required in the mid-nineteenth century as more parental responsibilities became legal obligations. As the state narrowed the parameters of acceptable parenting, removal of children from families became an everyday occurrence. Victorian parents would have been surprised to discover that their great-great-grandchildren could lose custody of their offspring for emotional neglect. Today, leaving children unsupervised for almost any time, under any circumstances, is criminalized.[100] Lowering the age at which minors can be tried as adults further limited the family's remit.[101]

As the definition of property vastly expanded, so too did theft. Removing customary gleaning, pasturing, and other collective rights on common lands in the eighteenth century made those rural poor who continued what had once been legitimate activities now guilty of larceny. Property rights were continuously created in new realms, especially the ethereal. Not until the early eighteenth century did it count as stealing to palm off someone else's ideas or even exact words as your own. But after that, countless violations of intellectual property began to be enforced.[102] The rights of persons to themselves expanded the harms others could do them. Unprotected by free-speech rights, classical age satirists in Greece did not attack their contemporaries for fear of being prosecuted for defamation.[103] Starting in the sixteenth century, slanderous, libelous, and other kinds of attacks on reputation became actionable in common law. Developing rights of personality and publicity allowed prosecution of those who would harm (or use features of) others' individuality.[104] As globalization and multiculturalism increasingly juxtaposed different religions, blasphemy laws that once seemed to be fading with secularization and indifference have been revived.[105]

Legal personalities, those with actionable rights, have also multiplied. Whether unborn children could be plaintiffs and, if so, starting at which point in gestation varied with a given jurisdiction's abortion laws. Singling out attacks on pregnant women that caused damage to their fetuses enlarged or at least deepened the pool of potential plaintiffs.[106] Making femicide a crime in itself (fifteen countries and counting), with especially stringent penalties, increased the number of women victims. The expanding roster of licensed professions (now 18 percent of the US labor force) gave more practitioners a stake in having their uncertified colleagues prosecuted.[107] The status of who or what could be a plaintiff expanded beyond the human, too. Trusts, corporations, municipalities, ships, nation-states, and other inanimate entities have received enforceable rights. Animals used to be pursued for harms they may have committed, but those who hurt them are now held liable.[108] Our relationship to animals more generally has become evermore the law's business, whether forbidding the keeping of pigs in big cities in the nineteenth century or determining which kinds of dogs are valid pets.[109] And nature itself—rivers and forests, for example—has become a plaintiff.[110]

Technological, social, and economic developments may have driven the law to respond by expanding, but the legal system itself also unfolded luxuriously under its own steam. Long-forbidden actions grew like Jack's beanstalk. As a specific form of theft, embezzlement emerged in English law in 1799, arising from a case where a bank clerk pocketed a customer's cash while noting it as deposited to the account-holder's credit. The customer was no worse off, but the bank had suffered a loss that existing law could not touch since the money had never actually been in its possession. From such humble beginnings, embezzlement expanded from a transgression that only those in certain specific relationships of trust could commit (a crime of betrayal) to a general offense applicable to anyone entrusted with property.[111]

From the sixteenth century on, perjury grew to mirror the increasing use of oaths, now sworn by witnesses to deliver the certain testimony that earlier had been ensured by ordeals and torture.[112] Oaths ceased being reliant on adherence to a particular or, indeed, any religion. At least in the common law nations, they became more commonplace elements of bureaucratic practice, not just reserved for courtrooms. Tax declarations, for example, commonly require an oath to their accuracy. With no less than eighteen sections of the US Code now dealing with perjury, more citizens have become potentially liable to it.[113] In the 1970s and 1980s, fraud expanded to cover circumstances where nothing was foregone or any laws violated, but where victims had nonetheless lost an "intangible right," such as the duty of public officials to provide honest and faithful services. From a narrowly defined action not applicable even when someone kept property entrusted to them, larceny has enlarged and can now be committed even by actions once seen as innocent, such as keeping money paid out to one by mistake. Bribery expanded in the 1990s to encompass also the lesser offense of receiving illegal gratuities.[114]

Laws once intended for specific purposes have grown to include a smorgasbord of behaviors. *Grober Unfug* (disorderly conduct), defined in eighteenth-century Germany for use against noisome street urchins, was extended to include everything from carpet beating after-hours to press offenses to Social Democrats' distribution of pamphlets.[115] Treason broadened from collusion not just with enemy nations but also with nonstate actors, such as terrorists.[116] The right to free speech is certainly more generous now than in the era when most criticism of the authorities was actionable, not to mention the restrictions imposed by blasphemy. But in other ways its limits have stiffened with additional restrictions ranging from hate-speech prohibitions to the broader definition of libel.[117] The right of public assembly has narrowed. The authorities tolerate less chaos than was allowed in eighteenth-century demonstrations and protests. Our earlier right of spontaneous assembly today requires all manner of permits and permissions, applied for beforehand.[118]

Even within their narrowed remit, modern penal codes still punish a panoply of behaviors, ceding little ground to the broad police powers of the early modern period. US states criminalize many acts that few citizens contemplate in the first place: selling untested sparklers, exhibiting deformed animals, leaving animal carcasses on public roads, cheating at cards, provoking dogs to fight, selling perfume as a beverage, training bears to wrestle, and frightening pigeons away from devices meant to capture them. Forbidding the removal of fire-safety tags from mattresses is often given as an example of allegedly excessive criminalization.[119] The concept of police power expressed the early modern state's expansive authority over its subjects but is usually thought to have been superseded by the rule of law with the rise of the modern *Rechtsstaat*, a state based on law. In fact, far from being anachronistic, such police powers continue in parallel to the penal code, now sometimes in the guise of administrative or regulatory law.[120]

Criminalizing proxy behaviors to get indirectly at underlying acts has bloated the penal code. Driving underage, driving while intoxicated, driving too fast, driving with defective equipment, and so forth are all separate crimes (implicit endangerment offenses) intended to punish dangerous locomotion without giving traffic police carte blanche to haul any motorist into court.[121] It took years after automobiles became common for speed limits to be instituted at all since motorists insisted that police worry instead about unsafe—not necessarily fast—driving.[122] That was but a blip on a broader development that has criminalized largely all automotive behavior. With driverless cars and the elimination of noisome human wetware from the transportation process, perhaps such laws will fade. Prohibiting proxy behaviors also motivates laws that forbid the possession of drug paraphernalia, tools useful in burglaries, or knives suitable for attacks.

Because penal codes are hemmed in by due process, authorities have also marshaled civil and other noncriminal codes to prosecute offenses. In California, almost as many acts have been criminalized outside the penal code as within it, including school principals failing to use required textbooks, teachers neglecting to bring first-aid kits on school outings, and citizens gambling on the results of elections. In Minnesota, 83 percent of recent crimes created by statute have been codified outside the penal code, 91 percent in Oklahoma.[123] The civil law requires only a lower standard of evidence, allowing greater flexibility and prosecutorial follow-through. Civil law is routinely used against offenses such as insider trading, terrorism, and pedophilia. Store owners, for example, can prosecute via criminal law for the return of stolen items. Using civil recovery laws, they can also collect up to five times their value.[124] Civil asset forfeiture—the confiscation of property allegedly involved in crime—has long historical roots in English law, not to mention biblical precedence. As of the 1980s, it was put to use again. In effect, it punishes while enforcing, inflicting drastic sanctions on those not yet convicted of crimes, such as drug selling or money laundering, while forcing them to prove their innocence, bereft of the penal code's protections.[125] More generally, authority has informally expanded the limits of its executory powers by punishing outside the law. Extrastatutory harassment, including death, is an unacknowledged weapon in the state's arsenal. Thousands have been killed in pacifying the favelas of Rio de Janeiro or in fighting drug use in the Philippines. In El Salvador, ten times as many criminals as police die in gunfire with each other, a figure that suggests routinized extralegal executions. In 2015, forty times as many US residents were killed by police than legally executed.[126]

Law has begun to punish formerly legal behaviors. Victimless-crime laws ban perceived moral failings even though arguably no one is harmed. Knowing of a possible crime without reporting it has become an offense in its own right. Misprision of treason, or failure to report plots or political crimes, was criminalized in late eighteenth-century Europe.[127] That offense has now expanded. Crimes of omission or the absence of action would once have seemed a contradiction in terms. Today, not reporting a crime or failing to prevent children in your care from committing one is actionable.[128] Good Samaritan laws punish those who do not help others in distress. Similarly, not protecting someone under our care has become actionable in Anglo-American common law. Such expansion of law's remit is clear in the common law nations, where protecting against harm is the basis of the penal code. In the civil law tradition, the tendency is, if anything, stronger. In Germany, the criminal law protects legal goods (*Rechtsgüter*), which cover—however much the concept harm may have recently expanded—an even wider spectrum: everything from traffic safety to the environment and international peace.[129]

More generally, the law has also expanded its remit by moving from acts to thoughts. It once punished only deeds already committed, hoping for deterrence by inflicting public agonies on perpetrators. It has since begun enforcing law preventively—anticipating and punishing action not yet undertaken. Intent is thus penalized much like act. New thought crimes have emerged, even as formerly criminalized ideas such as blasphemy and sacrilege became legal. In the seventeenth century, courts began punishing defendants not for the crime itself but simply for being suspected of having committed it (*Verdachtsstrafe*). Since the offense was a lesser one, sentencing was adjusted accordingly to something short of death.[130] Once endangering (posing a risk but not yet actualizing it) became a crime in its own right, the mere possibility of harm became actionable.[131] Inchoate crimes, which target intent, in turn massively expanded the range of outlawed actions. Attempts, conspiracy, and solicitation were added to their underlying acts as new crimes, thus quadrupling the number of substantive offenses. Merely talking about committing a crime, even if nothing came of it, could be punishable. If a transgression did result, conspiracy was added as an additional offense to the act itself. More than a quarter of all federal criminal prosecutions in the US now involve conspiracy.[132] In the United Kingdom, incitement (the British version of solicitation) blossomed into the new wide-ranging offenses of encouraging or assisting crime.[133] People were sent to prison for second-order inchoate crimes, such as conspiracy to solicit. To gather tools usable in burglary could be prosecuted as an attempt to attempt to attempt to commit larceny—three levels of offense.[134] Hate-crime laws increased the penalties for offenses motivated by a dislike of protected categories of citizens. They thus added a punitive premium for the emotion that sparked what would otherwise have been a commonplace transgression.[135]

Along with actual perpetrators, accessories and accomplices to crimes have increasingly been held liable, too—those who participated only vicariously or indirectly in the offense or knew of it without reporting it. Who counts as an accomplice has steadily broadened. Sometimes the intent of this expansion has been to spare perpetrators. In postwar Germany, various levels of accomplice liability were carefully parsed to relieve Nazi criminals of harsh sentences.[136] But in general the intent has been to rope in a larger circle of offenders. A horrific court case from sixteenth-century England punished the husband who tried to kill his wife with a poisoned apple but saw his daughter die instead as the treat was passed along to her. But the friend who had counseled him on how to murder and supplied the poison went free since the child's death had not been his intent.[137] Such fine distinctions were quickly subsumed. Already during the French Revolution, accomplices were punished as severely as those whom they helped offend. Up to this point, English law had not allowed prosecution of accessories except where the main offender had also been convicted, but as of 1848 they could be charged independently and, indeed, as principals.[138]

Jurisprudence has formulated a spectrum of complicity: direct and indirect participants, solicitors and facilitators, as well as accessories before and after the fact—those who obstructed justice, those who received stolen property, and the like.[139] An ecosystem of criminality developed around the offense. Accomplices could be punished even for trivial and tangential assistance: preparing food for the offender, holding his child, lending a smock.[140] In the common law nations, many counted as accomplices because all killings committed during a felony were deemed murders. Thus, in 2007 a man was jailed for life because friends used his car to commit a murder-robbery while he was asleep somewhere else, dead drunk.[141] Those who threatened but not did commit harm began to be punished. So were those who did nothing. When second offenses flowed naturally from the first, an accomplice to the initial crime automatically counted as participating in the latter.[142] Outlawing conspiracy allowed the authorities to prosecute groups for doing something that if undertaken individually would have been legal. French civil servants were welcome to resign individually but not in groups. A solitary walk was unobjectionable; many simultaneous walks became an illegal demonstration. Two people would be much more leniently sentenced if each one sold marijuana individually than if they hawked the same amount together.[143]

Law has expanded over the past many centuries. America has begun debating overcriminalization, the bloating of the penal code, and the metastasization of criminal punishments throughout statute.[144] If nothing else, multiplying and dispersing sanctions blur the moral message of right and wrong that law should convey. Indeed, they impede citizens from even knowing what rules they are expected to follow.[145] The survey here shows that evermore law is a long and broad development, not a problem only in contemporary America. Already in the first century BCE, Cicero complained of more law, less justice. Nor has the march toward more laws and more behaviors punished been uniform and inexorable. Occasional reverses have been booked. Early in the new millennium, the US narrowed the definition of government corruption, making it harder to prosecute.[146] White-collar crime—insider trading, for example—may have been circumscribed and therefore prosecuted less tirelessly in recent years.[147] Nonetheless, the overall direction is unmistakable.

This trend poses a paradox. Levels of violence and disorder have dropped dramatically over the past several centuries. The state has monopolized violence, building an evermore efficient apparatus of enforcement and punishment. And citizens have ever better controlled themselves, self-regulating their psyches as required by modern metropolitan life. Yet the number of crimes they are potentially liable for has increased. Even as the state has become a more subtle, regular, and ubiquitous sanctioner, even as citizens are evermore socialized into correct conduct, the number of laws and the range of behaviors they formally punish have also mushroomed. The need for law seemingly declined, yet its amount and sway increased. Why? Before we can answer that, we need an idea of what held true before the state began throwing its weight about.

Chapter 2
Crime before the State

Transgressions were punished long before the state assumed that task as part of its monopoly on violence. Gods were arguably the first police, though they were often indifferent and distracted enforcers. Besides smiting sinners directly, divinities also worked in tandem with the customary regulation that kin groups enforced on their members. Once sin and crime began to be distinguished, the former fell to the church, the latter to the state. But this change took a long time, and only well into the early modern era did the state start performing its role unchallenged by either church or kin.

Before states began to issue statute as the rulebook for their subjects, customary law and social norms formulated guidelines to live by. But above them were the edicts of the gods, binding on all believers. The earliest clan societies, uniting several kin groups, lived in fear of violating the precepts of supernatural entities, which were made known through the intermediation of shamans, witches, sorcerers, and other go-betweens. As societies enlarged, growing more complex, they united multifarious groups among whom less could be taken for granted. Accompanying this growing complexity—whether as cause or effect is hotly debated—religions emerged to enforce codes of conduct, from which morality eventually evolved. This molding of human behavior occurred either at the behest of moralizing high gods, such as the Abrahamic divinity or Allah, or by creeds that dispensed broad supernatural punishment through means such as karma in Buddhism. Policed by omniscient, omnipotent big gods, these complex societies developed cooperative habits that gave them advantages over less-sociable ones.[1]

God's role in law enforcement raised issues. Technically speaking, divinities had only limited sanctions at their disposal. If the consequences of transgression were overly specified, gods risked being unmasked as shooting blanks. Bad weather, illness, death, and other—in any case—likely events were the most plausible indicators of divine wrath, but their import was often hard to fathom. Nor is it clear why omniscient and omnipotent gods needed mortal justice. Often they did not, instead intervening directly to punish offenders. So annoying did the gods of Mesopotamia find humanity's constant din that they struck back.[2] Roman gods punished oath breaking directly. In sixth-century Gaul, perjurers were paralyzed, their right hand raised in oath, or they contracted gangrene in the offending limb or were struck dumb as God brought justice to earth.[3]

When the gods intervened directly, they also undermined human justice, and temporal authorities risked being cut out of the loop. A sincere confession, which in the early medieval Latin Church could be given to anyone, not just to priests, might set things right with God, eliminating mortal sanction. Twelfth-century Europeans pondered whether if sinners contritely confessed to gain absolution, a subsequent ordeal would exonerate them. A fornicating fisherman from Utrecht, for example, fearing he would be accused at the next synod, confessed to his priest. Having resolved to sin no more, he carried the hot iron without being burned. Repentant offenders, who had settled their affairs with God, were often miraculously saved from the gallows.[4]

The nature of their divinity influenced gods' relation to the law. Though the earliest gods demanded and appreciated tribute, they were often uninterested in making humans toe some moral line.[5] Polytheistic religions' confused command structure muddled who issued laws on what. Chinese gods could work against human purpose.

Greek gods countermanded each other, making unclear or contradictory demands. Gods often paid humankind no mind. Sometimes human prayer could compel them to react.[6] Other times secondary divinities (such as Prometheus) sided with humans and were punished for it. Pantheists worshipped gods whose influence was local and circumscribed. How did humans then know what divinities expected of them? The hierarchy of gods meant a ranking of edicts, too—some more pressing than others. Multiple near-omnipotent beings—such as the Greek gods—acting on no discernable basis of justice or morality unsettled their subjects.[7] Monotheism helped clarify matters. A single power issued commands binding on all members of the faith everywhere. But even such pronouncements required interpretation and could be mutually incompatible. Matthew contradicted and revised Moses's commandments.[8] And the Christian God could also be petty, or so humans thought. Renaissance Italians assumed that God, just like everyone else, pursued vendettas.[9]

Hoping to assert their exclusive connection to the supernatural, religions branded their rivals as mere sorcery. Secular authorities, too, mercilessly persecuted witches and sorcerers, competing claimants to power who had failed to assume the aura and trappings of true divinity. In Hammurabi's code (Babylonia, ca. 1750 BCE), the worst crimes were witchcraft and offenses against the administration of justice and religion. The Chinese penal codes hounded sorcerers.[10] Monotheism accentuated this tendency. Though enlisting miracles to persuade converts, Judaism and Christianity distanced themselves from the welter of competing doctrines that used what they dismissed as mere magic. Two forces reigned supreme, God and Satan, with only secondary room for demons, saints, wonder rabbis, and holy objects. The medieval church persecuted witchcraft and sorcery as pagan delusions, even as it considered that its own miracles proved God's existence.[11] Eventually it handed off punishing witchcraft to secular courts—in England, Scotland, and

Germany as of the sixteenth century. Heretics, too, were turned over to the secular powers for execution.[12]

The Jews' covenant with God promised them prosperity so long as they followed it or disaster if they did not.[13] In Leviticus, God detailed what he would inflict on disobedient Israelites: plague, famine, savage beasts, cannibalism.[14] The Old Testament forbade immorality, blasphemy, murder, usury, witchcraft, theft, seduction, bestiality, assassination, manslaughter, assault, kidnap, slander, bribery, perjury, treason, and riot. It treated all largely as offenses against God. Death was the punishment for many offenses, though it was often unclear whether God or human authority was to do the enforcing.[15] Those who afflicted widows and orphans, however, could be sure that God himself would kill them with a sword as punishment.[16] In the ninth century, Charlemagne invoked divine law to warn murderers that both God and he would punish them. As late as the sixteenth century, Martin Luther insisted that authorities enforcing the law acted on God's behalf.[17]

The gods punished directly but also at human behest, as when magistrates at Teos and Sparta invoked curses at offenders.[18] Oedipus pronounced a curse against the unknown killer of Laius, but, as it turned out, Oedipus himself was that killer. Roman law distinguished between *ius* (profane criminal law) and *fas* (sacral criminal law), the latter dealt with by the pontifex, the chief high priest. Early Germanic law codes may have distinguished between sacral offenses (violating the peace of gods and people alike by arson, homicide, fornication, and so forth) and profane, less-serious breaches of the peace of the people.[19] In the first century CE, Tacitus wrote that German priests, standing in for the gods, punished warriors.[20] Sacrifices—including of humans, as among the Egyptians, Nordics, Germans, and Incas—revealed how eagerly believers aimed to please their gods.[21] For Aztec gods, human blood was their nourishment.[22] Hopes of propitiating angry gods long remained a motivating force. The country-wide fast ordered in England in 1832 to atone for whatever sins had caused that year's cholera epidemic was only one such national self-flagellation that the British Parliament hoped would catch the Almighty's eye.[23]

Besides intervening in this world, gods could threaten punishment in the next. Only some religions imagined the afterlife as atonement. The Aztec and related Mesoamerican religions foresaw nothing but total extinction for all, good and bad.[24] For non-Axial religions—immanentist, not transcendent—which often saw postmortem life as but an extension of this one, no great shift was required. But Hinduism and Buddhism, where the law of karma punished this life's wrongs in the next incarnation, may have enjoyed a deterrent bounce.[25] Though the ancient Chinese did not link law to the divine, the Confucian ruler represented the gods, and good and evil were expected to be treated accordingly in heaven.[26] The Christian doctrine of purgatory, completed in the thirteenth century, added a wrinkle by blurring the gulf between the now and the thereafter. Sinners gained a second chance at postmortem redemption through penance. Others could intervene on their behalf through indulgences, the shaving of time off purgatory through monetary payments rather than through good works.[27] Excommunication—exclusion from the religious community—also blurred now and later. Hell loomed eventually, but in life, too, the excommunicant became a nonperson, the living dead. For believers, eternal damnation was an incomparably worse sanction than anything meted out on earth—not to mention the certainty of being found out. To the medieval mind, God's omniscience penetrated far deeper than Jeremy Bentham's panopticon, and straying led to consequences more severe than any possible secular punishment.[28]

Secular lawgivers piggybacked on transcendent sanctions, trading off between this- and other-worldly punishment. The church's power over the next life added muscle to its punishments in the here and now. Wihtred, the eighth-century king of Kent, threatened foreigners who refused Christian marriage with banishment, the

English with excommunication.[29] Physical punishment was costly, so invoking supernatural policing relieved hard-pressed secular authorities. Sanction after death may have lessened the state's need for immediate intervention, while its subjects' belief in strictures in the afterlife encouraged obedience in this one. Assuming that past attitudes can be extrapolated from the reactions of today's undergraduates in psychology lab experiments, humans who believed that gods would eventually punish transgressions felt less impelled to ensure that offenders received their just deserts now. And stern gods were better regulators of behavior than kind ones. A belief in hell's transcendent accounting, punishing sinners who had sidestepped this-worldly retribution, may thus have helped the state.[30]

At first, most offenses were sins, contraventions of divine will. Gods were therefore the ones to mete out sanctions. Vengeance is mine, the Lord warns in the Old Testament. Secular crimes scarcely existed independent of divine offense, oversight, and intervention. Sin and crime were separated from each other only gradually, and even today the distinction between law and morality throws up similar problems. Offenses could therefore have both legal and ritual consequences. Among the ancient Greeks, accidental killings required purification but no penalties. Involuntary manslaughter meant exile as a means of purification. Deliberate killings, in contrast, brought down both law and religion on the offender's head.

With the state's emergence as caretaker of secular order, crime was distinguished from sin. Churches pursued sin, states prosecuted crimes. Much sin became defined as crime. The Greeks punished arrogance and extravagance as criminal offenses. In 1650, England changed adultery from a church court offense to a felony without benefit of clergy.[31] In our own day, adultery has reverted to—at most—mere sinfulness, though technically it remains illegal in many US states. Usury went from sin to crime to big business, with only a faint echo of its disreputable past still audible in laws that set putative upper limits to allowable interest charges.[32] In medieval England, infanticide was treated as a sin, and church courts imposed penance.[33] The state later took even the youngest under its wing, though the dire straits faced by mothers who resorted to killing their offspring was often taken into account. A third of women indicted for infanticide in seventeenth-century Scotland were banished instead and never brought to full trial.[34] But in seventeenth-century Denmark and Norway, giving birth in secret (thus facilitating infanticide) was a capital offense. In Germany, sixteenth-century law reform increased the likelihood that infanticides would die, too. And in France at the same time, infanticides made up a fifth of all those executed by the Parlement of Paris.[35] Sin and crime still blended. The concern was not just with the killing as such but also with how it endangered the child's soul by depriving it of baptism.[36]

As crimes and sins separated out, so too did the respective modes of proof it took to be convicted in the West. Religious and secular parted ways during debates over trial by ordeal in the twelfth and thirteenth centuries. Ordeals called on God to indicate guilt or innocence and thus to intervene directly in human affairs. Compared to feuds and other private dispute resolutions, trials by ordeal had two great advantages: they were public decisions taken once and for all, and, in theory, they tapped into a supernatural source of certainty, allowing a definitive outcome.[37]

Though foreign to Roman law, ordeals existed globally, from Europe to Japan. Archaic Greece knew them, as did Palestine of the Bible.[38] The accused swore oaths invoking gods and their own reputations as reason to believe their claims to innocence, and they were backed up by compurgators—allies who staked their own reputations on the defendants' behalf.[39] Whereas oaths involved God indirectly as the ultimate character witness, ordeals (by battle, water, or fire) roped him in directly. Humans obliged God to testify through the ordeal's outcome as to the guilt or innocence of his wretched creations. Ordeals promised certainty, but practical problems still remained. If God determined the outcome of judicial combats, why seek out the best fighter? Why were women more often subject to trial by fire rather than by immersion, where the buoyancy of their adipose tissues compounded the likelihood of a guilty verdict?[40] How to explain miscarriages of justice, when ordeals gave patently false verdicts?[41]

Ordeals were eventually abandoned as people were persuaded to reason on the evidence of their senses to determine guilt, but first they were attacked for religious reasons. Medieval theologians worried over the tension between worldly proof and divine gravitas. Of course, an omnipotent divinity could intervene in human affairs. But why would he want to upend the laws of nature and perform miracles to settle petty disputes—and at human demand?[42] Ordeals were God intervening into nature, thus miracles, but they were not his free choice. His act had to correspond to an outcome dictated by human will—guilt or innocence. God should not be tempted or tested—that was the theological objection to ordeals.[43]

Ordeals eventually gave way to physical evidence and the jury. But even as the secular state's concern for religious transgressions ended and the supernatural's role in the judicial process was marginalized, God's calling card remained on the tray in the hall. The intertwining of divine and secular continues even today in the oath.[44] By swearing, we invoke a higher power while promising certain actions or attesting to the truth of our assertions. That humans thought they could oblige God to help keep them honest is what made oaths suspect to the apostles.[45] But the judicial system in the Latin West took a more robust Old Testament view of God's willingness to backstop mortal truthfulness. In taking an oath, we curse ourselves, calling down supernatural wrath if we lie. In seventeenth-century England, anyone violating the oath taken in a binding-over action risked God's anger.[46] Today a jail sentence for perjury is at stake, not our immortal souls. But the logic of trembling before a higher power remains.

The State Emerges

As divine and secular law gradually separated, crime fell to the state, leaving sin to church and conscience. Since the state came to handle punishment alone, hell—as a place of deterrent torment—played a less necessary role in mainstream theology.[47] Yet, seen in history's long scope, the state only recently awoke to what we regard as among its primary duties: laying down the law, punishing transgression, maintaining order. Law—natural, divine, customary—was, of course, older than statute. Outside the ancient empires, enforcing it was long left to religion and civil society. China, Greece, and Rome policed their citizens, but not until the early modern era was the state again able to do so in Europe. Recognizably modern policing arrived only in the late eighteenth century. Even today, small isolated societies such as the Inuits, or close-knit religious communities manage without overt policing, resolving matters—even homicide—informally between victim and offender's kin.[48]

Only gradually did the state command a role in resolving conflict. Disputes had been sorted by the interested parties, coming to agreement or feuding in its absence. Feuds eventually gave way to a public resolution of conflict in trial-like circumstances. Court procedure was well elaborated already in ancient Babylon, almost two millennia before Christ.[49] From the seventh century BCE, even before law had been written down, men acting as judges set up informal courts in Greece to adjudicate disputes between parties who would jointly choose a venue and agree to adhere to the judges' decision.[50] In the *Iliad*'s trial scene, the disputing sides find judges, a framework of adjudication, and two talents of gold for the best judgment. Such quasi-courts slowly managed to ground their decisions not just, as earlier, on the claims of the powerful to rule but also on laws that were accepted as applying to all citizens.[51]

As the decisions of these early Greek informal courts accumulated and were abstracted, they gave rise to a judicial framework.[52] Rules were imposed: parties to agree on arbitrators, decisions handed down under oath and binding, a settled issue not to be raised again, and so forth. Meeting regularly, arbitration tribunals developed into an early form of courts. Their decisions could be appealed to the Council of the Areopagus, which may deserve to be considered the first proper court. During the poet Hesiod's time, eighth century BCE, arbitration became public and compulsory. Each male citizen served as a judge in the year after turning fifty-nine.[53] Trials run wholly by the judiciary made a public duty out of formerly private matters. As of the seventh century BCE, the early Greek codes of Drako, Solon, and Zaleukos specified penalties rather than leaving them to the judges' decision. Forbidding victims' kin from seizing the accused and taking matters into their own hands, the Great Code of Gortyn (fifth century BCE) instead offered regularized procedures of public adjudication.[54] Communal negotiations were now subordinated to the authorities. Whether from self-interest or compulsion, the parties agreed to abide by rules imposed from above. The law gradually emerged as a body of strictures, independent of kin, with the state as enforcer.[55] Under the Romans, improvised public tribunals grew permanent in the second century BCE, authorized to punish serious crimes affecting the whole community. During the later empire, judges presided as state representatives, able to act independently of any charge brought by private parties.[56]

But even as the authorities promulgated laws, much remained left to self-help. Awarded a settlement in ancient Greece, defendants themselves still had to enforce it. Cases were heard before courts, but Roman plaintiffs acted as their own prosecutors.[57] In medieval common law, victims' widows and children personally dragged killers to the gallows, and a violated woman herself castrated and blinded the rapist.[58] Justifiable homicide is the polite fiction whereby a weak state agrees that certain killings are legitimate. Ancient Greek and Roman law defined justified homicide expansively, as did most Western legal codes for the next two millennia. A highwayman in the act, a robber using force, anyone stealing at night, someone robbing clothes at the public baths, a man having sex with another's wife, mother, sister, daughter, or concubine, a rapist of free-born women or boys: according to various codes, all could be justifiably killed on the spot.[59] The killer of a manifest felon would likely not be prosecuted in medieval England, or he would be protected against retaliation from the criminal's kin. Someone burning down a house in medieval Iceland could be instantly killed in the act, as could trespassers.[60] Absent reliable intervention by the authorities, self-help remained the victim's most likely source of satisfaction.[61]

Only gradually did the state grow able to define, police, and punish homicide. Early Chinese emperors might pardon murderers, but, recognizing that victims' families would still seek to avenge their kin's death, in the fifth century they began compelling the pardoned to move far away.[62] In medieval England, a husband could no longer kill an adulterer having sex with his wife, but as a trespasser the cad was still a sitting duck. In the late seventeenth century, catching a wife in adultery remained sufficient provocation to reduce a charge of murder to manslaughter.[63] Yet by the thirteenth century killing outlaws and obvious felons on the spot was considered frontier law in England, no longer allowed in most localities. Justified killings were eventually permitted only in self-defense. In the thirteenth century, a thief caught in the act could be killed with impunity only if he also posed a danger. And self-defense grew limited in turn. In England by the mid-thirteenth century, even if in danger, those able to flee committed a crime if they instead struck and killed in self-defense.[64] The duel, which we return to later, was also part of this story of restricting justifiable homicide. It allowed certain sorts of people to kill each other by following particular rules. But by the nineteenth century, it too was largely stamped out.[65]

Yet, as so often, the law here bears continuing traces of its past even in contemporary statute. Violent self-help remains tolerated today.

Several US states allow mere manslaughter charges for killing spouses caught in flagrante.[66] Until 1975, a French husband catching his wife in the act at home could justifiably kill both her and the lover. So could a Texan husband.[67] In Italy, sentences were reduced under similar circumstances until 1981.[68] Even severe assaults today are still less likely to lead to arrest, prosecution, and conviction if between related people—practically speaking, husbands against wives.[69] Temporary-insanity pleas are used as technical work-arounds to treat violence against women leniently.[70] Stand-your-ground laws permit citizens to take the law into their own hands to defend themselves. In many nations, such as Britain, such laws have been whittled back. The state jealously guards its monopoly on violence, forbidding citizens to act as their own avenging angels. But in the United States, the citizen's duty to retreat rather than to fight is defined narrowly, sometimes allowing lethal self-defense.[71] A similar logic is used when abused women invoke battered-wife syndrome to expand the parameters of the imminent threat they need to plead self-defense.[72]

Before the nineteenth century, the fundamental reality of enforcement and punishment was the state's absence. Some crimes, as we will see, did concern the state from the start—especially treason, where it was the target. But most violations were left for the interested parties to handle. Until the state imposed its judicial monopoly, offenses were dealt with largely in two ways: vengeance and compensation.[73] Compensation was the overarching concept because in effect restitution was provided by both methods, measured either in blood or in material value.[74] Restitution and vengeance alike righted the moral imbalance created by harm, either in the eye-for-an-eye logic of the lex talionis or by means of fungible values—money, oxen, slaves—that were considered equivalent.[75]

If all parties agreed, compensation resolved the issue once and for all. But feuding kin groups often fought on for generations, the original offense ever amplifying and expanding. In the seventeenth century, the Scottish authorities hastened to intervene immediately after the first killing, before feuds could snowball, each subsequent round of slaughter harming anew, stoking further revenge.[76] Since the offender's entire kin was accountable, feuds ratcheted upward. The stronger the kin, the longer the feud.[77] A single spared opponent threatened yet further revenge. Pushed to its logical extreme, a feud was truly resolved only once the opposing clan's last male had been killed. The family of Milovan Djilas, the Yugoslav Communist partisan and politician, for example, was almost wiped out in feuds with agents of the Montenegrin prince Nicholas I in the early twentieth century.[78]

Vengeance was a major obstacle to the state's hopes of pacifying its territory internally. During the Warring States period in China (ca. 400 BCE–200 CE) unbridled vengeance challenged the state's grip, with officials forced tacitly to condone it.[79] Feuds, in effect, negated the state—with kin groups treating each other as the primary political units and refusing to recognize any higher authority than honor. Hopes of taming vengeance's savagery encouraged the state to expand its role in administering justice.[80] Once embarked on the business of adjudicating disputes, the state therefore sought to curb vengeance while promoting and institutionalizing compensation instead. In the Hittite edict of Telepinus (ca. 1620–1600 BCE), a victim's family chose between retaliation and restitution. But later laws ruled out retaliation.[81] By the time described by Homer, half a millennium later, the Greeks had largely managed to stamp out blood feuds. In the *Iliad*, blood is never exacted for blood.[82] The Romans, too, suppressed vengeance early. And Sharia law restricted blood feud in part by permitting retaliation only after judicial authority had determined the culprit's guilt.[83] In the Old Testament, David rejected the vengeance taken by two of his followers on the son of his enemy Saul. He killed the killers who, mistakenly expecting to be rewarded, had brought him Ish-Bosheth's head.[84]

Slowly, wherever it could, the state wrested control away from kin. Compensation and vengeance ran parallel for many centuries.[85] By the seventh century CE, the Visigoths had followed the Greeks and Romans by taking disputes into the courts. In hopes of keeping the peace, the early Germans allowed restitution even for homicide.[86] Medieval kings offered restitution as an alternative to vengeance, in the Swedish Helsinge law in the early fourteenth century, for example. Merovingian laws ordered compensation for assault and robbery, set out procedures to clear those accused of homicide, and stipulated restitution so as to prevent feud. Charlemagne admonished the kin of killers and their victims to seek quick settlements, thus squelching dispute.[87] Over a thousand years, from the late Roman Empire to the imposition of a semblance of regularized policing in the early modern era, European states sought to suppress feuding.

England, with its centralized state and developed court system, was among the earliest to match the ancient empires' achievement. By the thirteenth century, feuds among the nobility had been brought under control.[88] On the continent, that took another two centuries. The medieval peaces—a church initiative—sought to multiply the holy days on which killings were forbidden, thus pacifying more of the year. A Saxon edict from around 1221 ruled that revenge could be exacted only on Monday, Tuesday, and Wednesday, but the rest of the week was to remain free of conflict.[89] Renaissance Italian families' savage vendettas were controlled only slowly by emerging absolutist states. In sixteenth-century Florence, peace treaties among warring families, enforced by posted bonds, sought to end feuds. In the fifteenth century, the Spanish monarchs Ferdinand and Isabella imposed the Santa Hermandad to enforce royal justice against their warring aristocrats.[90] The Imperial Peace Statute of 1495 in the Habsburg lands similarly outlawed feud and private warfare. And honor crimes were brought under court control in Russia.[91]

By the 1500s, feuding had largely been replaced by the official judiciary, at least in the European core, where the state was strongest. Even in a largely pastoral country such as sixteenth-century Castile, where only a quarter of males could read, lawyers litigated on behalf of a menagerie of plaintiffs over quotidian disputes.[92] Conflict resolution had shifted from bare knuckles to the courts. But in the peripheral worlds, where the state's sway was weaker, feuds continued: the Scottish Highlands, Friuli, Liguria, Valencia, not to mention islands such as Sicily, Corsica, and Sardinia. For more than five hundred years after its ninth-century founding, Iceland refined its elaborate system of law, but it never found a way of enforcing it other than by feud. When the Icelanders finally wearied of cycles of bloodshed in the thirteenth century, they invited the Norwegian king to establish order. Highland Scottish clans grew tired of fighting in the late sixteenth century. They asked the royal authorities to arbitrate disputes and threatened to arrest their own members who refused or reneged.[93] By the time of the revolution, French deputies still worried that if the penal code legitimized killing in defense of others, not just oneself, it would give carte blanche to what were by then considered Mediterranean habits of vendetta, known from Italy and Corsica.[94]

In Giuseppe Verdi's opera *La forza del destino* (1861), the brother of a seemingly wronged woman is delighted ("What great joy!") when her lover is healed of a mortal wound—but only because this affords the brother the chance to kill the lover once and for all, avenging the lover's killing of the siblings' father. Feud was hard to brake, the logic of its momentum unrelenting. Even deep into the nineteenth century, the Japanese government still authorized and rewarded private parties seeking vengeance.[95] Feuds continued unabated across the Mediterranean and Balkans. In eighteenth-century Corsica, with feuding men holed up in fortified houses, only women could till the fields. A century later, feuds endured, half of them lasting at least fifty years. Deep into the twentieth century, such disputes claimed hundreds of victims annually in the Balkans.[96] In Albania, dozens of families remain sequestered in their homes today, too fearful of vengeance to venture out. Clan feuds in Gaza claimed at least ninety deaths in 2006.[97]

Feud, however, was not anarchy. Where centralized authority had yet to impose rules, feud was a means of settling disputes. All—strong, weak, or equals—had to resolve differences knowing that an unacceptable solution would prolong the conflict and that fortune or recrystallizing coalitions might reverse today's outcome. Feuds were stylized rituals whose procedures limited the worst excesses. The talionic principle of an eye for an eye in Jewish, Greek, Roman, and Sharia law was meant to set an outer limit to vengeance. Sharia exempted singular organs—noses and penises—from amputation.[98] Where feud was most institutionalized, as in medieval Iceland, the rules on vengeance killing were incorporated into the law of the land. In early modern Germany, feuding was rule bound, including negotiations before hostilities and a challenge delivered prior to violence.[99] If followed, the feud's fundamental logic was self-limiting: reaction only in proportion to provocation. The feud might continue interminably, but without necessarily escalating. Only men and only adults usually could be killed. Icelandic law spelled out the allowable: immediate killing for sexual assault, say, but acts of vengeance over the subsequent year for less-serious blows. Those who violated truces became social pariahs. Feuds here were a stabilizing ritual that channeled conflict into formalized arenas for arbitration.[100] In Catalonia, prospective avengers registered their claim by letter to their victim, waited ten days, and targeted only the offender himself. Having withstood an all-out assault on its house for three days, a clan in modern Montenegro was considered vindicated. Thereafter, the feud unfolded more moderately as small-group attack and individual ambush. However awful, feuds moderated even worse horrors—the apparent paradox dubbed the "peace in the feud."[101]

Vengeance competed directly with the state's claim to be the only enforcer of order. In comparison, compensation had the advantage of quick and bloodless resolution—so long as all agreed. No wonder authorities preferred it to vengeance. A bull killed someone: the Old Testament recognized the owner's theoretical liability to pay with his own life but suggested ransom instead.[102] From the beginning, the law eagerly sought to regularize restitution. The earliest extant code (Sumerian from ca. 2050 BCE) tallied the precise cost of infractions: ten silver shekels, say, for cutting (off?) a foot. So did the Twelve Tables of Roman law. The sixth-century laws of the Salian Franks stipulated costs for stealing pigs, depending on their condition and age, and other animals, down to bees.[103]

Wergeld, the restitution paid in Germanic law for injuries or killings, precisely tabulated the cost of mutilation and dismemberment as well as the worth of different lives. Modern actuarial tables are less detailed than these medieval codes. Æthelberht's laws from seventh-century Kent finely calibrated prices, both by damaged body part and by whether the victim was slave, freeman, or priest. Front teeth were worth more than back teeth. Damage to incisors was legally weightier (counting as mayhem) than damage to molars or grinders, not only since it was more disfiguring but also because the loss of incisors disadvantaged victims in a fight. Different fingers and their nails had different prices. Whether ears were rendered deaf, cut off, pierced, or lacerated mattered, as did whether bones were laid bare, damaged, or broken and whether the penis was destroyed or pierced partially or fully. Such detail pertained not only to bodily injuries but also to every conceivable violation of women and other forms of property.[104]

These finely calibrated costings revealed how the law still was only the intermediary between kin groups negotiating what they owed each other.[105] Though less bloody, compensatory law—like vengeance—was ultimately incompatible with the state's ambitions to be the only actor to settle conflict. Restitution was therefore eventually suppressed, too. In ancient Greek and Jewish law, compensation was eliminated altogether.[106] Christianity, however, accepted restitution and thus obliged Christian states to spend the following centuries attempting to eliminate it. The state took its own revenge for being eclipsed by beginning to claim part and ultimately all of the compensatory payments for itself.[107] Early Anglo-Saxon law already distinguished *wite*, or fines that belonged to the king, from wergeld.[108] In early English law, communities unable to identify a killer paid *murdrum* to the king. Because a homicide breached the collective good of the peace, feudal lords claimed part of the wergeld paid to kin. By the twelfth century, compensation in England was paid to the church, king, or community, not to the victim's family.[109] In sixteenth-century Seville, mothers and widows could still accept compensation from the murderers of their sons and husbands. But highway robbery and treason were not thus atoned. By the seventeenth century, restitution had largely been eliminated, at least in northern Europe.[110] Rather than allowing injured parties to be compensated, the state itself now collected what had in effect become fines.

Restitution was thus largely eliminated from the penal code, its logic now confined to civil law and insurance. And yet reintroducing compensation to the criminal law remains today a widely discussed proposal, sometimes called "restorative justice." Reformers note that the victims receive nothing besides the satisfaction of seeing offenders punished.[111] If criminals restitute victims, it is argued, rather than making amends to and through a neutral state, they will better grasp the evil they have wrought.[112] Allowing offenders to buy themselves out of prosecution by compensating victims, however, is still considered beyond the pale, although it remains possible in Islamic law.[113]

Chapter 3
Crime as a Social Problem

That crimes were ultimately offenses against the community, not just against individual plaintiffs, was perhaps the most important conceptual breakthrough in law's development. Individual harm was self-evident but only tangentially the state's business. For millennia, such torts were therefore left to the parties involved to handle. The idea of a public crime, however, required both a sense of social damage—a tear in the communal fabric going beyond any individual's stake in the matter—and recognition that the state, as society's most plausible representative, was the proper actor to punish it. That insight took centuries to emerge.

With the state seeking to stamp out vengeance and restitution, a broader issue arose. If crimes merely pitted kin groups against each other, then private resolutions sufficed. But what about victims without family or others to speak for them?[1] More interestingly, what about actions that damaged not just the victim but also society? Many crimes targeted individual victims: theft, rape, murder. For them, private solutions were obvious and for centuries the only ones available. Yet other offenses, sometimes with no specific individual victims, were inherently attacks on society. Offenses against authority and religion were obvious examples of such public crimes.[2] But more mundane violations could also harm something beyond the individual victim. Embezzlement, tax fraud and evasion, espionage, perjury, perversion of justice, coining and counterfeiting, food adulteration, sedition, pollution, failure to school or vaccinate children: all such acts inflicted collective harm where restitution did not suffice. Even individual crimes had social consequences. Philo of Alexandria, a contemporary of Paul, considered adultery worse than murder because it harmed the soul, not just the body, and left behind victims among families, children, and the state.[3] Though suicide was seemingly the ultimate individual act, Durkheim argued, in fact it gnawed at the social principle of each person's inviolability.[4] Anything that undercut public trust in the currency long remained a capital crime—even in Quaker Pennsylvania of the eighteenth century. Clippers of coins, John Locke thundered in 1696, not only removed some silver but also undermined the public faith in government, turning robbery into treason and meriting death.[5]

Dante Alighieri regarded fraud and betrayal—betraying public trust—as socially more harmful than mere violence.[6] In a collectivist system ruled by religious caste (theocracy) or dictator (autocracy), an individual action might violate the communal order—privately worshipping false idols, say, or stealing property that by definition belonged to the collective. But the idea of purely individual transgressions wilts under scrutiny also in secular and politically liberal societies. They, too, enforce a common code of ethics. Citizens may be left to make decisions privately that earlier were publicly defined and enforced. Mores may have changed and relaxed. Yet inviolable moral precepts ground every society, even ours today.

Both Roman and then Germanic law focused on individual retribution and retaliation.[7] Yet the insight gradually spread that if society suffered damage, then it could take revenge. If society had been harmed in ways unrepairable by individual action, the state would stand in for its claim to restitution. Christianity's emphasis on forgiveness and on redeeming sinners shifted attention away from making criminals pay: not taking an eye for an eye but turning the other cheek.[8] Nonetheless, sins remained understood as actions against God, offensive not just to him but to all faithful. Sin had collective consequences. Crime went beyond individual malfeasance.

Religious law first broached the idea of an offense that trespassed against something higher, not just the immediate victim.[9] In early times, crimes foremost violated God's order. Sin and crime overlapped, and everyone—not just the miscreant—might end up suffering. The offended gods might punish or forgive. Hebrew law was divine, emanating directly from God. Cuneiform laws (of Babylonia, Egypt, etc.) were mediated by the ruler, who was their author. Adultery illustrates the difference. In cuneiform law, a husband could decide whether to punish his wife and her lover. But in biblical law the offense was against God, not the spouse. Death was the unavoidable sanction, with the religious authorities vouchsafing God's role as the offended party.[10] Genesis demanded that wild animals who killed humans be put to death—not because of the harm done but because they had violated the higher law that human life, made in God's image, is sacred.[11]

The state's stake in punishing crime thus went beyond individual justice to protect the common interest by enforcing the law. "All suffer injury when someone wrongs the state," Plato insisted. Demosthenes regarded deeds of violence as public crimes committed also against those who were not directly involved.[12] The Greeks saw some crimes as polluting all society, with individual actions taking on collective consequences. Like traitors and committers of sacrilege, murderers offended the community as a whole, not just victim and kin.[13] Crimes involving matters of public concern, such as charges against government officials, were processed in special jury courts (*dikasteria*).[14] In the Old Testament, rituals were prescribed to cleanse a community of the collective guilt arising from an unsolved murder.[15]

Most apparently, desertion or loss on the battlefield endangered the entire community and was collectively punished from early on. By the Roman *fustuarium*, a disgraced military force divided itself into tens, picking by lot one man from each group to club to death. The Germanic tribes hanged deserters in trees.[16] Other offenses that violated the community in early law included treason, incest, bestiality, and witchcraft leading to death.[17] In ancient Greece and Rome, aborting a healthy fetus was a crime against state and society for eliminating an economic and military resource.[18] In common law, maiming someone was illegal not so much because of the harm done the individual as for depriving the king of an able-bodied subject to defend the realm. Self-maiming was felonious for much the same reason.[19] As was homicide.[20] Murder had its obvious victims, but the social order also suffered when homicide proliferated. Fraud undermined the security of all financial transactions, not just the one in question. Thieves, as Kant explained this logic, hurt themselves as much as their victims. Undermining everyone's ownership, they hollowed out their own, too.[21] Individual crime inherently affected all of society.

Crimes with public consequences could thus not be left to individuals to handle. Private prosecution of public crimes misaligned the incentives. Why should victims pursue offenders if they would receive no restitution? Or, conversely, they might undermine public trials by defaulting to informal plea bargains or even by dropping (or only half-heartedly pursuing) a prosecution if paid off by the defendants.[22] Outlawing such side payments, known as "compounding" (in effect a circuitous form of restitution), the state sought to force dispute resolution into public forums. In sixth-century France, Merovingian kings forbade private settlements for theft.[23] In the thirteenth and fourteenth centuries, robbery victims who got their goods back from thieves and agreed to keep quiet could be prosecuted for *theftbote*.[24] Private deals to settle misdemeanors remained legal, but for felonies they were forbidden in eighteenth-century Britain. Courts fined those who sought to sidestep the judicial machinery by offering rewards for the return of stolen property rather than prosecuting theft officially.[25] Even today, police and retailers are at odds over whether shoplifters should be prosecuted or merely arm-twisted into making restitution.[26] In the US, offering to accept restitution for a felony itself became a felony. The state could prosecute on victims' behalf even without their consent.[27] Public crimes demanded public punishments.

Vengeance and restitution would no longer do since both took an individual approach to crime. Restitution grew incompatible with public punishment once the state began taking at first a cut and then soon all of compensatory payments, directly competing with the victims. From the vantage of vengeance, restitution's basic assumption—that money resolves every conflict—was profoundly amoral. Higher principles had been violated that money could not assuage. Do not accept restitution for a murder, the Old Testament commanded, but kill the killer.[28] Even where compensation was customary, vengeance lurked offstage. Medieval Icelanders happily restituted most offenses, but not the killing of family. "Kin should not be carried in one's purse," they cautioned.[29] How could money make good murder, rape, or assault—or adultery, defamation, and other loss of honor? How could restitution pay the price of living in fear of crime or for seeing other public goods violated?[30] For crimes that could not be compensated, early Germanic law demanded whipping or enslavement. Later, life itself became the tribute paid.[31] In the long run, excepting a few vestiges, as in Sharia law, the inability to compensate for certain offenses and the need therefore for public punishments became deeply embedded in our moral sense.

Vengeance in turn threw up a different dilemma. It refused any compensation other than an equivalence of pain and suffering. Like compensation, vengeance was pursued by kin groups, yet it gave voice to a collective system of value alternative to and competing with the state's pretensions to speak alone for society. Wounded honor was an inherently collective affront, an injury that both was created and had to be restituted socially. Dishonor injured its victims' social personae, affecting how they were seen by others.

All of society, not only the immediate victim, was involved. Vengeance was so pressing a motive and was so hard for the state to quell precisely because—tapping into the burning insistence on retribution—mere restitution could not assuage profound injury.

In the long run, neither restitution nor vengeance could master crime's social consequences. Public offenses demanded public punishments, and only the state could mete out such sanctions. Even those hoping to reintroduce restitution to modern penal codes admit its limits. Allowing restitution for rape, for example, would legalize sexual inequality, nor could crimes against humanity be restituted.[32] Some crimes are ultimately irreducibly public. As the state gradually assumed the adjudication earlier left to the implicated parties, it emphasized crime's collective nature. The shared moral codex underlying any society presupposed that violating its norms endangered everyone, not just immediate victims. Shouldering responsibility for punishing public wrongs, the state thus took over the role first played by God.

Most religions have penalized sins as offenses against the gods.[33] That collective offenses endanger all has been a leitmotiv across cultures and ages. In the Old Testament, crimes against God threatened all of Jewish society, requiring death for the offender.[34] After the Homeric period, the Greeks grew convinced that criminals' presence polluted society, endangering everyone and requiring the state to punish on behalf of the gods.[35] In *Oedipus Rex*, a plague looms because a killer remains at large. Once the Roman Empire converted to Christianity, heresy became an offense against the state, an aggression against everyone. Pagan sacrifice was made a capital crime as of the fourth century. Justinian's code of 529 CE held blasphemy responsible for famine, earthquake, and pestilence.[36] The Aztecs feared drunkenness as a violation that opened a portal for sacred wrath to enter mortal society. Peruvians were certain that violating Inca commandments hurt everyone, not just themselves.[37] Sodomy was thought to have provoked God to unleash the plague on fifteenth-century Venice.[38] In early modern Europe, swearing and blasphemy were considered dangers to all, not just to the individual sinners, as was bankruptcy by Dutch Calvinists.[39] English Puritans feared God punishing all for the presence of sin. Austrians of the same era were convinced that vice, frivolity, and wrongdoing had angered God, bringing on the Turks and inflation. Cotton Mather, the New England Puritan divine, told a convicted murderer he had to die lest the nation be polluted.[40] In our own day, the AIDS epidemic and other catastrophes have been blamed on sin.[41] The logic of collective affront is familiar and persistent.

In Hebrew law, public offenses demanded collective punishment. For idol worship or the serving of other gods, the entire community had to expiate. Stoning—definitionally carried out by the group—was often used for crimes considered a collective threat. Moses was commanded to bring out a blasphemer to be stoned by the congregation.[42] Banishment, found in Dracon's code in the seventh century BCE, was also common in early German and Nordic societies. It was collectively enforced: anyone was at liberty to kill a returning exile. Tacitus noted that the tribes of Germany still settled murder privately, but those who offended against the collective (by retreating in battle or deserting to the enemy) merited public punishment. Six centuries later, the Carolingians imposed public punishments, not just private restitution, for inherently collective offenses such as counterfeiting, false witness, and perjury. In Anglo-Saxon England, incest, witchcraft, and bestiality were treated as crimes punishable by the community, not just by the victims.[43] In eighteenth-century England, two-thirds of those convicted of forgery were executed. Other than murder, no crime was more severely punished.[44] For the Incas in the Andes, removing a bridge was a public offense on par with adultery, murder, or blasphemy, much as stealing bee hives was a capital offense among the Germanic tribes, whose only source of sweetness they were.[45] At the end of the Roman republic (ca. first century BCE) offenses earlier considered private (*delicta*) came to be seen as public. The concept of *iniuria* (a wrong or outrage) was expanded to include violating private homes or corrupting minors and women. Laws now outlawed adultery, electoral corruption, the bearing of arms, public violence, criminal gangs, and interference with the administration of justice.[46]

This logic of collective offense was also extended to crimes that on the face of it did not affect the entire community, homicide above all. Among the ancient Jews, a murderer's blood was needed to expiate this crime against both God and humans.[47] In Homer, however, homicide concerned only the victim's family, who pursued the matter. If the dying man forgave him, the killer could not be charged, and the victim's relatives were released from the obligation to prosecute. Despite his other reforms, the Athenian statesman Solon left homicide a private offense. But in the sixth and seventh centuries BCE, murder began to be considered a crime not just against the victim but also against the gods, who might be angered if it went unpunished.[48] The Roman state in turn made pursuing murderers its duty, no longer left to the victim's kin. Murder gradually became seen as an offense as much against king as against kin.[49] Even before the Conquest of 1066, the English monarch directly prosecuted weighty crimes, such as homicide by stealth. By the early twelfth century, the Crown had assumed jurisdiction over homicide and other serious crimes generally, forbidding private settlements. Killings and other felonies that had earlier been atoned for by restitution were now punishable by death.[50]

As caretaker of common interests, the state also began to decide whether to prosecute at all. In the early accusatory systems, victims challenged offenders and might themselves be punished in the same manner if they failed to prove the case. Later, third parties not directly implicated in the offense were allowed to file charges, too. As Solon reformed Dracon's code permitting any citizen to avenge the wronged, he institutionalized the sense that certain transgressions harmed the whole community.[51] The *graphe* allowed any male citizen, victim or not, to prosecute public offenses, such as military desertion, political bribery, temple robbery, idleness, theft, perjury, hubristic conduct, and sycophancy. One notable reform was to forbid parents to sell their children into slavery. Such rights had to be enforced by third parties since minors could not act against their parents?[52]

Roman public law increasingly upheld common standards that could not be set aside by an understanding between the parties. Under Augustus, whether to pursue adultery ceased being the decision only of the woman's husband or father. He could take the initiative, but so could third parties. A husband who took no action against his wife caught in flagrante could be punished as a procurer (*lenocinium*).[53] In seventh-century Visigothic law, the king could prosecute adultery if the husband, children, or other relatives refused to, and they, in turn, could be penalized for negligence. Charlemagne's capitulary of 802 punished adultery as a crime against the Christian community.[54] In the same spirit of forbidding offenses even in the absence of a direct victim, a woman who voluntarily aborted could be punished. Accessories to suicide could also be found guilty.[55]

Public crimes developed apace during the Middle Ages. Public utility, Pope Innocent III argued in the early thirteenth century, demanded that crimes be interdicted.[56] Charlemagne's tribunals had already ordered and enforced a peace rather than just mediating between warring parties, who might comply or not. Besides excommunicating the disputants, the medieval peaces mooted the idea of crime and disorder harming the "common utility."[57] Even restitution was harnessed to atone for collective damages. The proximate victims received their bit. But church and state increasingly also got a part—since the larger community too had been harmed. Sin offended God's honor, Anselm of Canterbury insisted in the eleventh century, and a miscreant's payment must reflect that additional damage.[58] An offense did not vanish just because the victim died or refrained from prosecuting. Judges had an obligation to persist, the fourteenth-century Italian jurist Bartolus argued, so as to defend the community.[59] From the thirteenth century on, witnesses could be compelled to testify. Otherwise, the canonist Hostiensis argued, the innocent would be damned, the guilty absolved, and crimes go unpunished.[60] As of the Sachsenspiegel (1221–1224), the most important compilation of law in the Holy Roman Empire, a general public proscription of offenses was absorbed into customary law.[61] Half a millennium later, when the French revolutionaries proclaimed that all offenses were attacks on the public, the idea of crimes as inherently social events had been long in the making.[62]

The Judiciary as Voice of the Public Interest

Out of the state's growing responsibility for punishment grew the now common distinction between torts and crimes—torts as harms that individuals restitute among each other and crimes as acts of collective concern. The Greeks only incipiently distinguished crimes from torts but did allow any citizen to bring charges on matters of public interest, such as treason, desertion, and embezzlement. This rule also applied where the victims were unlikely to speak up or where larger issues were at stake: maltreating orphans or seducing free women.[63] In the fifth century BCE, Solon allowed anyone to take legal action on behalf of a victim. Everyone helped enforce the law, especially where society was the injured party. Acting with hubris (obnoxiously and self-indulgently) was considered so offensive to the state that it was actionable even by a slave.[64] Among the fourth-century CE Goths, serious offenders were compared to wolves: outsiders to society and enemies of king, people, and God, to be killed on sight.[65] Crimes where the culprit was not immediately known or where the offenders—once identified—belonged to no group able or willing to punish them as one of their own could also not be left to private resolution. They required state intervention.

Theft, for example, early on became the state's business.[66] In England, with its accusatory judicial system, any citizen could pursue any offense, acting as a public prosecutor. The prosecutor, when that position eventually developed, had no powers beyond those of every male citizen.[67]

As crime became regarded as an offense against the public, the courtroom emerged as the arena where law prevailed. Three snapshots from larceny's evolution illustrate the development. In Roman law, the nocturnal thief (whose evil intent was presumed manifest) could be killed on the spot. In early medieval England, victims were obliged to sound the hue and cry, thereby enlisting the public's aid and alerting it that the criminal would be executed so that the accusers would not be mistaken for killers as they carried out the sentence. But by the thirteenth century, the right of private execution had given way to the duty of public trial.[68] Courts evolved from arenas of mediation in the ancient world to independently prosecuting institutions. Their task was now adjudication, no longer arbitration. Trials eventually emerged as the primary forum for administering justice.

After collapse of the ancient world, courts slowly developed once again in the Middle Ages, extending the state's investigatory and adjudicatory powers. Feudal lords dispensed justice over their subordinates. Emerging as the primus among lords, the king did the same to them—in England after the Conquest of 1066 and in France two centuries later. Settling disputes in his court, the monarch became the first quasi-professional judge, the place lending its name to the institution.[69] Eighth-century English statute warned subjects against taking the law into their own hands instead of going through courts. By the thirteenth century, French courts had changed from locals mediating among themselves to royal power imposing verdicts increasingly based on abstract concepts of justice and legality.[70]

Extrajudicial, indeed extraterrestrial, mechanisms of judgment such as oaths, ordeals, and combat were eliminated across Europe by the thirteenth century.[71] The jury system that then developed in England allowed what—from Roman law's perspective—must have seemed wildly capricious: letting bystanders decide weighty issues of guilt and innocence in private deliberations. Max Weber compared juries to oracles, neither of them required to give rational grounds for their decisions.[72] With the twelfth-century revival of Roman law on the continent, combined with canon law, the old accusatorial process pitting plaintiff against defendant gave way to the reintroduction of an inquisitorial approach. Inquisitional techniques had biblical backing. When word of Sodom and Gomorrah's sins reached heaven, God himself investigated.[73] The state, including at first also the church, now took over this role, acting through judges and prosecutors to pursue transgression. Germanic law had earlier been based on accusation, with the victim's kin initiating matters. In the inquisitorial procedure, in contrast, the state took the lead. Individuals might still start the process, but judicial officials then took over.[74] The state assumed the role of society's plaintiff.

Crimes had earlier been prosecuted only when someone had been harmed. Twelfth-century legal reforms now identified a public interest. An individual might not have a specific concern in a given crime, Hostiensis argued in the thirteenth century, but all had a general interest in every crime.[75] English criminal law shifted from largely private agreements on monetary compensation to royal courts and justice, with death as the usual punishment.[76] By the early fourteenth century, France had institutionalized the prosecutorial function in the person of the *procureur du roi*, who could act even without a private complainant. Two centuries later, he alone could seek serious criminal sanction, even given a plaintiff. By this time, the German lands were following suit. In the Carolina, the first German penal code from 1532, private parties could still initiate prosecution, but then an official public investigation took over.[77] Queen Mary's mid-sixteenth-century reforms in England decreed that plaintiffs could no longer terminate actions at will. Once a case was initiated, the authorities prosecuted it to its conclusion. Russia, too, shifted from private to public law, with harsh punishments instituted from the sixteenth century.[78] As late as the sixteenth century, extrajudicial settlements were still common in Poland and Hungary, and they remained so in Bourbon France and colonial North America in the eighteenth century. But the number of "bootless" crimes, those that private parties could not settle, gradually expanded, and the courts ruled supreme.[79]

The accusatorial system in England and parts of northern Europe relied on juries. Like the inquisitorial method, juries provided an alternative to oaths, ordeals, and other appeals to divine intervention. The defendant's peers instead decided the outcome.[80] Though less dramatically than in inquisitorial courts, where judges ruled, juries, too, extended the state's reach. Prominent local men, they served as the central authorities' proxies. Under Charlemagne, they had to answer the judge's questions about local crimes.[81] In tenth-century England, the leading local nobles were obliged to accuse and arrest those suspected of crimes. Two centuries later, under Henry II, this responsibility was given to a presenting jury, a forerunner of the grand jury, which reported crimes committed locally. By the thirteenth century, two-thirds of murder trials in England were initiated by the authorities, not by appeal from the victims' families.[82]

In other respects, too, England's accusatorial system concentrated initiative in the state's hands, following the continental lead. From the mid-fifteenth century, juries ceased being self-informing, and Crown officials instead collected the evidence presented to them.[83] Reforms in the mid-sixteenth century made the process more public. Plaintiffs continued to prosecute cases, but they were now obliged to testify. If there was no accuser, the justice of the peace became more like a public prosecutor. He actively investigated the crime, organized the case, and rounded up the accused and witnesses.[84] In the eighteenth century, the plaintiff still had to press the authorities to indict, prepare the trial, assemble witnesses, and present the evidence in court.[85] But by the nineteenth century, the English authorities finally took full responsibility for apprehending and prosecuting criminals.

As a further arrow in the authorities' quiver, the legal revolution of the twelfth century revived the Roman doctrine of *infamia*, now called *mala fama*. Ecclesiastical courts could prosecute notorious suspects in the absence of an offense, accusation, or accuser. Even without a harmed party, the community's sense of violation was actionable.[86] To avoid baseless accusations, plaintiffs had earlier "subscribed" to the potential punishment by undertaking to suffer the same if they failed to prove the accused's guilt. With victims understandably reluctant to become plaintiffs, a fully-fledged accusatorial system was hobbled. But from the twelfth century, a new system of denunciation before ecclesiastical courts allowed plaintiffs to accuse without having to prove they were right or to risk being punished if they could not. Judges could now proceed on the basis of denunciation or other evidence of notorious offending, gathering testimony and prosecuting on their own.[87] By the fifteenth century in Italy, prosecution on the basis of bad reputation, *malum famum*, was commonplace.

As the state became the primary punisher, sanctions were no longer carried out by victorious plaintiffs but by professionals acting for the court. In fifth-century Athens, the victims' families executed murderers. In Visigothic law, accusers sometimes tortured the plaintiffs but were liable should they die.[88] Stoning, as in Jewish law, meted out punishment by the community as a whole or at least by a representative sample.[89] But Plato already described a parricide's execution by public magistrates, who then stoned the dead body for good measure.[90] And in classical Athens, executions were carried out by a professional known as the "public man."[91] With the Romans, the public executioner became a fixture—arguably the second bureaucrat, after the tax collector, though of course even more socially ostracized. The Middle Ages, too, saw official executioners, sometimes moonlighters from other despised professions but full-time employees in larger towns. To judge the significance of this institution, consider that in China's Warring States era, kin were expected to take vengeance on official executioners who had fulfilled their duties against the family's relatives.[92] However strong our sense of filial piety, the idea that we should kill the executioner has long bowed before the state's authority.

Chapter 4
The State as Victim: Treason

Most crimes eventually became understood as collective problems to be solved by the state acting on society's behalf. But one offense—treason—definitionally concerned the state from the very start. Early on, even murder was left to the implicated parties to sort. Yet from the very onset, the state penalized treachery against itself in the severest manner. Other than sacrilege and blasphemy, treason was the first example of a truly public crime and set the scene for the broader development outlined in the previous chapter. Yet as a crime it became ever less important. Democratically legitimated regimes feared it far less than their autocratic forebearers did. Why revolt against yourself? And as their powers grew, states found more effective ways of protecting themselves short of the ponderous legal machinery used to deal with treason.

Treason has always stood apart from other crimes. It is founded in scripture, where humans are warned against cursing their rulers.[1] Romulus himself, Romans believed, had protected their city against subversion, presiding over the trials in person.[2] It is the only crime explicitly defined in the US Constitution. Traitors have often been punished by special tribunals, outside normal courts.[3] Dante consigned them to the lowest circle of hell, two notches below murderers. In ancient China, treason was the only crime exempt from the stricture that relatives not turn each other in. For all other crimes, family ties trumped obligations to the state: you were punished even for accurately reporting an errant family member to the authorities. For treason, in contrast, the state wreaked its vengeance not only on offenders but also on all their family.[4] Where faiths backed rulers, attacks on them threatened the divine, too. In medieval England, killing the king was compared to blasphemy against the Holy Ghost.[5]

Until recently, traitors died gruesome deaths. In ancient Egypt, treason was the only crime punishable by death. Traitors were thrown into pits in ancient Greece, banished or painfully killed in Rome, and even eaten in China.[6] In sixteenth-century England, they were dragged along the ground to the gallows, hanged until close to death, cut down and castrated, disemboweled alive, had their heart cut out and burned along with the entrails, and finally were beheaded, then quartered, each part hung on towers and the head set upon London Bridge.[7] As of 1814, traitors were allowed to die by hanging but were then still dismembered. If the king was in a good mood, they might merely suffer decapitation.[8] Death remained the punishment for treason long after it had been banished for other crimes, up to 1998 in the United Kingdom.[9] The traitor's family, too, was often punished. In fifth-century Athens, treason was a hereditary sentence, with descendants banished and despoiled. Roman law spared the children of traitors but confiscated their property and made their lives miserable.[10] An Aztec traitor's household was enslaved for four generations.[11] The Prussian Code of 1794 also held a traitor's children liable in case the state decided to banish or lock them up. In nineteenth-century Bavaria, a traitor's family had to change its now infamous name.[12] Deep into the twentieth century, the Soviets punished traitors' families.[13]

For treason to be a crime, a state was needed to offend against. As its primary victim, the state defined treason and did so according to its own nature. It classified certain acts as treasonous—ones that others might see differently, even as virtuous. A vicious spiral of self-referential criminality ensued. Almost any action, however innocent it seemed, has at some time been deemed treasonous. But one person's regicide was another's tyrannicide. Treason has always been an unstable concept. As the state consolidated its position, it abandoned its once-heavy reliance on the concept of treason for protection. Modern states invoke it rarely—not because they are weak, but because they are secure.

As long as the state and its ruler melded, treason was an offense against the person more than against the institution. Whatever the attendant pleasures of being a ruler, it was also very dangerous. In the first millennium CE, European monarchs were ten times as likely to be violently killed as the most endangered citizens of the developed world, young Black American men in blighted neighborhoods of the 1990s.[14] In the early Middle Ages, with the sixth-century Salic code, for example, attacks on kings were punished especially severely. Ming regulations singled out acts that endangered the emperor: incorrectly mixing his medicines, violating dietary prescriptions, poorly training his carriage horses, building his ships shoddily, and so on.[15] By the sixteenth century, regicide—the most obvious form of treason—had declined to largely modern levels.[16]

In sixteenth-century England, Henry VIII used treason shamelessly to hound his enemies—whether to attack his theological opponents as he broke with the papacy or against those who rejected his six marriages. Between 1532 and 1540, Henry's courts charged 883 people with treason. Of this total, 308 (38 percent) were executed, 287 of whom had openly rebelled, raising war against the king; 34 were victims of court politics, caught up in the destruction of the Boleyn, Pole, and Courtenay dynasties; and 394 were tried for treason in relation to the Reformation—Catholic martyrs and others denying the king's preeminence.[17] With each new wife from Anne Boleyn forward, Henry made it treasonable to question the validity of his latest wedding or to accept his earlier marriages.[18] In 1541, as he planned to divorce Katherine Howard, his fifth wife, he made it treasonous for a woman he intended to marry to conceal an unchaste sexual past, for his queen to cuckold him, and for anyone who knew of such transgressions to not warn him.[19] He also expanded treason beyond his person to include attacks on his policies as well. Opposition to Crown policy was criminalized; calling the king a heretic, schismatic, or tyrant was now treason.[20]

In stark contrast, modern America has made little use of treason. Had the Founding Fathers' rebellion failed, they would have been hanged as traitors themselves.[21] Unsurprisingly, they were as alert to tyrants' abuse of treason charges as to treason itself.[22] They knew how rival aspirant families had misused treason to settle scores in England and were aghast at the hideous punishments inflicted there, so they defined treason as a limited and abstract offense on par with other felonies.[23] Even with the specter before them of Shays' Rebellion (a tax revolt in western Massachusetts in 1786) and other insurrections, even with England in Canada, with Spain in Florida and claiming the Mississippi Valley, with France only recently relieved of the Ohio Valley—despite enemies seemingly all around—the Constitution's drafters formulated treason precisely and narrowly. They dealt with it in the Constitution to prevent the legislature or judiciary from expanding it at will.[24] Though they followed the model of the English treason act of 1351, in their definition they eliminated compassing (or imagining) the king's death not only to acknowledge the absence of a monarch but also to ensure that constructive definitions of treachery, extending from actions to mere thoughts, could not be used to settle scores between political factions. Simply holding beliefs or harboring intent, as was actionable in England, was ruled out. Overt acts were required as evidence of guilt.[25]

The fledgling nation did not define treason as harm to a nonexistent monarch but restricted it to "consist only" of levying war against the United States or adhering to its enemies.[26] As in English law, a confession or two eyewitnesses was required as proof.[27] Treason was not to be used to punish political opponents or in domestic infighting, and the sovereign ruler's person no longer played a role. Only acts intended to harm the nation were treasonous.[28] With a few exceptions, mere riots, without a demonstrable ambition to overthrow the government, were not actionable as treason.[29] Over the course of two and a half centuries of US history, only some two score traitors have ever been prosecuted.[30] No convictions were returned during World War I, and not a single person has ever been executed for this crime (admittedly with the intervention of a few presidential pardons).[31] Even after the Civil War, the North did not pursue the Confederates for treason.[32] Such insouciance in the face of what was once regarded as the worst possible crime spoke to the Americans' desire to leave behind the Europeans' frequent misuse of treason. It also showed Americans' confidence in their new republic. Its foundation was secure, and it faced few enemies. They were a people "singularly confident of external security and internal stability," in the words of the Supreme Court in 1945.[33]

Between these extremes on treason's historical trajectory—sixteenth-century England and modern America—two points emerge. First, treason reflects the nature of the state it offends. Second, except in the totalitarian dictatorships, treason has faded in importance, not just in the United States but also in all democratic countries. Because democracies are not one person's rule, they are inherently less prone to treason in its classic form—political assassination. The primary parties in modern democracies are broadly similar, and the rules of succession clear, so killing a leader merely means that someone quite like him or her carries on. In autocracies, by contrast, whether absolutist monarchies or dictatorships, killing the ruler pays off. Protected by a private army of thousands, Adolf Hitler survived some forty attempts, Fidel Castro several hundred.[34] Oppressive, unrepresentative, and weak leaders have been most likely to die violently in office. Their rule generated opposition, and they tolerated no dissent, but they were insufficiently ruthless or effective to suppress their enemies fully.[35]

The state eventually no longer needed treason laws to protect itself, instead amassing an arsenal of other weapons against attack.

Treason fell victim to the state's own success. More important, as the modern state became an element of an increasingly representative and eventually democratized political system, it served its citizens, not their rulers. Political change no longer came primarily through revolt, rebellion, or insurrection—acts threatening the entire system—but as piecemeal reform, broadly agreed. Seen in a Kantian or Hegelian perspective, treason thus became just another crime. It was self-rebellion, acting against oneself. Attacking a democratically legitimated system differed from transferring power among competing dynasties. Change in democracies came increasingly from within, as everyday "treason" or reform. The domestic aspects of treason—sedition—faded in importance. Treason in democracies instead focused increasingly on collaboration with enemies, or external treason.[36]

Over millennia, treason reflected the nature of the government authority it attacked. It spanned a broad array of actions against the people and their community in the Greek city-state, where state and society largely overlapped (as they did again in the totalitarian regimes of the twentieth century). It focused on affronts to the person and later the office of the sovereign in imperial Rome and even more so in feudal Europe. In the early modern era, treason was abstracted to cover attacks on the nation, not on its ruler. And modern representative democracies pared treason back largely to aiding and abetting enemies. Most recently, as sovereignty has in part transferred to supranational institutions—the United Nations, the North Atlantic Treaty Organization, the Hague, and the European Union—treason's boundaries have grown even hazier.[37]

Treason was once a much broader concept. A young and weak state was threatened by many acts.[38] When treason was the charge invoked between dynastic factions vying for preeminence, little hemmed it in. The ruler of the moment defined all enemies as traitors. Since traitors' lands escheated to them, medieval monarchs eagerly expanded the crime's remit.[39] In the fifteenth century, French kings used treason charges to redistribute subordinate lords' lands to allies.[40] The greater the sovereigns' leeway to define treason, the more enemies quavered. Pointing to the Chinese emperor, Montesquieu put it aphoristically: the less precisely high treason was defined, the more despotic government could be.[41] Few actions have not been thought treasonous: consulting soothsayers about the king's death, questioning the royal household expenditures, committing buggery, being a Jesuit priest, manufacturing bad shoes, and clipping coins—alongside, of course, aiding and abetting enemies and assassinating leaders.[42] In contemporary Thailand, insulting the king—via internet postings or bathroom graffiti, say—or even just speaking ill of his dog merits prison. In Myanmar, so does tattooing an image of the president on your penis—or even just claiming to have done so.[43] Since treason was definitionally a threat to the state, whatever the state thus defined became ipso facto thus. Traitors have come in all shapes and sizes: Christians under Rome, peasants in the fourteenth century, Jesuits in the fifteenth, both republicans and aristocrats in the eighteenth, Chartists in the nineteenth, Nazis and Communists in the twentieth, Islamists in the twenty-first.[44]

Before religious and secular power began separating in the early modern period, treason and sacrilege or heresy were much the same offense, attacking the highest authority.[45] The Greeks closely associated impiety (*asebeia*) with treason (*prodosia*), and temple robbers were targeted by the same law as traitors. The Romans regarded serious violations of divine law (*fas*) as a kind of treason against the gods. Criticism of the emperors, regarded as quasi-divine, was considered both impiety and treason.[46] In the Old Testament, the rebellions of Adam, Cain, and Saul were disobedience against God. The Bible instructed Christians to obey the authorities, who held their power from God.[47] In 1199, Pope Innocent III turned imperial laws on treason against heretics, now seen as traitors to God.[48] Henry VIII, both king and head of the English Church, distinguished only vaguely between treason and heresy. French kings in the sixteenth century equated heretics and traitors, confiscating the property of both.[49] In the seventeenth century, James I of England considered resistance to kings blasphemous. The Prussian legal codes of the seventeenth and early eighteenth centuries still defined treason as an attack on divine as well as worldly powers.[50] And French old-regime law recognized *lèse-majesté divine,* thought and speech crimes against God. It was from this that *lèse-majesté humaine* was derived by analogy once the prince and the state were conceived of as being separate.[51]

As long as rule by one lineage remained the norm, state and governing family overlapped, and treason was committed against the person of the ruler, not against the state in any abstract sense. Killing the leader was the essence of treason. Today, assassination is legally seen as but another murder. Because fathers, like hereditary leaders, were once invested with a quasi-supernatural authority, parricide too was once a worse crime than the simple homicide it is today. The Romans drowned parricides in a leather sack together with a dog, a cock, a viper, and an ape. So did eighteenth-century Germans, who added infanticide to the list of such crimes.[52] In ancient China, a broad array of kin elders were protected against parricide, and offenders were punished by the severest affliction, death by slicing.[53] Neither English nor US law singled out parricide[54] But in France parent killing was still a separate crime in the Napoleonic penal code of 1810. The convicted were executed with special humiliations: barefoot, wearing only a shirt, head covered with black cloth, the right hand amputated.[55] In Japan, parricide did not become a murder like any other until 1973.[56]

Similarly, seducing a leader's wife or adult daughter is today at most a private moral transgression with no legal implications. In the past, however, subverting the royal lineage's purity and claim to power by adultery, seduction, or rape was treasonous.[57] Philippe IV of France executed two minor nobles in 1314 for adultery with his daughters-in-law.[58] In 1536, Henry VIII prosecuted Lord Thomas

Howard for marrying the daughter of the queen of Scots, Henry's eldest sister. Had Henry died heirless, he feared Howard could bid for the crown. The new act made it treason to defile or deflower the king's sister, niece, or aunt or to marry them without royal permission.[59] This still holds. Adultery with the monarch's consort, eldest unmarried daughter, or the wife of the heir to the throne remains treasonous. Princess Diana's affair with James Hewitt, her riding instructor, posed the issue most recently. With treason still a capital crime at the time, both could theoretically have been executed.[60]

When state and society broadly overlapped, as in the Greek polis, more actions were potentially treasonable than later when the state crystallized into more specialized functions and was threatened only by specific acts.[61] Among the Romans, too, almost any offense seemingly of peril to the state was treasonous, although the emperor eventually became the focus of concern.[62] The Romans distinguished two concepts. *Perduellio* (wicked warfare) covered any action harmful to the people, as though from an armed enemy.[63] As Rome enlarged, former external enemies became internal subjects, and so the concept of treachery expanded as well.[64] About 100 BCE, it included also the *crimen maiestatis* (combined by Sulla into a single law in 81 BCE)—behaviors tarnishing the sovereignty or dignity of the Roman state or the emperor. *Maiestatis* encompassed *perduellio*, and together they included even negligent or merely reckless behavior. Under Augustus, the definition expanded to cover personal damages to the leader, such as slander of the *princeps*, his family, and other prominent citizens, alive or dead.[65] Counterfeiting, too, was treason because it desecrated the emperor's image on coins.[66] Wearing clothing in the imperial purple was a treasonous offense.[67] Already under the Romans, the concept of majesty thus shifted focus from the community to the person of the ruler, which was to dominate the Middle Ages and absolutism. The Lex Quisquis (397 CE) expanded treason to include almost any political utterance the ruler, his ministers, and favorites objected to.[68]

Treason in Roman law was action against ruler and people. Germanic ideas, as they merged with the Roman inheritance in the barbarian legal codes of the seventh century, instead emphasized the contractual relationship between ruler and follower. Loyalty was pledged, and breaking that pledge (*Treubruch*) was treason.[69] *Verrat* was equally evocative: bad counsel. The vassal owed his lord good advice and aid.[70] As feudalism spread, kings, solidifying their power as the primary lord, distinguished betrayals against themselves from those against lesser lords. English common law thus separated high from petty treason, reserving special sanctions for crimes against the king.[71] The German term for treason in general, *Hochverrat*, still retains a memory of high treason.[72]

As royal power solidified, treason focused on the monarch's person. In the late thirteenth century, the English king Edward II sought to define opposition from his barons, who wished to hold him to his feudal obligations, as treason. The kings slowly succeeded. If the monarch was society's linchpin, his demise was necessarily worse than others. A royal death involved the "whole nation in blood and confusion," in the words of an eighteenth-century English jurist. Every stroke against him is "levelled at the publick tranquility."[73] In the seventh century, Visigoths defined treason as actions against the people and the land as well as against the king. But at the close of the ninth century, King Alfred declared a man's treachery to his lord the one crime that compensation could not expiate.[74] The English treason act of 1351 (still in effect today and the model for the US Constitution's treatment of the subject) targeted violations of the king's person. It began with instructions to punish physical attacks against or plans (i.e., compassing) to kill the king, queen, and eldest son as well as rape of the king's wife, daughter, or daughter-in-law, thus compromising the lineage. Only then did it proceed to war against the king and his realm, adherence to the enemy, and the killing of high ministers.[75] The feudal king pushed aside lesser lords, concentrating treason law's protection on himself. His absolutist successors took this approach to its apogee. Even the subjects of a king who had become a tyrant, James I lectured them, had no right to resist him. No rebellion was ever justified.[76]

From Ruler to Nation

Yet this fixation on the sovereign's person could not last.[77] Whom or what did the concept of treason seek to protect? Was treason an attack on the person of the sovereign or on sovereignty itself, independent of its current holder? If treason law protected the sovereign person, then if he were deposed, allegiance remained with him. His usurper was a pretender. Tell that to the triumphant successor! But if allegiance was to the ruler on the throne—in other words, to the system not to the person—then the expelled sovereign was a has-been, and the current occupant the true king. Any attempt to reverse a once-treasonous shift in power would now itself be treason. Success cleansed treason. Being enthroned justified all earlier treason. Politics became a succession of treacheries. Each successful treason immediately flipped from crime to status quo. Treason was thus an inherently unstable concept. If allegiance was to the person, it could not survive his or her departure; if to the system, then the new regime automatically trumped it. Impotence or irrelevance were the possible outcomes.

As long as treason focused on the ruler, regime change became a parade of treacheries. When the current leader lost, he was definitionally succeeded by traitors turned kings, whose own rule was equally illegitimate and faced the same predicament with the next challenger. In ancient China, a ruler who had driven out his predecessor was considered to have polluted himself. To be cleansed, he had to sacrifice a victim—that person was dismembered, his limbs thrown out the city's four gates.[78] As long as competing would-be rulers battled, as in the European Middle Ages and early modern period, accusations of treason rarely rose above being tit for tat. "Treason does never succeed; and what's the reason?" the famous epigram asks. "When it succeeds, no man dare call it treason."[79]

Put another way, all political action short of slavish support of the powers in charge could be treason. As a judge, Richard Tresilian, a member of the court party during Richard II's reign, had advanced the king's cause in 1386. With the peers ascendant again the following year, he was impeached and executed. Having pronounced treason on others, the judge was now himself killed as a traitor. In Tudor England, treason charges flew fast and furious as lordly lineages sought to prevail. Competing accusations of treason inevitably arose, with the last word going to the victor of the moment. Most so-called traitors of this period merely had the misfortune of ending on the losing side of a civil war.[80] Much the same held true during the French religious wars of the sixteenth century, when lèse-majesté could be turned at times against the Huguenots and at others against the Catholics, depending on what prince appeared to be next in line for the throne.[81]

Besides the inherent anarchy of a personified definition of the offense, in time other forces also helped move treason's focus away from the individual ruler. Whom did the king serve? Himself, the people, something higher? Germanic and feudal law approached relations between ruler and subject contractually and reciprocally. "Thou shalt be king if thou dost right," as the Visigoths put it, "but if thou dost not right, then shalt thou not be king."[82] In post-Conquest England and France, the feudal relationship was reciprocal. If the king violated his end of the bargain, vassals could formally withdraw fealty (*diffidatio*) and then wage war against him, all without committing treason.[83] A king who became a tyrant lost legitimacy. To rebel against him was not treason. This was clearly spelled out in the various thirteenth-century compacts regulating relations between kings and their barons, most notably the Magna

Carta (1215).[84] That tradition had been overshadowed in late feudalism as one lord gained preeminence and enlisted the crime of treason for his own protection, but its fundamental logic reemerged in the contractarian political theories of the eighteenth century.

Even the absolutist monarchs' pretensions, spurning any criticism, were undermined in the sixteenth and seventeenth centuries as the religious persecution sparked by the Reformation prompted contractualist theories of government, and the natural-law tradition reemerged. Natural law insisted that transgression was not just what authority said it was but that the state itself could be considered a criminal if it violated those higher laws by which it should abide. Only those kings who governed according to higher principle could justify their authority. Tyrants could justly be deposed. John Ponet's *A Shorte Treatise of Politike Power* (1556) openly advocated tyrannicide against Mary Tudor because her rule contravened divine and natural law. Obedience was not to a personal monarch but to a constitutional sovereignty compliant with divine and natural law. In 1579, Phillipe du Plessis-Mornay, the likely Huguenot author of *Vindiciae contra tyrannos*, argued that it was treasonous for a king to commit crimes against his subjects.[85] Regicide might be reprehensible, but tyrannicide was justified. Oliver Cromwell's republic in mid-seventeenth-century England rested on similar constitutional assumptions. Kings derived power from the people. If they did not pursue their subjects' good, resistance was justified.[86] Even Thomas Hobbes allowed subjects to resist kings who harmed them directly.[87]

Whether the standard by which rulers were judged was a suprapolitical principle or an implicit contract with their subjects, they were held accountable to something other than their own wishes. This principle was institutionalized further with representative rule in the seventeenth century and then with democracy beginning with the eighteenth-century revolutions. Not every criticism or action against leaders was treason. Indeed, they themselves could be guilty of treason. Once rule was justified by a higher standard by which it could fail, traitors were distinguished from common criminals not just because they violated laws—both did that—but because they did not recognize the legitimacy of the law in the first place. Modern traitors rejected the entire system, claiming it had no purchase over them. Unlike common criminals, traitors also often claimed to be spurred on by a higher purpose, not by mere lucre.[88]

In Europe after the late Middle Ages, the object protected by treason laws thus shifted from the person of the sovereign to something more abstract, whether the Crown, the office of the monarch, the existing governmental system, or eventually the nation. As political systems increasingly justified themselves as pursuing the good of the ruled, the crime of treason declined. Why undermine a system that ostensibly helped you? Treason necessarily faded when political change could be effected by means other than resistance, rebellion, and overthrow of authority in that regular change was incorporated into the very functioning of government. As subjects became citizens and thus the ultimate sovereign, treason meant revolting against themselves.

Treason's focus continued to move from sovereign to sovereignty, from ruler to state. In the early thirteenth century, the Magna Carta codified how the English king shared power with his barons and was not a divine ruler, which helped bring forth the idea of the Crown as the bond between the kingdom (the barons who had to be consulted) and the king. The Crown, not the king, was sovereign.[89] Treason now meant action against the realm more than against the king. By the mid-thirteenth century, treason was seen in France as a crime not just against the ruler's person but also against the province as a larger entity independent of him. The ruler now represented the state; he no longer was the state.[90] By the early sixteenth century in England, kingship was no longer understood as a network of personal allegiance but, rather, as an office or a public capacity. The king assumed it, but it existed independently of him.[91] Under

Edward II in 1320, forging of coin was declared to be an affront not just—as the Romans had it—to the ruler but also to the people of his realm. Similarly, counterfeiting in sixteenth-century Florence was no longer a crime because, as with the Romans, it desecrated the emperor's image on the coin but because it impugned the credibility of the state's finances.[92]

A century later in Elizabethan England, the state grew fully recognized as a permanent and public entity, existing independently of the monarch. Only thus did the trial of Charles I in 1649 for treason make sense. He had warred against something independent of the monarch, namely "Parliament and Kingdom." The English civil wars of the 1640s crystallized out an impersonal concept of the state, where the kings' sovereignty was derogated to them by the people.[93] By the time of England's strife with its North American colonies in the 1770s, this idea was firmly in place. Colonist rebels levied war against the king, "though they have no direct design against his person."[94]

Protecting the Person of the Ruler

Despite this shift in the definition of treason, attacks on the sovereign's person long remained the primary concern. In 1813, the Bavarian penal code's first and worst example of treason was attacks on the "sacred person" of the king.[95] The Napoleonic penal code punished attempts on the emperor as parricide.[96] England took longer than most to shift attention from ruler to state.[97] In 1695, an English statute, passed in reaction to the bloody excesses of recent treason prosecutions, sought to hem in their scope by imposing due-process requirements. Even it, however, exempted attempts on the king's life.[98] A century later, after stones were thrown at George III, treason was specifically defined to include harming, maiming, or wounding the monarch.[99] Five years on, after another attack, attempts to assassinate the king were now to count as and be tried in the same less-restrictive manner as murder.[100] Two witnesses were no longer needed, making it easier to prosecute. In 1840 and 1842, several would-be assassins attacked Queen Victoria.[101] The treason act of 1842 therefore allowed prosecution of violence against the monarch without wheeling out treason's heavy legal machinery, treating such crimes by the laxer standards of conventional murder. The monarch's person could be better protected by making it a crime short of treason merely to bring into her presence firearms or other weapons or even just to alarm her. Easier to prosecute, these offenses also triggered more moderate punishments (transportation, hard labor, flogging, imprisonment) than the death prescribed for treason.[102] The 1998 treason act retained compassing the monarch's death (inherited from the statute of 1351) as the only treasonable action directed against his or her person. Attacking the queen would thus be treason only if it was evidence of wanting to kill her.[103]

Although special protection was sometimes still reserved for the head of state, treason's focus was clearly shifting from ruler to state. Nowhere did this transition occur more abruptly than Israel. Importing the English treason act of 1351 largely verbatim in 1943, Palestine under the British Mandate defined treason as "levying war against His Majesty." When it became a nation in its own right, the Supreme Court redefined the object of solicitude in 1959 to be the State of Israel.[104] Elsewhere the change was more gradual. The example of the French revolutionaries' shift from king to state as the protected object shows that ruler and system were being clearly distinguished. In the penal code of 1791, lèse-majesté, offense against the monarch, shifted to the newly minted category of crime against the nation, *lèse-nation*. In July 1790, the king—like all his subjects—was made to swear an oath to the nation. His flight to Varennes on 20 June 1791, as he sought to leave his subjects behind, revealed the king as no longer treason's victim but its primary culprit.[105] Like Charles I, Louis XVI died on the scaffold, a convicted traitor.

Napoleon backtracked slightly. The penal code of 1810 especially protected the emperor (his murder punished with the extra measures reserved for parricide) and his family (their killing punished as a capital crime), much like the Roman and medieval sovereigns.[106] In the late nineteenth century, the Japanese penal code cast its net even wider. It protected not only the divine emperor and his heirs but also his mother and grandmother, whose role in assuring the regime's continuity had, after all, been fulfilled long ago.[107] In Germany, as in Italy and Sweden, insulting the sovereign was still considered an affront to the nation, thus graver than disparaging private citizens.[108] Attempts on his life was the penal code's first example of treason.[109] The Belgian penal code of 1867 distinguished internal from external security. Recognizing that the king was not the state itself, though one of its officers, it added another category on crimes against the king and his family.[110] In the French Third Republic of the 1870s and then in Germany's Weimar Republic from 1918 to 1933, such feudal echoes dissipated altogether. In matters of personal safety, the president was treated like any other private citizen. Killing him, after all, did not lead to a change in government, merely a new election.[111] Fearing unrest, the Social Democratic leaders of the Weimar Republic bucked their party's commitment to abolish capital punishment, mandating it for conspirators who plotted to kill government members.[112] By the postwar era, however, the transition was complete. In the German Basic Law (1949), treason laws protected not the ruler and not even the nation but the fundamental political system, the constitutional order.[113] The current French penal code makes it treasonous to attack—among other aspects of the very broadly defined "fundamental interests of the nation"—the "republican form of its institutions."[114]

Born a republic, the United States was reluctant to offer its head of state special protections. Assassinating the president was defined as nothing more than murder unless the killing was part of a plot to aid and abet the nation's enemies.[115] A wartime statute in 1917 sought to change direction by outlawing threats against the president.[116] After John F. Kennedy's assassination in 1963, it was discovered that although federal law penalized threats against the president and the murder of other national officials, it had overlooked the killing of the president.[117] That omission was rectified in 1965, when investigating and prosecuting assassination were centralized in federal hands, though with punishments for it remaining the same as for conventional murder or manslaughter.[118]

Protecting the System

With political change, treason also changed. Battling barons, fighting for the crown, used treason to solidify power once they attained it. Endless bloodletting resulted. Hence, the 1495 treason act, passed after ten years of Tudor rule under Henry VII, in effect recognized de facto (not just de jure) governments. To avoid the killing of court officials as regimes devoured their predecessors, the act assured government personnel that they would not be prosecuted for treason as new monarchs ascended the throne or for past adherence to the king's enemies.[119]

At issue here was not the nature of the system but the identity of the ruling clan. When political change was threatened between different systems, not just by substituting royal lineages, however, the stakes increased. Treason was gradually whittled down from a welter of actions to focus on the primordial sin of fundamental regime change. Treason had once been vaguely defined as almost any conceivable action that hurt the body politic and community, especially its ruler. Gradually it came to focus on overthrowing government, aiming to change the system fundamentally, whether in collusion with foreign enemies or not.

Such fundamental change had earlier been almost inconceivable. Dynasties, not regimes, came and went. Early modern governments sought to protect themselves by passing inherently self-contradictory laws outlawing their own end. Anyone in a position to violate these laws could not, of course, care less. In the late fourteenth century, Richard II promulgated a statute making it treasonous to attempt to repeal his new law on treason. His successor, Henry IV, having won the throne in war, repealed it shortly thereafter.[120] Treason laws' inherent contradictions were accentuated once they were deployed to protect not just the ruler but also the system. The German peasants revolting in the sixteenth century fought not for a new king but for a new political system altogether. The same had been true of the English peasants rebelling in 1381 and then charged with treason against the realm.[121] The Holy Roman emperor thought the same as he expanded treason in the sixteenth century to include rebellion—threatening revolting peasants with decapitation or flogging.[122] He rightly worried that peasants wanted to end imperial rule *tout court*. After the peasant rebellion of 1525, the *Landesordnung* (territorial law) of South Tirol threatened all insurrectionaries with death.[123] The treason trial of Charles I in England in 1649, part of the establishment of Cromwell's republic, brought fundamental regime change. No longer did rival claimants to the throne succeed one another; hereditary monarchy ended altogether.[124] Treason was already cruelly punished, but under Charles II Cromwell's now defeated followers were subjected to even more spectacular suffering, probably in response to how they had overturned the entire order. The corpses of the mercifully already dead Cromwellians were disinterred, hanged, and beheaded.

Representative government and then democracy exacerbated the problem of treason's logical self-contradiction. How could treason be squared with the right of citizens to hold their leaders accountable? In democracies, allegedly based on natural law, actions that "would earlier have kept the hangman busy" were now understood as citizens' right to determine the regime that ruled them.[125] Far from being treason, criticism and change were baked into representative government. With freedom of speech a fundamental right, seditious opinions and even libel against the ruler could not be treason. And yet even democracies faced treason's fundamental incoherence: you cannot legislate across basic ruptures in legitimation. Only unsuccessful treason can be prosecuted. Successful treasons by their nature are not pursued.

Regimes with representative and especially democratic legitimacy allowed, indeed welcomed, criticism and reform. Yet they, too, drew the line at fundamental system change. Just as sovereign individuals cannot sell themselves into slavery without violating their freedom, so democratic regimes could not allow the undermining of popular sovereignty. That principle, in turn, rested on the assumption that popular sovereignty would never willingly surrender itself into the hands of some other system. Deciding whether one dynasty or another was to sit on the throne involved no basic principles, but to tamper with a regime constituted by its subjects' free choice was serious. Insofar as democratic regimes represented the general will, to question them was to thwart that will. A traitor to democracy was an enemy of the people. Starting already with the French Revolution, such reasoning was taken to its extremes in the populist pseudodemocracies of totalitarianism. Any criticism, however mild, was taken as tantamount to treason. Any transgression, however inconsequential or technical, was heresy.[126] Some liberal democracies, having surveyed the ravages of authoritarianism, therefore drew robust conclusions on protecting democracy against its own worst instincts. Militant democracy was the outcome—the doctrine that lesser civil rights, such as free speech or assembly, must occasionally be sacrificed since a democracy cannot tolerate political parties that aim to overthrow popular rule. In the postwar era, more than half of Europe's nations have banned a political party for such intentions, mainly but not only parties on the far Right.[127]

This logic existed already with the first quasi-democratic republic in ancient Rome. When the monarchy was overthrown and the republic installed, each citizen had to swear never to support a king or similar leader, making it treasonous not to back the existing system.[128] Similarly, in 1671 the New England colonists of New Plymouth defined treason as any attempt to alter or subvert the "Fundamental Frame and Constitutions of this Government."[129] The US Constitution of 1787 followed suit, guaranteeing the individual states a republican form of government and promising to protect them against invasion.[130] The French revolutionaries repeated this reasoning. They messianically regarded their regime as history's culmination. To question this conclusion was self-evidently treason. The French penal code of 1791 listed seventy-nine different crimes against the state.[131] In 1792, the revolutionaries decreed death for anyone proposing a return to monarchy or any other regime hostile to the people's sovereignty.[132] In the Napoleonic penal code, treason was defined as any "attempt to change the form of the government."[133]

But, of course, events overtake even the most ambitious intentions. The Roman emperors were not deterred by the republic's oaths. Revolutionary France was only the first of—so far—eight French regimes: five republics, two empires, and whatever Vichy should be called. Overturning a popularly legitimated system may be a primal political sin, but no regime is stronger than its ability to defend itself. Treason laws are only as robust as the regime that enforces them.

Treason Narrows

Once democratic governance became the norm, treason changed profoundly. Democracies had weaker reason to fear treason than less-legitimated regimes, except as outside attack or a wholescale upheaval from within. Democratically legitimated regimes' authority rested on doing their citizens' biddings. Why would anyone overthrow themselves? The short answer was that almost no one did. Treason moved from being a crime of the elite—nobles battling each other for power—to one of outsiders, cranks, and fabulists—the Lord Haw Haws and Tokyo Roses of the world. The longer answer must also take account of the circumstances of World War II and the Cold War. As nations became carriers of competing ideologies (as during the earlier wars of religion), working for a foreign power meant more than helping enemies fight one's homeland for pay. Traitors took sides in an ideological battle. The fifth columnists in the West—Julius and Ethel Rosenberg, Guy Burgess, Harold Philby, and others from that quaint era when art historians had access to state secrets—were anticapitalist true believers. The dissidents of the totalitarian regimes were their mirror image.

But in the longer *durée* of modern history, treason fell into disuse. By the eighteenth century, interest in it was so slight that standard legal texts ceased discussing it in any detail. No other major crime, German observers calculated early in the twentieth century, was committed so infrequently.[134] Prosecutions occurred mainly in wartime and other crises. The world wars and interwar era saw clashing ideologies demanding ever firmer allegiance and a precarious geopolitical balance, with nations fearing attack and invasion. Legislation protecting nation and state unsurprisingly tightened.[135] In the United States, sedition laws suppressed radical unions during the 1920s. An uptick in treason prosecutions followed the Kennedy assassination in 1963. The Cold War rekindled treason charges, as did the Algerian conflict for France.[136] But even then treason law remained little used, compared to the early modern era, although Islamic terrorism in the West from the late twentieth century on has put it back in the limelight.

Once a blunderbuss in the early modern period, modern treason narrowed to a few crimes, mostly involving enemy powers and local collaborators. Modern law commonly distinguished between foreign and domestic treason, or what Germans call *Landesverrat* (treason) and *Hochverrat* (sedition).[137] In liberal democracies, treason was restricted to a few actions: attacks on public authorities, insubordination in the military, sabotage, and more generally the aiding and abetting of the enemy. The external aspects of treason included obvious instances of assisting foreign enemies: committing espionage, serving in their military, admitting them illegally into the national territory. The presumption was that in democracies both government and citizens opposed the enemy.

In contrast, modern democracies deal with sedition, the domestic aspects of treason, in two ways. Much of what would earlier have counted as seditious is now accepted criticism and dissent and thus something the modern state must tolerate. But not all. Democratic systems that otherwise regard freedom of speech as foundational have also been quick to punish when matters stray onto treason's turf. Regarding words as treasonable acts in their own right stands in a long tradition. Following Roman law, with its emphasis on sedition and disloyal thoughts, the English treason act of 1351 expanded treason to include compassing or imagining the death of the king—a purely internal event perceptible only to traitors themselves and perhaps to God. How then to know whether someone was guilty? Two centuries later, under Henry VIII in the treason act of 1534 the offense was broadened to include attempts to imperil the king's person, accomplished by writing or a similar manifest act. Calling the king a heretic, schismatic, tyrant, or the like was now treasonable.[138]

Courts came to accept spoken or written words alone as overt acts proving treason. In one extreme example from 1460, a tavern owner was convicted for promising to make his son, should he behave, heir to the throne.[139] During the French Revolution, about a third of the many thousands executed died merely because of what they had said or written.[140] The American Founding Fathers avoided making mere expression treasonable, but state statutes considered allegiance uttered to the English king treasonous.[141] A US statute of 1917 protecting the president from threats criminalized verbal attacks on his person, thereby sanctioning speech, and criticism of conscription was punished during World War I. In cases during World War II, propaganda was accepted as action and thus potentially treasonous.[142] To prevent overreach, courts sought to distinguish between true threats and mere hyperbole. Yet even those who made conditional threats in private were indicted.[143] On the whole, however, free-speech protections encouraged the state to accept that criticisms, even ones like those once considered treasonous, were the price of democracy. The authorities worried less about the content of utterances and more about whether they sought to undermine public order. Criticism was fine, riot not.[144]

Prosecutions of overt treason were reined in. But the modern democratic state also redirected its powers into other channels, retaining its defensive capacities in new guises. Treason laws were no longer the only or even the main bulwark against the state's enemies. It now deployed new potential charges. Since these charges were not subject to treason's procedural restrictions, through them the authorities in fact had greater leeway. Following the US Civil War, no one was prosecuted for treason, but laws regarding other, newly defined crimes now punished much the same acts. Rebellion and insurrection were criminalized in 1862, seditious conspiracy in 1861.[145] Such attempts to make an end run around treason proper survived challenges in court, which portrayed them as treason in all but name.[146] In the 1940s, similar treason substitutes were passed that outlawed advocating the government's overthrow.[147] In the United States, treason was seldom prosecuted during the Cold War, in part because the Supreme Court tightened up requirements in 1954. The authorities instead pursued threats via other means: rebellion, insurrection, trading with the enemy, seditious conspiracy, advocating overthrow of the government, piracy, and espionage were among the crimes now rolled out against treasonlike activities.[148] Alger Hiss was convicted of perjury in 1950, the Rosenbergs of conspiring to spy in 1951.[149]

Britain invented the crime of treason-felony in 1848 to prosecute those whose actions earlier would have required accusations of sedition.[150] During World War II, the new felony offense of treachery allowed pursuit of espionage and disloyalty without treason's cumbersome rules of evidence and procedure.[151] The French penal code of 1994 devoted an entire book to the grandiosely named crimes and misdemeanors against the nation, the state, and the public peace. The book defines treason in 10 articles and then proceeds to another 227 distinct articles, many covering several different acts.[152]

Modern states also turned to practical techniques to protect themselves. No-go zones from which civilians were excluded or forbidden to photograph became common.[153] Although modern leaders may no longer be protected by as many laws, they have become far more insulated from their constituents, making them physically harder to harm. They are assassinated most often at stopping points during travel, including parades.[154] Modern weaponry has in effect banished leaders from the open air. Their workplaces and homes have been sealed off like fortresses, and they travel in armor-plated vehicles. Such protective technologies would have been the envy of the Borgias and, until recently, would have been used only by the most despised dictators, such as Hitler and Stalin.[155]

The rough and tumble that leaders were once expected to endure astonishes the modern mind. The same day in 1800 that James Hadfield tried to assassinate George III in the Drury Lane Theater, the king had earlier been the object of a near-miss shooting during a Grenadier Battalion field exercise in Hyde Park. That same evening, on the way back from the theater, George was pursued by an angry mob, which dispersed only when the Bow Street officers made arrests.[156] Security precautions were laughable by modern standards. In 1840, a drunk wandered into the White House to spend the night unnoticed. John Wilkes Booth shot President Abraham Lincoln while the police officer assigned to his theater box was drinking in a nearby bar.[157] After an unsuccessful attempt on President Andrew Jackson's life in 1835, the would-be assassin was released on (an increased amount of) bail since there had been no actual battery.[158] The French king Louis-Philippe was the object of seven assassination attempts between the autumn of 1834 and the following summer.[159] When Queen Victoria was shot at in her carriage in 1842 and the assailant escaped, she and Albert were sent down the same route the next day (at a slightly faster pace) to flush out the would-be assassin.[160] Though he was indeed arrested on the second attempt, it seems highly unlikely that modern leaders would thus be treated like tethered goats—nor does a body double seem to have occurred to the Victorian imagination. Victoria's reign was long, but the eight attempts on her life put to shame what modern leaders are expected to endure. In the spring of 1878, Kaiser Wilhelm I survived two assassination attempts within three weeks, both on the same boulevard, Unter den Linden. Napoleon III, however, was widely suspected of having fabricated assassination plots to suppress his enemies.[161] And Felice Orsini's attempt on Napoleon's life in 1858 certainly prompted a widespread crackdown and massive deportations.

A logically unstable concept, treason has undergone two divergent developments. As the state increasingly came to serve the people as the ultimate sovereign, treason largely dissipated. Regime change no longer involved switches among ruling dynasties, who sought to bolster their own legitimacy by wielding treason laws against their enemies, only to have the same eventually done to them. In a popularly legitimated system, treason was almost self-contradictory. As an offense, it continued as a pale vestige of its former self, largely reduced to collaboration with external enemies. What had once been the worst possible crime, one the state expended its main efforts suppressing, had largely vanished by the nineteenth century. But the state's repressive machinery against those who would threaten its stability or harm its leaders took new forms. The modern state relinquished treason law as an arrow in its quiver not because it was weak but because it was too strong and all-controlling to need it any longer.

Chapter 5
Parallel Justice

In history's long sweep, the state eventually asserted its prerogative to maintain order on its own. It imposed its monopoly on violence by banning parallel means of resolving disputes that had long coexisted with the official machinery, both predating it and often persisting even today. Civil society adjudicated its own disputes long before the state was in a position to intervene and continued to do so long after it became a competitor. The state's claims to monopoly were not as absolute as it often pretended. Sometimes it enlisted private efforts on its own behalf, as we will see later with policing. Other times it tolerated a continuing role for civil society.

In the state's judicial role, its primary rival was the family. The family's head, the paterfamilias, ruled supreme within it, largely autonomous of statutory interference. Over wives and children, treated as property, his was the final word. In the earliest eras, he could sell his offspring or adopt them away, treating them—and his spouse(s)—largely as he pleased. Only gradually, under the Romans, was killing children or slaves forbidden.[1] Roman fathers built prison cells in their homes for disciplining. In the eighteenth century, the Bastille was filled with errant offspring locked up at their families' request—the Marquis de Sade among the most notorious. Physical abuse of children was likely the most frequent form of assault in this era.[2] The father also chose both his sons' and his daughters' spouses.

Only gradually did the state make inroads on this patriarchal preserve. With Solon, children could no longer be sold into slavery;

with Christianity they were no longer exposed. By the eighteenth century, women began to be allowed to own property and conduct themselves as legally independent of their families, and they were eventually allowed to vote. In the modern era, children were emancipated from absolute paternal power, too. The state required fathers to let them be registered at birth, drafted, educated, vaccinated, and inspected. It began meddling in inheritance, forbidding primogeniture, enforcing equality of offspring. It took over divorce from the church. It sought to determine how many children families bore—more or fewer depending on its needs. The young were emancipated from their fathers at an ever earlier age, becoming full subjects and then citizens in their own right. In Roman law, a father's power lapsed only with his death. Today, the children's late teen years are usually the cut-off. Such changes came late and often remain incomplete. Marital rape was outlawed only recently and not everywhere. Spousal abuse remains widespread—officially forbidden but tolerated nonetheless. Parents can still waive statutory-rape protections for minors in some US states and elsewhere by consenting to child marriages. Even today, parents determine more than half of all marriages globally.[3]

Beyond the family as a judicial institution, however, more specific mechanisms of adjudication have also vied with the state's pretension to sole power. Vigilantism is a general aspect of this self-administration of justice, duels a more specific instance. Both sought to implement justice, as locally defined, by sidestepping the state's claims to omnipotence. Both therefore had to go, and both eventually went. Of course, all justice began as vigilantism, civil society administering itself. The spontaneous stoning of criminals in ancient Greece and Rome is an example.[4] The logic of ostracism was much the same, though not lethal—a vote taken against those who had aroused enough ill feeling among their fellow citizens that they were voted out of society for a decade. Only as the state successfully established its monopoly was vigilante justice disparaged as unworthy.[5]

The duel was founded on consent—that both parties thus agreed to resolve their differences. Why should something consensual be forbidden them? Consent removes some actions from the law's purview, making them a matter of private negotiation. At a certain age, sex consented to is making love. Without permission, it is rape. With the proper forms signed, someone who violates your body with sharp instruments is not committing assault but performing heart surgery, inscribing a tattoo, or piercing your ears. Consent does not always sidestep the law's prohibition, though. Even agreed to, certain sexual acts—involving physical damage, for example—remain assaults, not just sadomasochistic foreplay.[6] Female genital mutilation cannot be agreed to; male circumcision is contested. A surgeon who cuts off your fingers could probably be charged with mayhem or assault even if you had agreed.[7] Neither murder nor assault can be mitigated by the victim consenting to be harmed.[8] You cannot sell yourself even willingly into slavery, though becoming an indentured servant was once interpreted as expressing individuals' right to control their own affairs.[9] Whether you can hawk your sexual services depends on the jurisdiction, as it does for selling or renting your organs or gametes.

Invoking consent, the duel also sought to exempt its particular violence and death from illegality. Duelists sought to be spared sanctions, as other legal killings such as justifiable homicide and self-defense were exempted. But the state would have none of it. True, the duel helped tame aristocratic brutality, refining and replacing the vendetta in the Renaissance.[10] In that sense, it helped lessen violence. Yet because duelers aimed to fashion their own sphere of private law, the state ultimately could not tolerate their combat, any more than it could vengeance or feud. Duelers were, as one seventeenth-century critic put it, lawless condemners of authority.[11]

Duels were ancient. David and Goliath fought one, and in the medieval trial by battle God himself intervened to indicate guilt or innocence in cases where the evidence was ambiguous and truth difficult to discern.[12] Yet Augustine inveighed against gladiatorial combats, and the medieval church rejected the shedding of Christian blood in duels.[13] Eric Haakonsson, governor of Norway in the eleventh century, outlawed duels.[14] The Council of Trent in the mid-sixteenth century excommunicated dueling Catholics, and Protestants followed suit. Though the duel was found in the Germanic codes, Roman law knew it not. Judicial battle, with its appeal to God's intervention, was undermined with the rise of Roman law in the twelfth century and rare by the fifteenth.[15] Duels instead shed their supernatural aura to become yet another means of feuding and a test merely of skill, bravery, and luck. In Njál's saga of the thirteenth century, when Mord is challenged to a duel, his friends point out that he is likely to lose since Hrut is strong and brave.[16] By the sixteenth century, the modern secular duel had arrived: a vindication of honor, not an evidentiary technique, and no longer an element of the judicial system but deliberately outside it.

From the state's vantage, the modern duel actually had much to recommend it. Unlike feuds or vendettas, duels were first limited to aristocrats and restricted in scope. Duels were fought between equals over points of honor, which were slippery to legislate, prosecute, and punish. Challenges could not be issued up the social scale and were wasted if aimed down.[17] Compared to full-scale feuds, duels were orderly and conducted with discretion. Only two men fought, their interaction ritualized, with few chances of drawing others in and thus expanding the conflict. Duels also ended, once and for all, disputes that might escalate. Even if both parties survived, the duel settled their conflict.[18] Yet its aristocratic pedigree made it appealing to other social groups. With the middle classes emulating their betters, dueling democratized to become all the rage in eighteenth-century Germany.[19] Dueling scars became male adornment. The dueling associations of the Central European universities issued leather masks with strategically placed slits so that facial scars could be decoratively inflicted as fashion dictated. In eighteenth-century England, workers, too, settled conflicts with ritualized fistfights.[20] Even the democratic New World enjoyed such aristocratic vestiges. The American South was naturally fertile soil, but the habit also spread farther north. In 1804, Aaron Burr killed Alexander Hamilton in New Jersey shortly after Hamilton's son had died in a duel.[21]

The duel's popularity threatened the state's pretensions to monopolize adjudication. The absolutist state pacified unruly nobles in part by suppressing duels. Louis XIV managed to eradicate the duel among his courtiers, drawing them into the gilded panopticon of Versailles and undermining their raucously independent lives in Paris or the provinces.[22] The English upper classes abandoned duels early on. James I forbade challenges in the early seventeenth century. In the 1840s, officers who encouraged duels were court-martialed, and widows of duelists were stripped of their pensions. The last known duel with a lethal outcome in England was fought by two Frenchmen in 1852.[23] In eighteenth-century Massachusetts, judges were required to sentence duelers to death and then dissection. Peter the Great ordered the bodies of both the slain duelist and the winner hanged alongside each other.[24] In the 1830s, Alabama made aspiring lawyers affirm they had never dueled. To this day, would-be Kentucky state legislators must swear that they have never partaken in a duel.[25]

Statutes against dueling were but one facet of the state's attempt to suppress vigilante justice more generally. Vigilantism can be thought of in at least two ways. Before the state was able to administer justice, vigilantism improvised it. But once the state staked its claim, vigilantism competed with it. The benign view of vigilantism, as the provision of what the state eventually would do, sees it as delivering services the authorities failed at and relying on volunteer labor drafted only as required.[26] The English hundreds were one form of such self-administered justice, as were the twelfth-century Sicilian *Vendicatori*, the *Vehm* in early modern Germany, and today's many mafias. *Samosud* in Russia was the popular justice administered by peasant communities in the absence of much official policing. With *maling* in eighteenth-century Holland, crowds manhandled thieves caught red-handed, who were often spared only by being arrested.[27] The Regulators in eighteenth-century back-country South Carolina provided law enforcement where the state failed. "Jeddart justice" refers to Jedburgh, a Scotch border town where raiders were hanged without trial.[28] To this day, even well-policed states such as France and Germany allow private citizens to bring flagrant offenders to justice.[29]

Vigilantism not only enforced neglected laws but also often prescribed behavior dictated by sentiments of justice and morality that were popular though not on the books—and, indeed, often illegal. Because vigilantism competed with the state, it was inherently a relapse as citizens briefly took back the sovereignty they had otherwise yielded to the authorities. Long-standing vigilante movements were a contradiction in terms.[30] Vigilantes broke the law to achieve what they deemed just. Rough music, charivaris, and shivarees were of this ilk: humiliating those who had violated custom and tradition, such as old men who took young brides or henpecked or cuckolded husbands or wife beaters.

Vigilantism sometimes served broadly sympathetic causes: prosecution associations bringing felons to heel in eighteenth-century England; citizens uniting to bring order to lawless territory in the nineteenth-century American West; Guardian Angels patrolling inner-city neighborhoods ignored by the police; communities banding together to drive out drug dealers or flush out hoarded food during shortages; Queer Nation helping curb discrimination against sexual minorities; and the so-called Regulars in eighteenth-century New York State who—dressed in women's clothing—flogged abusive husbands.[31] Fictional accounts stand in this line: Robin Hood, the Three Musketeers, the Virginian, Zorro, the superheroes of comic strip, screen, and digital game.[32] In this spirit, vigilantism was often romanticized as expressing popular sovereignty, a form of temporary self-rule, like other social movements. If law were ultimately made by the people, so this logic went, why should they not also enforce it?[33] Vigilantism was democracy or self-rule in its rawest, least-mediated form.

Yet lynch justice often ruled instead. Hate-filled mobs bayed for blood while the state stood aside: when Protestants were massacred in the sixteenth century, Jews were slaughtered in pogroms, Native Americans were killed like wild animals, Blacks were hanged to teach them their place.[34] Orgies of violence, overpowering whatever the authorities may have done to quell them, vented savage hatreds.[35] Mob justice occasionally accompanied widespread social breakdown, as in St. Petersburg following the revolution of February 1917.[36] But it has equally been part of otherwise stable and functioning systems and often even a means to achieve goals the authorities tacitly accepted. The mob's motives could at times arguably be unobjectionable: when child molesters were publicly ostracized and driven out of communities; when a woman who refused to clean up after her dog on the subway in Korea was hounded by a massive harassment campaign.[37]

Named after Charles Lynch, a justice of the peace who supervised extralegal executions of Tory sympathizers during the revolution, lynch justice in nineteenth-century America marked the limits of the state's pretensions to enforce law on its own terms.[38] Lynching expressed a rough popular justice, with white crowds meting out vastly more severe punishments than the law foresaw on despised, often innocent, and almost invariably Black victims. Black men showing a sexual interest in white women unleashed the white vox populi's extraordinary savagery.[39] In the American South, lynching was a de facto parallel system of "justice" for much of the 1900s. In part, lynching filled a gap in the state's enforcement, but it equally gave voice to a different conception of law altogether, one that—neither legalistic nor universal but brutally retributive—upheld the property, racial, and sexual hierarchies defended by rural whites. More justice and less law, was how one Wyoming lyncher put it in 1902.[40] In the late nineteenth century, even the recorded number of such killings—and many lynchings likely went unrecorded—far surpassed official executions.[41] At a snail's pace, the state eventually suppressed this regime of terror. Lynchings declined from more than 150 annually in the 1890s to half that at the turn of the century and into single digits by the 1940s.[42]

But rather than being stamped out, southern whites' baying for blood was then arguably institutionalized within the state's judicial machinery. State executions increased as extralegal killings were eliminated, the authorities themselves thus satisfying the popular demand for retribution. The American South and Southwest, lynching's heartland, today have the highest execution rates in the country. The death penalty's popularity here gives voice to a form of community justice, now inflicted not directly by lynching but indirectly as the authorities respond to popular demand.[43] The continued popularity of capital punishment in China similarly sustains the Maoist doctrine of whipping up popular hatreds against enemies, slaking a widespread demand for revenge.[44]

Chapter 6
Why Punish?

Many motives, sometimes contradictory, have prompted crime's punishment, and they have historically shifted in emphasis and focus. The fundamental philosophical dispute has pitted retribution and a hope of delivering justice for the wronged against a more utilitarian concern with diminishing crime that was willing to employ techniques that did not necessarily treat the harmed as they deserved. An innocent good-faith buyer of stolen property, for example, was usually considered its legal owner. The need to keep markets unencumbered by endless disputes over title took precedence over the original owner's absolute title: efficiency trumped fairness.[1] These opposing positions have been argued in largely all eras. Though the two are theoretically exclusive, in fact some combination of justice and usefulness has motivated almost all state actions.

The kin groups who once settled disputes among themselves typically sought revenge and retribution. Harm needed to be set right, an out-of-kilter moral balance reequilibrated. Compensation was demanded for damage to life and limb, to intangible property (the monetary value of men's sexual monopoly over women), or to reputation. Ancient and early medieval law listed precise values: for each particular mutilation or for the rape of other men's wives, daughters, or female slaves. But how to deal with losses that were hard or impossible to compensate? Taking revenge at least gave the satisfaction of equal damage, a negative compensation for a loss that could never otherwise be made good. The talionic one-to-one logic of retribution sought to cap the otherwise potentially unbridled frenzy of revenge: an eye for an eye, death for death, amputations of the offending limb or member.[2] Even hell was imagined talionically: blasphemers hanging by their tongues, adulteresses by their hair.[3]

Beyond this logic, who sought to punish? That victims and their kin were keen on revenge is obvious. Less clear is why the state—concerned to maintain order and take a broader view—should also pursue retribution. When authority was the offended party, as with treason, then its motives were akin to kin's. For threats against the group as a whole—public harms—the group responded as a unit, as in the ancient Greek pollution theory of crime. But as the state assumed responsibility for regulating a group that was more variegated than kin, with multiple and contradictory interests, it necessarily became more concerned with order than with retribution. At that point, authorities were likely to have stepped back from avenging harm to considering instead their broader aims in prosecuting crime. Although vengeance might satisfy the individual or the kin, it also created disorder through ongoing feud that undermined social harmony. The state needed to be seen ensuring justice, but justice was more than retribution.

From a practical vantage, the state was as concerned to maintain order as to dispense individual justice. Ensuring justice was part of underwriting stability, but too narrow and individual a concept of justice, with no concern for social utility, undermined that order. Vengeance delivered a narrow form of justice for the harmed party, but the rest of society gained little and indeed suffered from continued mayhem in vengeance's wake. So was the answer a more utilitarian approach, which took the aggregate well-being of most citizens as its primary goal? That approach threw up problems, too. Social utility could be maximized only by violating primal notions of fairness and equity. Some offenders would be let off, some innocents punished—if that promoted order. From a utilitarian vantage, what mattered was the damage caused by criminals, not why they had offended. Not criminals' motives or intent but the harm they inflicted should determine their punishment, the Enlightenment philosophe Cesare Beccaria argued in 1764.[4] From this vantage, punishing a successful assassin made sense, but punishing one who had overslept or missed the mark, killing no one, perhaps did not.[5] It could be socially efficient to punish only mildly or even not at all if it did not deter future crime. Why bother prosecuting the aged death-camp guard?[6] If punishment prevented no offenses, what was the point? Bentham asked. It would just be "adding one evil to another." But if it did deter others, then the otherwise "base and repugnant" sanction was justified as "an indispensable sacrifice to the common safety."[7]

If preventing crime could be achieved by other means, then a utilitarian approach considered punishment unnecessary. If hanging someone in effigy deterred, Bentham argued, then actually stringing up offenders would be cruel.[8] But the same logic might equally dictate punishing even the innocent in pursuit of useful outcomes. What if hanging every ten-thousandth passer-by reduced crime? Either way, in this view punishment was set not in relation to the crime already committed (what was just and deserved) but in terms of what would prevent future offenses (what was useful). The two extremes of these divergent approaches—retribution and social usefulness—can be nicely juxtaposed thus: Why punish a prisoner who was certain not to offend again? the utilitarians asked.[9] In contrast, Kant famously argued that even in a society that had agreed to dissolve itself, the last capital offender should nonetheless be executed in order to square the moral accounts, however little consequence or effect this killing might have.[10]

Retributionists were concerned with desert, utilitarians with danger. But desert and dangerousness unfortunately often pointed in different directions. Some deserved punishment, though they no longer posed a threat. Others were real dangers, though they had yet to commit a crime. Did that mean sentencing on the basis of predicted offending—leniency for the now toothless monster but lengthy terms for those with vividly sadistic imaginations? Or, more mundanely, did it mean longer sentences for the recently unemployed, who were revealed by statistical analysis to be more likely to offend?[11] Once the tie between offense and its punishment was cut, seeking instead some socially beneficial outcome, all bets were off. Why punish attempted murder less than completed homicide when the would-be killer was as morally culpable and dangerous as the one who succeeded?[12] However, a desert-based approach struggled to explain why a particular crime merited precisely this or that punishment. Did an eye balance the moral books for an eye? Why death for theft? For that matter, why death for any of the other two hundred capital crimes in eighteenth-century England?

Treating criminals as they supposedly deserved also produced dysfunctional outcomes. Branding criminals on the cheek in eighteenth-century England prevented them from resuming normal life.[13] Torturing to extract confessions crippled suspects who later proved to be innocent. The law requiring that forgers be executed, London bankers complained in 1830, encouraged juries to let them off, thus endangering the property rights the law sought to protect. When arrests for domestic violence were mandated, reporting the crime dropped off.[14] Overly harsh punishments could spur more crime, not deter it. In Russia, Montesquieu observed, where both robbery and murder were punished by death, thieves killed their victims. Why spare a witness?[15] In Qin era China (third century BCE), rain delayed a group of convicts en route to a military camp. Since the punishment for arriving late was death, there was no downside to the revolt they decided to stage instead.[16] The recent intense scrutiny of pedophilia, it has been argued, has ironically helped sexualize childhood, thus perhaps exacerbating the crimes it seeks to avoid.[17]

The dispute between justice and utility has been ongoing, tipping one way or the other. The polarities have been presented here abstractly and ahistorically. But the themes are discernable in almost every epoch. Just deserts or socially useful goals? Justinian's sixth-century Digest focused on desert, defining justice as "a steady and enduring will to render everyone his right."[18] Kant amplified this central principle of Roman law, insisting that punishment should pursue no goal other than meting out what is deserved.[19] Contemporary retributionists resist the utilitarian neglect of desert, insisting that punishment instead articulate society's moral outrage.[20] Utilitarians in turn not only have promised beneficial outcomes from punishment but have also sought to conquer their own moral high ground. The state has no more right to inflict pain and death, they have insisted, than do its citizens. Only the pursuit of a broader social goal—less crime—could justify sanctions. Mere retribution, without seeking to reduce crime, Hobbes argued, is but an act of hostility by the sovereign.[21] Locke considered punishment justified only insofar as it makes repairs or seeks to avoid future crime.[22] All punishment is evil, Bentham agreed, and allowable only if it prevents some larger harm.[23]

Merely imposing just deserts could lead to pointless retribution, unconcerned with actual effect—Did crime increase afterward, did offenders transgress again? Sheer utilitarianism, at the other extreme, could tinker amorally, punishing without fairness or justice so long as the outcomes were desirable. In practice, most punishments have evaluated both the damage done as well as the intent behind the act. We do not punish for just the harm caused (otherwise accidental damages would be penalized as harshly as intentional ones) and only rarely for the intent alone (otherwise the would-be killer or even the sadistic fantasist would be jailed for as long as the actual murderer). Evil intent has generally prompted harsher punishments for the actions it motivated and sometimes, as we will see, has been penalized by itself. Conversely, harms caused accidentally or inadvertently have been punished less severely or not at all (except under strict liability in the common law world, where intent and negligence are irrelevant).

The motives prompting punishment have often been classified as to whether they look backward, to atoning for crimes already committed, or forward, to avoiding future offenses.[24] Thus, revenge, restitution, and other measures to reestablish moral balance sought to rectify past injustice. They were concerned primarily with the individual criminal and with society only insofar as they aimed to restore its overall ethical equilibrium. Incapacitation, deterrence, rehabilitation, and prevention, in turn, aimed to improve the future. They were concerned more with bettering society than with making offenders pay. Individual criminals were reformed or incapacitated. Those incapable of reform had to be incapacitated, at the extreme by death. If they were used as examples, others' behavior might be affected. Incapacitation aimed less to punish than to render offenders harmless, halting any further predations.

Deterrence looked forward, but it affected the future only insofar as making criminals' present circumstances publicly miserable did in fact discourage others from emulation. Its logic was that even if offenders were not capable of rehabilitation and only suffered by being punished, others contemplating their fates might be reformed and avoid crime—a second-order rehabilitation.[25] Rehabilitation, in turn, acted on present criminals, expecting to improve their future conduct. Finally, prevention most actively shaped the future by intervening, not just to reform today's transgressors or merely to make the environment less prone to crime but to anticipate future acts and discourage potential criminals or punish them beforehand by laws on inchoate offenses.

The dividing line between backward- and forward-oriented punishments has been imprecise both conceptually and historically. Already Plato discussed punishment in terms of learning virtue and deterring future acts rather than just in terms of taking vengeance for the past, which he dismissed as a primitive, animalistic motive.[26] Yet retribution has remained a motive in the modern world. Indeed, it enjoyed a renaissance in the twentieth century, with desert weighing heavily in determining punishment.[27] Conversely, even when administering just deserts retributively, punishment can deter if potential offenders understand that they are likely to be caught and sanctioned. All human punishments, "in a large and extended view," the English jurist William Blackstone wrote in the eighteenth century, are more intended to prevent future crimes than to expiate past ones.[28] Whatever its immediate motives, a well-functioning system of justice deters.

Any given punishment could be motivated in different ways. Largely all punishments could be retributive, except in cases where offenders actively welcomed the outcome—as with murders intended to prompt capital punishment, thus disguising a suicide. In religions where killing could be forgiven but self-killing could not, suicide by murder followed logically—at least if God were thought too obtuse to see through the ruse. Swedes, especially women, killed others to achieve suicide without eternal damnation. Theirs was the predominant form of homicide in Stockholm in the late seventeenth century. The victims often were children, innocents who did not have to repent their sins before death. Muslims in the Philippines have masked their desire for death in jihadist attacks that lead to their killing. Suicide by cop is a short-cut variant.[29]

If suffering were required, then retributive punishment of masochists was definitionally impossible. Indeed, exoneration would be the only feasible sanction. That logic cropped up as the authorities sought to deal with suicidal murderers of the sort just mentioned. Paul Johann von Feuerbach's draft of the Bavarian penal code in 1810 commuted execution to lifelong labor in chains if the offender was aiming to commit suicide.[30] In Denmark, torture was first added to the death penalty in hopes of deterring would-be suicides. When that did not work, capital punishment for those who sought death through murder was abolished altogether in 1767—a penal enactment of the old joke where when the masochist says, "Hurt me, hurt me," the sadist says, "No."

If rehabilitation were painful or unpleasant, even it could be retributive—as is often true of prisons.[31] Carried out in secret, many punishments merely incapacitated, while when carried out in public they also deterred—both the offender (except when executed) and others. Shaming punishments definitionally had to be public and were both retributive and deterrent. Besides being retributive, death and banishment could also be both incapacitating and deterrent. So could certain kinds of mutilation, especially the so-called sympathetic talionic punishments: amputating thieves' hands, pederasts' testicles, rapists' penises, or blasphemers' and slanderers' tongues.[32]

Death could be retributive and deterrent but never rehabilitative. Nor could a true life sentence in prison—or at least it did not matter even if it were.[33] Fines, depending on their level, could be retributive, deterrent, or compensatory or all three, but unlikely rehabilitative.[34] Prison could be retributive, deterrent, incapacitating, preventive, and perhaps even rehabilitative. Forced labor could be compensatory, deterrent (and even better than execution since it lasted longer), and possibly rehabilitative.[35] Banishment has been understood both as incapacitating and—by the ancient Greeks—as rehabilitative because part of a purification ritual. In the British penal colony of New South Wales, banishment also rehabilitated the many convicts, who subsequently became useful citizens.[36] And retributive punishments implemented fairly and firmly could have deterrent and thus utilitarian effects by demonstrating that the justice system worked and would punish miscreants.[37] Looking just at the punishment did not always reveal the motives behind it.

Nevertheless, the broad historical trend has been from retrospective to prospective approaches, from retribution to rehabilitation. Blips mar the smooth curve of any long-term evolution. It is always difficult to date developments precisely, nor do they occur everywhere simultaneously. But we can discern a rough outline. Starting in the sixteenth century, the newly powerful and effective core European states enforced the law more harshly than ever before as they refined their own powers of imposing justice. But having rattled its sabers, the state needed less to demonstrate its ferocity as its prowess improved. That trend toward greater moderation has continued largely into the present. A detailed study of any subperiod will naturally unveil many variations in this large-scale development. Physical mutilation, rare in the late Middle Ages in England, revived under the Tudors.[38] Having faded with the Enlightenment philosophes, a retributive justice was revived by Kant and then Hegel in the nineteenth century. From the early nineteenth century, US prisons pursued rehabilitation. Overcrowding in the post–Civil War period ended such efforts. Rehabilitation returned in the twentieth century but again was abandoned by penal theorists and practitioners in the mid-1960s.[39]

Starting in the 1970s, retribution made a comeback, both among reformers who thought that punishment's social utility had been overemphasized at the expense of basic notions of justice as well as in penal practice. Now came mandatory minimum sentences, enhanced sanctions for habitual offenders, reduction of parole, and, above all, the late twentieth century's massive expansion of incarceration.[40] In the Islamic world, punishments have become notably harsher in recent decades, with executions, stonings, and merciless lashings. Criminals are still executed in public in China, Pakistan, and the Middle East.[41] Compensation and restitution have also enjoyed second lives in the form of "restorative" justice, focusing more attention on victims than did retribution or social utility. Community-service requirements, too, have offered a mild form of restitution to society as a whole.[42]

Nonetheless, in a long historical trajectory it is hard to overlook two fundamental developments. Most obviously, though punishment had long been civil society's task, it finally became the state's largely exclusive province. Less undeniably but nonetheless true, the state has been more concerned with society's overall functioning than with individual justice—except insofar as a fair judiciary is necessary for a well-run system. The state's attention has turned evermore to punishment's social utility. Preventing future offenses has become more pressing than atoning for past acts. That has meant a shift from retributive justice to the prevention of crime. A moderation of the ferocious inflictions of the past has, in turn, been one welcome outcome.

Chapter 7
How to Punish?

Punishments have varied along with the motives prompting them. Exchanges of value—whether in specie or goods—made atonement a transactional arrangement. Offenders paid the costs they had imposed. With vengeance, death was the currency of justice. Feuds were often long and sanguinary. Nonetheless, the logic of restitution limited overly bloody revenges. A dead goose laid no golden eggs. Most of the punishments of the past are no longer used: mutilation (though male sex offenders are sometimes chemically or physically castrated), branding, shame, and humiliation (though public registries of sex offenders and chain gangs still exist), torture (in many nations), banishment (in most nations), and death (in many nations). The punishments that remain, at least in the West, are imprisonment and an endless array of fines.

Banishment

Most simply, criminals have been rendered harmless by getting rid of them, either by death or by banishment, outlawing, deportation, or exile. The Incas made many crimes capital for this reason. They never fined or confiscated goods since what was the point of allowing a poorer but still dangerous criminal to remain?[1] The etymology of the term *exterminate* suggests a combination of execution and banishment—death as the ultimate bringing beyond the boundary: *ex terminus*. Execution separated the criminal once and for all from society; exile served the same purpose less absolutely. Plato envisioned a form of imprisonment far from human habitation. The Greeks practiced ostracism, a popular vote to banish dangerous citizens for a decade.[2] Both Greek and Roman law allowed a choice between death and banishment.[3] Exile could be temporary, as among the Greeks, who regarded it as a form of purification. Or it could be perpetual, as in ancient Egypt, where an ultimate punishment, debaptism, also eradicated criminals' names, obliterating offenders in both this world and the next.[4] For serious crimes, such as parricide, the Greeks cast the offender's body out of the city, denying it burial and any postmortem home.[5] The Chinese both banished—physical removal—and excluded, a kind of internal isolation in shame. With excommunication—a form of spiritual banishment in the Middle Ages ("God's outlaw")—exile acquired a new dimension.[6]

Banishment followed a certain topological logic that made it suitable in some times and places but largely useless elsewhere. It worked well in a sparsely populated world with abundant destinations for exiles—ungoverned spaces.[7] But as the nation-state, with its territorially defined sense of sovereignty, arose in the early modern era, most spaces belonged to someone. Frontiers became borders, and formerly liminal territories were now apportioned.[8] In such denser and more clearly delineated circumstances, your neighbors implicitly had to cooperate in any banishment meted out as punishment and might indeed display their hostility precisely by giving your internal enemies refuge. In small tribal societies, banishment could mean physical as well as social death. Among the Jews, *karet* was to be cut off from the people, and so flogging was considered preferable.[9] Bereft of their property, exiles from ancient Athens lived hard-scrabble lives.[10] At first, exile made a virtue of necessity—to escape vengeance a killer had to flee. In ancient Greece, *atimia* was a form of outlawry. Anyone might kill or plunder those so sentenced, thus encouraging distance. In largely unpoliced societies, outlawing offenders was the best that could be done with those who escaped apprehension.[11]

Nonetheless, in antiquity exile was a well-regulated condition. Rules governed, for example, how shipwrecks cast up on forbidden shores should conduct themselves. If they kept one foot in the water, they were spared until they could depart again. Recidivists, tried in territories they were banished from, mounted their defense from a boat, with the judges sitting on the beach.[12] In the Old Testament, exiles went to one of six designated and signposted cities of refuge, where they were protected from avengers and lived rent free until their case had been resolved.[13] Cain, though threatened with wandering the earth, was in fact taken under God's protection, as indicated by a mark put upon him (but protected from whom given that the only other humans alive were his parents, Adam and Eve?). He settled in neighboring Nod, east of Eden, where he founded the city of Enoch and a dynasty, including a great-great-great-great-great grandchild Jubal, father of all who play stringed instruments and pipes—not a bad outcome for the first fratricide.[14]

Before modern nations patrolled their borders and transported offenders, outlawing, banishing, or exiling criminals helped keep them from one particular place, without necessarily specifying where they should be. Outlawing was less precise and possibly less effective than banishment or exile. The ancient Chinese spelled out in sentencing how far defendants had to remove themselves. In medieval Iceland, a small island nation, outlawry in practice meant banishment. Along with fines, it was the most common sanction.[15] Medieval exile could mean having to go live in a certain place, such as a monastery, or being forbidden to linger anywhere for more than a few days and thus sentenced to perpetual wandering.[16] The early modern Spaniards often removed those sentenced to hard labor to Africa. The eighteenth-century Parisian police gave first-time petty offenders the option of returning to their native provinces—banishment lite.[17] Other than killers, exile was often used to remove political enemies for whom normal penalties seemed inappropriate. Ovid was banished from Rome, and this function remained well into the Middle Ages.[18] The Bourbon monarchs sent nobles who had fallen out of favor at court abroad or, for lesser offenses, to their provincial estates. The French revolutionaries made clear that old-regime refugees were never welcome back. The Napoleonic penal code banished political criminals, but until midcentury the lack of suitable French territories left this exile a largely theoretical option.[19] The English began transporting ordinary criminals to the colonies in the early seventeenth century. In an era when prisons were porous and inefficient, banishment was a more reliable incapacitation—excarceration instead of incarceration. A century later, having tallied up the exorbitant costs of domestic prisons, they started deporting convicts to Australia.[20]

In medieval England, vastly more convicts were outlawed than hanged. In the seventeenth and eighteenth centuries, almost all (97 percent) noncapital criminals in Amsterdam were banished. Banishment from Paris was also far more common than imprisonment.[21] With the revolution, the French began exiling political prisoners to Guiana in South America, and then after 1848 and the Commune of 1870 they set in motion waves of expulsion to other places as well, such as New Caledonia. After 1885, they transported hardened criminals to colonial penal settlements—the bloodless guillotines, so called because of their high mortality. Having once begun, the French continued this practice long after others had ceased, well into the 1930s.[22] Before the American Revolution, three-fifths of all English male convicts were transported. Even in the 1830s, about one-third of convicts went to other colonies.[23] The English convict transports arguably fell victim to their own success. New South Wales became a prosperous colony with a largely free population. As of the 1840s, the residents grew reluctant to admit more transportees.[24]

On a larger scale, groups defined as enemies, whether religious, ethnic, or political, were banished. Jews were expelled from England in 1290 and from Spain in 1492, followed by Moriscos (descendants of Muslim converts) in 1609. French Protestants, the Huguenots, were forced out of the country after 1685. Native Americans were expelled from their ancestral lands across the nineteenth century, as were other first peoples in the English settler colonies. The Turkish genocide of Armenians in 1915 occurred in the guise of forced population transfers. Greeks and Turks expelled each other in mutual population transfers in 1923. The Madagascar Plan, proposed in June 1940 by the Nazis as a means of ridding Europe of Jews, was a last delusional fantasy of large-scale banishment. The mass killing of Jews in death camps began in mid-1942 when it became clear, as the German advance into the Soviet Union bogged down after Stalingrad, that merely pushing them eastward out of Europe was no longer an option.[25] Such "excisionary violence," with banishment and extermination the endpoints on a continuum, has arguably characterized not only totalitarian regimes but also the colonial policies of otherwise modern liberal states. In the relatively moderate guise of ethnic cleansing, where deportation but not death was the aim, excisionary violence has been practiced over the past two centuries in most European nations, in the partition of India, and in British-ruled Palestine.[26]

Internal exile was used instead of prison. In the sixteenth century, the Florentines sent convicts to malarial areas around Pisa and Livorno. Corfu—now the playground of yacht owners—was a Venetian penal colony. More generally, *confino* was a form of internal exile to remote locales.[27] Carlo Levi wrote memorably of his time in exile to a small village in Lucania under Mussolini in *Christ Stopped at Eboli* (1945). The Russians put Siberia to use. Because the tsars exiled political prisoners, a stint in Siberia became a Communist badge of honor, Vladimir Lenin taking his nom de plume from the Lena River. The Soviets, in turn, adopted both internal and external exile, using domestic passports to eliminate freedom of movement. Large swaths of the country were turned into de facto penal colonies, with harsh terrain hampering escape as surely as barbed wire.[28] In imperial China, exiles from one province were always sent to a particular twinned province. Only in the early twentieth century did internal exile begin to be dismantled here.[29]

However common in the past, banishment has largely ended today. Pursued too vigorously, it created its own problems, as when the Chinese discovered in the nineteenth century that they had banished so many prisoners to Ili in Xinjiang that the local governor worried they would ally with "outside barbarians" to foment rebellion.[30] Prison and camps took over the incapacitation that banishment had once achieved. Exile today is a polite fiction, allowing peaceful regime change in autocracies. Former dictators flee prosecution, taking themselves off on last-minute flights to friendly neighbors, trailing mistresses, wardrobes, and suitcases of cash. The Ugandan dictator Idi Amin was emblematic of modern exile—a well-upholstered pariah, holed up as guest of the Saudis on the top floors of the Jeddah Novotel.[31] Exiles today tend to be ideological refugees, given shelter in sympathetic nations—such as the Allende Chileans, the Tanzanian socialists, and the Kurdish independence fighters in Sweden during the 1970s. Today's sanctuary cities in America protect undocumented immigrants, who are viewed sympathetically as victims of circumstance and harsh federal immigration legislation. Embassies, too, at times give sanctuary to prominent dissidents abroad, and churches continue their role as places beyond secular law.

But in other respects exile has become morally impossible. Banishment assumes that transgression in one place is inconsequential elsewhere, that no common legal and moral standards hold everywhere. Though having committed serious offenses, criminal exiles were tolerated abroad. That is no longer possible. Though Socrates drew the opposite conclusion, he put his finger on the problem when he refused an offer of exile, preferring compulsory suicide: Why would foreigners put up with his ideas if his fellow Athenians did not?[32] Real criminals can no longer be banished. Far from accepting exported miscreants, a vigilant abroad requires they be kept at home. Australia has recently drawn the logical consequence, preventing pedophiles from traveling abroad by refusing them passports.[33] A universal moral codex by and large holds globally, and a violator of it in one place would only exceptionally be tolerated elsewhere. The banished have vanished.

That shift in turn has led to a revival of domestic exile. The residence of sex offenders in the US, for example, is regulated much like the Soviet system of internal banishment. They are required to register, and their neighbors are notified, free to draw their own conclusions. The restrictions on their housing (proximity to schools, parks, and the like) are often so expansive that nowhere suitable remains.[34] In New York City, only 14 of 270 homeless shelters can receive released sex offenders. Those who cannot find a bed in these overcrowded facilities often remain in prison.[35] Thanks to GPS monitoring, not just residence but movement too can be restricted.[36] Domestic banishment also continues in another sense, at least in the United States and Britain. With the increased use of true life sentences, either multiple or without parole, prison has become a means to remove offenders permanently from society, with no expectation of rehabilitation. In 2012, a third of all Americans serving life sentences had no prospect of parole.[37] Sentences in the United States also sometimes explicitly remove defendants from their local communities, as in the aptly named Project Exile.[38] In addition, European countries are increasingly deporting foreign criminals after they serve their sentences, back to homelands they often never or only long ago lived in.[39]

Fines

For millennia, imposing payments as compensation for offenses was the most common sanction. But it wasn't until the state began collecting such payments that they became fines. With the rise of the prison in the eighteenth century, compensation was partly eclipsed, for serious offenses at least. Nor has it received anything like the scholarly attention lavished on incarceration. But in the modern era, monetary restitution, now in the form of fines, has again become a widespread sanction.[40] Precisely how common is hard to measure. In absolute terms, the sheer volume of levies, such as parking tickets, probably makes fines seem more important than they are. Some nations, such as the US, or the East Bloc in its time, used fines less than others.[41] For indictable offenses in Britain, fines peaked at almost half of all punishments in the 1980s, falling subsequently to half that. But they almost definitionally make up the bulk of punishments imposed on organizations.[42]

With vengeance and restitution, the disputing parties agreed on an exchange of value or death to resolve matters. Two millennia before Christ, Eshunna's code in Sumeria threatened fines and death as its only sanctions.[43] At first, monetary compensation was paid directly by the offender to the victim. Only later did the state insist on its cut, eventually imposing pecuniary sanctions as an alternative to more direct bodily chastisement.[44] The word *fine* itself comes from the final settlement (*finalis concordia*) negotiated by the offender with a medieval king so that he could be released from prison. Prison was not the punishment as such but merely the means by which the criminal was encouraged to pay the fine.[45] In medieval England, felons' property reverted to the king. If accused felons refused to plead one way or the other, they were subjected to *peine forte et dure*, being pressed to death with weights. But if they endured this torture, thus dying without being convicted, their estates were saved for their heirs.[46] In Norman England, amercements were penalties payable to the Crown for misdeeds.[47] Among the early Germans, part of the mulct went to the king. Scandinavian rulers started collecting their part of wergeld in the Middle Ages.[48] In eighteenth-century America, fines imposed for biting, gouging, or maiming were paid half to the victim, half to the state.[49] The authorities ultimately took everything, transforming compensation into fines in the modern sense. Restitution was now due the community, no longer to the individual victim. Today, only civil fines and judgments for damages recall the original sense of victims being compensated.[50]

Once fines in the modern sense had emerged, the state faced a choice. It could levy them to make offenders pay for externalities, pricing their behavior through what in effect was a tax baked into the cost of doing business. Fines on polluting industries or for workplace accidents have been of this ilk—forcing offenders to pay some part of the costs of their actions without necessarily halting those acts altogether.[51] The Factory Act of 1844 in Britain required employers to fence in dangerous machinery and enforced this by imposing fines. In effect, it remained the employers' decision whether to fence or to pay the fines.[52] Fines on the nineteenth-century sex trade raised revenue, presupposing that prostitutes would continue business in order to pay.[53] Fines on those who shirked civic duties similarly taxed the negligent. Eighteenth-century Londoners could buy their way out of their required participation in the watch by hiring a substitute. In the American colonies, citizens who refused or failed their tasks as constables or sheriffs were fined. Traffic and other everyday fines, too, are much like post hoc licenses.[54]

But fines have also been used to compel. If raised to exceed the value of the offense, fines can be an indirect means of coercion, compelling offenders to change behavior. Were acts the state wished to discourage to be priced or penalized?[55] Sometimes pricing could be used to punish. Though not obliterating the person, fines could extinguish someone economically. The Romans exorbitantly valued damaged goods when they wanted to compel restitution of the actual objects rather than just have damages paid.[56] Henry VII used bonds and recognizances to coerce his nobility, four-fifths of whom were at some time indebted to him. When Lord Abergavenny was fined £70,000 for unlawful retaining, it was not with the expectation that he would pay but as leverage to relieve him of £500 annually. Convicted of blasphemy in 1676 and fined 1,000 Marks he could not pay, John Taylor was effectively jailed for life.[57] Up through the 1940s, prisoners in the southern US, fined several times their possible annual earnings, were in effect enserfed by being leased to mines, railroads, quarries, and farms.[58] Under China's one-child policy (recently relaxed), fines for a second baby, set at thrice parents' annual earnings, rendered their offspring de facto stateless, bereft of rights to housing, school, and work.[59] In the early 1990s, the US government began to impose corporate fines that were actual punishments, not just retrospective licensing fees. Once merely slapped on the wrist, polluters were now often compelled by unaffordable fines to obey environmental legislation.[60] Punitive damages follow a similar logic, intended not just as compensation but as sanction for wrongdoing.

Unpayable fines as a means of coercion contradicted the state's interest in revenue. Steep fines to compel obedience were less lucrative than small fines routinely imposed for minor offenses. In the third century BCE, Romans built a temple to Venus from the fines paid by adulteresses.[61] The medieval state derived much of its income from minor fines. In the thirteenth century, judicial fines generated one-eighth of the English monarch's revenue. Wessex law doubled fines for stealing on Sundays or religious holidays. In sixteenth-century Shetland, feudal lords imposed fines for meticulously specified actions and varied them by time and place, so that bloodying a shopkeeper's nose on a Sunday night rather than a Monday morning could be an expensive proposition.[62] Today, financially strapped US and UK municipalities treat speeding tickets in a similar spirit, as profit centers.[63] So did the East Germans when they fleeced Western drivers passing along the transit routes to Berlin, and so do Chinese localities when they fine prostitutes.[64]

Since large coercive fines were but an indirect means of compulsion, as the state grew better able to twist arms directly, the need for them faded. Fines could be diminished without weakening the state's overall ability to compel. Already the Romans limited how much magistrates could fine. In the seventeenth century, the French Parlement restricted fines to a quarter of the defendant's estate.[65] English courts of the same era hewed to a rule deriving from Magna Carta of fines not being so high that defendants had to sell the tools of their trade. Rather than impose a heavier fine, which in effect meant lifetime prison, Blackstone advised, the courts should physically imprison or whip the defendants.[66] When in 1687 for political reasons the duke of Devonshire was fined £30,000 for striking someone near the king's palace (a median fine for assault was two shillings, six pence), the Lords judged this fine oppressive and illegal. In 1689, England prohibited excessive fines, followed a century later by the US Constitution's Eighth Amendment on cruel and unusual punishments.[67]

Whether treated as tax or a means of indirect compulsion, fines relied on the already existing machinery of sanction without which they lacked bite. In fact, fines were only a quasi-sanction. Even as restitution to society, not merely to the individual victim, fines were often not seen as punishments in the fundamental sense of pain equitably inflicted for retribution or deterrence. For offenses that are gravely immoral—such as rape and murder—payment strikes the modern mind as a wholly inappropriate punishment. Restitution between individuals undercut the state's ambition to enforce laws applicable to all. In a similar way, fines ran in parallel and sometimes at cross purposes to the regular system of retributive sanction. Above all, they were hampered by their social inequity.

Bodily pain was the state's primary leverage over the poor, either directly by inflicting distress or alternatively by prison's slow confiscation of their mortality. The rich also had property on the line, but they could more easily shrug off a loss of property than the poor could forfeit years. Inequalities of money dwarf those of chronology. The starkest disparity between the time-wealthy teenager who stands to lose a life in jail and the ninety-year-old would rarely be more than six to one. As property themselves, slaves owned none. Unable therefore to be fined, they were instead whipped, castrated, or otherwise mutilated according to early medieval codes. Freemen unable to afford a fine were flogged.[68] In the thirteenth century, rich offenders able to pay compensation were more likely to be prosecuted for tort violations, but the poor, who could offer nothing but their pain, more likely for crimes. A New Hampshire statute in 1682 had those below a certain poverty line whipped rather than fined.[69] Deep into the nineteenth century, workers—with little to offer the fine collector—were jailed for violating labor contracts.[70] Since a rich person could effectively buy the right to slander others if fines were the only punishment, Kant suggested that they be obliged to kiss the hand of the poor whom they had insulted.[71]

Judiciaries through the ages have wrestled with the inherent unfairness of punishments premised on property. The Romans happily fined the gentry and beat the poor. The Greeks, in contrast, substituted prison in place of fines for those who could not pay.[72] Talionic sanctions have at times been considered an egalitarian alternative, preventing the wealthy from buying their way out. However harshly, they treated rich and poor alike.[73] Sixteenth-century Florence trumpeted the egalitarian virtues of direct corporeal punishments for all citizens, rich or poor. The absolutist monarchies, asserting their power through spectacular public punishments, could scarcely be bothered to impose the merely indirect suffering of fines.[74] Only if they could not afford the five-shilling fine were drunks in colonial Massachusetts locked into the stocks for three hours. Russian peasants feared fines and (if they could not afford them) prison more than they did bodily pain, which could be endured. Whipping remained a common punishment in Russia far longer than it did in the West.[75] In the 1930s, fines were rarely used in nations such as Italy, Bulgaria, and Poland, where most people lived outside a cash economy.[76] Reformers imposing smallpox vaccination in the nineteenth century pondered the unfairness of allowing wealthy resistors to pay fines instead and appreciated the equality of directly compelling all to contribute to herd immunity.[77] Because fines favored the affluent, they were regarded warily in socialist nations, though they were happy to seize assets.

Like bail, fines raised problems of fairness. If others paid on the offenders' behalf, they allowed them to avoid atoning. Early on, fines permitted the well-off to escape. A wealthy Roman, slapping the faces of passers-by as he perambulated, was followed by a servant, who paid on the spot the requisite fine for his indulgence.[78] But in a money-based economy, if fines were correctly calibrated and perhaps paid in installments, most people could afford them, and they were not strikingly unfair. In ancient Rome, women, children, and slaves could not be fined since they owned nothing.[79] Yet medieval English law assumed that even slaves could pay fines, and by the eighteenth century fines were a ubiquitous punishment.[80] Today fines have become the commonest sanction. Even allegedly socialist China punishes half of all criminal offenses by fines.[81] Sanctions have become more moderate, and most citizens are sufficiently well-off to be punishable in their property, no longer just in their person.

Yet the inequality problem has not vanished. In the early twentieth century, the first motorists, who had to be wealthy to enjoy this new sport, happily paid a succession of £10 speeding fines. Rich motorists were occasionally sentenced to jail to make sure they did not just pay their way out of trouble.[82] To account for this fundamental inequity, fines have sometimes been reengineered as a fairer and tougher coercive device.[83] They have increasingly been tailored to the offender's circumstances. Plato suggested fines graded by wealth for his ideal community.[84] Following the Scandinavians in the 1920s, income-staggered fines were adopted also by others, such as the Swiss and the Cubans. In northern Europe, fines are often set in relation to daily wages.[85] Finnish millionaires have been slapped with five-figure speeding tickets. Estonia has trialed giving speeders a choice between cash fines and forfeiting their time by the roadside under police supervision—both more equal and possibly more deterrent for drivers in a hurry.[86] Maximum penalties for insider trading—a rich man's offense—leapfrogged in the US from $100,000 in the 1960s to $1 million in the 1980s to $5 million in the new millennium.[87] Corporations have faced the same logic. The European Union has threatened to fine information-technology and social media businesses in relation to annual revenue. For a company such as Google, a 10 percent fine of annual revenue would be $9 billion.

Finally, fines pose the issue of fungibility. As restitution, fines have priced almost every action, even those that the modern mind resists considering compensable—such as Sharia law's acceptance of payment for murder. If nothing else, this pricing of everything undermines the facile idea that only the modern market economy alienates humans by attaching a monetary value to all things. Wergelds, due for killing someone, expressed the social hierarchy of the early Middle Ages in precise monetary terms. In seventh-century Kent, Æthelberht required only that a man who had stolen someone else's wife pay her wergeld and supply a new woman, much as if he had run over his neighbor's dog while backing out of the driveway.[88] Medieval law was the equal of today's actuarial tables in its subtle distinctions among harms and their cost. Marxist legal theorists, such as Evgeny Pashukanis, in effect agreed, arguing that punishment in bourgeois society and more generally law and morality are founded on the idea of exchange, whose logic reaches historically much further back than the origins of capitalism.[89] With the introduction of specific performance, it is modern law that arguably has sought to retain a sense that some actions cannot merely be compensated. Instead of just paying damages, offenders are forced to restore matters to their preharm state. Already early Roman law set aside victims' claims that stolen items be restored to them and offered only restitution in money.[90] The Anglo-Saxon systems limited specific performance to equity law, especially for land

and other singular goods. Specific performance achieved its highpoint in the nineteenth-century civil law codes, which took as their default making damages whole again, not just paying for them.[91]

Death

Forward-looking motives prompted even more different sanctions than backward-looking ones did. Before mass media, deterrent punishments had to be brutal and public. Carried out in secret, an execution only incapacitated. But a hanging in the town square was thought to concentrate the subjects' minds, not just amuse the rabble. Early states could caution their subjects against transgressing mainly through theatrical cruelty, amplified by word of mouth. The mass public trials held by the totalitarian regimes in the Soviet Union and China served similar purposes.[92]

As crimes were recognized to have broad implications for society as a whole, punishment both retributed for wrong and aimed to prevent its reoccurrence. Death has historically been the most consistently used penalty, still on the books in one-third of all nations today. Vengeance commonly demanded it, and the state, with its first forays into adjudication, in fact curtailed capital penalties as it sought to reduce mayhem and bloodshed. But as the state itself took over punishing, it wanted to demonstrate that it, too, could administer justly harsh penalties. Death quickly became among the truest arrows in its quiver. By the standards of its day, the Old Testament decreed death comparatively sparingly, for perhaps some thirty types of crimes. Islamic law knew only three capital crimes: robbery, adultery, and apostasy.[93] But of the 359 articles in the Chinese emperor Wu's code, 409 statutes related to the death penalty.[94] And Dracon's code (seventh century BCE) used scarcely any other punishment. Dracon thought small offenses deserved it, and he knew of no worse punishment for the serious ones. The Greeks considered capital punishment insufficient for deliberate parricide, the worst form of murder, so they stoned such killers' corpses at a crossroads at the city's edge, then hurled the body beyond its boundaries.[95]

Death, in fact, came as a welcome relief from the preliminary tortures inflicted on many criminals. William the Conqueror abolished the death penalty, judging it overly lenient. He preferred to treat his enemies as slaves, blinding and castrating them.[96] Even today, the logic of retribution suggests that some crimes—such as genocide—perhaps deserve more than simple death.[97] Beccaria put his finger on the problem: since the human body could suffer only so much, the most enormous crimes were not adequately punished by pain alone.[98]

As we have seen, when defending against a common danger, the state readily assumed the authority to punish drastically on society's behalf. Having once regarded death as merely an efficient method of incapacitation, Roman law began to aim higher, hoping to set a deterrent example. Under Tiberius (d. 37 CE), it sought to prevent those sentenced to death from committing suicide before the state exacted its due.[99] In the fifteenth century, the Russian state spoke for the communal interest, even at the expense of crime's victims, by forbidding compensation (by money or enslavement) for especially heinous offenses, insisting instead on death. In 1537, Christian III of Denmark demanded capital punishment for all homicides (other than accidents or acts of self-defense) because kin's ability to pay restitution was undermining deterrence.[100] This spirit of capital punishment serving the common cause infused the commission reforming German penal law in 1906 when it described capital punishment as an act "in which the majesty of the state achieves its most powerful expression."[101]

But death has been more than just another sanction, and its use contentious. Its origins were theological—a sacrifice to appease the gods.[102] Its finality lent it gravity and moral import. The state illegitimately assumed God's role in deciding life and death, said the death penalty's opponents. But the authorities were just using their most potent weapon to protect the community, came the riposte. After all, the state sacrificed soldiers in extremis for the common good.[103] Why did it not have analogous moral authority to battle and kill internal enemies? Did capital punishment undermine the broader goal of reducing crime? Did the state contradict itself by killing to punish killing? Such have been the debates.

However much we pride ourselves on our humanity and compassion, capital punishment has faded as much because the state no longer needed it as thanks to any groundswell of popular revulsion. Quite the contrary: in most countries, the death penalty was and remains popular. In ancient Rome, capital punishment asserted republican freedom: a citizen could be executed only after trial by his assembled peers.[104] When death sentences were first restricted starting in the nineteenth century, reformers were acutely aware of bucking public opinion. The French revolutionaries, who otherwise changed so much, kept the death penalty. Massive public campaigns resisted its abolition when that was proposed in France in 1906. The death penalty was finally ended in 1981 despite continued support from two-thirds of the public.[105] Capital punishment remains in effect in many nations—in some as an instrument of state terror, in others thanks to its popularity. Having been all but abolished in America during the early 1970s, the death penalty made a comeback, especially in the South and the West. Unlike for other punishments, juries rather than judges pronounce sentences in capital cases, and officials who advocate capital punishment are often elected by a public eager for retribution.[106]

In Western nations, capital punishment has been abolished largely at the instigation of the professionals involved and allied elite opinion. In recent times, social elites have only rarely favored capital punishment—in twentieth-century Germany up through the 1950s and in contemporary China.[107] Iran may be on the verge of flipping, though elsewhere among the Middle Eastern autocracies capital punishment remains widely used. The death penalty became a human rights issue in Europe only long after it had been abolished, sometimes for self-serving reasons, such as sparing former Nazis, but also in revulsion at the Third Reich's mass murders.[108] Niklas Frank opposed the death penalty for everyone except his father, Hans Frank, chief jurist of the Nazi Generalgouvernement in Poland, who was hanged at Nuremberg.[109] And, indeed, the Allied imposition of death at Nuremberg complicated efforts to abolish it subsequently at home—in Britain, for example.[110]

Even so, which higher principle took precedence? The state not killing or the state justly punishing evil? Whose lives mattered most—victims' or criminals'? By the 1840s, British proponents of retaining capital punishment had turned the sanctity-of-life argument in their own favor, arguing that by not executing murderers, the state was not taking victims' deaths seriously.[111] "Treating criminals humanely is in effect tolerating the inhumanity that they have shown their victims," was how a Chinese pro-death activist recently put it.[112] That is the standard argument, fighting fire with fire. Yet even those who oppose everyday death sentences ponder the extremes. Urged on by strong popular and press demand for retribution, the Norwegian Parliament overwhelmingly reinstituted the death penalty after World War II for traitors and collaborators with the Nazis. "Humanism and mercy for traitors betrays the people" read the banners in massive demonstrations in Oslo in 1945. After the genocide in 1994, Rwandan authorities were dismayed to discover that only the Hutu killers tried at home could be sentenced to death, whereas those tried before the International Criminal Tribunal were spared. Saddam Hussein was never brought to an international tribunal because the Iraqis and Americans insisted on the possibility of capital punishment, and, indeed, he was eventually executed.[113]

Prison

In China, prison became a primary form of punishment already during the Han period, two centuries before Christ, though at other times it was not.[114] In Europe, however, before the seventeenth century prisons were generally places to warehouse those awaiting trial.[115] Exceptions included the Greeks, who used prison in some instances as a punishment, and in Rome an indefinitely postponed execution might leave a prisoner languishing in jail for life. In medieval England, oath breakers and thieves could be locked up for forty days. In thirteenth-century Languedoc, the Catholic Inquisition imprisoned heretics, hoping for confessions.[116] Monastic orders often shut in rogue monks.[117] Debtors were imprisoned in ancient Rome and medieval Europe to persuade them to pay up. In early modern England, they made up easily half of all inmates. But since they were held as part of a civil process, they were not felons or punished as such.[118]

Prison gradually became a sanction in itself, not just the helpmate of real punishments. From the late thirteenth century, both the number of prisons and the crimes that landed offenders there increased. In the early sixteenth century, the English common law listed 180 imprisonable offenses.[119] As of the eighteenth century, prisons were finally a punishment in themselves. The first to abolish death entirely, Tuscany's criminal code of 1786 left imprisonment as serious crime's main sanction. Largely financed and often run by the inmates themselves, early prisons were porous holding pens that barely separated miscreants from society. Prisoners were expected to pay for their own upkeep, entitled to better conditions for extra fees, and reliant on charity if unable to pay.[120] As late as the early twentieth century, when the suffragettes were jailed, Britain's prisons had three classes, like its trains. The bottom two are easy to envision. First-class inmates enjoyed books, newspapers, visits, and mail as well as better food, drink, and cells, permission to wear their own clothes, and the right to hire other prisoners as servants.[121]

Prisons were expensive to build and to run. Revolutionary France cut corners by converting nationalized church properties.[122] Mutilation, torture, death, exile, and flogging had been cheaper, but inflicting pain and even death eventually lost favor. Banishment worked only if penal colonies or expansive territories were at hand. Using male prisoners for military ends, as galley slaves, for example, raised questions of motivation and reliability—much like for mercenary troops. The Chinese practice of enlisting criminals in military exile to defend the country's borders suffered from obvious inherent contradictions.[123] The nineteenth century reshaped the armed forces on a universalistic nationalist basis—the male citizen's self-interested duty. With exceptions, such as the French Foreign Legion, it was now thought nonsensical to entrust the nation's defense to society's outcasts. The refinement of sail in the eighteenth century and the end of the need for oarsmen turned galleys into hulks that now housed prisoners whose muscle power was put to use elsewhere.[124]

Already in the 1700s houses of correction aimed to reform the recalcitrant poor—vagrants, the idle and disorderly, obstreperous servants, unmarried mothers, and the like. As of the mid-seventeenth century, convicts who earlier would have been killed were now imprisoned.[125] The English were ahead on the prison curve. After 1853, as transportation to Australia ended, prison became the main punishment for serious offenders.[126] By the early 1800s, 60 percent of those sentenced were imprisoned; by the 1860s that portion was 90 percent. In late eighteenth-century Paris, only 10 percent of sentences were for jail. But in the revolutionary penal code of 1791, prison became the most common punishment. By the early nineteenth century, imprisonment had become the standard punishment for noncapital crimes in Germany, too.[127]

To cut costs, inmates were put to work. Prisoners built the pyramids, and the Romans used them on public works or in the mines.[128]

Workhouses were an early iteration of what was to become the prison. Galleys made criminals part of the nation's defense. Labor was central also to nineteenth-century prisons, both for what it brought in and for its disciplinary effects. The Chinese and Soviet camps often worked prisoners to death. Inmates in the American South, Blacks a majority among them, were worked ruthlessly.[129] To this day, the American prison-industrial complex remains a large corporate presence.[130] But inmates were rarely a first-class labor force: work shy, asocial, unmotivated, uncooperative, and hence uncompetitive. Like eighteenth-century workhouses for the poor, prison labor rarely paid for itself.[131] At the same time, prisons' subsidized labor competed with the free market.[132] Already with the first workhouses, nonincarcerated workers and private employers complained of publicly subsidized goods sold on the open market.[133] US law specifically forbade prison labor from competing with the free market. That labor has therefore been tolerated largely to make products consumed by the state itself—license plates, uniforms, and the like—or for public works.[134]

Prison was in effect a fine levied in terms of time. By itself, it could not guarantee a change of behavior. Just as someone might regard a fine as the price of offending, so too an inmate might consider a stint behind bars the cost of doing business, especially if he could pay a fall guy to take the hit. In early modern Europe, debtors often preferred prison to settling their accounts: sometimes they had no choice; at other times they did. When debtors were no longer imprisoned in Britain as of 1869, those who refused to pay up, though they had the means, could be jailed.[135] Conversely, in Sharia law, debtors could be imprisoned to determine whether they had the funds to meet their obligations; if not, they were released since what was the point of coercing them to do something they could not? More recently, plaintiffs hoping to conceal substantial assets in divorce cases have been willing to suffer jail.[136] A similar trade-off between time and money held for fines. In the 1950s, more than half of US jail inmates were atoning for unpaid fines, as remained true in Scotland in the

1980s.[137] Further complexities lurked. The state had long inflicted pain on offenders. Inmates' lives could of course be made a living hell, too, but if torture were the goal, prison was an inefficient and costly way to go about it. Jail incapacitated offenders in an era when banishment was no longer possible. Why not then rehabilitate them, so that prison did not become a breeding ground for further criminality? Prisons, in other words, were inefficient means of inflicting pain and an expensive and possibly dysfunctional form of incapacitation. Why bother locking up criminals if prisons did not improve them?

From such considerations sprang the rehabilitative turn incarceration took in the eighteenth century. Since prison without rehabilitation was basically torture, and since inmates were the state's for a long time, why not attempt to redeem them?[138] By itself, prison promised to discourage certain bad habits: drinking, gambling, concubinage, whoring. A regular schedule of meals, sleep, and work—even if just the treadwheel's make-work—inculcated industrious discipline. Enforced solitude at least isolated inmates from bad influences and might encourage them to ponder their crimes.[139] Prison was to be a spiritual ordeal from which inmates emerged purified. The Philadelphia system of extreme isolation therefore became popular. Prisoners lived and worked wholly alone, hooded when they left their cells, receiving only a single visitor and letter annually. England's Petworth prison had stalls built to keep them apart even in chapel. In Pentonville, the guards wore padded shoes so as not to break the silence.[140] Yet total isolation was costly and took a heavy psychic toll on inmates, who often committed suicide or went insane. From such failures emerged a moderated approach, pioneered at Auburn prison in upstate New York, where inmates were isolated in their cells only at night, working communally during the day.[141] Yet all such ambitions for rehabilitation have failed. Today's prisons—overcrowded, understaffed, replete with society's least favored—perform what is at best incapacitation and at worst—in maximum-security institutions—a form of torture.

Chapter 8
Moderating Punishment

Seen in a long historical view, punishments have—with some fluctuation—become more moderate. Durkheim argued that as societies became more complex and interdependent, they would naturally scale back punishments.[1] Like all general explanations, this one is unable to account for why harshness has fluctuated historically or why it has varied among cultures that were otherwise seemingly similar. In China, castration, the last remaining mutilating punishment, was ended around 220 CE.[2] The Western state's embrace of moderation began only after an initial turn first to greater violence under absolutism. When punishing was a communal activity, vengeance often ran amok. Here, the state exerted a calming influence, suppressing feuds and eventually outlawing them. As the state began to take over punishment, however, it needed to prove its mettle and show that it could administer justice. The punitive ferocity of the early modern period was unleashed as the state asserted its authority and ability to enforce. Capital punishment expanded in the eighteenth century to even trivial transgressions—thefts of trifles and the like. In 1688, some fifty crimes were capital in England, and by 1820 more than two hundred were.[3]

Public punishments reached their violent extreme in Europe sometime in the 1700s.[4] Moderation had begun earlier, perhaps already in the fifteenth century, but with the absolutist regimes of the early modern era they at first grew more severe again.[5] The Enlightenment philosophes were eager reformers. In 1762, Voltaire exposed the gross injustice done to the Protestant Jean Calas, falsely accused, tortured, and executed for having killed his son, a convert to Catholicism. Cesare Beccaria's book on punishment became a runaway global bestseller, advocating moderate, regular, and predictable punishment as more effective deterrence than occasional public dismemberment. The state now had more and more effective tools, so why rely on horrendous public sanctions?[6] Mercy sprang less from a change of heart than from the state's developing prowess.

In the Middle Ages, mens rea, the doctrine that an intent to offend was a prerequisite for punishing the act, created new offenses of planning and conspiracy. Yet it also moderated sanctions that had earlier been levied on the act alone, even if it had been accidental or unintentional. Equity law, with its roots in Roman and canon law, softened the often harsh consequences of applying the common law literally. Confessions were no longer required for conviction or torture for their extraction. Offenders could be tried on evidence that would earlier not have passed muster and sentenced to lesser punishments.[7] Spectacular public deaths were gradually considered more deleterious than deterrent. The US Constitution specifically forbade cruel and unusual punishments in 1787. Torture was eventually outlawed in all nations, at least on paper. Disgusted with the Inquisition's excesses and the Reformation's pursuit of its own heretics, the Enlightenment philosophes saw torture as barbaric. Prussia led the way, abolishing it in 1754. By the late eighteenth century, it had been forbidden in most European nations—at least if we ignore the torture of serfs in eastern Europe and of slaves in the colonies.

The right granted clergy to be punished only in ecclesiastical courts, which could not impose death, was extended in fourteenth-century England to all men who could read (using generous and often ritualized literacy tests) and thus claim, even if implausibly, to be of the cloth.[8] In 1487, this right—benefit of clergy—was extended to all men, and in 1623 to women. Nonclergy could invoke it once, and to prevent repeat claims they were branded on the thumb with an M for "murder" or a T for "theft." In the sixteenth century, about 20 percent of all felons sidestepped execution through benefit of clergy. In the early eighteenth century, capital punishment was extended by removing benefit for various crimes (petty thefts and shoplifting, attacking deer, cutting down trees, etc.). Yet at the same time the literacy requirement for benefit was removed, thus extending it to everyone, literate or not.[9] Though on paper the law may have been harsh, the number of executions declined after the mid-seventeenth century.[10] Awash in in capital crimes, England undercut their effect through benefit of clergy and other mitigations. In seventeenth-century Sussex, 80 percent of those found guilty could have been hanged, but at least two-thirds were thus spared.[11]

During the seventeenth and eighteenth centuries, death was less invoked for property and other minor offenses and reserved instead for homicide and other serious crimes.[12] In the American colonies, William Penn's Great Act in 1682 limited death to murder alone at a time when the British homeland had more than 200 capital crimes. Those 200 were then reduced to 8 by 1841.[13] The Prussian penal code restricted capital punishments in 1743 and executed only murderers after 1794.[14] Most northern US states confined the death penalty to murder starting in the 1780s.[15] With the new French penal code of 1791, the panoply of capital crimes (from sodomy and murder to minor theft and the cutting down of trees) was pruned, leaving just various forms of murder and theft.[16] In China, from 800 in the Qing dynasty (1644–1911), the number of capital crimes fell to 130 in the penal code of 1908 and to 10 in the 1950s—part of the twentieth-century reforms intended to follow Western models of moderation.[17] Today, some 70 are on the books. The US has 46 capital crimes, mostly variations on homicide.[18] Nations that retained death sentences cut back dramatically on executions—from 72 per million in colonial America to 1.8 in the 1990s. The Chinese remain enthusiastic executioners, killing thousands annually. But even they have recently narrowed the range of capital offenses under the slogan "Kill Fewer, Kill Cautiously."[19] Even for major transgressions, such as treason, death became less common throughout the world. Most nations eventually no longer applied it at all.[20]

The technology of death was also refined.[21] Capital punishments came in a wide variety over the centuries: poisoning, strangling, drowning, stoning, asphyxiating, boiling, precipitating, impaling, hanging, crucifying, and burying. Beheading was among the earliest techniques, reserved in Roman law for nobles and the reason why such punishments are called "capital."[22] The Chinese, in contrast, regarded strangulation, leaving the body intact, as superior.[23] With its semiautomated decapitation, the guillotine brought the nobility's privilege to the masses. Commoners, too, escaped the vagaries and humiliation of the noose or the mishaps of unskilled or inattentive ax-wielding executioners.[24] In the twentieth century, Americans accepted gas, the electric chair, and then lethal injections as neither cruel nor unusual.[25] Earlier, as the use of execution declined, intermediary punishments developed, more severe than fines and less than death. The Byzantine Empire mutilated instead of killing. Emperor Wen in ancient China whipped rather than mutilated. The Reichslandfriede of 1103 prescribed the loss of hand or eye for large thefts.[26] After 1600, thieves in France were sometimes branded rather than mutilated. Less visible parts of the body than the face were gradually chosen for scarring or mutilation.[27] To preserve their economic value, slaves in nineteenth-century America were whipped rather than imprisoned or executed. Galleys, workhouses, and transportation joined death and mutilation. Transportation was introduced on a large scale in late seventeenth-century England thanks to dissatisfaction with death.[28]

Banishment and transportation were in turn eventually judged excessive, too, their use declining by the mid-nineteenth century. Indeed, transportation at times hardly deterred. The actual passage, though not easy, became less harrowing by the mid-1700s. The prospect of jobs and a future was often better than the offender's situation at home. By the 1870s, deportation to the South Pacific island of New Caledonia was considered so desirable that French inmates assaulted and murdered guards or fellow prisoners in hopes of being banished to paradise.[29] Flogging, balls and chains, solitary confinement, and other physical chastisements were gradually abandoned, too.[30] Punitive excesses were tempered early in England, though well into the eighteenth century more convicts were executed there than in other European nations. The breaking, drawing, quartering, and mutilation still common in France ended, leaving only hanging. Pressing with weights was abolished in 1772, branding in 1779. In Prussia, strangling and burning were not abolished until forty years later, and in the 1830s most executed bodies were still also broken on the wheel or decapitated.[31] Yet where punishments remained public, sentiment was turning. Reformers feared that the spectacle of death fed the crowd's bloodlust more than it edified.[32] In Germany, physically chastising the convict before execution was thought to arouse the crowd's sympathy, and so it was eliminated in the late 1700s.[33] By the nineteenth century, executions had been moved from the public square to the comparative seclusion of the prison.

Instead of death and other savageries, prison became the favored sanction. In late eighteenth-century England, public whippings declined as prison sentences became routine for theft.[34] Yet prison could nevertheless be retributive, even barbarous. Perhaps the Victorian era's (and our own) overcrowded, undermanned, chaotic, and violent prisons were shortcomings of the original intent. Even so, certain aspects of incarceration squarely aimed to inflict pain. Some prisons were deliberately more unpleasant than others. Into the nineteenth century, German prisons flogged inmates on entry and exit (*Willkomm und Abschied*) as well as on the anniversary of their offense. The practice of *schwerer Kerker* in Austria put inmates in chains, permitting almost no communication.[35] British Victorian jail diets were so meager as to constitute scientific starvation. Pointless treadwheel labor made sentences even nastier experiences.[36] The Philadelphia system's solitary confinement would now be considered psychologically so harsh as to be retributive. Today's US supermax institutions take this tradition to its extreme, but now with no ambition beyond controlling prisoners and inflicting psychological pain.[37]

Prison itself eventually came to be considered harsh and ineffectual. By the end of the nineteenth century, more than half of British offenders, especially first timers and the young, were fined rather than incarcerated.[38] As prison was thought to breed further criminality, the number of those jailed was reduced. Parole, probation, and other halfway solutions instead kept the convicted within the carceral loop without actual lockup.[39] The prison's foundational idea, that isolating the inmate from society would serve to rehabilitate, was here reversed. The responsibility for social molding and control was instead returned to society.[40] Already in the late nineteenth century, Belgium and France began suspending first timers' sentences, releasing them on good behavior. In France, inmate numbers were thus halved between 1887 and 1956. Alternatives to prison were developed in the late twentieth century using house arrest, conditions of residence, halfway houses, periodic imprisonment, treatment programs for addiction, electronic controls on movement, community service, and boot camp. Prisons themselves were differentiated by adding more loosely structured and policed arrangements for inmates unlikely to abscond as well as specialized institutions for juveniles.[41]

Punishments were moderated for several reasons. As authority was exerted on its subjects' behalf, law became less of an outside imposition on civil society and more the expression of its own will, thus giving less cause to contravene it. Such moderation began already in the sixteenth and seventeenth centuries, long before democracy, so we cannot see an immediate cause in a specific political system.[42]

Yet it did coincide broadly with the rise of more representative government. It seems also to have been part of the civilizing effect that historians have identified as a general ameliorating influence on violence starting in the early modern period. As measured in homicide rates but also in many other respects, levels of violence in European society began declining in the sixteenth century. The absolutist state's monopolizing of the tools of violence, the repression of vengeance and private adjudication and their replacement by courts, the decline of honor culture with its insistence on a personal righting of the moral balance upended by an offense, which in turn was connected to a growing liberation of individuals from the demands of their immediate kin groups—all such factors led to the broad and dramatic decline of homicide rates over the past five hundred years.[43]

Nor could the penal code diverge too far from common sentiments of right and wrong without provoking resistance and becoming hard to enforce. To preserve order, the state had reason to keep those it was policing on its side. On the whole, maintaining order was a popular cause. Laws have often favored the powerful: harsh measures against poaching or against lost rights over commons or against smuggling, for example. But ensuring that criminals who preyed on fellow subjects got their due was a welcomed state function. Popular sentiment was therefore likely to have influenced punishment even before politics were formally democratized. Law enforcement is invariably a pas de deux between state and civil society, each relying on the other. The more a legal system appears to its subjects as legitimate and justified, the more they follow its precepts voluntarily rather than out of fear of the consequences of disobeying.[44]

Conversely, as the state became more powerful and confident, it needed less to exert its force overtly. Durkheim advanced an axiom that punishments were harshest where society was primitive and government absolute.[45] The interplay between society and state in determining punishment is, of course, one of the leitmotivs of this book. But Durkheim's idea that absolute government was also omnipotent misses the mark. The thrust of modern governance has been precisely the increase in its effective power over society, even as it has discarded the trappings of absolute dominance. The modern state's ability to persuade, jostle, inculcate, and arm-twist its subjects—who grew more literate, rational, and self-aware as education spread—into obedience proved more effective than drawing and quartering in the town square. At its most savage, the state's law enforcement in fact undermined its own ambitions to effective control. Violence begat resistance. We have noted how harsh punishments spawned further crime as offenders sought to avoid execution by eliminating witnesses. The henchmen of Truman Capote's true-crime novel *In Cold Blood* (1966) became killers so as to leave no witnesses. Even those who committed mere property offenses in China during the 1980s often murdered their victims to avoid the testimony that might subject them to the ever-harsher punishments threatened for such offenses.[46]

Harsh punishments also made it hard to convict. The law of accomplices was first developed to spare secondary participants from what seemed like an unjust death.[47] When lay moral intuitions rejected disproportionate sanctions, the prosecution's ambitions were hindered. In nations with jury systems, where decisions fell to the accused's peers, drastic punishments at odds with popular sentiments of justice were often not enforced.[48] In medieval England, the great majority of defendants tried for homicide were acquitted.[49] For crimes where conviction meant death, few defendants pled guilty. In eighteenth-century England, they were actively discouraged from doing so in capital cases. With so many capital crimes, many offenders were tried but few convicted—in part thanks to inevitable difficulties of evidence and proof but also in part because juries deliberately nullified outcomes they considered needlessly bloody.[50] Although members of early juries were jailed for not returning the verdicts demanded by judges, jury nullification eventually became an accepted mechanism to rein in overly harsh prosecutions. Juries either found defendants guilty of lesser crimes or innocent altogether.[51] When punishment for defendants pleading benefit of clergy was changed in 1699 from branding on the thumb to branding on the cheek near the nose, courts often balked. So long as rape was a capital crime, no one pled guilty, and few were convicted. When the punishment for grand larceny increased to transportation to America in 1718, defendants were less willing to plead guilty.[52] Forgers and counterfeiters were hard to prosecute in the early nineteenth century when death was their reward. The Bank of England therefore proposed lesser sentences to maintain its conviction rates and thus plausible deterrence.[53] Early nineteenth-century French laws punished quarantine avoiders so harshly that they were rarely applied (whereas the moderate English system of fines for the same offense was consistently enforced).[54] Even under the Nazi regime, Germans were reluctant to report looting to the authorities once it became punishable by death.[55] An overly vindictive state, bereft of sympathy, undercut its own purpose.

Chapter 9
Crimes of Thought

Punishments were moderated as the state expanded its power. Enforcement's brunt bore down ever less on its citizens' bodies, both in outright physical pain and in the psychic anguish of time lost in prison. Yet the state did not step back from probing and controlling its subjects' lives. Quite the contrary. It moved beyond mere transgressions by act to delve into citizens' inner lives, their thoughts, inclinations, proclivities, and—most intrusively—the likelihood that they might offend in the future. So far we have looked at crimes as tangible acts committed: killing, stealing, burning, cheating. But thoughts, ideas, beliefs could also offend—if they were prohibited. And so eventually could intentions, plans, and conspiracies, even inclinations and proclivities to do what the state forbade.

The state had little ability to plumb its subjects' true state of mind. By torturing, it could elicit confession or repentance but never know how sincere. How far into the individual psyche could the state penetrate, and why should it bother? The state could hope for outward conformity, and it often rested content with that. But even in secular modernity, the state has shown an interest in what goes on in citizens' minds, seeking to penetrate and influence that.

With overt, tangible offenses, human law could and eventually did handle matters. But thought crimes—not easily known—tested secular law's limits. Speech and writing expressed underlying thoughts and beliefs and, by being public, could influence others in unwanted ways. But because subvocal, thoughts were definitionally without effect on others, their very presence unknown. Why pursue such an offense? And how? The Fourth Lateran Council in 1215 specified that unknown crimes should not be subject to inquisition. Only those publicly charged with heresy were to be pursued, not offenders accused in secret, much less those who kept their thoughts private. In 1484, the Spanish inquisitor Tomás de Torquemada decreed that those whose heresy was unknown to others be allowed to abjure and do penance in secret, too, thus never being exposed as heretics.[1] "The thought of man shall not be tried, for the devil himself knoweth not the thought of man," said Chief Justice Brian at the end of the Middle Ages.[2] Given the impossibility of penetrating the black box of any human mind, were such pronouncements just the state making a virtue of necessity?

How could the state or church police an interior state of mind when it knew only outward signs—acts or words? Even if it knew of an interior transgression, what could it aspire to? Punish the thought or conviction retroactively? Ensure that whatever heterodox believers really thought, they at least mouthed the right opinions? Or seek to change the offender's actual beliefs and thus future acts as well as thoughts? With conventional transgressions by act, no one expected offenders to become good and never offend again. Retribution cared only that they suffered. Deterrent punishments naturally sought to prevent future crimes, but more by terrifying potential offenders into obedience than by necessarily changing their dispositions. From society's utilitarian vantage, whether citizens behaved out of fear or goodness mattered less than that they toed the line. In modern parlance, society was a behaviorist—concerned with outward acts more than with inward beliefs. Yet rehabilitation at its starkest, as in totalitarian brainwashing, did in fact seek to change past offenders into a future law-abiding and right-thinking citizens.[3] Citizens' inner and outer states were to correspond, both acting and being good or at least in conformity to the law. Such attempts to penetrate deeply into citizens' psyches therefore provoked opposition as violating human autonomy, or—overreaching—they simply tended to fail.

Retributive punishment for thought offenses made little sense, given that no one had been harmed by purely private ideas. Punishing to deter or incapacitate heterodox thinkers might warn others off entertaining similar deviations, but it also publicized the presence and possibly even the popularity of precisely the ideas to be stamped out. To punish thoughts meant to seek to convert or persuade the offender. If successful, the influence would lead to a genuine and lasting change of mind. Or it might mean merely outward assent to a position still rejected at heart. How would persuaders know?

In Islamic law, male apostates were jailed for three days in hopes of reviving their faith. If they did not then reaffirm it, they were to be executed. In the Middle Ages, Dominicans tortured suspected heretics less to find out what they thought than to make them recant.[4] At the end of their travails, the monks remained equally ignorant of the heretics' true convictions. In seventeenth-century Virginia, the authorities' inability to do much beyond eliciting outward signs of conformity was laid painfully bare. Those who absented themselves from twice-daily prayer were first punished by loss of wages, whipping, and the galley, and those who spoke against the Christian faith were executed. These measures, however, judged only on external indications. Ministers therefore also interrogated suspected heretics on their faith and knowledge of it. Those who refused to submit were whipped and made to confess to the congregation. For a third infraction, they were flogged daily until they confessed, asked for forgiveness, and sought instruction from the minister.[5] Despite this escalation, the religious authorities still remained uncertain what their victims actually believed.

Authorities have always found it hard to know who entertained heretical ideas, how firmly they held them, and if they could be dissuaded. Crimes of thought were inherently harder to detect, much less eradicate, than conventional offenses by act. Much normal crime is opportunistic, succumbing to a momentary weakness. Offenders of thought have rarely been motivated by what would be the equivalent—a whim or passing fancy. Unlike conventional criminals, they have usually been moved by conviction. The heterodox have often been educated, conscientious, well-meaning people, idealistic and unbribable, too. Of course, some have sought to reform a religion or bring down a political system. But they have equally seen themselves as the only ones truly understanding the thought system in question, seeking to return it to its roots, core, or true mission.[6] Attacked as heretics or traitors, they claimed to be true believers or patriots. Many statesmen started as traitors; many religious leaders as heretics. Christ was accused of blasphemy for insisting before the Sanhedrin that he was the Messiah.[7] George Washington would have hanged for treason had England won the Revolutionary War.

Since their religions made no exclusive truth claims, polytheistic regimes of the pre-Axial age could most easily accommodate variant beliefs. The Romans folded deities from conquered cultures into their pantheon of cults and gods. Not every belief was taken equally seriously, but they all could be accommodated so long as they tolerated one another. A single god, demanding unwavering adherence, however, undermined polytheism's workaday toleration. The Abrahamic monotheisms made exclusive and mutually incompatible claims to absolute truth, all while refusing to consider polymorphous beliefs worthy competitors. For the Jews, Jupiter was not just a foreign god, but no god at all.[8] Christianity was even more universalizing than Judaism, less attached to any particular nation. Universalizing ideologies—whether religious or, later, political—saw ideological dissent in binary terms. They were ecumenical in the sense that anyone willing to believe was welcome as an adherent but intolerant in insisting on the sole truth of their way, the falsity of any other.

Many more people would ultimately be killed for political principles than for theological beliefs. But outside the totalitarian regimes, the secular powers would never match the intensity with which religious heresy was pursued. The stakes were higher for heretics than for political dissidents—eternal damnation, not just death. Nor could political persecutors assuage their consciences with the belief that the pain they inflicted was for the sufferer's own good in the next life. Augustine insisted the church must compel the true faith. Heretics had been led astray. Christians should force them to see the light, not indulge their errors with a misplaced sense of mercy, thus losing them forever.[9]

Heretics also had the advantage over many political dissidents in appealing to ultimate authority. A common claim of religious transgression was that it understood the truth, which—as orthodoxy—had become encrusted by institution and ritual. Only the heretic tapped straight into the godhead.[10] The heresies that eventually became Protestantism shared a belief in their direct access to God's truth. Hence, they rejected many sacraments, the cult of saints, pilgrimages, salvation by good works, and above all the clergy as intermediaries between the laity and God.[11] The most extreme sects lost even a sense that sin was possible, allowing them to believe that unbridled sex, including incest, would restore their lost purity.[12]

Religious Unorthodoxy

The first thought crimes were theological. Disobeying God was the original sin. When crime and sin were largely the same, worshipping deities other than your own people's god was among the first offenses. At first, such transgressions had little to do with the state as such, nor did gods need the state's laws and powers to punish them. The ancient Greek gods sometimes administered justice, though these spiteful and all-too-human deities mostly quarreled among themselves, wreaking occasional havoc on human society.[13] In Euripides's play *Bellerophontes*, Zeus dispatched the main character with a thunderbolt for his atheism.[14] When Gideon pulled down the altar of Baal and desecrated the other local gods whom the Jews had begun worshipping while in Canaan, his father saved him from his people's wrath by insisting that were Baal a god, he could defend himself.[15] Why the God of the Jews needed mere mortals to take up his cause when blasphemed was left unexplained.[16]

Sin, irreligion, immorality, and crime were at first largely indistinguishable. *Crimen* could mean both "sin" and "crime."[17] Both sins (in the broad sense of being irreligious and immoral) and crimes violated laws given by god(s) and enforced either directly by them supernaturally or indirectly through authorities, whether religious or worldly. Attacking the leader, who was also god's earthly representative, transgressed both religious and secular authority. Heresy and treason were thus much the same offense—attacks on leaders. In ancient Greece, sacrilege and treason were closely related, the temple being the home of the state's protector.[18] Sins such as blasphemy were treated like secular transgressions such as murder or theft, as violations of the divine order, and enforced by the authorities. Blasphemy in Greece was a portmanteau offense, including speaking ill of the gods, disturbing the peace, and dishonoring principles of government. Sacrilege was punished with death in the Lex Julia, along with embezzling public monies. Adultery was considered a sacrilege in Roman law, a defiance of marriage's inviolability.[19]

Sin and crime were eventually separated out. The transcendent religions of the Axial Age—Buddhism, Confucianism, Jainism, then Judaism, Christianity, and Islam—desacralized this world. God and the divine were elevated to a higher plane, no longer interacting much with the mortal and certainly not on a daily basis.[20] By the nineteenth century, the legal reformer Anselm von Feuerbach was able to argue that God could not be insulted and that he certainly would never stoop to exacting revenge for injured honor.[21] The Greek and Roman gods had constantly meddled in human affairs. The Western Christian world was eventually, after kings and popes had sorted their relations, ruled by secular law, with religious precept only at a remove.

If the divinity did not intervene, religions themselves could only persuade. They could censure and influence believers. Excommunication had an effect only insofar as the spiritually banished remained sufficiently adherent to agree that it imposed a cost on them. If used too often, as among seventeenth-century Jewish communities against Sabbatian heresies, its effects were shrugged off.[22] Only those who still accepted the orthodoxy could be punished by it. For similar reasons, religion's most effective leverage, hell, failed to work for those whose faith had changed or faded. Besides such voluntarist measures, religion could enforce its precepts only when it allied with the state, turning sin into crime.

Religious orthodoxy and the state therefore intertwined. A language, as the old joke goes, is a dialect backed by an army. So, too, a sect becomes religion only once it can enforce itself. Once a persecuted faction, the Christian Church eventually promulgated its doctrine by law. With the Roman Empire converted under Constantine, the church could determine the content of faith in this world with more than just threats for the next. Christianity came in variants, so in 325 the Roman emperor chose among them, calling the Council of Nicea to formulate the first creed.[23] The Theodosian legislation of the fourth century made Catholic Christianity the religion of the empire. Other Christian faiths were now branded as heresy. Heretics and pagans were stripped of the right to worship or hold civil office and fined for their beliefs. Trinitarianism was Christianity's central theological dispute, an attempt to reconcile monotheism with Christ's peculiar status as partly human, partly divine. It did not become orthodoxy until the Council of Chalcedon in 451.[24] In 453, the constitution of the emperors Valentinian III and Marcian subjected pagans and heretics to confiscation and death. After 376, imperial constitutions forbade secret meetings of heretics. From the sixth century on, those who failed to denounce heretics were also condemned.[25]

Long persecuted, Christians now went after each other. After Nicea, Constantine issued an edict against heretics aimed at Novatian schismatics and Gnostics.[26] A millennium later, that cycle repeated itself with the Reformation. Just as treason wipes the slate clean by its own success, so victorious heresy becomes orthodoxy. Though hounded to near extinction, Waldensians, Hutterites, and other sects sowed their seed in those areas where Protestantism later flourished.[27] Severely persecuted by Catholics, mainstream Protestantism in turn went after many of its own bewildering array of sects. Luther had at first rejected coercion in matters of faith. As he gained power, however, worried by the excesses of Anabaptists and other schismatics, he changed his position. John Calvin's vicious hounding of Michael Servetus to a gruesome death in 1553, who had already been persecuted by Catholics for his views on the Trinity, was among the worst examples.

So long as religion was considered society's cement, belief was a public issue. Incorrect thoughts threatened order and stability. If God insisted on human society's purity, individual deviations became a collective problem. Heresy could spread like disease and had to be stamped out. The threat of divine wrath at sin obligated human authorities to police themselves. Chinese rulers anxiously scanned the heavens for omens and signs of supernatural displeasure that required a recalibration of their policies.[28] Romans were largely indifferent to theology so long as order was maintained, but Christians feared that wrong thinking affected the entire community. Heresy threatened God's wrath through famine, earthquake, and pestilence. Theologians of the eleventh and twelfth centuries insisted that a universal, uniform faith alone won God's favor for the Christian world. Emperor Maximilian issued the first imperial law against blasphemy in 1497 because he feared epidemics, famine, and natural disasters.[29]

As we have seen, both treason and heresy were first regarded as defiance of collective religious and political authority. In 1199, Pope

Innocent III treated heresy analogously to treason. Both were crimes against the ultimate authority, whether secular or religious.[30] Heresy was not just an individual crime but, like treason, also offended against the community of faithful. Only subjects or citizens could be traitors since foreigners were definitionally unable to betray a ruler to whom they owed no allegiance. Foreigners could be enemies, of course, but not traitors. Believers may quibble whether Søren Kierkegaard was right that pagans could not sin. But atheists probably cannot sin—unless it turns out they are wrong, and God exists.[31] Similarly, only believers could become apostates and heretics.

But non- and other-believers could blaspheme or verbally assault sacred values. Early Christianity drew such distinctions imprecisely. Pagans were routinely lumped with heretics in the Roman Empire. Religion, sorcery, magic, superstition, and witchcraft were interlaced. Christians took witchcraft very seriously as a competing faith, necessary to root out. "For rebellion is as the sin of witchcraft," says the Bible.[32] As of the fourteenth century, black magic and pagan rituals were considered heresy, which thus elevated superstition to a theological challenge.[33] In medieval France and England, necromancy aimed at the royal line was treason. In the early seventeenth century, James I of England drastically punished witches.[34] The Ming Chinese outlawed private ownership of celestial instruments to predict the future. In sixteenth-century Muscovy, both witchcraft and religious dissent were serious crimes, along with treason and revolt. The Massachusetts Bay Puritans made witchcraft a capital crime.[35]

Resonances of such hierarchies persist. Few today see sorcery as a valid competitor to religion. When in the Republican presidential primaries of 1980 George H. W. Bush called Ronald Reagan's supply-side policies "voodoo economics," the description was regarded as an uncontroversial commonplace, even as Vodun's practitioners accused him of slander.[36] Nations with official state religions decide which variants they recognize as legitimate competitors. In Germany, both the Society of Friends (Quakers) and Scientology are classified as sects, not religions. European authorities question whether such would-be religions qualify for state subsidies (or can collect religious taxes). In the US, tax exemptions have been the main issue: whether to grant Scientology standing as a religion has been the remit of the fiscal authorities.[37]

Transgressions against the faith eventually became crimes against the state. In the fifth century BCE, the Greeks began punishing the impious and those who refused to recognize the gods.[38] Plato argued that even well-meaning citizens who committed impieties should be put to death if after being instructed and admonished for five years in a house of correction, they had still not repented.[39] Socrates was only the best remembered of such victims. The Romans cared little for religious orthodoxy. Good citizens engaged in the cults, but Roman law knew few theological or sacral crimes. Transgressions were punished largely if they were also a public offense, such as theft from the temple. Unauthorized revelation from the Sibylline book of oracles was a capital crime, and neglecting private shrines was actionable. As the Romans began persecuting Christianity, they sometimes made sacrifices to their gods obligatory. But they regarded religion mostly as a matter of public order. Citizens were expected to go through the motions of adherence, but their actual beliefs were of less concern. Roman syncretism, assimilating the foreign cults swept up by imperial expansion, hampered any narrow orthodoxy.[40]

Christianity's challenge to the state cults threatened public order even as the Romans took little interest in its theological claims. They viewed Christians as another annoying, standoffish sect that shunned public festivals, sacrifices to local deities, and homages to the emperors' statutes. Neither the Christians' portentous prophecies of unbelievers' fates nor rumors of secret bloody and sensual rituals helped their image. Rome firmly regulated and occasionally suppressed Christians along with the Bacchantes, the Druids, and followers of the cults of Isis and Serapis.[41] Christians, however, proselytized effectively, universalizing Judaism's monotheism and its unwavering claim to the truth. They ignored the Roman state, which, besides persecution, had few tools to deal with a belief that despised worldly power. Once the emperors converted to Christianity in the fourth century, religious and political power aligned. The state now policed orthodoxy, and heresy and blasphemy became among the most commonly prosecuted crimes.[42]

Church and state together battled heterodoxy through the Middle Ages. Pope Gregory IX decreed that blasphemers undertake public penance in church, while secular authorities fined them. Secular laws against blasphemy followed in the early thirteenth century.[43] Forbidden to shed blood, clerics farmed out heresy's punishment to the state. In England, Henry VIII combined political and religious power in the same hands, and the two forms of dissent became indistinguishable. Objecting to his variant of the Reformation was both heresy and treason.[44]

Religion began to be exempted from the state's concern in the Elizabethan era. Francis Bacon promised that the authorities did not seek to "make windows into men's souls." And in 1570, the queen agreed that all subjects who were obedient to her laws would be free from "any molestation to them by any person by way of examination or inquisition of their secret opinions in their consciences for matters of faith, remitting that to the supreme and singular authority of almighty God, who is only the searcher of hearts."[45] The right to remain silent was invoked in this era to protect religious dissidents from persecution, indirectly allowing them freedom of conviction by not having to testify to their variant beliefs. That innermost thoughts need not be divulged to secular authorities was invoked by Thomas More in his trial in 1535.[46] Extremists such as the Arians and Anabaptists were persecuted, but Catholics and Puritans only if also their activities threatened political dissent. Though adopting the Thirty-Nine Articles as official doctrine in 1571, the Elizabethan church did not rigorously enforce them. Catholics attended established churches or paid fines for recusancy and went to mass in private. The state demanded only outward conformity and pro forma obedience.[47]

Insofar as the state wanted heretics to repent or convert, it could not just execute them. With thought crimes, capital punishment indicated failure, so heretics were often imprisoned and tortured in hopes of conversion. Used to extract the truth, torture also served to persuade. Dead heretics, Thomas Aquinas pointed out, could not do penance.[48] The Spanish inquisitors repeatedly urged the accused to examine their consciences, identify the charge against them, and confess. Only then were formal charges brought.[49] Because particular thoughts were not an ineradicable part of humans—as ethnicity would later be considered—they could be changed and did not seal their thinker's fate.[50] Only those who valued their convictions above all else faced death. Luther came to consider Anabaptists, who rejected the state and its coercions, blasphemers and seditionists, calling for them to be killed. Not everyone was cut out for martyrdom, however, and many convicted heretics lived after recanting.[51]

From Theology to Politics

Over time, faith grew private, no longer a threat to the state. Dissidence moved to politics instead. We have followed this development with treason. Threats originally posed to the person of the ruler were later aimed at the system as politics ceased being a dynastic matter. With the spread of representative government and later democracy, some degree of political dissidence was baked into the system as reform, with only outright attempts to destroy it outlawed. Only in the totalitarian regimes did political dissent retain a theological aura, with even trivial acts regarded as mortal threats. Nonetheless, liberal democracies, too, took an interest in citizens' political thoughts. Nationalism sometimes presupposed an adherence to the community that prompted the state's concern with its members' beliefs, not just their conduct. The faithful congregation found its counterpart in the patriotic nation.

Political dissidents could be traitors or revolutionaries, more dangerous than ordinary criminals. Just as assassination was not merely another murder, so politically motivated crimes were "less reprehensible morally but more dangerous to society than the same act would be if due to revenge or some other personal motive," as the British police said of the suffragettes in the early twentieth century.[52] The French revolutionary penal code of 1791 made political crime an offense against the state, not the ruler: *lèse-nation*, no longer lèse-majesté. Seeking to change the system was treason. Those undermining the state attacked their own people and so ultimately themselves. Opposing the people's will, they stood outside the community.[53] Democracy's opponents were enemies of the people. This was the logic taken to its extreme in the totalitarian populisms.

But dissidents could also seek to improve, not overthrow. In this guise, they were considered political criminals. In recognition of their social status and benevolent intentions, nineteenth-century Europe punished them more leniently than ordinary offenders. Starting in the 1830s, France softened its treatment of opponents. Both Left and Right despised Louis-Philippe, the bourgeois monarch. Legitimists hated him for overthrowing the last Bourbon king, republicans for his narrowly upper-middle-class backing. The Orleanist regime responded with comparatively moderate laws, though robust by modern standards. It curbed free speech and writing, required authorization for associations, and controlled weapons. The July Monarchy's reforms marked the growing lenience of laws on political crime. Political opponents were now regarded as honorable, sincere citizens, not as criminals.[54] Madame Germaine de Staël, the *salonnière* and writer, was allowed to remain in France, though not in Paris, and visitors to her home near Auxerre were monitored but not prohibited. Napoleon III, though authoritarian, treated opponents of his coup moderately, exiling some, allowing others to remain in France under surveillance.[55]

The suffragettes of the late nineteenth century were emblematically political criminals. They advocated violence yet often hailed from prominent families. Unlike the Chartists and Fenians, earlier working-class political prisoners in Britain, suffragettes were radicalized insiders. They exploited that position, daring the authorities to treat them like drunks and other low-level offenders.[56] Using cat-and-mouse tactics, they pushed the authorities to respond forcefully, hoping to win public sympathy. They heckled, demonstrated, threw stones at meetings, broke windows, disrupted religious services, burned mailboxes, slashed paintings, rushed the House of Commons, picketed politicians' homes, held hunger strikes, and committed public suicide. Even assassination may have been discussed.[57] Fined, they did not pay. Ordered to provide sureties, they refused, requiring the government to keep them in jail.[58] On hunger strikes, they obliged the police either to undermine their own authority by releasing them or to force-feed them, with the attendant bad publicity.[59] Hunger strikes had long been one of the truest arrows in the political criminal's quiver. Strikers in effect took themselves hostage, leaving the authorities with bloody hands by requiring them either to let the strikers die or to torture them by force-feeding. Even God had been the object of a hunger strike by Saint Patrick.[60]

Yet lenient treatment of political offenders had its limits. The more authoritarian, the more twentieth-century regimes have treated political prisoners akin to ordinary criminals, refusing them the courtesy of a special status.[61] And even liberal democracies have shown their harsh side. Unlike on the continent, the Anglo-Saxons generally did not recognize political crime as a special instance or grant leniency for such offenses, however well intentioned.[62] Nor did they regard ordinary crimes as in any sense justified through being provoked by political oppression. Historians may regard crimes committed by

Blacks in the United States, whether slaves or their descendants, as protests against a deeply unfair system, thus political. But at the time they were met with lynching and oppression, certainly not treated with any understanding.[63] The rise of nationalism and the ideological conflicts of the interwar and Cold War decades posed quasi-theological political conflicts once again, undermining the nineteenth century's lenience toward political offenders.[64]

British prime minister Margaret Thatcher held out against Irish Republican Army hunger strikers in 1980. She refused to recognize their political status or to force-feed them. Almost a dozen starved to death.[65] Contemporary terrorists, who have been willing to commit mass murder by suicide, have failed to win status as political criminals or its attendant sympathy. If anything, they have provoked the state to treat them worse than ordinary offenders—held, interrogated, tortured, and sometimes sentenced without benefit of due process, as at Guantanamo. Ransoms for release can be paid for victims of criminal kidnap, but under United Nations regulations and in some countries, such as Colombia, under threat from the Revolutionary Armed Forces of Colombia, it is a crime to do so for politically motivated abductions. "If it's criminal, it's legal," was one British bureaucrat's laconic summation.[66] In such respects, terrorists have been treated much like anarchists in the late nineteenth century and fascist collaborators after 1945, as enemies beyond the pale.[67] The lenience with which the nineteenth century treated political prisoners evaporated in the following era.

Ever Inward

Ideological systems, whether religious or political, punished thought, not just deed. Why? So long as subjects acted lawfully, did it matter what went on in their minds? Did orthodox behavior require orthodox belief? Were not laws enforcing church attendance or party membership enough? And why were the authorities so curious about their subjects' thoughts? To ensure that everyone was truly virtuous, both thinking and acting correctly? Or were the authorities utilitarians, worried that wrong thoughts undermined society's cohesion? Knowing what was in people's heads, let alone changing it, was an intractable problem. Identifying, reforming, or at least incapacitating heretical thinkers, in contrast, was a practical proposition.

Acting lawfully merely means obeying rules. Being good, however—whether in a religious or a secular moral sense—requires a correspondence between interior and exterior states. Sin and morality look to the motivations behind the act, the law to the act itself and to the attitudes impelling it only if they indicate its character.[68] To avoid sin, according to Locke, inner conviction must correspond to outer behavior; lawfulness only means acting correctly.[69] In Kant's distinction, morality rests on human autonomy, the law on external compulsion. The law can make people behave correctly, but only morality or belief can make them good.[70] States reached the outer limits of their powers at this distinction. Perhaps they could compel subjects to act lawfully, but making them good was doable, if at all, mainly through institutions that were only partly under the states' sway: churches, families, schools.

Authorities have always been keen to know the inside of their subjects' heads. In a fragment of an ancient Greek play, possibly by Critias, King Sisyphus speculated that divine omniscience had been hatched as a concept because mortals could not know each other's minds. People who feared that gods knew their innermost thoughts would be good, prompted by a kind of universal panopticon principle.[71] This logic underlies recent theories of how large, complex societies, uniting unrelated strangers, emerged under the auspices of omniscient "big gods."[72] Gods were often all-knowing. Janus could look two ways at once, Buddha four; the Egyptian god Horus appeared as a sharp-eyed falcon; and Greek gods' bodies were often covered with eyes.[73] The monotheistic gods were even better enforcers: omniscient, omnipotent, and morally infallible. According to the medieval theologian Peter Abelard, God, able to pierce humans' inner minds, punished the sin with no need to await the act.[74] In comparison, even the mightiest mortal rulers were weak. Political and religious heretics could be known only if they revealed their thoughts by word or deed. Otherwise, unorthodoxy remained their secret, its punishment a matter for God—if anyone. Such were the Marranos, forcibly converted Spanish Jews; Moriscos, their Muslim analogues; and the Nicodemites, Protestants who attended Catholic mass.[75] Confession was the best and—other than indirect revelation by act—usually the only way of knowing the black box of the mind.

But even confession, especially if produced by torture, could mislead. The Greeks allowed evidence from slaves only if extracted by torture—even preferring this testimony to the uncompelled offerings of freemen.[76] But was confession under duress authentic? Or a desperate ploy to end the agony? The tortured body was not a reliable conduit to the soul. Medieval torturers solved the problem as best they could by requiring that a forced confession be repeated in the courtroom. Those who recanted off the rack started over again—though, for what it was worth, no more than thrice.[77] In sixteenth-century Seville, one observer thought that women who still did not confess after being stripped naked were probably innocent since why else would they accept such humiliation? But this was a logic that could be applied at any stage. At which level of agony did the tortured finally reveal the truth? Michael Servetus, the antitrinitarian Protestant whom Calvin hounded to a horrendous death, asked to be beheaded before being burned lest the flames persuade him to recant.[78]

The most fervent heretics, convinced of their own righteousness, were especially willing to play fast and loose with the observable truth. Protestants in sixteenth-century England, for example, perjured themselves. Ninety-eight percent of Lollards, an early

Protestant sect, who were tried as heretics abjured. Many of them then relapsed, so their initial recantations were likely insincere. Even Joan of Arc recanted at first. Hearing saints' voices rebuking her, she rescinded her recantation and was burned alive.[79] Giovanni Valentio Gentile, an Italian Protestant in Calvin's Geneva, was arrested for heresy in 1558. Concluding that he had recanted out of fear rather than conviction, the judges voted for his execution.[80] The sentence was commuted, but the point remained. Ultimately no one could know the authenticity of a forced confession, and those doing the confessing or recanting might well still retain their heretical core beyond reach of their suffering.

Torture was of course often used as punishment in its own right. Ancient Persians tortured not to extract confession but to intensify suffering.[81] But its main role in Western law was evidentiary, to reveal truth in the absence of better sources. Greek and Roman authorities tortured only outsiders, including slaves, but not citizens, over whom they had other leverage. Slaves, beholden to their masters, would tell the truth to others only under duress.[82] Citizens, however, were valid witnesses in court. If they lied on the stand, they risked being charged with perjury, pronounced legally infamous (*atimos*), and fined.[83] That perjury eventually became a serious crime is the price we have paid for avoiding torture. During the Middle Ages, ordeals and other divine interventions brought resolution to trials.[84] When in 1215 the Fourth Lateran Council forbade ordeals for ecclesiastical trials, it left a yawning evidentiary gap. Through ordeals, God had revealed the guilty: their hands blistered, their bodies buoyant. Without the ordeal, the Roman-canon law's standard of evidence was hard to meet: two eyewitnesses or a confession. With death as the likely punishment, few confessed voluntarily. To force a confession, torture therefore became crucial for conviction.[85]

Medieval courts tortured to unveil innermost thoughts but also to solve crimes without witnesses. In Europe's inquisitional systems, confession became the queen of proofs. Not only did the defendant's admission seal the case, but for crimes that were unknowable in any other way confession was the only access to them. With offenses such as simony and concubinage, the only witnesses were themselves implicated and unlikely to sing.[86] Other offenses, such as heresy, might be unknown to anyone other than the offender, though blasphemy, like slander, required an audience of at least one. How then to make suspects confess? Torture was required because the inquisitional system demanded firm proof. Abolishing ordeals had moved God out of the judicial process. Torture was meant to reassure that the standard of proof remained exacting. With mere mortals now sitting in judgment, confession—even if elicited by torture—became the capstone of evidence.[87] Where judicial torture remained uncommon, as in England, it was largely because the standard of proof was lower. English authorities tortured, too, but unenthusiastically. Persecuting the Templars in 1310 and unable to find competent Englishmen for the task, Edward II imported continental torturers.[88] Not English humanity but the legal system explains the difference. By Roman law standards, the jury system applied lax standards of evidence—whatever would convince a dozen compatriots. It did not need torture.

New crimes were formulated that were not capital and therefore required less-definite proof for conviction. When seventeenth-century Germany began to punish those who were merely suspected of offending (*Verdachtsstrafe*), the standard of proof was adjusted accordingly, and torture to confession (inherently unlikely with a crime of suspicion) was no longer required.[89] Circumstantial evidence was taken evermore seriously, displacing confession. As the quality of the evidence required to convict was lowered and the range of both offenses and sanctions expanded, torture was less fit for purpose. An increasingly powerful state, punishing subjects for more acts in more ways, could afford to abandon such blunt instruments. Fundamental to torture's eventual demise was also that certain interior crimes—religious and many political heresies—fell out of the state's remit.

The authorities no longer had to plumb souls, though that still left broad scope, as we will see, for other occult crimes.

Torture in the West today is used largely on outsiders but now mainly in a forward-looking interrogational mode, aiming to extract information about anticipated events rather than confessions about past transgressions.[90] Having supposedly banned torture, our own era (ignoring totalitarianism) has seen it revived. Some democracies have developed techniques of "clean" torture that tacitly acknowledge their illegality by inflicting pain without leaving physical traces.[91] The state has repeatedly confronted supposedly existential threats from actors it regards as outsiders, beyond the protection of due process: outcasts and organized criminals subjected to "third-degree" interrogations by American police (legal until 1936); Algerian nationalists taking the independence struggle to French soil in the 1950s; Islamic extremists waterboarded—or worse—at covert rendition sites, beyond the law's protection.[92] Ticking-bomb scenarios have been invoked to convince skeptics that torture was necessary, despite the damage to institutions and morality.[93]

Torture to elicit confession was among the first, crudest, and commonest techniques the state used to penetrate its subjects' interiors. It was the flip side of the voluntary laying bare of souls that the church also began demanding of the faithful. Confession and inquisition arose simultaneously as mirror aspects of the church's attempt to illuminate and mold the soul. When the Fourth Lateran Council abolished ordeals in 1215, paving the way for torture's reintroduction, it also made sacramental confession a routine element of lay religiosity, an annual obligation of all Christians.[94]

At first, confession was a public event, Christians seeking forgiveness collectively through the church's intermediation.[95] Sinners who made peace with the church contritely endured its penitential punishments: praying, fasting, undertaking pilgrimages, paying fines, chastising themselves, wearing clothes that indicated their faults, and the like. In return, they expected the church to intercede for them with God.[96] As of the mid-sixth century, beginning in Ireland, confession was also held privately, penitent to priest. In this form, it was required as of 1215.[97] Public confession had channeled the sinner's redemption through the church, which intervened with God. Private confession put the sinner in more direct relation to the divinity, though still through a priest. Canon lawyers called confession the *forum internum*, the "internal court," to distinguish it from their own external court of law.[98] Absolution resolved sin, while crime was left to the secular authorities. Protestants eventually denounced Catholic confession as a wheeze, promising redemption through mere ritual. They emphasized true confession and contrition's ability to bypass established authority as sinners pleaded directly with God.[99]

Confession's privacy was reinforced with the sixteenth-century invention of a place for it to occur, the confessional. Confessions were now both private and at least nominally anonymous, encouraging penitents to reveal all. If confession had earlier dealt with the frictions of rural life, the tensions and violence of local communities, it now concentrated on interior sins, often sexual, with masturbation a particular church preoccupation.[100] Sinners were reconciled to God, no longer to the community. Even before the Reformation attacked penances as mere empty ritual, confession focused on interiority. Early medieval confessions involved two meetings with the priest, the sinner first confessing and then after penance returning for absolution. But as absolution was extended to the laity starting in the late tenth century, confession was compressed to a single meeting where penance and absolution were dispensed together. Attention thus shifted to the sinner's attitude at the time of confession, the contrition expressed even before having undertaken penance.

A presumably apocryphal story illustrates the change. Having raped his daughter, a man asked for severe penance in confession. Given seven years, he demanded more. The priest instead reduced his penance, and this downward haggle continued until it arrived at but a single Paternoster. By this point, the man was so mortified by shame that he died on the spot, going straight to heaven.[101] The Reformation turned confession even more inward.[102] Luther distinguished between acts that harmed the community (adultery, murder, theft, usury, slander, wrath, enmity), which were to be handled by public or sacramental confession, and "the secret sins of the heart," or sexual fantasies. The latter could be dealt with between individual sinners and God. Insofar as they wanted the comfort of confession, they could also confess to any Christian, ordained or not.[103]

Neither forced nor voluntary confession provided certain knowledge of interior states, however. Only a truthful confessant aligned interior conviction with outward profession. Others were conflicted. Neither priest nor torturer knew whether conversion or confession or repentance was meant wholeheartedly. The problem with torture lay epistemologically not with those who had in fact offended. They resisted the pain—or not. The innocents, in contrast, saw no reason to suffer for deeds they had not committed, and so they served up whatever they thought the interrogators wanted to hear, and often much more. Soviet police, for example, became alarmed during the late 1930s as torture stimulated detainees' imaginations, and the evidence suddenly suggested that subversion was even more widespread than the authorities feared.[104] On the scaffold, the executioner never really knew whether he was killing a stubborn heretic or a genuine innocent.

Imposing orthodoxy, religious or political, some regimes welcomed public confession or recantation as a ritual of allegiance by which dissenters acknowledged their reentry into the fold, affirmed the official creed, warned potential transgressors, and reinforced the official message of ideological unity—all regardless of what the heretic actually thought. The authorities often settled for the mere appearance of a change of heart. The Inquisition threatened to torture Galileo unless he recanted his heliocentric beliefs. They forbade him to write more about them and kept him under house arrest for the rest of his days, which suggested they were under no illusion as to his true thoughts.[105] More cynically, the forced self-criticism of the Soviet mass trials turned confession into an empty exercise in abject humiliation that could scarcely have convinced even the most credulous true believer. When interrogating suspects, Chekist secret-police officers were advised not to seek evidence but to ask first what class the suspect belonged to. From that all else followed.[106] Chinese Communists, in contrast, seem to have continued the Confucian tradition of self-criticism, seeking to change their enemies' convictions.[107] Either way, totalitarianism's insistence on alignment of inner and outer states, belief and act, meant that confession again took on a role akin to that in the post-Lateran world. Objective proof of guilt or innocence based on third-party evidence paled in comparison to extracting an admission from the sinners themselves as part of their forcible rehabilitation. Bereft of any real proof of guilt, the mass show trials of the 1930s were often based on confession alone. In the post-Stalinist 1960s, confession was downplayed, and proof reinstated in importance.[108]

Short of confession, the authorities had only external signs of thought offenses to go on. Specific acts, indicating forbidden attitudes, were treated as offenses: following certain ritual practices (or refusing them), owning particular writings, or tuning in to specific media.[109] Refusing to swear an oath or pledge betrayed internal attitudes. When the church began requiring annual confession, it gained insight into parishioners' ideas, such as those of heretics too guileless to lie, and also flushed out dissenters, such as Cathars, who shunned such sacraments.[110] Even moderate Protestants rejected many of Catholicism's rituals, sacraments, and liturgy. Eating meat on Fridays or refusing to fast during Lent, they gave themselves away.[111] In ideological systems, otherwise commonplace transgressions became fraught with new significance. Once Stalin had declared socialism achieved in 1933, petty offenses such as begging threatened to undermine the new system and were considered political crimes.[112] A bribe is the price of doing business in a conventionally corrupt system. In an ideologically saturated one, bribery often became a crime against the state. Economic crimes were counterrevolutionary in Maoist China. In the 1980s, they were depoliticized as normal offenses. Nonetheless, even today smuggling, foreign-currency speculation, public-property theft, and bribery remain political offenses in China. As actions against socialism and thus the state, they are punished by death.[113] And assassination, as we have seen, is not just murder. Even in secular, allegedly unideological Western nations, it is difficult to shake the residue of such sentiments and to treat the killing of a leader as mere homicide.

Chapter 10
Obliged to Be Good

As the state turned its sights to human interiority, probing thoughts to punish the offending kind, new vistas opened up. Being good presupposed a congruence between inner inclination and outer act. So long as the state punished only acts, it could hope for law-abiding but not necessarily virtuous citizens. Crimes of thought and their policing raised the possibility—last seen when the authorities had been concerned with sin as well as crime—that goodness, not just propriety, might be the outcome of their interventions.

Apart from habit, custom, and informal sanction, at least three kinds of rules have enforced behavior: religious precepts, moral exhortations, and laws. Each was transgressed in its own way. Sin scoffed at divine edicts or the church's will. Immorality transgressed ethical or moral codes. Crimes violated laws—rules that, neither divinely enjoined nor necessarily ethically informed, had been issued by recognized authority. Religion, morality, and law have often reinforced each other. Once the gods stopped enforcing and the church gave up its temporal power, the law commanded the largest battalions. Nonetheless, religion and morality still undergird the law. Religion, morality, and law today steer in different directions on only a few issues: abortion, euthanasia, homosexuality, and polygamy. Despite increasing secularization, the law continues to enforce morality. "Besides interfering with people who wish to have abortions, commit homosexual acts, visit prostitutes, take drugs, get drunk," as one scholar listed the still controversial instances in 1976, "it also interferes with people who wish to steal, rob, evade income taxes, assault, and murder."[1]

Ideological regimes, religious or political, have punished wrong thoughts for at least two reasons. First, the thinkers needed to be saved from themselves. That was Augustine's logic. Since eternal damnation awaited heretics, compelling their conversion did them a great favor. Second, wrong thoughts might harm society collectively either by angering higher powers (or—in the secular, political version—by defying ineluctable laws of history or biology) or by undermining its sense of community. As we have seen, the concept of crime as a collective affront has deep historical roots—back to the Greek pollution theory at least. Medieval heretics were persecuted not just to save themselves but also to protect other Christians.[2]

Western societies no longer consider thought crimes a communal danger. As the distinction between sin and crime was elaborated, and as religious and eventually political beliefs were moved from the state's auspices into the private sphere, what individuals thought or believed became a matter largely for them alone. The same held, but to a lesser extent, for the collective danger posed by wrong thinking. If some thoughts motivated wrong action, they undermined society. The individual adulterer might not harm anyone, but widespread philandering threatened to hollow out the family as an institution. Perjury, contempt of court, and tax evasion did not necessarily cause immediate widespread harm but undermined the penal code's deterrent effect.[3] The state might no longer enforce religion, but it did police morality. In much the same way, though the authorities did not suppress political criticism, they did insist on maintaining order. Treason, as we have seen, has been narrowed to the point where only actual attempts to destroy the state are punished. Most opinions may be freely expressed. The concern with speech has shifted from its content—now only rarely actionable—to the circumstances and form of its expression: whether it threatens unrest or disorder. Around the time of the Peterloo massacre in 1819, the English authorities began paying less attention to whether public statements were libelous and treasonous and more to whether the assemblies where they were uttered were riotous.[4] Contemporary debates over hate speech focus less on the precise—usually risible—claims advanced in that speech and more on the circumstances of their utterance and their consequences in acts.

Does the modern state legislate morality? Founded contractually for its citizens' common good, the state, many think, pursues order, not virtue. Society has therefore banned only those actions that harm it, undermining public tranquility. Sacrilege, even unbelief, are no longer its concern, though blasphemy may disturb the public peace and can be prosecuted on that basis, not as an offense to God or religion.[5] Nor are many behaviors pursued that harm no one, or even those that affect only the person doing them: adultery, sloth, fornication, gluttony, inebriation, masturbation, and other acts that once called down the law's wrath. The private realm of permissible behavior and cogitation has undeniably expanded. Yet what that realm includes and what remains regulated depend on how order and harm are defined. As some behaviors became private, others were recognized as of public concern.

By themselves, religion and later morality lacked strong means of secular enforcement. Big gods enforced sanctions and encouraged prosocial behavior.[6] But on earth law played little role in voluntary communities of the likeminded, bound together by belief but with no official ability to coerce. Among the early Christians, morals and faith guided believers without legal sanctions. As a gathering of the likeminded with no tools of compulsion, the early church could enforce its precepts only through private punishments (penance, fasting, pilgrimages, sartorial markings) that believers agreed to submit to, along with whatever psychic toll was imposed by the conviction that they had fallen from God's favor. Mennonites, the Amish, Mormons, Orthodox Jews, and other religious communities that enforce behavioral norms not enshrined in statute continue like this today.

Convinced of their own virtue and ability to guide behavior by example rather than by precept, political ideologies, too, have succumbed to the illusion that they could do without the law. Punishing them treated humans as animals, Marx thought. Under socialism, people would recognize their own wrong-doing and reform themselves. Somewhat unexpectedly, Marx's view of what abolishing the state would actually look like was akin to the United States of the early nineteenth century.[7] Later Marxists believed that law was needed only in bourgeois systems, to defend property against the dispossessed. Law, along with morality and the state, would be superseded under socialism's wholly novel arrangements.[8] Early in the Soviet Union, the police were considered a bourgeois and capitalist institution and thus nothing for socialists.[9] That was the myth of the state withering away in the coming Communist nirvana. Castro thought that socialist Cuba could do without lawyers since revolutionary justice was based on moral convictions, not legal precepts.[10] Yet these political ideologues, just like the religious ones, soon discovered how handy the law could be. Unhampered by due process, the so-called actually existing socialisms attacked their class and ideological enemies mercilessly. The state must be democratic for the proletariat and dictatorial against the bourgeoisie, Lenin decreed.[11] In the theocracies, morality and religion were enforced by law, often backed by terror.

Early on, religion regulated even behaviors that would later be treated as ethical or legal concerns. Thus, theocracies policed a wider range of conduct than we now recognize as pertaining to either morality or the law. The Old Testament decreed death for encroachment on the tabernacle, idolatry, blasphemy, Sabbath breaking, assault on parents, contumacy, murder, manslaughter, negligent killing, adultery, concealed unchastity, rape, homosexual acts, bestiality, prostitution, incest, stealing from God, kidnapping, and serious perjury.[12] Religion sought to control personal conduct (diet, hygiene, dress, grooming, and other ways of combatting uncleanliness) as well as beliefs (apostasy, sacrilege, heresy, blasphemy), economic and legal relations (usury, perjury, breach of contract, forgery of documents), supernatural and semireligious behaviors (sorcery, witchcraft, magic), morality (adultery, incest), quasi-emotions (greed, pride, envy), and family relations, including women's rights.[13] As if that were not enough, religion also claimed to govern belief, sin, grace, and other inner states. Today's theocracies punish a similarly expansive range of actions, many of which are elsewhere considered private issues or matters of indifference.

Polytheistic religions were not very good at setting consistent ethical precepts. Gods disported themselves with little coherence and even less willingness to set a good example. Among the Aztecs, as the four sons of Ometeotl fought each other for control of the universe, Huitzilopochtli beheaded his sister when she tried to murder their mother, who had become pregnant out of wedlock. The Egyptian god Seth killed his older brother, Osiris, to become king of Egypt and then had to fight his nephew, Horns, to retain power. Deities raped, seduced, and cheated. Osiris sired the god Anubis by the wife of his brother, Seth, and Seth in revenge raped his young nephew, Horns.[14] The monotheistic religions were practically prim in comparison, issuing universalist law codes and punishing a wide variety of behaviors—drinking and gambling in Islam, for example.

Whether mono- or polytheistic, divine precepts were often ethically indifferent, even immoral. Gods were spiteful, vengeful, petty, peevish, and cruel. They were often envious of humans—when mortals were too happy, for example.[15] What they commanded was not always ethical, and far from all sins were immoral.[16] Why gods were not more moral has long been a puzzle. The concept of an "act of God," describing the unpredictable, overpowering forces insurance companies refuse to reimburse for, hints at the dilemma. Job tries our understanding as he endures God's injustice. Accustomed to mercurial divinities, even the Greeks were often stumped by how unjust the gods could be. In the *Theognidean sylloge*, Zeus is asked the question we pose of Job: Faced with a just person suffering undeservedly, can we still worship the immortals?[17]

It may be sinful not to pray or worship, but it is hardly immoral. Nor was Jonah being immoral when he disobeyed God by taking a ship in the opposite direction instead of going to Nineveh to preach.[18] Dietary injunctions and other rituals were morally indifferent. Whether we believe in the unity or the trinity of the godhead may be theologically significant, but not ethically. Some taboos still in force today are likely rooted in a deep premoral past: laws against suicide, incest, bestiality, necrophilia, and parricide, against improper burial or disposal of corpses, and perhaps against cannibalism. Nor should we read much morality into the first three or four of the Commandments: that only the God who issued them may be worshipped, that he must not be figuratively represented, that his name must not be invoked except to worship him, and that he must be worshipped on a particular weekday.[19] These orders were the trade-unionist aspects of divinity, with religious but no ethical import. Adultery and coveting others' possessions we today regard as mere moral transgressions. In contrast, not stealing, killing, or bearing false witness remain core legal and moral prohibitions.

Religion at times contradicted morality outright. The elect saw their behavior as inherently virtuous, regardless of how immoral. Subjects who claim direct access to the divine are the state's worst nightmare: unruly, supremely self-assured antinomian anarchists, irrepressible in their mischief. In the twelfth and thirteenth centuries, the Free Spirits of northern France and the Rhine Valley were convinced that, thanks to their immediate relation to a pantheistic god, they had no need of the church and its sacraments. Sinless and thus unbound by conventional morality, they allegedly indulged in spectacular feats of sexual promiscuity, even incest. Intercourse with the illuminated, they cunningly claimed, restored a woman's virginity.[20] The

Ranters of seventeenth-century England believed they were incapable of sin and so welcome to indulge in fornication, incest, adultery, orgies, cursing, whoring, drunkenness, and blasphemy.[21] The Jewish messianic rabbi Sabbatai Zevi made similar claims to direct connection with the divine. Claiming to be the messiah, he married a former prostitute and radically reformed rituals. In 1666, he ordered followers to celebrate his birthday rather than fast on the Ninth of Ab, commemorating the Temple's destruction. Sexual extravagances were also reported among later Sabbatian heretics.[22]

But as religious and secular administration grew separate, so did law and religion and later morality as well. Morality increasingly crystallized out the ethical components of religion, leaving behind the sectarian and ritualistic aspects. Eventually it too was statutorily enforced. Compared to what would have been the Jews' theocratic commandment of religious injunctions if they had had a state, the Romans scarcely enforced religious matters. They did forbid violating the chastity of the Vestal Virgins, who stood in constant contact with the gods if they remained pure.[23] But it was still long before religion and morality were clearly distinguished. The scholastics of the twelfth and thirteenth centuries recognized natural law, but not morality, as something separate from religion.[24] In the sixteenth and seventeenth centuries, natural law, in all its variations, supplemented or replaced the divine as the ultimate authority. By the Enlightenment and especially with Kant, a secular morality had developed with little connection to organized religion, indeed often opposed to it. Voltaire's philosopher Zadig claimed that all religions aimed at a lowest common denominator of ethics. At the same time, sin also came to approximate immorality as religious teachings became more generally ethical and less concerned with theological doctrines.

For Hobbes in 1651, crime was still a subspecies of sin, "consisting in the Committing (by Deed, or Word) of that which the law forbiddeth, or the Omission of what it hath commanded." Every crime was a sin, but not every sin a crime.[25] In the early seventeenth century, Hugo Grotius, too, hardly distinguished between law and morality. Sin and crime remained conflated. Laws in the eighteenth century still prohibited what were regarded as sins or moral failings: committing adultery, having sex outside of wedlock, working on the Sabbath or not working at all, begging, bear baiting, and cock fighting.[26] But in 1689 Locke separated the two. The magistrate's mandate was the public good. Being covetous, uncharitable, or idle: though possibly sins, these were not crimes. No harm ensued, nor was society's peace disturbed.[27] Law's concern was only with actions that hurt others. The Enlightenment philosophes, such as Beccaria, distinguished between secular punishment in this world and divine justice in the afterlife.[28] The French Constituent Assembly's Law of 8–9 October 1789 declared that the law should prohibit only actions harmful to society.[29] The Bavarian penal code of 1813 distinguished rigorously between law and morality. Law should not deal with acts that violated people's moral obligations to themselves. Masturbation, sodomy, bestiality, and fornication were immoral, but laws punished such sins only if they violated others' rights.[30] Adultery was treated as a breach of contract and dealt with in the code's article following that on attorneys who failed to pursue their clients' interests. It was punished with a maximum of three months' jail.[31] In France half a century after Locke, however, Montesquieu still counted offenses against religion and morality as two out of four forms that crime took, alongside actions against public tranquility and individual security.[32]

Enforcing religion long remained the law's task. The church developed its own courts whose remit included blasphemy and heresy. By 1500, such courts were found throughout Western Christendom.[33] Technically a royal institution, the Inquisition pursued the church's enemies until 1834.[34] Secular authorities eventually entered the field, too. Early in the thirteenth century, several European states instituted death against heresy, which they treated as a secular crime.[35] In seventeenth-century England, blasphemy was a common law offense and in 1697 also began violating statute. Christians who denied the Trinity, claimed there was more than one God, or rejected the Bible as divine authority could not hold office and suffered other legal disabilities and jail if they repeated any of these offenses.[36] Yet the state cared for public order more than for theological purity. Cromwell's mid-seventeenth-century Puritan republic faced even more extreme nonconformists. Reformers themselves, the Puritans could have enforced orthodoxy only hypocritically. But dissenters such as the Ranters, who believed that God was everywhere and that no authority deserved obedience, gnawed at society's moorings.

In 1650, the House of Commons took aim at Ranters with an act punishing those who believed that, thanks to their immediate relationship to God, moral distinctions no longer applied to them, salvation and damnation were irrelevant, and they were incapable of sin. A month later, another act ended all requirements of uniform religious belief and practice. A variety of Christian practices was now tolerated, but extreme dissenters were still beyond the pale—Ranters and Socinians (who rejected Christ's divinity and original sin). In effect, forms of Christianity that were both religious and moral were accepted, but those sects that refused to toe the line of morality and social order were not. This distinction held even after the monarchy was restored in 1660. Christians sects that did not threaten the social order were tolerated. Only those who refused to swear oaths (Quakers) or considered themselves the sinless elect were not. They were punished not for theological deviations but for threatening stability. When John Taylor was convicted of blasphemy in 1676 for calling Christ a bastard, a cheat, and an imposter, he was put in the pillory with a sign saying "for blasphemous words, tending to the subversion of all government."[37] Blasphemy was now punishable in common law because Christianity was part of the social order. But it became enforced by law less as a religious doctrine than as a set of behavioral precepts—more morality than theology.

Morality and religion were conflated. Resting on both, the social order would be undermined if either were violated. In 1675, Chief Justice Hale warned that to deny religion was "to dissolve all those obligations whereby civil society is preserved." A century later, in 1797, Justice William Henry Ashurst said of blasphemy that it was not just an offense against God but against "all law and government from its tendency to dissolve all the bonds and obligations of civil society." Another century on, in 1908, Justice Walter Phillimore allowed that humans were free to think, speak, and teach as they pleased in religious terms but not in moral ones.[38] Purely theological issues had now been left to God, but beliefs with this-worldly consequences—morality—remained the law's concern. That is broadly where the issue has remained ever since. Some still think that morality cannot be taught without religion.[39] But in the main, doctrinal matters have been shifted to the private sphere, out of the state's purview. Outside the world's remaining theocracies, religious practices concern the law only if nonreligious norms have also been violated: bigamy among Mormons, animal cruelty in Santería sacrifices, child neglect by Christian Scientists shunning medicine, truancy among homeschooling Seventh-Day Adventists, infibulation of Muslim women.

Blasphemy, however, has remained on the books in many countries. Thirty-two nations (eight in Europe) still retain antiblasphemy laws. Another twenty punish apostasy.[40] France abolished blasphemy in 1791, and the US never instituted it as a federal crime.[41] Yet it remained in place as a state-level offense. Even colonial Pennsylvania, otherwise religiously ecumenical, outlawed blasphemy. Massachusetts prosecuted it as a capital crime until 1692.[42] By 1951, federal law and First Amendment rights together made prosecutions for blasphemy unconstitutional. And yet as of 2009 it remained law in Massachusetts, Michigan, Oklahoma, Pennsylvania, South Carolina, and Wyoming. On this basis, in 2007 Pennsylvania rejected a bid to name a company "I Choose Hell Productions."[43] Until 2008, blasphemy remained a crime in Britain, but only against Christianity. This helped the authorities in 1989 when they were pressured to join the fatwa issued by Iran's Ayatollah Khomeini against Salman Rushdie for his treatment of Muhammad in his novel *The Satanic Verses*.[44]

Blasphemy obviously remained a religious issue in theocracies. But to secular societies, blasphemy marked the boundary between free speech and civility, a matter of order and propriety, not theological doctrine.[45] Modern blasphemy laws no longer protect specific doctrines but prohibit the insulting of religious feelings or the inciting of hatred against religious groups.[46] They have become a form of collective libel legislation, protecting minority communities from attack.[47] In 1922, an Australian judge found that while respectful denial of God's existence was not blasphemous, scurrilous and offensive attacks intended to outrage Christians were. In 1978, a British court convicted of blasphemy the publisher of James Kirkup's poem about homosexual sex between Christ and a centurion.[48]

Muslims, whose religion—like some variants of Protestantism—forbids depictions of God as idolatrous, have especially policed blasphemy. Cartoons depicting Muhammad in *Jyllands Posten* in 2005 cast the complacently tolerant Danes as the new Satans of international politics.[49] With the slaughter in 2015 of twelve journalists by Islamist gunmen at the offices of the Parisian satirical magazine *Charlie Hebdo*, free-speech fundamentalism found itself unexpectedly on the defensive against a more cautious consideration of religious sensibilities. Muslims in Europe—however quick to anger and kill—were also downtrodden minorities. Did that give them claim to deference for their cultural singularities? Mormons endured a whirlwind of blasphemy in the wildly popular musical the *Book of Mormon* in 2011.[50] Their official response was commendably restrained. "You've seen the play," the billboards proclaimed, "now read the book."

From Theology to Morality

Yet even as religion was reduced to a public-order issue, ethics were still enforced by law. Individual habits with no immediate social consequences were privatized as citizens' choices: gluttony, sloth, cupidity, and most sexual behavior other than rape and pedophilia. But new immoralities came to be restricted by law, as we will see. Morality was informal social sanction that broadly reinforced what statute also dictated. Did the law need morality as a backup? Or were formalized, democratically decided rules alone legitimate, with morality therefore archaic and redundant?

The Enlightenment's debates over atheism posed such issues first. Could society function without a commonly accepted sense of sin? Could atheists be moral? Even the philosophes found it hard to shake off the basic assumptions of a fundamentally religious era.[51] Hobbes endowed the Leviathan with a strong state church—not for religion's intrinsic value but to secure order. Though religiously tolerant, Locke banished atheists because—considering that they accepted no higher power—their oaths and promises meant nothing.[52] If people did not believe in a punitive God, Voltaire feared, society would crumble. That was the gist of his often misunderstood assertion that bereft of God, we would have to invent him.[53] Though a generation younger, Pierre Bayle had already cast off religion's social role. Morality was not necessarily based on religion. An atheistic society would function civilly and morally so long as it punished crimes and honored laudable acts. We have no right, he insisted, to assume that an atheist is less moral than a believer.[54]

That the irreligious could also be moral was discovered only slowly. In the developing world, vast majorities still refuse to accept that one can be both moral and yet not a believer.[55] Even today, we continue to insist on religiously observant leaders. Outside China, few public figures dare to openly acknowledge their atheism.[56] Similar issues were raised when James Fitzjames Stephen and John Stuart

Mill crossed pens in the nineteenth century. Punishments voiced society's moral revulsion, Stephen thought, whereas Mill allowed sanction only if citizens directly harmed each other.[57] These issues arose again in the 1960s in debates fought as Britain reviewed the criminalization of (male) homosexuality. Did society need the glue of a common moral codex to undergird formal statute and avoid ethical anomie? Patrick Devlin famously argued that it mattered less what moral values society held so long as they were widely shared and enforced.[58] Both sides back then broadly assumed that gay sex was immoral; at issue was whether it should also be illegal.

Should the law enforce morality? Did purely individual transgressions even exist—ones with no consequence for others? Conservatives insisted that individual acts—divorce, sexual unorthodoxy, blasphemy—weakened society's bonds.[59] But what level of harm should be punished? Most expansively, not just tangible harm but offense, too, was actionable. Acts that merely offended others, even without damaging them, could be condemned. That risked leaving the penal code responsive to society's most delicate souls. They might feel impaired just by the possibility that somewhere someone was doing something disturbing.[60] Without a semiobjective criterion of harm, the definition of offense would endlessly expand. In 1957, the Wolfenden Committee (Parliamentary Committee on Homosexual Offences and Prostitution) in Britain solved the problem by deft distinction. It simultaneously demarcated a private sphere where actions—in this case male homosexuality—were permitted even if offensive to some but advocated more stringent penalties for street prostitution, regarded as a public harm.[61]

Nevertheless, society still rested on moral and behavioral norms. The law dealt originally with crime, sin, and immorality, all together. As the three were gradually separated out, it focused on violations of statute, not of theology or morality. Depending on how "to bear false witness" is defined, twentieth-century British law embodies either three and a half or four and a half of the

Bible's Ten Commandments.[62] Today, the law is much larger than morality, prohibiting many more actions. Yet it has also narrowed. Large swaths of once illegal conduct are now solely a matter for ethicists or theologians. Purely theological transgressions are rarely legal issues any longer. Many acts once considered immoral are now often legal: adultery, homosexuality, prostitution, abortion, suicide, euthanasia. And not all immorality is illegal: lying, cheating on your spouse, bullying, standing by while someone drowns. Conversely, most crimes are not immoral: jaywalking, driving with a broken tail light, failing to withhold employee Social Security deductions. The distinction between illegality and immorality has become a commonplace.[63]

As philosophers explored the various moral codes in effect across the globe, their relativity caused lawyers to fear hitching statute too closely to ethics. Montesquieu emphasized the multiplicity of legal and political systems. Locke and Kant sought to separate law from morality, John Austin and Bentham (who considered the idea of natural rights "nonsense on stilts") to free their utilitarian codex from it entirely. The French Revolution, invoking what the revolutionaries insisted were natural laws, scared many, prompting conservatives such as Edmund Burke and Friedrich Karl von Savigny to draw sharp distinctions between law and morals.[64] Starting in the late nineteenth century, legal realists, for whom the law was only what the authorities decided, unlinked to anything transcendent, made the separation watertight.[65] The law sought to wall itself off from religion and morality and to remain untainted by what it regarded as outmoded behavioral prescriptions. The Austrian legal philosopher Hans Kelsen insisted in the early twentieth century that morality was culture specific, without a common core. The law could not be founded on such relativistic quicksand.[66]

Nonetheless, despite the most astringent legal theorists' distaste, the legal and the moral still overlapped. True, the law expanded to include more actions only tangentially related to religion or ethics, but its core remained the fundamental tenets of morality.[67] Do not kill, lie, assault, cheat, or steal. Blurring the line between law and morality became a problem mainly when statute enforced those aspects of morality that did not involve protecting others from direct harm. Should the law require us to perform acts that benefit others? To avoid acts that cause indirect harm to others or harm to ourselves? To shun acts that offend others or that are regarded by them as immoral?[68] These were gray areas where law and morality overlapped, where cultures differed in which ethical precepts they enforced legally, and where changing social mores, striving to be recognized in legal reform, first had an effect.

Morality has obviously varied—sometimes dramatically—among and within cultures. Such differences have tended to concern sex and women: homosexuality, pedophilia, adultery, bigamy, divorce, contraception, abortion. The law often limped along, barely keeping abreast of evolving mores.[69] In the US outmoded detritus still litters state penal codes, technically outlawing a wide range of behaviors: adultery, fornication, sodomy, and (in some state or municipal code somewhere) just about any form of sexual behavior short of the missionary position within marriage and solitary masturbation. In 1948, Boston police arrested 248 adulterers. Massachusetts successfully prosecuted an adultery case in 1983, and as of 2012 the offense remained on the state's books as a felony.[70] Nevertheless, a common core arguably united most behaviors considered morally significant: promise keeping, truth telling, protecting innocents from violent attack.[71] That punishments should be proportionate to offenses approximates a human constant.[72] The endless debates over natural law at least served to distill plausibly quasi-universal rules. And law helped reinforce morality when it was used expressively to undergird society's ethical precepts.[73]

Even today the law is based more on morality than is often recognized. Hospitality law, how to treat aliens, what the Germans call *Gastrecht*, has evolved from a moral obligation to a legal duty in international law.[74] The obviously unethical is usually illegal as well, but morality also informs everyday economic transactions. The law of contract depends on the concept of good faith. The US Uniform Commercial Code defines good faith as "honesty in fact in the conduct or transaction concerned."[75] All commercial systems rest on the (moral) assumption that those engaged in exchange can rely on each other's promises. Such promises may be reinforced in law. The blossoming of contract law in the nineteenth century put some steel in the velvet glove of promises made in the free market by its interacting parties.[76] But without good faith, systems of exchange would collapse.[77] More generally, good faith transactions—keeping promises, performing what was agreed upon, and the like—were behaviors enforced at first by custom and religion in self-governing communities. When the law began regulating these actions, they long kept religious forms. The standards of due care in the law of negligence, of fair competition, and of fair conduct of a fiduciary: all involved a concept of fairness and reasonableness that—though applied by courts—ultimately rested on moral intuitions.[78] In the continental civil codes, contracts were explicitly premised on morality. Those that were immoral could be declared invalid.[79]

Relations of law to morality had long been given voice in two sets of distinctions. Where both morality and law forbade the same actions, they targeted inherent evil, *malum in se*. Where the law alone prohibited conduct that might not be immoral, it created the *malum prohibitum*.[80] *Mala in se* were fundamentally unethical actions, directed against life, health and bodily security, personal liberty and dignity, property rights, as well as the constitutional order and safety of the state. Sins they were not, but the term *moral turpitude* was often used to describe them.[81] *Mala prohibita* were forbidden acts or regulatory or civil offenses. Plato distinguished between curable and incurable offenses, Aristotle between natural political justice (having the same force everywhere) and legal political justice (important only once laid down in the law).[82] The distinction had become formalized by the late fifteenth century and then rendered orthodoxy by Blackstone in the 1760s.[83] Despite being ridiculed by Bentham, the distinction remains in good standing, cited by the US Supreme Court as recently as the 1950s.[84]

Related, though not identical, was the distinction between torts and crimes, emerging after the thirteenth century in common law. Before this point, crimes could be pursued both by private parties and by the king, and the law could impose either compensation or corporeal punishments.[85] Torts were harms that could be assuaged through compensation alone. Before the state assumed responsibility for justice, most transgressions had been treated as torts—even ones, such as homicide, that later became crimes. They were settled between the disputant parties through an exchange of value. Torts were actions society preferred to regulate, whereas crimes were forbidden outright. One priced acts; the other prohibited them. Torts were not worth the bother of criminal sanctions. Or, because certain offenses might enrich the offender more than they harmed society, they were more efficiently dealt with by recouping their social cost through fines. Crimes, in contrast, were acts whose cost society was unwilling to monetize and collect, therefore to be forbidden altogether. Punishing crime aimed not to reimburse victims but to deter others. Sanctions inflicted real suffering. Crimes were actions society sought to eliminate wholly (rape and murder), whereas torts might have some social utility (the economic efficiencies of turning a blind eye to polluting or workplace accidents) and should be discouraged and reduced but not wholly forbidden. It sufficed if their cost was internalized, borne by the offender.[86]

The boundary between morality and law has constantly shifted across history. Many behaviors have boiled off the core of immorality to become legal: sex between racial groups, drinking, adultery, homosexuality, to some extent abortion and prostitution, to some extent the use of inebriants other than alcohol. Incest may be moving toward a crossing of the ethical Rubicon.[87] Polygamy is ambiguous. Monogamy has historically been the exception. China and India, together composing well more than a third of humanity, did not forbid polygamy until the mid-1950s.[88] Outlawed in the West, it remains present throughout the Muslim world, in parts of non-Muslim Africa, surreptitiously among Mormons, as well as in more recent demands by urban hipsters for civil unions of threesomes.[89] Bestiality has been decriminalized in some nations (although animal rights may end up trumping claims to human erotic self-expression). Euthanasia, once considered murder, is legal in several jurisdictions. Attempted suicide is less commonly punished than earlier and has been decriminalized in some sixty nations, mostly Western.[90]

Tax avoidance may be morally suspect, but tax evasion is illegal, too. Working on the Sabbath was once irreligious, immoral, and illegal, but, overall, Sabbatarian regulation has declined.[91] Yet surprising numbers of laws still shape economic activity according to religious fiat. In allegedly secular Sweden, taxis charge even more on Lutheran high holy days than on weekends or nights.[92] Signs on playgrounds in the Calvinist parts of the Outer Hebrides discourage children from using them on Sundays.[93] Blue laws still regulate liquor sales on Sundays in the US. A popular movement in Catholic Bavaria seeks to reverse their few exceptions to Sunday closing laws. Communism sought to upend inherited moral instincts about property (or theft, according to the anarchist Pierre-Joseph Proudhon). The Soviet Union punished theft of state property more harshly than theft of private possessions, often with death and with no chance of amnesty, but the penal codes of most Communist states still prohibited conventional larceny.[94]

The law does not just reflect social value judgments; it helps shape them. Durkheim wrote that the collective consciousness is not offended by an act because it is criminal, but that it is criminal because society abhors it.[95] This oft-quoted bon mot did not, however, spare him the paradox he thought he was sidestepping. Yes, as he rightly pointed out, the quality of the criminality that society shuns is hard to define, but cleverly turning the tables does nothing to solve the causal problem. Why does the collective consciousness decide that something is abhorrent and therefore criminal? And, having done so for its own inscrutable reasons, how can things ever change? In fact, seen historically, not only has the law changed continuously, but changes in statute have also driven views of what offends. The law has taught us right and wrong, not just mirrored our views thereof.

The realm of the illegal and immoral has not just shrunken but also expanded. Many once legally indifferent behaviors are now outlawed. Two centuries ago, a man who refused a duel would become a social outcast. Today, one who accepts the challenge risks a charge of attempted homicide.[96] Honor killings—once an imperative—are no longer permitted or acceptable. Conventional industrial waste disposal—that is, polluting—has become broadly illegal. Tobacco use is increasingly forbidden, almost like other drugs, even as other inebriants have become tolerated. Primogeniture once kept the family intact and men on top. Today, anyone who insists on leaving all assets to an eldest son would be regarded as peculiar and in most developed nations denied his or her wish.[97] Theft of intellectual property became a crime starting in the late eighteenth century and expanded massively through the twentieth, though in the digital age it has become something of a misdemeanor and even morally valorized as justified use.[98]

White-collar crime, once treated more leniently than physical offenses, is taken more seriously.[99] Whereas being tough on crime is often a conservative cause, economic offenses have riled the Left—just as the women's and environmental movements brought their own rosters of new offenses to be prosecuted. In the 1960s, corporate executives from major American businesses, conspiring to fix prices, went to jail for the first time. In the 1970s, the US began prosecuting bribes paid to foreign authorities—once regarded as a cost of doing business. Insider trading has been criminalized, even though it was earlier considered a normal—if a bit sharp—business practice or at worst a violation of tort or regulatory law.[100] In 1934, insider traders could be required to disgorge only illicitly procured funds. By the 1960s, they could be fined as well; as of the 1980s, they were slapped with treble damage sanctions and jail. Prison sentences have become a regular occurrence in the US business world.[101] Wall Street executives, pillars of their Connecticut communities, are perp-walked for the news cameras as they are taken to be booked. And as sentencing reform diminished judicial discretion and pegged punishments to the dollar value of the harm, prison stays for crimes such as securities fraud have lengthened to rival those for murder.[102]

Many now illegal acts have also become immoral: slavery, wife beating, marital rape, child labor, child marriage, child abuse, cruelty to animals. Pedophilia, considered normal (within limits) in ancient Greece, is today regarded as the single most immoral and illegal act, potently stigmatized. Once prized as manly behavior, hunting endangered megafauna has become both illegal and immoral.[103] Now illegal and on the cusp of also being immoral are actions such as insider trading, price fixing, bribing, and antitrust violations. Driving drunk is illegal and increasingly regarded also as immoral. Some jurisdictions have harnessed popular sentiment to state enforcement by prosecuting hosts who allow guests to depart inebriated. Endangering consumers by knowingly selling deficient products is considered immoral. The days of caveat emptor (buyer beware), when consumers bore most risk in a purchase, are long gone. Sexual harassment is criminal and has recently also become regarded as immoral, not just a lark that women ought to tolerate. Abortion remains morally fraught but also illegal in many places and circumstances. Polluting is not just illegal but has become immoral, too. In surveys, it often ranks as more serious than traditional offenses, even murder.[104] This new view is arguably colored by older theological concepts of pollution as a transcendent violation. Ancient ideas of despoiling the sacred order were broader in their understanding of taint than modern biological and chemical concepts, though today deep ecologists come close to this older view.[105]

Law has sometimes directly enforced moral obligations. Certain duties became required of citizens: providing testimony in court, paying taxes, serving on juries and in the military. Perjury became a crime in England in the mid-sixteenth century. The act did not just undermine the court system but was also morally tainted since it violated an oath.[106] The medieval English law of hue and cry obliged all within earshot to join in pursuing a felon.[107] Hit-and-run laws today impose a duty not to leave an accident. Owners have obligations to those they invite onto their property. But, otherwise, there has been little legal requirement to help those in need.[108] Drawing up the Indian penal code in the 1830s, Thomas Babington Macauley argued that the law could not specify what bystanders had to endure to help strangers. Should they be required to go one hundred yards to caution someone against fording a swollen river, or a mile? The law should only keep people from doing harm, Macauley concluded, leaving morality and religion to encourage the good.[109]

But Good Samaritan paragraphs in civil law codes have demanded more.[110] The moral obligation to provide aid where there is no risk to the bystander is a legal duty in several European nations.[111] Israeli law requires aid in traffic accidents.[112] Already the German penal code of 1870 required citizens to help the police on request, and the Nazi regime broadened this obligation into a citizen's duty to aid others. In 1954, the German Great Criminal Senate declared the duty a moral obligation and "an imperative command of Christian doctrine."[113] The equivalent French legislation was initiated in 1941 by the collaborationist Vichy regime to encourage Frenchmen to aid German occupiers wounded by resistance fighters.[114] Since then, such statutes have been regularly invoked in Europe. The estate of David Sharp, who perished on Mount Everest in 2006 as forty other climbers passed him by, could have sued in France but not in Britain.[115] The English-speaking world became aware of Europe's Good Samaritan laws after Lady Diana's death in Paris in 1997, when the French authorities considered prosecuting the paparazzi who chased her car and then stood by photographing her as she lay dying.[116] The law of the sea has also long recognized a duty to help those in distress.[117]

Is moral evolution eventually reflected in the law? Or do changes in statute help shape ethics? Those remain open questions.[118] Authorities have often struggled to punish what most people do not regard as immoral offenses. Early modern popular opinion commonly refused to consider smuggling, poaching, or gleaning (once it had been revoked as a right) as crimes. They were "social crimes," more illegal than immoral.[119] Smuggling was once widespread across Europe, and the state's concern to prosecute it was too obviously self-serving in the early modern era, when tariffs were a major source of revenue.[120] It was thus more akin to tax evasion today than to the peccadillo we now—in an era of much freer trade—consider it. Nonetheless, as late as 1964, when *Goldfinger* became the third hit James Bond movie, its villain still transported gold across borders by smuggling it as the bodywork of his car.

Sometimes the law has been a teacher. Making something illegal has less reflected a moral shift than helped to create it. The authorities' vigorous suppression of dueling likely helped change opinion on something once held in favor. In the United States, tax evasion began to move into the realm of immorality when it was made a felony in 1924 and then in 1952 when its prosecution changed from merely a means for the state to recoup the income foregone to a tool of general deterrence.[121] Other fairly technical offenses, such as insider trading, antitrust violations, and bribery, which were scarcely known to the public beforehand, became morally condemnable in the wake of outlawing them.[122] Conversely, when law did not reflect popular morality, enforcement bogged down.

Juries nullified verdicts, refusing to convict those whose actions, although illegal, did not seem immoral. In so doing, they expressed society's broader sentiments. The growing acceptance of euthanasia was revealed when it took the US authorities four attempts to convict Jack Kevorkian in 1997 for assisting the terminally ill to die.[123] In the 1920s, prohibitionists thought they were bringing law and morality into alignment by forbidding the sale of alcohol, but, in fact, their moral intuitions turned out not to have been widely shared.

Chapter 11
From Retribution to Prevention

Punishing was one thing, preventing another. If the state could head crime off at the pass, it would save itself enormous bother. But how to do that? Deterrence was the oldest of the state's preventive tools. Although it remains in steady use, it is blunt, unwieldy, and unpredictable. More promising were the authorities' hopes of forecasting the criminal character, thus anticipating who might offend, where, and when and acting to prevent this. But that raised its own issues. Despite hopes for more, it turned out that the authorities were almost entirely unable to get inside offenders' heads to make useful predictions about crime—except based on their past behavior, on the assumption that what had already happened would continue in the future.

Heretics and political dissidents were often rational, well-meaning, stubborn people at odds with the official ideology. The dissident mindset was indicated by a verbalized thought, an act, or a ritual. The authorities sought to punish and thus to change not any one act or idea but the person who could think and behave in a certain way. They aimed at the underlying personality and its core of belief. Over time, beliefs were increasingly relegated to the private sphere. Religious divergence mattered only if it disturbed public order. Political dissent was channeled into the appropriate machinery of controversy in systems growing evermore democratic. So long as it steered clear of sedition and treason, it was not a crime.

That left certain offenders as the primary concern. The easiest to deal with were opportunists, weak-willed but not evil people who fell for temptation. Deterrence might hope to persuade them to stick to the straight and narrow. But habitual offenders, inherently likely to transgress, were tougher nuts. With ideological crimes, the state had aimed at belief systems that underpinned acts. With more conventional offenses, its focus remained on an underlying behavioral stratum, the character of the criminal, the personality that prompted such offenders habitually to offend.

Only the state could prevent crime. Private parties seeking vengeance or compensation for particular offenses had no concern to anticipate others. True, the bodies of the dead were often displayed to publicize the resolution of feuds, to halt further vengeance, and possibly to discourage potential transgressors.[1] But, by and large, kin groups had little concern to head off crimes more generally. Prevention was a public good that only the state could deliver.[2] As with disease, prevention beat cure. For crimes feared as endangering the entire community, prevention was an urgent necessity. Charlemagne's ninth-century capitulary defined adultery not simply as sin but also as a crime against the Christian community, to be punished so that "others may have fear of doing the same: so that uncleanness may be altogether removed from the Christian people."[3] And for crimes that were inherently hard to discern, prosecute, and convict—such as simony and clerical concubinage—prevention was the best tack.[4]

"Have you ever been punished before?" the Danish comedian Storm P. is asked. "No, always afterward." That was historically the nub of the matter. Preventing crimes, not just punishing them post facto, was complicated. Making an example of offenders by sanctioning them severely and publicly might deter others. Hardening the environment to make it more resistant to crime (locks, lights, cameras) impeded all forms of offending, whatever their motives, but beyond such rudimentary tactics, preventive action by the state meant identifying potential offenders and stopping them in their tracks. The authorities had to penetrate more deeply into subjects' lives and thoughts, anticipating wrongdoing, and intervening before it was realized. Law enforcement had begun as a private matter, the authorities only gradually assuming the task. With the ambition to prevent crime, an interventionist state actively plunged into civil society, aiming to manage it.

The preventive enterprise focused on communal harms, seeking to provide a public good. It therefore raised once again the classic utilitarian dilemma: Are individuals mere ends to a larger goal? A man should be hanged, as the dictum had it, not because he had stolen a horse but that horses might not be stolen.[5] Even as rudimentary a preventive strategy as deterrence was not necessarily just. It often made a harsh example of offenders who happened to be unlucky. "Altho' *one* suffereth, *numbers* are protected and relieved," an eighteenth-century Philadelphia judge explained the logic; "the punishment of a few is the preservation of multitudes." In the eighteenth century, capital punishment was intended less to sanction the immediate culprits than to warn off others. The proper end of punishment, William Paley wrote in 1785, is "not the satisfaction of justice, but the prevention of crimes." Asked how to treat the Gordon rioters in 1780, Edmund Burke recommended hanging only six of them, but with maximum publicity.[6]

Initially, when the state had little power or capacity, deterrence was its best preventive tool. The few offenders it got its hands on were publicly and savagely punished to warn others. In China, the Legalist school elevated this logic to a maxim: strict and brutal laws might sound abhorrent, but precisely their stringency meant that once having had their initial deterrent effect, they would not require enforcement any longer.[7] Life for most people was nasty and brutish; punishments had to be worse. The scaffold delivered a theater of horror, and prisons were made even more ghastly than offenders' everyday lives. Civil society still only imperfectly socialized subjects to moderate their impulses, curb their appetites, and discipline their most unruly instincts. Life was horrid; the state had to be even more so. To deter, punishments also had to be public to broadcast the message. Savagery in the town square caught everyone's attention. Medieval Germanic law punished crime after the fact, imposing compensation. This deterred only indirectly insofar as potential offenders preferred avoiding having to restitute. Roman law, however, had used exemplary public punishments deterrently, and this practice was revived in the Middle Ages. In his capitulary, Charlemagne aimed for deterrence in punishing murder and adultery with death.[8] Medieval canonists advised hanging bandits in the neighborhoods they had haunted to dissuade their peers. Hostiensis, the thirteenth-century bishop of Ostia, noted that "the infliction of punishment creates terror and deters others from sinning."[9]

For lesser crimes, shame helped prevent, too. In *1001 Nights*, being paraded disparagingly (sitting backward on a donkey, for example) was the commonest sanction. During the Western Middle Ages, offenders were publicly humiliated by marks that proclaimed their offense: branding on the thumb or cheek for those spared the gallows via benefit of clergy, red tongues sewed on false witnesses' clothing, yellow crosses for Cathars. Those condemned to penitence attended church carrying rods, which the priest used to beat them in front of the congregation.[10] In seventeenth-century Scotland, fornicators were seated on tall repentance stools. After such offenses were decapitalized in late seventeenth-century Massachusetts, adulterers and the incestuous were mock executed, forced to stand in the gallows for an hour, then branded with the letter of their crime. Women who had consorted with the Nazis had their heads shaved in postwar Europe.[11] In our own era, public sex-offender registries are officially intended to allow neighbors to protect themselves, but shaming perpetrators is a motive for their existence, too.[12] Chinese sentencing rallies, sometimes attended by huge crowds, inflict mass humiliation.[13]

Yet shame worked only insofar as the targeted actually suffered the emotion. Only offenders who were tied into social networks whose values they shared and whose censure they felt acutely were likely to be affected. In effect, shame punishments presupposed what they hoped to achieve. Those who felt shame were already motivated to behave. The brazen—or anomic—were less likely to be pained by publicity. The shame of receiving public alms, for example, did not necessarily spur the poor to industriousness. In 1697, England made poor-law pensioners wear badges. When this failed to discourage all but the neediest, paupers had to enter unpleasant and demeaning workhouses.[14] Harshness was required, the Poor Law Commission agreed in 1834, because the effect of shame was "quickly obliterated by habit."[15] Punishment and shame in effect worked at cross-purposes. As Durkheim pointed out, being sanctioned desensitized recipients and weakened their moral backbone, making them more likely to reoffend.[16] Relying too much on prison thus undercut hopes of having a reformative effect, leaving its function as primarily to incapacitate. That, in turn, opened the question of what to do when sentences expired and inmates rejoined society.

Death was the most useful deterrent—for others. Other harsh punishments could also prevent. John Stuart Mill favored the death penalty precisely because it delivered the same deterrence as life imprisonment but less cruelly.[17] Enlightenment philosophes who opposed capital punishment proposed a lifetime of hard labor as an alternative. In 1907, French prime minister Aristide Briand considered lifelong solitary confinement equally deterrent.[18] The Tuscan penal code of 1786 replaced death with *ergastolo*, a life of solitary confinement in chains, which many considered worse.[19] But these expensive solutions were beyond the administrative ken of early modern states. Public shows of force were among states' few means of rattling cages. "Killing a chicken to scare the monkey," was the Chinese slogan.[20] Death was made agonizingly spectacular to trumpet the message that crime did not pay.

Imperial Rome asserted the state's might through grotesque public death. Offenders were condemned to gladiatorial combat or thrown to the beasts in public games. They were burned alive or crucified to prolong the agony.[21] For offenders, death was often the least of their woes, a welcome relief from horrific tortures: burning alive as in Rome or boiling alive as in eleventh-century Spain or being sliced to bits as in China.[22] If lucky, the condemned were dispatched early in the process. Breaking on the wheel could proceed from the head down if the authorities wanted to be merciful, but it could also go from the feet up to prolong the agony. Arsonists in early modern France were rewarded for naming accomplices by being strangled before burning, as were women torched in eighteenth-century England. Even then, such mercies were performed surreptitiously so as not to dilute the deterrent effect of the public spectacle. In 1749, Frederick the Great of Prussia instructed executioners to strangle criminals secretly before breaking them on the wheel, thus preserving the deterrent effect while minimizing pain.[23]

Punishments became increasingly public and spectacular. The pillory was an early public sanction. Criminals were exposed while the crowd hurled insults and worse. In England, Ann Marrow lost both eyes when pilloried in 1777 for having impersonated a man in marriage to three different women.[24] Recidivists were punished ever worse—an ear sliced off in the first instance, a foot in the second, hanging for a third offense. Public whippings were added. The wheel was mentioned first in France in 1385.[25] Following the Roman example, the absolutist monarchies of the eighteenth century again staged spectacular deaths to demonstrate their might and glory. Gruesome public punishments reached their apogee perhaps in 1757 when the would-be regicide Robert Damiens was broken, eviscerated, and drawn and quartered in Paris—the scene immortalized for a modern audience by Foucault's prurient pen portrait.[26]

In the course of execution, such unfortunates were of course killed many times over, and death was often specifically added to death. For good measure, Peter the Great had the corpses of viricides (women who killed their husbands) hanged after their execution. In many European nations, executions were made even more painful by breaking offenders on the wheel first.[27] Criminals' corpses were often also desecrated. Plato argued for parricides to be stoned after execution.[28] In 1751, the English decided not only to execute murderers but also to dissect them afterward.[29] Not until 1949 did Scotland formally abolish drawing and quartering traitors posthumously.[30] Into the nineteenth century, executed bodies were publicly displayed for weeks and months as they rotted.[31] Though less adept at spectacular punishment than the continental regimes, the English stood out for sheer numbers. They applied the death penalty to a dismayingly large range of offenses. Homicides, arson, rape, and major larceny were givens, but they also executed for felling trees, attacking deer, stealing hares, hunting at night, buggering men or beasts, practicing witchcraft, and committing all manner of petty thievery. Defrauding the mail remained a capital crime until 1835.[32] In the early nineteenth century, England had 223 capital crimes in its statutes, France 6. The English sentenced to death proportionately five hundred times as many as the Prussians, executing sixty times more.[33]

At some point, however, this rudimentary deterrent lost its luster. Eighteenth-century reformers were appalled at its barbarity, whether it achieved its goal or not. The rowdy, unruly crowds at executions seemed to be enjoying themselves immoderately, their worst instincts stoked by raw violence.[34] Intended to demonstrate the state's awful majesty, public executions had instead turned into carnivals—both literally as mortification of the flesh and metaphorically as bacchanalia. Even worse, the mobs were often feeling sympathy with the condemned, undermining brutality's deterrence.[35]

By the eighteenth century, then, sheer brutality was no longer thought to deter. That change in attitude shifted—without undermining—the logic of deterrence. Beccaria and the Enlightenment philosophes argued that deterrence could be achieved without immorally making an example of some criminals for the public good. Certainty of punishment was more preventive than its cruelty.[36] Knowing that most offenders were likely to be caught, convicted, and punished would do more to dissuade than random savage affliction of a few misfortunates. In fact, as we have seen, the utilitarian reformers advanced an ethical argument for their own position. Whereas retributive punishments were just the state taking vengeance, thus wreaking more havoc, only punishments that deterred future offenses could be justified.[37] Medieval canonists had already argued that efficient prosecution and sanction were good deterrence—without the need for bloodshed. In the 1760s, Adam Smith agreed that preventing crime was done best by enforcing just laws rigorously.[38] More recent reformers have concurred. Knowing that a well-functioning system delivers equitable justice impartially in itself deters without the immorality of making some offenders serve the public purpose of scaring others off from crime.[39]

Enlightenment reformers did not object to public punishment so long as it was not too brutal. Putting criminals to hard work in public in special uniforms or in mines where the public could visit was considered deterrent. Beccaria thought lifelong slavery deterred more than death.[40] In the long run, however, publicity went the same way as brutality. Punishment moved out of the limelight. In 1783, London magistrates abolished the procession to Tyburn, though not the actual hanging, which still drew large crowds. Public hangings in England ended in 1868, six years after public whippings.[41] The French revolutionaries were at pains to avoid the spectacles of the old regime. The guillotine's semiclinical efficiency was intended not only to democratize death but also tone down the circus atmosphere, marrying deterrence to decency. Torture was ended as part of executions, and decapitation was permitted as the only technique, though beheadings were still performed in public.[42]

But after the excesses of the revolutionary Terror, any publicity proved too much. Executions were shifted from the town square to the prison courtyard and were now attended by only a few officials, not the rabble. In 1851, the new Prussian penal code brought executions within the prison walls. By the 1830s, most northern US states executed only inside prisons, England three decades later. The last public execution in the United States occurred in 1936 in Kentucky, in France on the eve of war in 1939.[43] And already by the late eighteenth century, public punishments were falling out of favor more generally. In England, the pillory was abolished in 1837. In the 1830s, the last old-style public punishment ended in France when convicts sent to the prison ships at Toulon or Brest began being conveyed in closed carriages, no longer paraded through the streets.[44] Spectacular deterrence persists in some nations. Prisoners are still killed publicly in the Middle East and in China, where mass executions are scheduled on public holidays and festivals.[45]

Administered away from the public eye, how could punishments still deter? In the absence of brutal spectacle, would potential offenders understand crime's consequences? Legislators in Washington State forbade published accounts of executions in 1909, thus eliminating even the vicarious experience.[46] Foucault echoed Beccaria by claiming that concealing sanctions shifted them from everyday experience to the realm of abstract consciousness. Punishment's effectiveness now resulted from its inevitability, not its visible intensity. The certainty of punishment, he thought, discouraged crime.[47] But that glossed over the inherent contradiction that hidden penalties could not deter crime. Punishment did not become more certain by virtue of being carried out in private. Punishments that were both certain and public were equally thinkable. And if the public did not know that sanctions were administered, how could its ignorance influence its behavior? The Norwegian government in London exile during World War II reinstituted the death penalty to discourage Norwegians from collaborating with the occupying Nazis. But how would those who were meant to be deterred from treason hear of this threat in a legally effectful manner when the only means it was conveyed were clandestine BBC broadcasts that few were likely to hear?[48]

More likely to be deterrent was the severity of sanctions. But that could also brutalize society, implicating the authorities in the same kinds of actions they were punishing and promoting further violence as offenders realized they had little to lose. Speedy justice swiftly administering punishment might also deter, but it threatened the rule of law, whose gravitas could not be hurried. In their periodic "strike hard" (*yanda*) campaigns starting in the 1980s, the Chinese—much like Europe's absolutist rulers—assumed that harsh public punishments swiftly carried out especially deter.[49] But on the whole, deterrence was never more than a crude first approximation of what the state really sought—the ability to discover and punish but even more so to predict, anticipate, and thus head off crime.

Intent and Mens Rea

Using the law to prevent crime, even with rudimentary means such as deterrence, presupposed first of all that potential offenders knew what was forbidden so that they could choose to avoid it or not. Next, it assumed their free will, the conscious choice whether to transgress. More precisely, it rested on the presence of an interval separating the intent and planning of an offense from its execution, during which an intervention might work. If crime were an automatic reflex produced by social conditions (the Marxist view of it as inherent in capitalism) or biological impulse (Cesare Lombroso's theory of the innate offender and its countless variations), it could be prevented best by social engineering: reforming society to improve criminogenic conditions or eugenically tinkering with human nature to breed out antisocial impulses. Socially or biologically determined crime could be prevented only by wide-scale reform of society or its members.

At the other end of the spectrum, if crime were spontaneous—committed by weak characters succumbing to temptation—then social reform promised little relief. Wholly opportunistic offenses were hard to anticipate and deter. At best, you could target-harden the environment against offenses—whether impromptu or planned.[50] Between such extremes of total determinism and utter fortuity, deterrence and prevention relied on potential offenders pondering their options before executing them and, it was hoped, concluding that—all in all—the anticipated crime did not pay.

Intent, liability, responsibility, and prevention were intertwined. Crimes heavily determined by strong natural urges (incest, sodomy, debauchery, baby snatching, sometimes bestiality) were often considered less blameworthy than those committed with intent.[51] Blaming social, biological, or other deterministic forces for crime lessened individual responsibility. Nor could such crimes be prevented except by modifying the underlying causal mechanisms. Conversely, one-off, spontaneous events were unpredictable and unpreventable. But in between these two extremes, individuals could be held liable—evermore so as their motives were deliberate and intentional. Peter Abelard, the medieval theologian, thought that all actions, without a consideration of their motives, were morally indifferent (*adiaphora*)—even violations of the Ten Commandments.[52] Their intent thus determined their nature. A focus on the intent, the mens rea, behind offenses made them more like sins. To be meaningful and thus worth punishing, sins had to be voluntary and deliberate acts. No will, no sin, said Bartolomeo Fumi, the scholastic philosopher, in 1547.[53]

Many, possibly most, debates over crime have concerned whom or what to hold responsible. At one extreme, at least in the common law world, strict liability punished all harm caused regardless of why or how it came about. That was social utility speaking. At the other, only harm that was both intended and actually carried out was penalized. That was justice making itself heard. But many actions lay in between: the accident befalling in a moment of inattention, the killing that resulted even though just a beating was meant.[54] Intent, strengthening responsibility for acts at one extreme, and the insanity defense, removing responsibility altogether at the other, were opposing pendants, stretching the continuum of behavior—willed and involuntary—in opposite directions. A focus on mens rea sought to mediate the two extremes, punishing transgressions, but only when the requisite intent revealed moral culpability.[55] Was society liable for crime, as the Enlightenment philosophes argued, because it created the poverty that sparked delinquency? Or were vagrants the authors of their own misery, spongers on society, and therefore to be treated harshly by the law?[56] Most agreed that no one was liable for actions they had been forced to perform under duress, therefore not their volition. Yet what counted as compulsion? Being physically compelled was clear. But what was the psychological equivalent? Legal codes have long tolerated men killing spouses or lovers caught in flagrante. Only recently and not everywhere have the supposedly irresistible imperatives of the honor code no longer trumped the law.

The insanity defense amplified such considerations: In what frame of mind were offenders not culpable? Incapable of intent, neither the young nor the mad nor eventually animals were guilty. Roman law assumed that insanity exculpated crime.[57] In the thirteenth century, the English jurist Henry of Bracton exempted infants and the mad from culpability, and insanity became grounds for granting felons royal pardons. By the mid-1700s, acquittal by plea of insanity was becoming common in England.[58] In 1800, after George III was attacked by an obvious lunatic, the law was changed to ensure that defendants who successfully pled insanity were committed to an asylum, not released, as they formerly were.[59] Having been a get-out-of-jail card, the insanity defense now led to life-long lockup. Over the following years, the burden of proof shifted back and forth between prosecution and defense. The M'Naghten rule in the 1840s was the result of Queen Victoria's displeasure when the assassin of her prime minister's private secretary pled insanity. It required the jury to assume the defendant was sane unless proven otherwise. The US Model Penal Code of 1962 shifted the burden to the prosecution, which had to prove a defendant *not* insane if the issue were raised. That decision was reversed in 1984 after public outrage when John Hinckley, President Reagan's would-be assassin, was judged not guilty because insane.[60] Today the insanity plea is used only sparingly, and those who succeed rarely see freedom again.

Intoxication ran a similar course. The Greeks increased fines for drunken assaults, but the Romans considered intoxication reason to punish less harshly.[61] Yet overinebriation could also be a double-edged sword: both a crime on its own and an exacerbating factor in other offenses. In the Penitential of Theodore, written by the archbishop of Canterbury in the late seventh century, someone who killed while drunk was twice guilty: of the self-indulgence of intoxication and of homicide. Yet half a century later in the Penitential of Ecgberht, the archbishop of York gave drunken murderers the same moderated punishment as those who killed in anger. Early in the nineteenth century, the enhancing effect of intoxication had vanished from English jurisprudence, replaced with the mitigating influence it retains today.[62]

As intent was increasingly taken into consideration, the range of offenses broadened from acts to inclinations. A crime intended rendered the offender clearly blameworthy. Even a dog, as Oliver Wendell Holmes put it, can tell the difference between being stumbled over and kicked.[63] Intent distinguished such actions from accidents and from acts that—though not fortuitous—were not premeditated or planned. The offender's mens rea, the intent, determined the nature of the act. Without a culpable mens rea, an act could not be a *malum in se*.[64] At the other extreme, intent alone—even without much of an overt act—could be a crime in itself, as with treason, conspiracy, and inchoate offenses. Someone who had no motive for a crime or refused to admit one became an enigma.[65] A concern for the mens rea behind the act thus deepened the problem raised by Locke and Kant on how inner and outer states corresponded. Being good meant more than acting lawfully. It required also wanting to do so. Taking mens rea into account, offenses arose when an inner bad intention correlated with an outer transgression. Without bad intent, the act—though harmful—might be legally irrelevant or even innocent. Conversely, with evil intent an otherwise legal act could be actionable.

Absent an intent to commit a crime, often none had occurred. With the concept of holy sin (*aveirah lishmah*), Jewish theology recognized that intentions decided the nature of the act, which could be blameless however seemingly heinous. Jewish women staked their honor to save their people: Lot's daughters became impregnated by him in order to save the human race as the world seemed doomed; Tamar pretended to be a prostitute to entice Judah, her father-in-law, to impregnate her, thus continuing the family line; and Yael seduced Sisrah before killing him and saving the Jews.[66] In the modern era, receiving stolen goods was unlawful only when you knew their provenance. Treason in US law was committed only by those who intended to harm their country, not by those who inadvertently aided and abetted an enemy even though their motives were patriotic—Jane Fonda in Hanoi or Edward Snowden in Moscow.[67] Of course, some crimes were inconceivable without intent. Rape, burglary, waylaying, fraud, and treason could not be committed by mischance. An attempted crime definitionally involved intent. Unlawful assembly meant joining a group in public intending to commit an offense. An insurrection aimed at public goals was treason but aimed at private ones merely a riot.[68] Many acts were defined by the perpetrator's motives. Killing someone could occur with or without intent, by mistake, in self-defense, or on purpose. The victim was dead regardless. But whether you were guilty of murder, manslaughter, or negligent homicide depended on the intent with which you had, say, run the red light. Burning down the neighbors' house could be arson or an accident.

Larceny was once defined as the simple possession of stolen goods, whether the accused had stolen them or not. But in the thirteenth century, Bracton, inspired by the Romans, insisted that there be an *animus furandi* as well, an intent to have stolen. In the late eighteenth century, larceny began to be conceptualized in terms not of having the goods, but of having intent. Those who took lost money thinking that the owner was unidentifiable were innocent, but if they believed the owner could be traced, they were guilty of larceny.[69] Depending on what transpired in the offender's mind, the very same act was criminal or innocent. Theft came to be parsed into a variety of actions: borrowing without consent, taking with intent to repay, taking for temporary use, taking with the intent of returning to gain a reward, and so forth. Each hinged on the culprit's mental state.[70] Someone who offered child pornography or drugs for sale could be charged even if turned out that the goods were in fact innocuous.[71] In these cases, it was the intent that was sanctioned. Someone who stirred sugar that he thought was poison into another's tea could be guilty of attempted homicide. Offenses are today punished more severely if motivated by hatred of certain categories of legally protected people (based on race, sex, age, homeless status)—in other words, according to their intent.[72]

Like modern strict liability, early law tended to punish the act regardless of its motives, if any.[73] In the Homeric epics, a homicide's intentionality did not influence the treatment of the killer. The same restitution or punishment applied, regardless of motive.[74] In a case of death by javelin at a fifth-century BCE Greek sporting event, much effort went into explaining how the victim, by running into the javelin's path, caused his own death and none on distinguishing between accidental and intentional acts. Roman law punished attempts as though they were accomplished crimes.[75] Focused on compensation for harm, early Germanic law was likewise uninterested in intent or in deterring future offenses. Regardless of why, the act had caused damage, and that had to be made good. No more composition was paid for an intentional harm (instigating a serf to kill someone) than for one caused negligently.[76] The authorities sought above all to quell blood feuds, persuading defendants to accept compensation instead. They also hoped to present themselves as firm enforcers of laws applicable to all. Not surprisingly, they were reluctant to get caught up in the niceties of intent. Ensuring restitution for victims, who would otherwise be avenged, was their immediate concern.

Before the twelfth century, criminal intent was not the main focus of law enforcement. The Leges Henrici Primi, a compilation of English law from the early 1100s, stated that even if an archer killed inadvertently, he should pay, for "he who commits evil unknowingly must pay for it knowingly."[77] In the sixteenth century, English common law punished only acts, not intent. "The imagination of the mind to do wrong, without an act done, is not punishable in our law, neither is the resolution to do that wrong, which he does not, punishable, but the doing of the act is the only point which the law regards; for until the act is done it cannot be an offense to the world, and when the act is done it is punishable."[78]

This disregard of intent came out in that feature of early law perhaps most perplexing to modern sensibilities: the punishment of animals. In the Code of Hammurabi, oxen that gored people were stoned. Ancient Persian laws specified amputation of ears, legs, or tails for dogs that bit. Hebrew law condemned homicidal wild animals to death.[79] Plato's laws prosecuted animals that shed human blood. Even inanimate objects that harmed (lightning bolts cast by gods excepted) were treated similarly.[80] Deodands were things that having caused death were forfeited to God via the king—carts, boats, mill wheels, cauldrons, and the like. Since the act, regardless of intent, was what mattered, why not hold liable a pig that ate a baby or a horse that threw its rider? Or block up a well in which someone had drowned?[81] Even here, however, intent at times crept in. For damages done between fighting animals, the Romans punished the one that started the scrap. The Roman jurist Ulpian considered animals subjected to men's sexual advances partly culpable if they had not run away. And raped animals were duly punished—a burro in sixteenth-century Seville was hanged, his sodomizer burned.[82]

And yet the distinction between the accidental and the intended was intuitive enough to have long been given voice in statute. Though early law may not have distinguished clearly or consistently between deliberate and accidental acts, it did so often. In the Old Testament, someone who killed accidentally could seek refuge in one of three cities, but intentional murderers could not.[83] Both the Old Testament and Middle Assyrian law treated extramarital sex differently according to intent, depending on whether it was adultery or rape. Both were killed if willing adulterers, but if the woman had been coerced, only the man was.[84] Ancient Chinese law also classified crimes according to motivation and recognized intentional murder.[85] Both Plato and Aristotle distinguished between premediated and unplanned homicide, but Plato demanded that the attempted murderer be tried like those who succeeded.[86] Athenian law separated premeditated from accidental killings, with intent required for murder and unintentional homicide punished only by exile.[87]

Roman law distinguished *culpa* (unintentional harm) from *dolus* (intentional harm). The Twelve Tables singled out numerous intentional acts for sanction.[88] A thief caught trespassing at night, his intent to rob thereby evident, could be killed on the spot. Unintentional acts were discounted: if a weapon "escaped from the hand" of the offender rather than being thrown, sacrificing a sheep sufficed for expiation.[89] Sharia law distinguished willful from accidental homicide. Germanic law, too, changed in this direction. Seventh-century Visigothic law had moved beyond early precedents to distinguish between culpable and other killings. And in ninth-century Wessex, someone who killed a man inadvertently with a spear carried over his shoulder paid the wergeld but not a fine.[90]

The resurgence of Roman law in the early Middle Ages helped emphasize intent as constituent of crime, as did canon law. Medieval theologians assimilated crime once again to the concept of sin, where both act and its motivation mattered. In the fourteenth century, the Neapolitan jurist Lucas de Penna argued that just as sin could be merely a thought, so the crucial element of an offense was its intent, which the act itself merely indicated.[91] Canonists agreed: without intent, no guilt. With Bracton in the thirteenth century, intent became integral to defining crime. Someone who killed by misadventure was to be acquitted. New techniques adjusted the legal outcome to the criminal's intent by expanding the royal pardoning powers. Even if offenders had acted without intent, the law still found them guilty, and they forfeited their goods. But the king could now pardon them, sparing their lives.[92]

That not every similar act was also legally equivalent became broadly accepted. Those who killed inadvertently or by accident differed from those who acted on purpose, deserving less punishment, if any. But to show mercy where it was due, the authorities had to probe the accused's psychic state. Scandinavian law of the twelfth and thirteenth centuries distinguished conscious "acts of hand" from unintended "handless risks."[93] Taking jurisdiction over homicides in the early twelfth century, the English Crown categorized them as culpable, excusable, and justifiable. Killing without intent or in self-defense (though defined very restrictively) was excusable or justifiable.[94] Juries often acquitted defendants who did not, they thought, merit death for killing. Conversely, as of the late fourteenth century, the English king was forbidden to pardon killings committed with malice aforethought. Nor, as of the fifteenth, could he pardon *mala in se*.[95] Not just the act but an evil intent, too, was now required for a felony to have occurred. By the late sixteenth century, the distinctions had emerged between murder and manslaughter and between voluntary and involuntary homicide—dependent on the motives animating the act.[96]

Intent as Offense: Inchoate Crimes

The concern with criminal intent continued apace as the development of inchoate crimes greatly expanded the law's reach. Inchoate (or nonconsummate) crimes were offenses of intent. They were actions designed to lead to another substantive offense, even if the latter did not occur. If an act was dangerous enough to forbid—so ran the logic—surely the state should also criminalize attempts at it. Many offenses had inchoate aspects. In the common law, burglary was defined as trespass with the intent to steal. Thrusting a finger through a window sufficed to make someone a burglar. Criminal assault was an attempt to commit battery combined with the present ability to do so.[97] The US Model Penal Code defined bribery to include those offering money or soliciting or agreeing to accept it from another even before anything had changed hands.[98] British law defined fraud in terms of making false representations intending to cause gain or loss. The Italian penal code of 1889 made it a crime to associate with others in order to commit a crime as well as even to declare an intent to offend. These inherently preparatory actions occurring before any actual harm had been inflicted were punishable.[99]

Crimes of preparation were inchoate offenses. Possessing otherwise harmless items might be illegal if it indicated criminal intent: implements of forgery, counterfeiting, arson, or burglary (screwdrivers, pliers, crowbars, and other tools found in most cellars); narcotics and their paraphernalia; certain kinds of arms (sawed-off shotguns, automatic weapons, tear gas, even toy weapons); gambling devices; and pornography.[100] New York law eventually recognized

153 distinct possession offenses. In 1998, one in five prison sentences there was for possession. A highly flexible charge, constructive possession, a form of second-order offense, could be leveled against even those who happened to be in the car or house where the implicated items were found.[101]

Lying in wait, searching, following, and enticing were crimes of preparation. Belonging to criminal organizations or associating with known offenders was penalized.[102] Loitering for purposes of prostitution, enticing minors to secluded places for nefarious reasons, transporting females across state lines for immoral ends: all were in themselves anticipatory crimes. British law punished sexual grooming of minors, defined as meeting or traveling to meet a child with whom one had communicated at least twice, for sexual purposes.[103] Otherwise innocent actions were punished as proxies for likely offenses. In seventeenth-century England, possessing shipwrecked goods with the identifying marks painted over was, in itself, punishable—whether they had been obtained legally or not. Today, those who import more than a certain amount of cash without declaring it can be prosecuted as likely drug dealers or money launderers, whatever the truth of the matter. Possession of a certain quantity of illegal drugs is taken to indicate an intent to sell, not just to consume. Even an innocent conversation with someone planning an offense can be proof of conspiracy.[104] The intent behind an act could heighten the severity of the offense committed. Trespass becomes burglary if done with further offenses in sight. Simple assault can be aggravated if carried out with the intent to rape, kill, or maim.[105]

Pursuing inchoate offenses was integral to the state's hope of preventing crime. The earlier the authorities intervened, getting out in front of the act, the less damage ensued. Attempts, solicitation, and conspiracy were inchoate crimes—acts aiming to bring about another offense. Criminalizing even unsuccessful efforts at crime, penal codes developed separate provisions for attempts. Conspiracy reached back even further than attempts into the preparatory chain of events leading from intent to commission.[106] Solicitation and incitation, in turn, delved still earlier than conspiracy, criminalizing what may have been only hot air. They were second-order inchoate crimes—attempts to conspire to offend. The US Model Penal Code penalized attempts to solicit, punishing even solicitors who had failed to communicate their criminal scheme.[107]

Yet intervening earlier in the causal chain threw up problems. Was an intent to commit a crime itself an act? If so, was it culpable? Or were intentions merely states of mind that accompanied the legally pertinent behaviors?[108] Either way, how did one know of intent except as expressed in acts? How far up the causal nexus of events could one reasonably assign guilt? Was a daydream, a fantasy, or a stray thought of causing harm culpable? Which thoughts were actually dangerous, which harmless musings? How far down along the progression from conception through planning to execution did the offender become guilty? Most agree that, having fired a shot, even if it missed, the would-be assassin was guilty at least of an attempt. But what about renting the hotel room with the necessary sightlines, buying the gun, taking target lessons, discussing the killing with others, hatching the idea, or even just at first forming a dislike of the victim? At what point did intent move from wishful thinking, fantasy, or desire to become the beginning of the act?[109]

Conversely, how far down the chain of events did renunciation or repentance still absolve the inchoate offender? Having occurred, few ordinary crimes were expunged by an offender's change of heart. A thief who returned a stolen object, even before its absence was discovered, was still guilty of larceny.[110] Some jurisdictions exonerated those who voluntarily broke off and thus prevented a crime that was being conspired about, prepared, or attempted.[111] With crimes of intent, renunciation could in practice exonerate, so long as no one else knew about it. But up to what point did renunciation get the potential offender off the hook? The closer to mere intent the law intervened, the more a change of heart had to be allowed for.[112]

What if the intended crime was conditional on other events that affected its likelihood? Did that diminish liability? Agreeing to murder someone if you won the lottery: Was that an attempt, regardless of the vanishingly small chances?[113] Since actual harm was not required for culpability, ambiguities multiplied. Was trying to murder someone with a voodoo doll an attempt? Was putting sugar in a potential victim's tea, thinking that it was poison?[114] When Dorothy Sayers's fictional detective Lord Peter Wimsey self-immunized against arsenic in *Strong Poison* and then ate Turkish delight powdered in it, he caught the would-be murderer Urquhart in an attempt even though he was not in fact poisoned.

Was intent itself culpable? Inchoate crimes punished not the final offense but the intent to commit it or something close to that. Anglo-American law has tended to require an act, refusing to punish mere intent. Whether a treasonous intent alone, as suggested in the English treason act of 1351, was punishable without an overt act has been hotly debated. In the fourteenth century, on rare occasions when defendants were convicted on the doctrine of *voluntas reputabitur pro facto* (the intention is to be taken for the deed), in fact a completed deed was also required.[115] The US Model Penal Code required proof of an overt act to show that a conspiracy was not just in the minds of the participants. More recent European law, in contrast, has not generally required overt acts to prove conspiracy.[116] German law regarded attempted treason as tantamount to its consummation. The Napoleonic penal code held much the same. But in 1832 this interpretation was moderated to cover only the attempt and its execution, lessening the punishment for the preparatory stages.[117]

Either way, even if the first dawning intent was not punishable, very closely subsequent acts were: incitation, solicitation, conspiracy, attempts. That still distinguished even the inchoate crime from sin, which could be committed by intent alone. In the Sermon on the Mount, Christ warned that those lusting after women had already committed adultery in their hearts.[118] In the fourteenth century, Lucas de Penna located the nub of the crime in the intent. The act was an incidental, practical feature, an external manifestation that revealed the criminal's state of mind.[119] But how could intent be known except through act? This dilemma was touched on by the story of the schoolmaster who warned his charges, "Boys, be pure of heart or I'll flog you."[120] Inchoate crime resembled sin in its focus on thoughts and not just acts. Aquinas argued that humans could judge only external acts, not inner thoughts. Divine law alone could ensure both internal and external goodness.[121] Hobbes argued that the intent to steal or kill was a sin known only to God. It became a crime apparent even to mortals only when manifested in an act.[122]

Without any other way of knowing intent, acts betrayed a state of mind. The law made use of them for that purpose. Nighttime trespass, for example, automatically signaled an intent that permitted offenders to be punished on the spot. In eighth-century England, a stranger who left the road without signaling his presence by shouting or blowing his horn was assumed to be a thief and could be slain. In sixteenth-century Nuremberg, anyone on the street after dark could be locked up for suspected burglary. An English act of 1851 imprisoned those caught at night with lockpicking or other burglary tools.[123] Yet sometimes it was frustratingly difficult to prosecute even those whose nefarious intent was clear. According to fourteenth-century English law, someone who ambushed another seemingly with intent to kill and left him for dead had committed only a trespass, subject merely to a fine. The same was true for someone who attacked with intent to rob, wounded his victim, but took nothing (probably because there was nothing to steal). However obvious his intentions, someone who had as yet done nothing but lurk menacingly was indictable only as a disturber of the peace or a nightwalker. In a case in 1859, a defendant lit a match near a haystack but extinguished it once he was spotted. He was acquitted of attempted arson, though convicted of extortion.[124]

Treason, as we have seen, was arguably the first inchoate crime, patterning the law of criminal attempt.[125] Treason had to be tackled preventively since, if successful, it allowed no second chance to prosecute. Attempting, planning, discussing, possibly just thinking treason—all were punishable.[126] Dionisius, the fourth-century ruler of Syracuse, executed a captain for having dreamed of slitting Dionisius's throat—for surely he contemplated assassination while awake, too.[127] The seventh-century Visigothic code punished not just overt acts against the ruler but also intent and opinion, expressed as maledictions, insult, and slander. Both the Edict of Rothar (643) and the ninth-century laws of King Alfred made plotting against the monarch high treason.[128] Whether the English treason act of 1351 punished the mere imagining of the king's death is debatable, but the statute of 1354 outlawed disloyal words.[129] Richard II's statute of 1397 did sanction compassing the king's demise even without an overt act, but it was quickly repealed for punishing mere intent. Nevertheless, at the trial of the duke of Buckingham in 1521 words alone were held sufficient to prove treasonous intent.[130]

Attempts were classic inchoate crimes. Taking part in the run-up to a crime, anticipating its committal, thwarted offenders remained as guilty from intent as their more successful peers. A fumbler who missed the shot was arguably as much an assassin as the expert marksman who hit his target. The threat that attempters posed to society was as great—possibly more so as they tried again—as that from successful offenders. However unfair it was to punish offenders and attempters equally, the same sanctions for both made sense for a society seeking to protect itself. And if mere intent was culpable, then morally speaking would-be and actual offenses deserved equal punishment. The Nazi regime punished attempts the same as crimes, reversing the mitigation built into the imperial penal code, and this position lasted well into the postwar period. The US Model

Penal Code, too, proposed punishing attempted and executed crimes the same.[131]

Early states did not at first consider attempts to be crimes. Ancient China's Ten Abominations, developed in the sixth century, included plots against authorities and parents, but other systems took longer to include attempts.[132] Ancient Egyptians recognized the intent to commit crime, regarding it a moral fault, yet punished only the act itself.[133] Greek law considered plotters, contrivers, and instigators of murder as willful killers but treated them leniently by allowing their burial after execution. Planning homicide was distinguished from killing with one's own hand, and the planner could be guilty of planning alone. Yet Roman law lacked even a term for attempt and prohibited only completed acts.[134] Nor did early Germanic law properly recognize attempts. Drawing a sword or knife was punished as an attempt, and instigating a crime was forbidden, like the actual carrying-out. But the more general concept was absent.[135] In medieval France, someone who intending to murder managed only to wound was prosecuted merely for blows and harm. The outcome remained more important than the impetus. The penal charter of Brussels in 1229 charged archers who managed to kill with homicide, but merely fined them if they missed.[136]

Slowly, however, intent became a determinative element. Both the Carolina in 1532 and the Ordonnance de Blois in 1579 recognized criminal attempts. In the seventeenth century, the Star Chamber in England busily punished attempts, whether poisoning or waylaying to murder.[137] By the late eighteenth century, the formal doctrine of criminal attempt existed. Defendants had earlier been convicted even where an offense had failed, but not on the basis of a generalized theory of culpable intent or attempt. In 1784, however, a defendant who had set a lit candle amid flammable material was convicted of arson even though the house had not burned down.[138] By the early nineteenth century, solicitation was also formalized as a concept in common law. Someone who incited servants to steal from their master, for example, was guilty even if the servant refused.[139]

From here, inchoate crimes were pushed back up the causal chain of events. In the mid-nineteenth century, the common law nations punished someone for an attempt only when they had performed the last proximate act to the crime itself—firing the gun, for example.[140] Over time, courts began to grant authorities more leeway to catch offenders before it was too late. The standards employed today are those of proximity: the dangerousness of the offenders' behavior and how close they come to accomplishing their aim. More recently, the equivocality standard has been added, gauging how dangerous offenders are by what they have already done.[141]

The doctrine of legal impossibility once curtailed too lush an efflorescence of inchoate crimes. A case in 1865 involved a man accused of stealing, but from an empty pocket, so that no theft had occurred or was even possible.[142] Other cases involved abortions given to women who were not pregnant, bribes to sway court cases offered to those not actually jurors, shooting a stuffed deer out of season, guns fired into empty rooms, and the peddling of what proved to be uncontrolled substances.[143] The would-be offenders were let off the hook because they had been mistaken about what they were doing. In the twentieth century, however, legal impossibility was whittled down. It was thought unfair to exonerate culprits who had clearly intended to offend.[144] The definition of inchoate crime thus expanded as crime grew increasingly subjectified. Even if someone merely thought they were doing something illegal, then they had committed a crime.[145]

The number of inchoate crimes has in the meantime mushroomed. Conspiracy has become more broadly defined. In England, it dated from the thirteenth century but became commonly used after the seventeenth. Already in the Middle Ages, unlawful assembly—defined as three or more people congregating for nefarious purposes—was outlawed.[146] The seventh-century laws of the Wessex king Ine determined the type of criminals by the size of the group and escalated the punishments accordingly: thieves if up to seven, a band of marauders if up to thirty-five, and a raid if more. Modern antiloitering laws, targeting gangs, prostitutes, or teenagers, follow this venerable tradition.[147] In the thirteenth century, those who defended and supported heretics were also considered and punished as such.[148] Conspiracy was an elastic category. Behaviors that were legal when done alone were outlawed when undertaken collectively. No criminal action had to result; the preparation sufficed. Large-scale conspiracy charges were first leveled against workers who were using collective action to wrest concessions from employers.[149] Today, the US federal code specifies at least twenty-eight different forms of conspiracy. They range from agreement to commit or attempt a crime to rather more tangential connections to the offense: agreement to solicit or aid in a crime or its solicitation, attempt, or planning; aid in planning an attempt; and agreement to aid in the planning of a solicitation of a crime.[150]

Double-inchoate offenses were once considered a conceptual tautology: attempts to attempt, conspiracies to conspire, and so forth. But penal codes have expanded to actions otherwise not criminalized. Attempted assault, for example, which can be legally deconstructed as an attempt at an attempt at battery, is a double-inchoate crime in several US states. A Wisconsin man who invited a child into his car for sex was not guilty of enticement since the boy did not enter the vehicle, but he could be prosecuted for attempted enticement.[151] If possession was already a double-inchoate crime (an attempt to use), then conspiracy to possess was a triple-inchoate offense.[152]

More and more statutes came to focus on intent. Making it an offense to cross state lines or to enter a building with certain goals in mind criminalized otherwise innocent actions. The offense of enticing a minor over the internet allowed intervention even prior to a crime of intent, conspiracy, or solicitation.[153] Even substantive crimes have come to be phrased in inchoate terms. The British Fraud Act of 2006 criminalized the dishonest making of false representations for gain. It replaced the traditional result crime of obtaining property by deception. In the new formulation, no property need have been obtained, no loss or gain created. All that was required was the dishonest making of a false representation that intended to cause harm.[154]

In the new age of terrorism, inchoate offenses have been punished even when they did not go beyond preparation. Terrorists willing to strike even though they will die are unlikely to be deterred. Suicide killers date at least to the Assassins of the eleventh century—trained and motivated Shiites who attacked Sunni variants of Islam and sometimes Christians.[155] But as the tactic has become more common, the need to deter has increased. Preinchoate, preparatory, facilitative, associative, and other offenses only distantly connected to the act have been made actionable. Since successful suicide bombers cannot be convicted, the planners have been targeted. Indeed, even those who have not provably planned terror have faced sanctions. Britain imposed preventive detention on merely suspected terrorists. As due-process objections were raised, the rigor with which it was applied decreased. But the restrictions on possible terrorists remain far more drastic than for any other suspected offenders. Non-British terror suspects have been detained indefinitely. When that proved legally objectionable, control orders on house arrest restricted the potential terrorists' movements, communication, association, and other activities. At times, they were forcibly relocated to remote regions.[156]

The UK Terrorism Act of 2006 prosecuted anyone preparing to give effect to an intention to commit terrorism or helping others do so.[157] In other words, it criminalized conduct before it even became an attempt. It also forbade giving or receiving training and being present where it took place. Such statutes went beyond making it illegal to help commit actual or attempted offenses. They prohibited activity even without a crime (a terrorist act) and where the targeted behaviors were unrelated to any specific act: buying maps, getting railway timetables or computer manuals, or asking the price of certain chemicals. Responsibility was thus imposed at a very early stage, when would-be offenders had not yet decided precisely what they intended and before the agreement required for conventional conspiracy charges.[158] Defining offenses widely and vaguely, the range of indictable actions has expanded. Recent British antiterrorism legislation has punished statements that are likely to be understood by some of the public as direct or indirect encouragement of commissioning, preparing, or instigating terror.[159] Possession of money or of unspecified other property, including documents, has been criminalized if the accused intended terroristic uses of it or even thought that others might do so.[160] Even for other serious crimes, recent British legislation has grown studied in its deliberate vagueness. Those "involved" in such acts are liable: not only anyone who committed or facilitated the offense but also someone who merely "conducted himself in a way that was likely to facilitate the commission by himself or another person."[161]

The legal net has recently expanded further into inchoate crimes of omission. Laws on crimes of omission punish those who have performed no act, on inchoate crimes those who have caused no harm. The two intersect to define what would seem to be the absolute minimum form of an *actus reus*: harmless inaction. Inchoate crimes of omission statutes target those who fail their duty of responsibility to dependents even when, as chance would have it, no lasting harm resulted. Guardians have been prosecuted who housed dependents in filthy and unsafe conditions, who left them alone in freezing or overheated cars, who neglected to provide medical care. Other instances include those who failed to report illegal activity, even though fortuitously no lasting harm ensued: money laundering, environmental offenses, treason, domestic violence, or the like.[162]

Preventing Crime

Defining intent, not just acts, as criminal was one early move in the state's larger game of preventing crime. We have seen that deterring through public punishment was rudimentary at best. Ritualized brutality in the town square worked poorly. Nor did pursuing inchoate offenses deter as such. Having ignored sanctions for committing crime, potential offenders were unlikely to fear punishment for attempting it. But outlawing inchoate crimes did seek to prevent by intervening early. All deterrence prevents, but not all prevention deters—that done covertly, for example. As countless embroidered samplers attest, prevention beats cure. Indeed, preventive law was likened to preventive medicine.[163] The analogy from disease to crime holds only partly, though (retrospective punishment of offenses is not remotely as good as a cure), so the advantages of prevention for crime were arguably even greater than for illness.

The virtues of prevention could be argued at various levels. At the most general, social conditions caused crime. The immediate offenders could be deterred, incapacitated, or rehabilitated. But the ultimate culprit was society. Social conditions—whether poverty, inequality, exploitation, familial breakdown, or anomie—caused crime. Social reform therefore promised to diminish offending. The belief in the virtues of social engineering is ancient and has become evermore pervasive. Crime in this view is like disease, to be cured not punished. The prevention of crime aimed at by most active policy makers has, in contrast, been narrower and more modest. It has sought not major social reform, much less revolution, but techniques to nab offending in the bud.

Offenders form their intent, prepare to carry it out, and finally commit the act. Laws sought to interrupt this causal chain at various points: closer to the intent or to the act. Penalizing the act, laws have been retrospective, dealing with faits accomplis. Aiming at intent, they have hoped to prevent. Post facto punishment of already committed acts remained blind to incipient offenses and—purely reactive—contributed little to lowering the overall incidence of crime except insofar as it deterred. Preventive interventions, aiming at intent, investigated, judged, and punished mental states that might not have led to results if left alone but foiled crime in those instances where the intent would have been followed by act.

Prevention thus moved the philosophical basis of punishment away from the idea that offenders should make good the harm done and that retribution righted society's moral balance. With prevention, justice ceded pride of place to a victorious utilitarianism, concerned primarily with order and tranquility. The Enlightenment principles commonly thought to govern sanctions faded. Punishments no longer fit the crime. Nor were they announced clearly and determinately in advance for precisely specified behaviors so that, as sovereign citizens, potential offenders could calibrate their own conduct. Sentences grew increasingly indeterminate and discretionary, tailored to offenders, not to crimes, and fine-tuned for rehabilitation more than for justice.[164] The clear relationship between offense and sanction was severed. Once the goal shifted from just retribution to effective prevention, the crime did not necessarily determine its punishment.[165] A crime might not be punished at all if that promised to spare society an offense to come. Or the state might impose punishment even on someone who had committed no tangible act. Prevention overturned many of justice's usual assumptions. Criminals were defined not by what they had done but what they might perhaps do. Attending to intent broadened the state's remit.

Preventing crime meant identifying criminals before they acted. The easiest prediction was based on past behavior. Many criminals committed more than one offense. That criminal tendencies were not evenly distributed across society was not a new insight when fear of dangerous classes gripped the urban bourgeoisie in the nineteenth century. Nor was it when Lombroso formulated his theory of habitual offenders or today when statistics on recidivism inspire three-strikes and other serial-offender laws to clamp down hardest on those who commit most crime. Already in ancient Athens, a third conviction for perjury led to loss of citizens' rights. Rome kept registers of suspicious and dangerous individuals. The *infamia* doctrine punished those whose character was blemished by moral turpitude.[166] In eighth-century Wessex, repeat thieves had feet or hands amputated. The imperial Chinese added the *cangue,* a kind of portable wooden stocks around the neck, for repeat offenders. The Carolina, the first German penal code from 1532, had a graded scale of increasingly harsh punishments for recidivists. Death as an incorrigible followed a third burglary offense in colonial Connecticut, after two rounds of branding. Whipping was the rule for a third incident of drunkenness.[167]

Modern methods of identifying people, undercutting their ability to game the system by using aliases and the like, have allowed contemporary statistics to pinpoint just how much crime is committed by how few.[168] Since the 1970s in the United States, 6 percent of offenders have committed half of all crime. In 1986, 3 percent of Minneapolis street addresses were the destination of half of all police dispatches. For robbery, criminal sexual conduct, and auto theft, fully 100 percent of dispatches went to 5 percent of all locations.[169] Conversely, 95 percent of urban space is altogether free of predatory crime.[170] By targeting crime hot spots, the authorities could anticipate and prevent crime. By policing St. Giles, as a London police commissioner put it early in the nineteenth century, they were policing St. James.[171]

Prevention targeted not the offense but the kind of person who might commit it in the first place. It punished character more than crime. This approach had a venerable pedigree. Roman law allowed judges to accept as proven any information about offenders allegedly known by everyone to be true.[172] Among the sixth-century Franks, someone identified as a criminal by upstanding community members could be convicted on that basis alone. Under Charlemagne, the Rügeverfahren permitted judges to begin an inquest on the basis of an offender's reputation.[173] Early medieval law allowed only those of good reputation to swear oaths to clear themselves. For others, it demanded compurgators to stake their reputations alongside the suspect, many of them if the accused's character was not spotless. On occasion, more than a thousand were assembled. As the Roman law inquisitorial process was reintroduced in twelfth-century Europe, ecclesiastical courts accepted the doctrine of *mala fama*, "bad reputation."[174] An ecclesiastical judge could now try a suspect without a specific accusation or accuser.[175] Freemen were sorted according to their reputations, leaving the bad eggs with less legal standing. Twelfth-century German courts could prosecute on repute (*Leumund*), with officials swearing to the blemished standing of the accused.[176] A notorious suspect could be accused without other evidence, required to swear a purgative oath, and punished on failure to do so. Priests suspected of living in sin and eventually heretics, too, were targeted by such techniques.[177]

Prevention targeted the offender more than the offense. To get out in front of the act, the state had to grapple with the actor. But how? Blackstone lauded preventive over punitive justice as superior in all respects. The matter, he thought, was simple: preventive justice merely meant obliging those persons whom there was "probable ground" to suspect of future crimes to assure the public that they would not offend.[178] Rarely had a seemingly innocuous phrase glossed over complications so glibly.

How to anticipate the future offender? Two approaches promised help: psychology and sociology. Offenders might be predicted psychologically if discernable traits revealed a propensity to crime. Lombroso's theory of the born criminal was influential in the late nineteenth century, harnessing biology and its degeneration to explain how the criminal psychology was formed. Countless other now discarded theories such as phrenology also claimed to discern transgressive proclivities through somatic or psychological indicators.[179] More recently, criminology has sought to predict dangerousness, identifying those who threaten to become offenders. In the 1960s and 1970s, measures targeting dangerousness, apart from any actual offense, were introduced in response to shocking crimes committed by released inmates. Sociopaths were identified as those who inflicted suffering and injury for fun, lacked compassion and impulse control, saw themselves as victims, and resented authority. Nonetheless, having failed in the past reliably to identify the criminal mind, now chastened psychiatrists also cautioned that testing for dangerousness was almost impossible and that standard psychiatric diagnosis was largely irrelevant. A major study of a large group of the supposedly criminally insane in 1966 in New York revealed them to be sad old men far more often than predatory psychopaths.[180]

Besides magic and witchcraft, torture has been the most venerable attempt to probe the soul's secrets. The psychological sciences sought to follow suit more methodically, yet their promise disappointed. Fearful of false positives, clinicians tended to forecast conservatively who among their patients might offend, thereby hobbling their predictive acumen.[181] Excepting the seriously mentally ill and perhaps drug abusers, few psy-forecasts managed accurately to predict future offending.[182] Even new technologies have done little to improve this track record. Psychological testing has recently claimed to reveal subconscious attitudes by measuring microsecond differentials in answering questions that confirm or challenge prejudices or assumptions. Minute gestures indiscernible to the naked eye, when agglomerated by the thousands, allegedly reveal characteristics such as sexual proclivity. Penile plethysmographs and their vaginal equivalents unmask involuntary sexual arousal—imperceptible in some cases even to the subjects being tested—to detect potentially reoffending pedophiles, rapists, and sadists.[183]

Hopes of reading others' minds likely only shortly postdated Eve's encounter with the serpent. The correlation between lying and arousing the sympathetic nervous system was operationalized already in ancient China. Suspected liars had to take a mouthful of rice and spit it out.[184] Those with dry mouths found the task harder than normally salivating innocents. It was a trope of racist ideology that Blacks and Jews—both allegedly incapable of blushing—were inferior because their interior states were less visible to others.[185] Mechanized lie-detection technology began with Lombroso's hydrosphygmograph to measure pulse rates, followed by John Larson's polygraph in the 1920s, correlating deception with increased blood pressure. The polygraph was sold to police and public as a means of getting at the truth that sidestepped the need for more primitive and violent techniques.[186] Other methods followed, all sharing the assumption that somatic reactions revealed inner states through a Pinocchio response, whether respiration rates, epidermal conductivity, voice stress, heat around the eyeballs, fleeting facial micro expressions, or millisecond hesitations.[187]

MRI scans and electroencephalography went further, measuring something seemingly closer to the inner workings of the brain, though still merely a heightened metabolic activity in certain cerebral areas.[188] Such technologies assumed that lying was more arduous (a greater cognitive load) than telling the truth, thus stimulating the responses detected. They all were unable to distinguish dissembling as such from other brain activities. Nor were they able to locate deception in specific and specialized areas of the brain. Moreover, liars could also game the system, all the more so when they knew what investigators were looking for. On the basis of no particular evidence, it is, for example, widely believed that liars avert their gaze, so those hoping to appear truthful now catch and hold their interlocuter's eye.[189] Perhaps we are entering a new era of predictive investigation, but attempts to discern individual thoughts by involuntary physical responses have yet to prove very successful.

If the psy-sciences did not fire prediction's magic bullet, that left sociology. Potential offenders could also be identified by extrapolating from statistically characteristic behavior of groups they belonged to. Regularities were identified to induce forecasts of conduct, using the logic of social science developed by the nineteenth-century Belgian astronomer Adolphe Quetelet, who thought that society followed patterns as discoverable as nature's.[190] Offending was linked statistically with various characteristics to develop a sociological criminal type. Membership of a group was associated with certain behaviors, which in turn could be used to define the group.[191] The group could thus be targeted, and individual members deemed potentially culpable—though merely for sharing the features for which the collective name was shorthand. Armed with—at best—probabilistic social science, prevention thus focused on the criminal more than on the crime. Did offenders belong to high-risk groups? Were they recidivists? Did they have a propensity for certain crimes? A penchant for repeated transgressions? A disposition for specific victims? Most generally, were they dangerous, posing an ongoing threat? The answers determined the appropriate punishment more than did the nature of any (eventual) offense, thus weakening retributive justice's link between act and desert. Retributionists' focus on culpability for the act treated each offense alike, even those committed subsequently by the same person. Targeting some people as especially dangerous and even treating recidivists more harshly, in contrast, meant punishing the person as much as the act.

In this logic, those predicted to recommit were to receive different sentences from onetimers.[192] Kleptomaniacs and drug addicts should be treated more harshly than one-off opportunistic offenders even though, acting under a psychological compulsion, they were—according to a retributive logic—less culpable. Sentences of treatment rather than punition also made sense if they promised less crime.[193] Inchoate crimes were by definition those that had not been consummated. Of interest, therefore, was perpetrators' intent and what it revealed about their state of mind, inclinations, and personality. Someone who would attempt, conspire about, solicit, or incite a crime posed a threat. Anyone willing to attempt an offense was likely to repeat it. Punishing attempts aimed foremost to neutralize threatening individuals and only secondarily to deter their offenses. That offenders were dangerous mattered more than whether they were guilty.[194]

Sociological or actuarial prediction raised particular problems. It was static. The characteristics that defined someone as likely to offend—poverty, unemployment, residence in certain neighborhoods—could at best predict lifetime, not imminent, risk.[195] Conversely, predicting lifetime offending on the basis of recidivism, as three-strikes laws claimed, was hampered by the tendency for transgressing to drop off with age. Former serial offenders were locked up just as they lapsed into crimogenic senescence.[196] To avoid unacceptable false negatives—releasing some apparently harmless persons who then went on to offend—meant tolerating many false positives, which kept innocents behind bars.[197] The former set off political fireworks; the latter were rarely heard from again.

Not only did actuarial forecasting overpredict, but its logic was also circular: those who had stolen were likely to have been unemployed; the former unemployed were therefore potential thieves. Not-yet offenders thus had their future behavior forecast on the basis of demographic, economic, and social traits they shared with already offenders. They were held accountable for characteristics that had proven correlative for past culprits, though not yet shown to be causally determinative for them. In effect, they were punished for the crimes of others. Even sophisticated sociology could not surmount the dilemma famously identified by David Hume: how to break out of correlation into causality. However refined the actuarial calculations, they still took a leap of faith from past behavior to future actions.

Since the popular mind confused correlation with causality, crime prevention reinforced the conceptual shorthands we call stereotypes. That the overwhelming majority of rapists are men does not mean that all men are rapists, except perhaps in the fevered imagination of Val in Marilyn French's pathbreaking feminist novel *The Women's Room*. But that African American men are charged with crimes disproportionately to their presence in the population has been used to justify the racial profiling that subjects them to more than their fair share of preventive encounters with the police. Similar discrimination confronts Middle Eastern travelers at airports. Such prejudices have been conceptually cemented throughout history, leaving traces in our vocabulary. *Vandals, barbarians, philistines, peons, banshees, troglodytes, plebians, Huns, sycophants, thugs, villains, beggars, buggers, coolies, bohemians, berserkers, boors,* and the other n-words of yore—all were used at one time or another for ethnic, national, or (quasi-) occupational groups now immortalized for their pejorative traits. In 1682, Louis XIV banished all "Bohemians" and "Egyptians" from France, by which he meant Roma.[198]

The inherent unfairness of this sociological logic meant that laws based on it faced obstacles. That many women, not just prostitutes, were swept up in police dragnets and inspected for venereal disease in nineteenth-century England helped marshal opposition to the Contagious Disease Acts. Vagrancy laws are ancient, permitting police to harass or jail largely anyone found in public.[199] Antiloitering laws give police broad discretion to target otherwise legal activity, such as "wandering or strolling around from place to place without any lawful purpose or object."[200] Broadly speaking, any car driver is fair game for police attention.[201] In recent years, courts have struck down some such statutes as too vague, all-inclusive, and broad, thereby justifying the targeting of racial, ethnic, and sexual groups only tangentially correlated to the relevant crimogenic characteristics. In response, the statutes have been refocused on more specific behaviors, such as loitering with various intents. Or they have been aimed at crime hot spots rather than at entire cities—all to avoid violating the rights of innocent bystanders who happen to share certain characteristics with the gang members or other groups being targeted.[202]

Psychological and sociological techniques of predicting and preventing crime alike raised problems. Modern law enforcement has therefore tended to retreat to the simplest means of forecasting of all: past behavior. Past actions were empirically and morally a more solid foundation for predicting future acts than actuarially based demographic or sociological correlations.[203] How often and how seriously someone had already offended have become the most heavily weighted factors in predicting future transgression.[204] Absent a belief in atonement or remorse (hard to test for its sincerity), past offenders were assumed likely to repeat their crimes, thereby condemned to a vicious circle.

However prevention formulated its predictions, it thus focused more on the criminal than on the crime. Unlike reactive policing, with culprits who could in theory be identified, prevention did not know who was going to offend. Yet it had to narrow its focus to only some citizens. Even before any crime had been committed, it too needed suspects. Bad characters, habitual offenders, dangerous classes, social parasites, objective enemies, recidivists: through the ages, such designations were shorthand for characteristics considered indicative of likely criminality.[205] *Profiling* is today's word for this use of extrapolation from demographic, social, ethnic, economic, behavioral, or other indicators to identify likely offenders.

Rehabilitation and Discretion

Opportunistic crime could be prevented by target hardening the environment, not by altering the offender's nature. Both rehabilitation and prevention instead focused on the character of the criminal. Rehabilitating offenders meant going beyond retributive infliction of bodily pain to an attempt to change them. It assumed that offenders' transgressions expressed a character flaw. Rehabilitation has usually been presented as an ameliorative and even humanitarian approach. But as Foucault famously noted, rehabilitation means that the state no longer just inflicts discomfort; it now seeks to transform the soul.[206] Already in 1835, Alexis de Tocqueville had argued something similar. Absolutist monarchies chastised their subjects physically, he held, while republics left the body alone to delve straight for the soul.[207]

When did the state adopt a rehabilitative ambition? Foucault located this sea change in the late eighteenth century with the aspiringly all-powerful absolutist state and then the French Revolution. Yet ambitions to change, not just to chastise, offenders have long been with us. Shame punishments in ancient China aimed at moral improvement or "self-renewal." The Greeks, like the Chinese, banished criminals to improve them and allowed their return once they were purified by absence. Plato suggested rehabilitating the impious by isolating them in prisons far from home.[208] Once the Roman Empire Christianized in the fourth century, it persecuted heretics in part to convert them. Augustine, as we have seen, insisted on the duty to convert otherwise damned heretics.[209] Saul the persecutor of Christians became Paul the apostle. God wants sinners to repent, not die, as Wazo, bishop of Liege, preached in the early eleventh century.[210] Inspired by Aquinas, the interrogators of medieval heretics insisted that their willful errors were reversible. Converting them was the goal.[211] Seventeenth-century Dutch houses of correction aimed not to punish but to reform. Transporting criminals to the colonies from seventeenth-century England was thought to offer a second chance.[212]

As Foucault pointed out, rehabilitative outcomes were expected from prisons when they were first constructed on a large scale in the early nineteenth century. Finely parsed techniques of solitary confinement were meant to mold inmates' souls. The very words used for prisons indicated the ambition: *houses of correction* and *penitentiaries*—the latter derived from *penitence*, or the guilt and remorse that medieval inquisitors sought from heretics. Sixteenth- and seventeenth-century

European states already sought to rehabilitate vagrants and the idle, prostitutes, unmarried mothers, street urchins, and the like.[213] But conversely, already by the mid-nineteenth century, as prisons grew overcrowded, rehabilitative ambitions faded quickly.

In the twentieth century, however, rehabilitation was rehabilitated. Indeterminate and individualized sentencing attempted to rope prisoners into their own improvement.[214] Nonfixed sentences allowed authorities to reward good behavior and punish bad. Inmates remained inside for times that depended less on how they had offended than on their subsequent behavior. As reformers in 1870 put it, the prisoner would be redeemed "through his own exertions" or not at all.[215] In the 1880s, the German reformer Franz von Liszt argued for the virtues of preventing future harm by sentencing according to the danger the convicted posed, not the offense they had committed or the punishment they might deserve. Sentences had to be individualized and discretionary, tied to behavioral outcomes, and not just an arbitrary duration. Failing to change, prisoners would have to remain inside. Incapacitation was the necessary corollary of unsuccessful rehabilitation.[216] Pushed to its logical extreme, indefinite and discretionary sentencing assumed that being incarcerated was the normal condition, release exceptional. All citizens were on parole.

Parole and probation implemented this approach. Release was contingent on prisoners behaving themselves. For preventive reasons, one prisoner might be kept in jail for longer than another, despite their having committed the same crime. Institutionalizing indeterminate sentencing through parole and probation started in the early nineteenth century, first in colonial Australia, then in the United States, shortening the sentences of well-behaved inmates. At midcentury, US states experimented with good-time credits for juveniles in reform schools and by the 1890s for adults. By the 1920s, most US prisons had indeterminate sentencing or parole.[217] Germany followed suit in 1935, but Britain not until the 1960s.[218]

Rehabilitation remained penal orthodoxy through the 1970s, before losing ground to neoretributionist reforms. Especially in the US and Britain during the 1960s and 1970s as crime increased, the response was harsh and retributive. Prison sentences were lengthened, jails were filled, and public shaming was once again used punitively. Rehabilitation was declared a largely bankrupt ideal, giving way to just-deserts punishment, and penal ambitions were limited to incapacitating offenders. Victims clamored for retribution, grabbing the spotlight from offenders and the state's hopes of resocializing them. Certain victims (of rape and domestic violence, for example) managed to turn retribution into an appealing goal even for the Left, which was normally resistant to what counted as a conservative cause.[219]

Sparked by rising crime rates in the 1960s as well as by shocking individual cases of savage acts committed by offenders on parole, retributionism certainly had a conservative slant, but it was encouraged also from the Left by reformers worried by the discriminatory potential of individualized punishments. The Right insisted on harsh determinate sanctions for brutal crimes. The Left rediscovered the Enlightenment egalitarianism of a clear moral bookkeeping that specified the consequences of transgression, not permitting class or status to differentiate punishments, imposing no demands of behavioral conformity beyond serving the sentence, and allowing sovereign citizens to make their decisions accordingly. The rehabilitationist project was also eroded by the widespread belief that a permanent underclass was forming and by cultural relativism's undermining of the bourgeois self-confidence required to set the norms to which offenders should be schooled.[220] In the late twentieth century, the goal increasingly became to punish criminals in proportion to their deeds, regardless of any effect on their subsequent behavior.[221] Sentences were determined at conviction; parole was ever less available. Even Sweden cut back on its use.[222] Mandatory-sentencing guidelines prescribed minimum durations, including fixed terms, and required that prisoners serve most of their time ("honesty in sentencing"). Punishments were increased for recidivists, and prison was evermore seen as merely incapacitating inmates, with few ambitions to help them change.[223]

This punitive turn was taken especially in the English-speaking world, whereas Europe retained more of the rehabilitative ideal. So did this turn upend Foucault's theory that the authorities' concern to mold their subjects' interiors was a permanent sea change and not just a secular oscillation?[224] The shift to determinate sentencing may have undercut early release, but the same retributive current also introduced civil commitment and other means of individualizing and extending sentences. Sex offenders were often kept inside if it was feared they would recommit. In Britain, offenders were sometimes sentenced to life with periodic review even for small crimes in cases of past sexual offenses or mental derangement. In Germany, *Sicherungsverwahrung* (preventive detention) allowed the authorities to keep prisoners deemed dangerous locked up beyond their sentences. In Italy, "security measures" achieved much the same.[225] In most nations, the mentally ill could be institutionalized for as long as deemed advisable. The decline of indeterminate sentencing made such measures necessary, permitting authorities to adjust prison terms to prisoners' attitudes and progress.[226] In other words, individualized sentencing actually continued despite neoretributivist reforms, but it was now harnessed to more, not less, punitive ends. Sharpened sentences for repeat offenders were similarly a form of upside indeterminate sentencing, the mirror image of parole. When punishments determined purely retributively seemed inadequate for still-dangerous offenders, they were extended.

Whatever its oscillating fortunes, rehabilitation required individualized punishments. Reforming offenders meant taking account of their specific circumstances. Rehabilitation was in effect resocialization or socialization come too late. The state undertook late in life what family, school, church, and community had evidently failed at. Not surprisingly, it was work done by the psy-sciences and their practitioners: psychologists, psychiatrists, therapists, social workers.[227] As we have seen, individualized sentences undermined the Enlightenment ideals of predictable and standardized punishments for specified offenses that treated all citizens equally, allowing them to know and anticipate the consequences of their actions. When the United States began experimenting with individualized sentencing in the late nineteenth century, the French regarded its indeterminacy as cruel and unusual.[228] Many critics today agree, noting that ethnic and class prejudice condemns minorities and the poor to disproportionately harsh sentences.[229] But cookie-cutter punishments, although abstractly fair, also ignored particulars of the offender who was to be rehabilitated.

The Enlightenment reformers had advocated consistency and equality before the law, but treating all who had committed the same offense in the same way could also be unfair. A theft prompted by necessity and one committed on a lark did not merit the same punishment—nor did perhaps a first offense and a repeat by a practiced thief. Were the law not just to react blindly but punish according to offenders' guilt and chances of resocialization, then it had to discriminate, treating superficially similar acts according to their varied motives, background, and context. Sanctions had to fit the criminal, not the crime.

How did the authorities know whether someone had been rehabilitated? As with sin, at stake was the congruence between inner state and outer act. The worth of human beings depended, John Stuart Mill argued, not only on what they did but also on what manner of people they were who did it.[230] Rehabilitating criminals, the state was in the business of producing good humans. Remorse was often demanded. Juries, judges, and parole boards looked for it. Convicts prepared to turn over new leaves were well advised to make a show of it.[231] Inmates who convinced their keepers of a change of heart were rewarded. When some proved to have gamed the system, offending again after release, the communal feeling of betrayal helps explain the backlash against probation in the 1970s. But, short of knowing interior states, the only outward measure of inner conformity was recidivism. If the state could not produce morally good former convicts, then perhaps it could at least turn out ones who did not run afoul of the law again.

Strict Liability, Negligence, Risk

Not only did the law elbow its way into citizens' heads, criminalizing their intent to harm before any actual offense, but it also broadened its remit to punish acts without any intent at all. In theory, a crime involved both the intent to do wrong and the carrying out of that wrong act—both mens rea and *actus reus*. As we have seen, the law came close to punishing the mens rea alone, and we return to this situation with respect to sex crimes in the next chapter. But it also punished acts alone, regardless of their motivation. The earliest laws often did not differentiate between purposeful acts and those that were unintentional or accidents. Only later did the law take intent into consideration. That initial approach, of punishing the act regardless of why it occurred, returned with the concept of strict liability.

Strict liability punished actions society wanted to eliminate wholly, regardless of why they had happened. Starting in the late nineteenth century, it was adopted widely as dense urban civilization's precariousness reinforced the necessity of discouraging harmful behaviors outright.[232] In theory, punishing on the basis only of negligence led to a socially inefficient underpricing of risk. If those engaged in potentially dangerous activities followed only the standard of due care required, they would escape liability for harm caused nonetheless. In contrast, holding them accountable in every instance—negligent or not—forced them to price in the true cost of harm.[233] The development of strict liability placed the burden of risk on those best able to reduce it, the cheapest-cost avoider—in the case of product liability, for example, on producers.[234] A spate of flooding disasters involving mines and reservoirs in the mid-nineteenth century spurred on the use of strict liability in the United States.[235] Manufacturers were later held accountable for product defects (food adulteration), and highly hazardous enterprises, such as nuclear power and aviation, were governed by strict liability.[236] Statutory rape and bigamy were also strict-liability offenses. Regardless of how good a reason someone had for thinking a child was of age or that their partner had been properly divorced, sex or marriage, respectively, was verboten. Bartenders who served the underaged were liable no matter how mature the customer appeared, how convincing their fake ID. Having to prove culpable intent for each such act would harm the public more than unfairness to the occasional innocent offender.[237]

Vicarious liability extended this logic, holding the head of a corporation responsible for the actions of underlings. The aforementioned bartender would be strictly liable; the absentee owner of the establishment vicariously liable.[238] Regulatory offenses were often of this nature, too. They brought the penal code to bear on offenses such as the sale of adulterated food or drink, child labor, and environmental violations.[239] As of the mid-1980s, the statutes regarding such violations dramatically expanded in the US. Violations of federal agency rules were now routinely punished as felonies, with more than three hundred thousand federal regulations thus enforced. Accomplices, too, were held accountable for the acts of their co-offenders, even though they themselves had neither done nor even intended to commit a crime.[240]

Not only was intent criminalized, but the number of other mental states that rendered actors culpable also expanded. Offenders were increasingly held liable for negligence, not just for deliberate harms.[241] Though offenders had not intended harm, they were guilty if they had not sufficiently anticipated its likelihood. They were punished not for intent but for not having the knowledge of the potentially dangerous situation or the insight they should have had.[242] A certain standard of conduct was expected from law-abiding citizens, and those who failed to achieve it were penalized.[243] The concept of negligence thus punished offenders not for their intent but for their ignorance. It discounted the mens rea normally required for a criminal offense, thereby broadening the range of punishable acts.[244]

Negligence had long been prosecuted. In Hebrew law, a bull known to be dangerous that gored again was to be stoned, and its owner killed, too. Roman law punished negligent behavior that might lead to injury.[245] If a beast's owner refused to curb it, Wessex laws of the eighth century allowed those whose crops it damaged to kill it. A century later, owners of animals that repeatedly caused harm were punished on a sliding scale.[246] By the nineteenth century, however, animals were acknowledged to lack intent and ceased being punished. They were no longer treated as purposive actors, but now largely as property. Their owners were culpable if they had acted negligently, allowing their charges to harm.[247]

Though of venerable concern, negligence was increasingly put to work as technological sophistication multiplied the consequences of inattention far beyond the realm of dangerous domestic creatures. From the 1870s in Europe, laws began holding liable those who increased risks of harm to others.[248] By the 1920s, criminal negligence was being identified as separately punishable. Reckless-endangerment statutes later in the twentieth century took matters a step further. Negligent offenders did not realize the danger they put others in, but reckless offenders ignored it; they were consciously negligent.[249] Ignoring the potential consequences of actions also became punishable, as did bringing about even the possibility of danger. If an act or omission by someone who did not mean to endanger another created a risk, that person could still be punished.[250] British law did not punish endangerment as such. But the US Model Penal Code included a general offense of recklessly engaging in conduct that placed others in danger of death or serious bodily harm. German law punished not only the endangering of life and property but even abstract endangerment, including slander that might stigmatize someone.[251]

Moreover, general endangerment offenses did not require proof of actual or likely danger. They criminalized activities that raised unacceptable risks. Even nations that did not criminalize endangerment generically did so in practice, heading harm off before it occurred by punishing those who put others at risk. Speeding and dangerous or drunk driving were offenses everywhere, so the laws against them were in effect preventive measures that punished the posing of risk.[252] As even risk was criminalized, only few actions now escaped the authorities' interest. After all, almost every behavior or action posed some danger. Likely offenders could be considered threats even if they did not actually commit a crime.[253] Was not the mere act of being put at risk not also a harm in itself: a driver speeding, a surgeon operating after drinking, a pilot flying without enough sleep? Even if the harm did not materialize, these actors could be offenders. Being exposed to heightened risk might be considered a harm as such.[254]

The law thus narrowed from its earlier blunderbuss approach. It now left many behaviors to the private sphere, where citizens made their own decisions, largely unencumbered by official attention. But in those areas still subject to law and in those newly brought under its umbrella, the authorities both broadened and deepened their remit. At first, most harms had been punished regardless of intent. The requirement of a mens rea then narrowed crimes to intended acts, sanctioning only those that deserved it. At the same time, the concern with intent also prompted the authorities to delve into citizens' minds, punishing them for their thoughts and ambitions, not just for their acts, and padding the roster of possible offenses. Meanwhile, negligence and recklessness also reversed the focus brought by the mens rea requirement, once again punishing acts regardless of intent.[255] Civil law nations were happy to prosecute even acts presupposing no intent, such as negligent arson, while the common law countries upped the ante with strict liability, where the act alone, regardless of intent, was actionable. More behaviors than ever thus fell under the authorities' purview, and the state also drilled into its subjects' minds, seeking to ferret out intentions and anticipate crimes in the making. The ever-expanding law may have provided the blueprint, but the boots on the ground belonged to the police, the sharp end of the state's enforcement stick to which we now turn.

Chapter 12
The State as Enforcer: From *Polizei* to Police

Most middle-class white Westerners regard the police as sheep do border collies: something they rarely encounter or need worry much about, so long as they stick to the center of the flock and do not tarry, dawdle, or stray. Such people pass years, decades even, without meeting uniformed officers face-to-face. If they do not drive, the frequency of their already rare interactions diminishes further. If they do not live in neighborhoods targeted by zero-tolerance enforcement, that effect is amplified.[1] Policing happens at society's margins, to the disenfranchised, poor, racial minorities, and the outcast. For them, the police are all-powerful and all-pervasive in their lives. Well-socialized burghers, in contrast, confront the state's enforcement arm infrequently because—policing themselves as part of the behavioral compact that assures their station—they rarely cross the invisible lines that trigger a statutory response.

Yet policing did not always hover at society's periphery. It was once largely synonymous with government itself. The term *policing* shares its etymology, not coincidentally, with *policy* and *polity*, and they in turn with *polis*—or more precisely *politeia*, Greek for "governance of a city." As we have seen, crime used to encompass many behaviors that are now decriminalized: reclassified under private law, relegated to the private realm, considered merely sins or minor infractions—or redefined as normal, such as being Protestant or gay. In tandem, policing once also intervened much more broadly. The police used to administer activities that today are not regulated much or at all (sartorial strictures, Sabbatarian rules, morals, religion, usury) or that are now the province of other arms of government (zoning, health and safety, child protection, social services, food and drug safety, transportation, animal control, competition).

In its older, all-encompassing mode, to police was to govern, to supply the basic infrastructure of a well-regulated society. Today, "police states" mean totalitarian dictatorships, unfettered by rule of law or due process. In the early modern era, a police state meant the opposite. It was a tautology, repeating itself, a "state state." In sixteenth-century France, *police* was defined simply as the government of a republic.[2] What the political theorists of absolutist government in seventeenth-century Germany called *Polizeiwissenschaft* is best translated as the "science of governing." To police was to administer. An echo of this tradition lingers in the Anglophone notion of "police powers"—the quaintly antiquated public-order and welfare regulations that were once among the police's most important duties.[3] But, on the whole, the English did not entrust the same sort of broad regulatory powers to their police as did the continent.[4] In contrast, the Scots, the American colonies, and, later, the US federal states gave police powers a remit more akin to Europe. Nineteenth-century America used morals-related regulations to criminalize behavior of the sort once targeted in Europe by *Polizei* strictures.[5] In that sense, the English police were both later and more modern—narrowly specialized in enforcing law and maintaining order—when first set up in the late eighteenth and early nineteenth centuries.[6]

On the continent, in contrast, early modern policing combined enforcing law and maintaining public order with a Noah's ark of regulation. The Romans had already pointed the way. Their city prefects kept order, but they were also responsible for fire hazards, public buildings, religious ceremonies, public meetings, prostitutes, beggars, and foreigners as well as more generally for health, safety, and morality. Only in the fifteenth century, with their first laws on

Polizei, did Europeans get back to that place.[7] These laws entrusted the police with a groaning smorgasbord of responsibilities: potable water; animal control; regulation of prostitutes, foreigners, vagrants, nonconforming religionists, and other undesirables; sartorial and sumptuary laws; Sabbatarian and opening-hours rules; flood abatement; food supply and adulteration; weights and measures; manufacturing; hiring, firing, and behavior of servants; purchase and sale; guardianship; fire prevention; mendicancy; rubbish and waste removal; price controls and profiteering; usury; embezzlement; pawn brokers; public drunkenness; arms and weapons; cursing; adultery and concubinage; commerce; fairs and markets; street cleaning and lighting; passports; transport; building codes; public works; bridge maintenance; wet nurses; poor relief; illicit publications and censorship; public houses and amusements. The police also enforced regulations to ensure salubrity: against immorality, blasphemy, drinking, cursing, and gaming. Weddings were closely regulated: who could be invited, what to wear, how expensive the gifts could be, how much food, drink, and music was permitted.[8] When not otherwise occupied, local executioners pitched in to dispatch stray dogs and pigs and to enforce regulations against lepers and prostitutes, sometimes gambling, as well as public defecation and blasphemy. It would arguably be easier to list what did *not* belong to the police's remit, which included largely everything other than perhaps defense and foreign policy.[9]

Nor did this panoply of functions evaporate entirely under modernity's sun. In early nineteenth-century Toulouse, the police still combined the functions of family court and counseling. Officers took evidence from complainants whose daughters had been seduced, whose husbands squandered their earnings, whose jilted lovers had stolen their wardrobes, and the like. The French gendarmerie helped out in times of natural or other disaster.[10] In Denver in the 1860s, the city marshal removed a noxious slaughterhouse and tannery from the town center. Stray dogs occupied much police attention. Officers lodged the down and out and returned errant children. When the Russian police took care of abandoned children, even deep into the twentieth century, they had little choice but to welcome them into their own families.[11] In the mid-nineteenth century, New York police counted cellar dwellers, inspected steam boilers, cleaned streets, and administered elections.[12] The English phrase "If you want to know the time, ask a policeman" revealed that few people owned a watch in the nineteenth century but also cynically assumed that most bobbies had lifted a timepiece off a drunken reveler.[13]

Writing in 1915, an American visitor was astounded at the range of activity still pursued by German police. Prussia had separate police departments for insurance, mining, water and dikes, field and forest, cattle disease, hunting, fisheries, trade, fire, politics, roads, health, and buildings—among other things. Berlin had twelve police departments. Only two—uniformed officers and the detectives—performed functions also handled by their English law enforcement colleagues. The others supervised markets and sale of provisions; inspected foodstuffs; controlled public assemblies; abated nuisances; oversaw lodging houses, cafes, and amusements; regulated druggists, vets, and other professions; and kept watch on certain banks. Division Eight oversaw censorship of theaters, control of concerts and movie theaters, and the employment of child actors. Meanwhile, the Paris police inspected mushrooms as one of their duties, and it remained their task to check on buildings and factories, scrutinize prices, and verify the quality of produce.[14] To this day, the French gendarmerie collects meteorological data and regulates veterinary clinics and abattoirs.[15] The Chinese police, tasked also with public-health matters and census registration, investigated citizens' homes and backgrounds.[16] Even the London police licensed chimney sweeps, shoeblacks, and messengers; kept tradesmen honest; inspected weights, bridges, and lodging houses; and enforced nuisance laws. They could even be asked to wake people in the morning for work.[17]

Even today, the police continue to provide many services and community functions—if only because no other institution answers the phone 24/7/365 but largely because most police work still involves maintaining order more than solving crime.[18] The vast majority of calls today to the police do not report crimes at all, much less serious ones.[19] Many are requests for help in emergencies that might quickly deteriorate but do not yet involve law breaking: domestic disputes, children on the street alone at night, noises scaring an elderly couple, drug overdoses and miscarriages, and accidents of all sorts.[20] The more developed the country, the more police respond to noncrime situations. Arrest is only the third most common outcome of their interventions (after doing nothing and advising how to avoid repeating the incident), occurring some 14 percent of the time.[21] Even when offenders are arrested, it is mostly over bread-and-butter stuff. Only 10 percent are charged with serious offenses. In the main, police interact with the public over drunkenness, disorderly conduct, assault, drunk driving, gambling, vandalism, and similarly pedestrian matters.[22]

Nonetheless, policing has narrowed significantly from its blunderbuss role in the early modern era. The Enlightenment's reformers held that the state was to provide the legal framework, thereby defining the acceptable, and maintain order but not otherwise use its police powers to regulate the particulars of civil society. Citizens were left free to arrange matters as they saw fit within legality's parameters.[23] Ensuring order, not promoting welfare, became the police's new role. In the Prussian general code of 1794, the police's tasks were to maintain public peace, security, and order and to prevent danger to the public.[24] Though that remained a broad remit, many of the police's earlier duties gradually either were not regulated at all or fell to other state agencies. The police's main role became to ensure order, prevent offenses, and solve those crimes not deterred.[25] Having once been the state's Swiss Army knife, police became a rapier. Perhaps the closest they come to their earlier duties today is regulating traffic, which brings them into frequent contact with many different citizens. Yet policing as such has not diminished. Yes, it has narrowed its scope to the more precise modern sense of dealing with crime as violations of the penal code, but what this specific definition encompasses has expanded and dramatically deepened.

On its way to this new role, policing changed entirely. In Europe's old regimes, up through the eighteenth century, offending was widespread and common, committed by many, not just by an easily identifiable criminal class, and tolerated in large measure for lack of effective means to counter it. The interested parties themselves, not the authorities, did most enforcement. Cases were often settled informally outside of court. If they reached trial, the unfortunate pendant to lax and indifferent enforcement was harsh deterrent punishment of the few who had been nabbed. Policing was sporadic, localized, and violent.[26]

With the growth of official policing starting in the eighteenth century and a judicial system able to handle the heightened throughput, enforcement became professionalized. Property-owning volunteer constables or their paid proxies were replaced by uniformed, salaried officers. Detecting crime and maintaining order became routinized, spreading into poor communities, too. Rather than making examples of a few, catching and sentencing as many offenders as possible were the new goals. Punishments were moderated but inflicted more regularly and predictably. Prosecution became the state's duty and the citizen's right, available to anyone who had been victimized, not just to those who could afford to pursue matters.

Policing had earlier enforced the authorities' will, suppressing not just mayhem and disorder but also unrest and revolt. Tsarist police in Russia were notorious in this regard. In early nineteenth-century

Austria, police still beat civilians for showing disrespect to the ruling house.[27] The unrest that roiled European cities in the eighteenth and nineteenth centuries doubtless helped spur the authorities' plans for regularized police forces.[28] In the French Revolutions of 1830 and 1848, the gendarmerie helped restore order—and was temporarily disbanded thereafter in acknowledgment of the unpopularity that act had won it.[29] But in a longer view, in increasingly democratic societies the police could not be partisan. To avoid raising hackles, they had to maintain order and enforce the law impartially. That order and legality benefit those at society's pinnacle hardly needs mention; that they equally and possibly especially favor those with few other means to protect themselves from violence and chaos bears repeating.

From its beginnings in the early nineteenth century, the English police recognized the virtues of being unpartisan. Unlike the older continental European forces, established to shore up dynasties and regimes, English policing was instituted less to take sides than to enforce the king's peace.[30] The bobbies were carefully controlled, largely unarmed, trained to win public sympathy, and subject to strict rule of law. They were citizens in uniform, not much more powerful than their civilian peers.[31] Marinated in an atmosphere skeptical of standing armies and anything in uniform, the American police were at first scarcely an arm of the state at all and more an extension of civil society. Officers were selected to reflect the social, national, and ethnic composition of those they policed. They were closely tied to local machine politics. Second-generation residents of New York City suspected Irish officers of favoritism and investigated to see whether they were arresting their fellow brethren in due numbers.[32]

As policing became a regular feature, seeping into society's interstices, an implicit compact was struck between citizens and officialdom. The rule of law applied to police as much as to civilians. Punishing violations of the criminal code was their remit and their legitimacy rested on keeping to that. Rules on how to collect, process, and use evidence became detailed. *Lettres de cachet* of the sort issued by the French king before the revolution, locking up miscreants indefinitely without specified charges, were no longer tolerated. Most nations eventually forbade coercion, the third degree, unauthorized eavesdropping, and similar techniques.[33] The job of the police was to uphold the law. If the law was fair, all citizens benefitted. When the police favored or persecuted some groups, their authority suffered. If anyone other than offenders felt victimized, the deal would be off. What counted as legitimate, enforceable law evolved as the state extended its powers yet took account of custom and habit. Social crimes such as poaching and gleaning ceased being enforced strictly on behalf of landowners. Laws that clamped down on workers' pleasures—drink above all—were policed only sporadically.

Police and citizenry needed each other. Short of an omniscient police state, civilian cooperation was crucial. Police were like fish swimming in the ocean of the people, as the current Chinese authorities have repurposed Mao's analogy of the People's Revolutionary Army.[34] The police did not just replace civil society's self-policing but also enlisted that function on their own behalf. Even in the modern era, most crime reporting originated with the public, not with gumshoe detective work. Some crimes, such as domestic violence, were likely to remain unknown if not reported. Tips, sightings, snitching, and reports were needed to resolve cases. According to one study, 93 percent of arrests were the outcome of citizens contacting the police. Unless victims or witnesses helped identify offenders, the likelihood of an arrest fell to 10 percent.[35] The most-wanted posters (and their TV variants) that used to festoon post offices were emblematic: appeals to the public for leads. Hotlines to report crimes were widespread. Volunteer patrols helped the police. Even the supernatural pitched in through its mediums.[36] And if citizens were not mobilized directly by the authorities, then they were indirectly by insurance companies, obliging them to lock their homes and cars, report thefts, and register stolen goods. Night watchmen in early modern Europe rattled doors, checking to see if they were locked as required by law.[37] Today officers collect data from neighborhood-surveillance cameras to track suspects. Warnings against abandoned luggage alert the public on public transport to possible terrorist bombs. Open registers of sex offenders presume that their neighbors will—if they have not already driven them away—help police them.[38]

Indeed, self-policing has remained a cornerstone of police work. As far back as the thirteenth century, English subjects were required to report treasonous plans they knew of—not tarrying more than two days or attending to their own business beforehand. Medieval Christians were expected to report heresy on pain of being suspected themselves.[39] Indonesia has updated this practice with Smart Pakem, an app allowing Muslims to denounce heretics from their smartphones.[40] In the West, anyone who knows of crimes such as domestic violence, especially if victims are unlikely to report them, is encouraged to alert the police, "thus marking that these offences are not a private matter between the parties involved," in the words of a Swedish bill.[41] The German legal code criminalizes knowing of plans for serious crime without reporting it.[42] The common law nations achieved much the same by defining accomplices broadly. Reporting requirements became standard for professions likely to see child or elder abuse.[43] Banks have to disclose large cash transactions, corporations disposal of toxic substances. Those who are not informers are accomplices—that is the logic.

A successful police system is one citizens want more of. Order and security are our first demands of the authorities. True, some forms of enforcement were inherently unpopular. Public support for the English police suffered in the early nineteenth century when they enforced laws that in effect targeted the poor for being poor—being drunk in public or sleeping in the open (thus classified as vagrant).

The working classes resisted bans on their pleasures: drinking on Sundays, street betting, gaming, dog- and cockfighting, hare coursing, rat baiting, and other animal sports (though fox hunting was of course not prohibited).[44] Attempts to enforce Sabbatarian rules in New York City that had been passed in Albany by provincial lawmakers stretched the police beyond what they could or wanted to do and undermined their popular support.[45] Today, the sense that ethnic minorities are singled out for unfair scrutiny and enforcement undermines support in their communities, hampering the compliance and cooperation on which successful policing necessarily rests.[46]

But laws that were not inherently biased have generally been popular. When the seventeenth-century English imposed binding-over orders on each other, which required good behavior on pain of punishment, they were yearning for more policing in an era before the state could deliver. Access to the law and its protection of their meager property were what the English poor desired in the eighteenth century. Many of the *cahiers de doléances* (list of grievances) drawn up before the French Revolution complained that small towns and villages hardly ever saw police patrols and demanded enlargement of the *maréchaussée* (local mounted force).[47] The Prussian habeas corpus law of 1848 forbade house searches at night. Upright burghers protested that when they reported a theft, the goods were long gone by the time the police finally showed up the next day.[48] Resisted at first, London bobbies soon became popular, the public complaining that they were not doing enough to maintain order. Assaults on police dropped by two-thirds during the late nineteenth century.[49] At first, bobbies could arrest only for crimes they had witnessed. Londoners pressed for changes, which passed in 1839 and allowed police to take suspects into custody for broader reasons. As theft's main victims, the nineteenth-century poor were eager to prosecute their losses in court.[50] Even though they dislike tax increases, citizens have been known to vote to finance expanded police patrolling. Faced with neighborhood disorder and crime, most residents have supported foot patrols and other up-close forms of policing.[51] Minority residents of US cities often receive unwanted and undeserved police attention, yet they have also backed more and stronger enforcement—of drug laws, for example.[52] Just anecdotes, these stories nevertheless illustrate a truism: in stable modern societies, many more suffer from crime than from police misconduct.

Making the Police

Like the rest of the state's crime-fighting functions, policing was largely a modern invention. True, in ancient Egypt policemen patrolled marketplaces, armed with sticks and baboons trained to chase wrongdoers. In Athens, a troop of Scythian slaves, brandishing whips and small sabers, was marshaled to guard public meetings, control crowds, and make arrests. Yet, their duties were rudimentary at best. In Rome, *aediles* could chastise citizens in specific remits—flogging actors, for example, because their duties included policing performances at the public games. The *tresviri capitales* were magistrates responsible for public jails, executions, and order in the streets, but they lacked their own means of coercion.[53] Only in the early modern era did recognizable police appear. Even in an ancient civilization such as China, where the wealthy had kept private guards at least since the eleventh century, state policing is scarcely a century old. Arguably, it began only in the post-Mao period.[54]

At first, the police were largely volunteers, citizens keeping order in their own communities. The sixth-century Frankish king Clothar sought to shift the burden of pursuing thieves from the family to the larger territorial community, punishing those who did not pitch in.[55] Thirteenth-century England set watches manned by constables—part-time volunteers who enforced the hue and cry. A crime discovered, the alarm was sounded. Pursuit followed, and if the culprits were caught and arrested, sometimes they were summarily executed.[56] Local communities in medieval Spain formed *cuadrillas*, town leagues, to guard common pastures against interlopers while also keeping an eye on road traffic. In seventeenth-century London, constables were male householders who served a year at a time, fulfilling the obligations of the Statute of Winchester (1285) to police their communities. By the eighteenth century, the gentry were hiring substitutes to serve their time or paying fines, which were then used to employ others. The system's inherent amateurism was thus mitigated as those who served at length acquired expertise.[57]

Parishes also began imposing taxes instead to salary permanent watchmen. By 1800, the City of London's constables were hired men for the most part.[58] At the time of the revolution, French policing was not yet entirely a governmental function. As of 1792, Parisian officers of the peace, armed with white sticks, arrested offenders and brought them before justices of the peace. Ordinary citizens could be ordered to help and jailed if they refused. Nor was policing yet professionalized in the United States, where a law in 1789 allowed marshals to compel local citizens to do their part on a *posse comitatus*. Volunteerism lasted even into the era of professional police. Nineteenth-century Toulouse had *dixainiers*, local citizens who broke up brawls and reported disorder, alerting the official police. Unpaid and sporting no outward signs of authority, they were rewarded by exemption from national-guard service and billeting troops. Russian peasants mainly policed themselves, as did largely autonomous communities of Latvians, Estonians, Jews, and other minorities in the East European countryside.[59]

Informal policing remains even in our own day. Volunteer security personnel patrol gated communities, organize block watches, and escort the elderly at night. And as new crimes have multiplied, ordinary citizens have begun serving as indirect enforcers: tenants who sue their landlords for unwarranted rent increases; the maligned for libel and defamation; consumers who win triple damages for prosecuting antitrust violations; retailers, hoteliers, and restauranteurs who police and enforce offenses against their businesses; citizens who sue fraudsters against the government.[60] Class-action suits allow groups of citizens who share only their victimhood to enforce the law.[61]

Authorities also outsourced the legwork of policing: to knights in medieval Europe, hundreds in England, samurai in Japan, *potwaris* in India, *hans* in China, and vigilantes in nineteenth-century America. In the sixth-century French Merovingian kingdom, those helping track down thieves were given a cut of the goods retrieved. In sixteenth-century Florence, *banditi* killed or captured banned persons. Prussian Junkers administered justice—using the term loosely—on their estates until 1872, Russian landed aristocrats until 1918.[62] Even when enforcement was authorized by the state, the personnel carrying it out often remained volunteers, with the restrictions that imposed. The justice of the peace in England, *länsman* in Sweden, and *Schultheiss* in Germany: all were legal amateurs acting as judges who had to herd their fellow subjects in the right direction while not poisoning their own reentry to civilian life.[63]

In eighteenth-century England, thief takers—frequently former criminals—made a lucrative business of apprehending offenders and reaping rewards when they were convicted—often of crimes the thief takers themselves had instigated. Visiting Assisi in 1786, Goethe was shaken down by the *sbirri*, armed thugs who acted as agents of courts and were paid via fees and rewards. In 1798, London merchants prevented pilferage from the docks by financing a marine police force that was so successful it became a public body two years later.[64] François Vidocq, who ran the Sûreté in the early nineteenth century, was a former criminal hired just for that expertise. In the American West, gun slingers such as Wild Bill Hickok and Wyatt Earp were employed to keep order as cowboys whooped it up on payday. The difference was often slight between them and proper outlaws such as John Wesley Hardin, Billy the Kid, and Jesse James.[65] In the early twentieth century, mining companies and other corporations broke strikes and enforced labor discipline with private police. Having started by supplying security for presidents and the army, Pinkertons then worked for the railroads, which as inveterate border crossers were served poorly by territorially organized policing.[66] Even today, American bounty hunters are privateers fulfilling a public function when they track down bail jumpers.[67]

Indeed, private policing continues in robust health. Far from having been displaced by their official colleagues, such forces are everywhere: university, school, and mall police; private and corporate guards; airline security; even mercenary quasi-military personnel sent into war zones.[68] Despite the state's massive expansion into enforcement, so unquenchable is the demand for security that private forces today outnumber official police, often several times over—almost three in the United States.[69] There are ten times as many private investigators and detectives as FBI agents. Twice as much money is spent on private policing in the US as on public. Even in statist China, a third of all policing is private, although these forces are owned by the Ministry of Public Security. In Shanghai, private forces are half as big as the official police; in Beijing, the numbers are largely equal.[70] Not part of the state's monopoly of violence, private police are restricted in their powers—unless they are deputized or are regular police moonlighting. But nor are they hampered by the due-process limits imposed by criminal procedure or regulation. Private-security forces in the US are not subject to the same curbs on conduct as official police. As agents of property owners, they can exclude or eject the unwanted from private premises in a way regular police cannot from public spaces.[71]

Recognizably modern police forces were established in the late eighteenth century on the continent, followed half a century later in Britain and then in the United States. The earliest was perhaps in France in the mid-1600s.[72] By the early eighteenth century, the *maréchaussée*, mounted officers, had arguably become the first national police force—some three thousand men, doubled in size after the revolution. Paris in the late seventeenth and early eighteenth centuries was well policed by the standards of the day. In 1667, the traditional night watch was replaced with a professionalized uniformed force reporting to the central government. Centralized police became the norm already under Louis XIV. It was continued by the revolutionaries and the two Napoleons.[73] By the late eighteenth century, some three thousand officers patrolled a city of six hundred thousand, the largest and best-organized force in Western Europe. Only about half were police in the modern sense. The rest were garbage collectors, firefighters, censors, architects, and the like.[74] London became as well patrolled only half a century later.[75]

Early on, police and army were scarcely distinguishable. Both served the ruler, putting down unrest and maintaining order—sometimes against external enemies, other times against domestic troublemakers. In autocracies, both forces were often made up of foreigners to avoid sympathy and fraternization when used domestically. Vikings protected the emperor in tenth-century Byzantium. The Swiss Guards quelled unrest for the pope and the French king, among others. After the revolutions of 1848, the police in Vienna often were Czech or Moravian. In southern Italy, the carabinieri usually hailed from the North, sporting an inbred feeling of superiority.[76]

With nationalism and democracy, however, such disjuncture no longer worked. Citizens were now rallied for the patriotic cause against foreign enemies and recruited en masse to the military. The police, too, began reflecting the population they kept in line.[77]

Barracked officers were separated from civilians, but police generally lived like and among civilians when off work. True, Russian police were recruited heavily from the army and rarely natives of the region they supervised. London bobbies were deliberately enlisted from the provinces. But New York City cops were chosen from those they would police, leading to an informal rapport but also, predictably, more corruption.[78] The gendarmes in France under Napoleon were supposed to know their local area so well that they implausibly could go to any point in their districts with their eyes closed.[79] More recently, radios and cars have centralized police, who swoop in only when summoned. The backlash against such distancing has prompted a return to community policing. Foot and bike patrols in local neighborhoods now allow citizens and officers to cooperate in maintaining order.[80]

Military and police have become separated. The peacetime British army in the eighteenth century fulfilled discrete functions: suppressing smuggling, putting down riots, and crushing insurrections.[81] Only in extremis was the military—eventually an emanation of the nation, even when a professional force—marshaled against civilians. In the Peterloo massacre of 1819, constables, unable to control a crowd of sixty thousand demonstrators in Manchester, called in the hussars. When a dozen civilians were killed, the authorities realized that the old system of repression no longer worked. Victorian Britain used the military against civilians only twice: during riots against the ban on Sunday trading in 1855 and during the parliamentary reform agitation of 1866–1867.[82] In the early twentieth century, troops were deployed mainly in industrial disputes.[83] The Emergency Powers Act of 1920 allowed the British army to protect food and fuel supplies. In the United States, the Posse Comitatus Act of 1878 restricted the use of the army for domestic policing duties, something that had become widespread in the South after the civil war.[84]

The separation between military and police took longer elsewhere. In the late nineteenth century, Russian authorities transferred cases to military tribunals if necessary for public order.[85] In the early twentieth century, Budapest's uniformed police were still a military troop, armed and barracked like soldiers, ready for service at a bugle call. The Italian carabinieri, originally a sixteenth-century branch of the Piedmontese army, remained part of the military after Italy's unification. It reported to the Ministry of War and, for its more purely policing functions, to the Ministry of the Interior. Much the same held for the French gendarmerie and the Spanish *guardia civil*.[86] In Germany, the Social Democrats proved disastrously willing to use the Freikorps (demilitarized troops employed domestically) to suppress the revolution of November 1918. The Freikorps' murder of Communist leaders soured relations between the two major parties of the Left, later undermining hopes of a unified opposition to the Nazis. The Third Reich continued blurring the lines, turning the police into the "internal army."[87] In the developing world, militarized police are still used as, in effect, an occupying army, as when Brazil's federalized police invade favelas and battle drug gangs. Recent terrorism has also meant that semi-militarized gendarmeries have expanded, especially in border security.[88]

National guards bridged the gap between police and the military, deployed in emergencies without seeming to pit army against citizens. In 1842, after riots were quelled by the army, Cincinnati created a reserve militia police guard.[89] More recently, the police, locked in an arms race with offenders, have adopted military equipment and tactics, blurring the line again. Even as the state monopolized violence, pacifying society, armaments technology forced it to weaponize at home as military battlefield kit leaked to criminals. Nineteenth-century police were armed with sticks and swords. London inspectors were allowed to carry pocket pistols as of 1829, and constables could draw revolvers from 1883 on.[90] The British police still generally do not carry arms when on patrol, but they use body armor and updated weapons such as batons, rigid handcuffs, and incapacitating spray. Trained officers (5 percent of the force) are armed.[91] German, French, and US police are armed as a matter of routine.[92] Legitimized by the "war" against drugs and then terrorism, SWAT teams and other paramilitary units have been used against civilians.[93] In the United States, deployment of such quasi-military teams increased fourteenfold in the late twentieth century, often for nonemergencies such as drug searches. Their tactics, weapons, and attitudes have been adopted by regular police forces, too.[94]

Crowd control upped the ante. Authorities fear mass unrest far more than individual crime. To deal with unruly crowds, violent crimes, hostage situations, and terrorism, police forces everywhere have ratcheted up their technological prowess, maintaining special units for emergencies. Water cannons and tear gas are used to disperse crowds. French forces especially have been armed to the teeth. Gendarmes use the army's standard assault rifles, submachine guns, and pump-action shotguns. In extreme situations, they marshal heavy weaponry, helicopters, armored vehicles with machine guns, and chemical, biological, radiological, and nuclear protection equipment.[95] Since the late 1990s, the equivalent forces in the US have used surplus military hardware against civilian protests—armored vehicles, ballistic helmets, tactical vests, night-vision goggles. In the 1960s, Britain, too, developed paramilitary forces to control crowds, strikes, and riots. Deployed against striking coal miners in the mid-1980s, they sported shields and helmets, later water cannon, tear gas, and plastic bullets, and eventually robocop armor.[96] But there has also been technological de-escalation. Less-lethal weapons have been developed: stun guns and tasers, water and sound cannons, tear- and other gas. Hydraulic equipment and kinetic devices, stun grenades, and barricade-breaching technologies have joined the armamentarium. New technologies of crisis defusion have also been developed: mediation training and hostage negotiation.[97]

Professionalizing the Police

Seen in a long historical sweep, the likelihood of an offender being punished has moved from possible through plausible to at times even probable. The dark figure of undetected crime remains obscure—more so the further into the past we go. To claim that the proportion of crimes committed that are also convicted is increasing would be a supposition. But we do know that the percentage of those indicted who are also punished is growing. The early modern state, as we have seen, punished the few criminals in its hands in spectacular ways to trumpet its deterrent message. But as the justice system and the police were able to accomplish their mission more effectively, punishment shifted from sending a message to would-be criminals to dealing with those offenders in its grasp. The state was in a position to affect their behavior—whether merely by incapacitating them or perhaps also by reforming them. The more prisoners in the state's hands, the better it could influence overall criminality.

How the justice system upped its game can be gauged by its growing ability to deliver known offenders to their just deserts. Just 10 to 20 percent of accused killers were convicted in fourteenth-century England.[98] More than 40 percent of those tried in seventeenth-century Sussex were acquitted, 30 of them in late seventeenth-century and early eighteenth-century Norfolk and Suffolk. Figures for all of England from the sixteenth to the eighteenth centuries were similar.[99] Conviction rates in Bavaria in the early nineteenth century hovered between 40 and 50 percent.[100] By the nineteenth century in France, they had climbed to 70 percent.[101] And modern judiciaries convict even more efficiently. In Japan today, 90 percent of those tried plead guilty, and acquittal rates are miniscule.[102] In Europe and the United States, the percentage of prosecutions leading to convictions are uniformly higher than 80 percent, sometimes significantly so.[103]

The judiciary became more efficient in prosecuting criminals for reasons explored later in this chapter. More fundamentally, crime and sanction increasingly aligned from the eighteenth century on. Punishments were moderated, and death sentences grew rare. Juries no longer felt morally compelled to acquit petty criminals who otherwise faced the scaffold. In a virtuous circle, the more offenders the state found and prosecuted, the less it had to rely on deterrence in the form of grotesque barbarities. The scissors gradually closed between what the authorities did to the wretches they caught to discourage other would-be criminals and what popular opinion regarded as proportionate sanction.

Even without juries to buffer an insistent prosecution, continental Europe's inquisitorial systems had built-in circuit breakers in the form of pardons and amnesties. They were tripped when crime and sanction seemed out of synch or when the numbers of the indicted simply grew insurmountable. The Theodosian Code mentions thirteen amnesties granted between 332 and 413 CE. The Spanish Crown's pardons extended even into the American colonies. When Louis XVI left Paris for exile in June 1791, he deplored how the National Assembly had stripped away his prerogative to pardon and commute sentences. His subjects, he lamented, would no longer regard him as their common father.[104] Even in republican times, that tradition continues. The French prison population has largely been stable since 1988 thanks in part to a series of mass pardons marking national holidays or presidential inaugurations. Although the timing of their use differed from the Western experience, China had an even more luxuriant tradition of "great acts of mercy" by which entire cohorts of offenders were pardoned on a regular basis—every three years, for example, during the last four decades of Emperor Wu's reign, from 128 BCE on.[105] Overall, pardons today are rare, but they remain as a curiously patriarchal remnant of once-feudal relationships. As punishments aligned with offenses, the need waned for royal pardons (followed in republics by their presidential and gubernatorial versions) to take the edge off earlier barbarities. Perfect legislation, as Beccaria pointed out, eliminated the need for pardons. Clemency should be the task of the legislator, not the sovereign.[106] The state could finally enforce just, measured, and—above all—if not likely then at least not implausibly improbable punishments.

Starting in the nineteenth century, police numbers and budgets marched steadily upward. Figures began being kept in the 1930s, showing that police ranks per capita have multiplied almost everywhere.[107] Some nations centralized their forces; others left oversight to local entities. Regardless, the police slowly professionalized and bureaucratized. Having begun as volunteers, officers were first salaried and then subjected to modern bureaucracy's usual processes of examination, training, discipline, and meritocratic advancement. In the early nineteenth century, the Russian tsar's political police force was staffed by personnel so ill educated that they quite literally could not understand the regime opponents they interrogated.[108] That had to change.

Maintaining order, providing evidence to prosecute offenses, and preventing crime were, in that order, largely what police did. The medieval hue and cry did rouse citizens in immediate pursuit of an offender, but grappling with criminals in flagrante diminished as part of police work. Today, only about a tenth of radio calls to patrol cars raise even the possibility of law enforcement in the narrow sense—stopping a burglary, catching a prowler, making an arrest, or investigating something suspicious.[109] In New York, even in poor neighborhoods in the high-crime 1980s, 40 percent of patrol officers made not a single felony arrest per year, and 69 percent made no more than three. In London, an officer might encounter a burglary in progress once every eight years. Direct crime work took up as little as 3 percent of patrol officers' working hours.[110]

In the twentieth century, the French police boasted an ability to find their culprit anywhere in the nation within twenty-four hours. Such powers developed only slowly. Continental police could inspect and arrest. In 1666, the officers of the Châtelet, the most important police headquarters in Paris, were given the right to enter homes and other buildings. Bearing arms was also concentrated largely in their hands, though not wholly—thanks to resistant nobles.[111] In the Anglo-Saxon nations, police had few powers beyond those of civilians. In seventeenth-century Sussex, the old hue and cry, obliging all citizens to help corral offenders, gave way to the need for written warrants, sworn before a justice of the peace and issued to a constable. This requirement made rounding up more of a duty for officials. In the eighteenth century, constables began making arrests and bringing offenders to court and jail. They also searched for the accused and at times for stolen property. Nonetheless, bringing offenders to justice still remained the task of victims.[112]

Robert Peel founded the London police in 1829. He wanted his bobbies regarded as but members of the public who were paid to give full-time attention to duties that were in fact incumbent on all citizens.[113] In colonial America, attacks on constables and sheriffs were frequent, and they lacked any effective power to arrest suspects who resisted. In mid-nineteenth-century New York, officers who misused firearms (killing a fleeing suspect, for example) were arrested by their colleagues like any civilian. Citizens had much the same powers of arrest as any official.[114] Both New York and London officers could be sued in ordinary courts for false arrest. In the United States, officers and citizens alike could arrest for misdemeanors committed in their presence. Both could arrest for felonies they had witnessed and for those they had probable cause to believe had occurred. But if the felony turned out not to have taken place, the civilian, but not the officer, was considered to have committed an offense. Some US states also permitted shopkeepers, hoteliers, restauranteurs, and the like to arrest and detain suspects until the police arrived.[115]

In many US states today, ordinary citizens may still arrest for misdemeanors committed in their presence and for felonies they have probable cause to believe have occurred.[116] Indeed, in certain respects, citizens retain greater powers over each other than do the police. Authorities are bound by due-process restrictions on searching and seizing evidence without warrants; citizens performing arrests are not.[117] Even today in Britain, policing is theoretically a private matter, with the officer in principle but a uniformed citizen. In the mid-1980s, almost a quarter of criminal court cases were prosecutions by nonpolice agencies, such as local authorities or the Royal Society for the Protection of Cruelty to Animals, as well as by individuals.[118] Citizens also retain powers to use proportional force, though not to detain, by relying on the doctrines of self-defense, defense of others, and defense of property. The right of self-defense remains since even modern police cannot always be everywhere. Even today, citizens must take responsibility for their own safety.[119] Ultimately, the modern state relies on a vestige of vigilantism.

And yet police were granted significant powers from the start. Constables in the late seventeenth century could arrest and imprison, break into houses, and disperse unruly crowds. Eighteenth-century London watchmen freely stopped odd people at night: a man selling cheese in the street at 3:00 a.m., for example, or carrying a sack of coal in the wee hours. Night watchmen looked out for suspicious people and arrested prostitutes and vagrants. Police in eighteenth-century Paris checked pedestrians at night and interrogated irregular characters, especially if they carried packages of potentially stolen goods.[120] German cities were well policed within their walls, and it was the suburbs where delinquency flourished as authority petered out.[121]

Over time, such powers were enhanced. The Anglo-Saxon common law gave police but few powers of arrest beyond those of every citizen. True, only police could execute arrest warrants, but most arrests were made without one. Yet only police could execute search warrants and sometimes search without one. And they could command bystanders. English civilians could arrest without a warrant for serious crimes such as murder. Constables, however, could arrest on suspicion alone. For minor offenses (being drunk and disorderly, for example), they needed no warrant.[122] Such powers expanded in the nineteenth century. The Metropolitan Police Act of 1829 empowered London bobbies to apprehend loose, idle, and disorderly persons whom they merely suspected of evil designs. Their New York colleagues could arrest those seemingly intent on a felony and their powers to search citizens for stolen goods were modeled on the London statutes. The portmanteau concept of disorderly conduct gave police on both sides of the Atlantic broad discretion. Being tasked to regulate traffic also gave London police expansive powers to disperse crowds and to keep thoroughfares open.[123]

Secret Police

"When a man marries his mistress, he creates a job vacancy" is a bon mot often attributed to the financier Jimmy Goldsmith but coined in fact by the multiwedded French actor Sacha Guitry.[124] So, too, with the police. As they became rule bound, regulated by law, and tasked with enforcing order in increasingly democratic societies, the need arose for special forces to sidestep the established procedures that now hobbled official inquiry. Once a uniformed police presence became commonplace, its deterrent effect lessened. Undercover police now became the joker in the deck. Pinkerton's plainclothesmen deterred because no one could be certain whether one was lurking nearby.[125]

Secret police were used against occult crimes in particular, especially theological and political unorthodoxy. The ancient Greek sky and thunder god Zeus, who was not omniscient, ran a spy service of thirty thousand immortals who roamed the earth, noting unjust deeds. Aristotle recommended a system of spies to keep tabs on dissidents.[126] Starting in the thirteenth century, Franciscans and especially Dominicans (God's dogs) were also early covert enforcers—trained to ferret out heresy, operating Europe-wide, and answering directly to the pope.[127] Many of the techniques later perfected by the modern secret police were first tested by the Inquisition: evaluating evidence of forbidden thoughts such as ritual practices or refusal to participate, ownership of prohibited writings, association with other suspects, statements to others. Nonheretics were obliged to report and testify; confession was extracted by threatening punishments or implying that others had already revealed all; grace periods were promised those who confessed now.[128] Under Henry VIII, Thomas Cromwell used his network of spies to report on subjects' theological shortcomings and doubts about the king's marital extravagances. Sometimes informants pretended to be fellow prisoners to gain the trust of papists and other enemies of the throne.[129] In Renaissance Florence, tracking aristocratic families' plots against the Medicis was the secret police's main function, as under Nicholas I in Russia.[130] Joseph II, Holy Roman emperor in the late eighteenth century, used his undercover police to keep tabs equally on his own officials and on revolutionaries.[131] The Bourbon secret police in the early nineteenth century kidnapped and sometimes murdered political opponents in exile—as does the Russian government to this day.[132]

As democratic winds began to blow across Europe, the autocracies feared revolution. In quiet times, the secret police mostly tracked the opposition press, followed and sometimes censored books and theater, and kept an eye on political meetings. The Prussians banned all German-language papers imported from America, fearing democratic tendencies.[133] But as protest quickened, things turned nastier. The French *police speciale* and the tsar's Third Department, dating to the sixteenth century, were among the most notorious of Europe's political police forces, ruthlessly suppressing opposition.[134] The English Special Branch was established in 1884 in response to bombings by Irish republicans. Despite much posturing about French-style plainclothesmen being an arm of autocracy, even the British found them useful. In 1842, a small detective force was established surreptitiously and not publicly acknowledged until the 1870s. From the late nineteenth century on, the British police, much like their continental counterparts, made clear their interests in political enemies.[135] Before unification in the 1870s, the German states collaborated across their multiple borders to track liberals, socialists, and Communists.[136] World War I marked a watershed, with the state now massively keeping tabs on its soldiers and citizens, including by intercepting and reading mail to measure the pulse of public opinion. If the Russian monarchy had forty-nine police officers reading the public's letters in 1913, the Soviets had ten thousand doing this work seven years later.[137]

Agents provocateurs were especially resented, embroiling the state in similar questions of complicity as its use of informers and entrapment for regular crime. Joseph Fouché, in service seriatim to the revolution, the Directory, and Napoleon, spearheaded the deployment of political undercover agents.[138] So active were the secret police under Napoleon III's Second Empire that all seditious affairs were said ultimately to have been their doing, much as Louis XV had been assured that wherever three people met, a police spy was at hand. Indeed, during the 1880s the police prefect financed the first Parisian anarchist newspaper, writing articles in it that prompted bombing attempts.[139] The Lyon police maintained a certain secret society so as to have conspirators to arrest or release as government policy demanded.[140] When Captain Renault ordered the "usual suspects" rounded up in *Casablanca*, this was the tradition he drew on.

Detective squads were also established to collect evidence and track down offenders. Detectives thus did what is commonly considered police work, but precisely because most actual patrol work was not like that, separate detective outfits were needed. One of the first was the criminal investigation division set up in London in 1842. Detectives' work habits and tasks differed sharply from the regular police: no uniforms, regular beats, or schedules. Detectives were reactive, delving deeply to solve crimes post facto. They were in close contact with the underworld, so corruption and graft were common among them. Like vice control, detective work was a tangle of mixed motives and quasi-legal temptations.[141]

The detective quickly became star of the most popular literary genre ever, barring perhaps the romance. The public was gripped by the narrative thrust, intellectual puzzles, and dramatic punch of the common law world's courtrooms. Dueling attorneys presented competing narratives and their evidentiary backup to a jury of everymen. Starting with Edgar Allan Poe's *Murders in the Rue Morgue* in 1841 and Wilkie Collins's *Woman in White* in 1859, detective fiction became the reading public's staple.[142] Charles Dickens is said to have invented the word *detective*, identifying Inspector Bucket in *Bleak House* (1852) as a "detective officer."[143] Introduction of the jury trial to Russia in 1864 made possible the use of fictional court cases with their inherent drama, presented as theater, to educate citizens in the early Soviet Union.[144] By the mid-twentieth century, a quarter of all English-speaking fiction and television programs were crime stories.[145] Poe's narrator may have emphasized his detective's almost preternatural reasoning, but Dupin himself pursued evidence with unbridled empiricism.[146] Sherlock Holmes spoke often of deduction, but his method was as inductive as scientific method insisted.[147] In *A Study in Scarlet* (1887), Watson noted Holmes's excellent knowledge of chemistry, anatomy, biology, and geology but also his profound ignorance of literature and philosophy. "Data! Data! Data!," Holmes exclaimed in "The Adventure of the Copper Breeches" (1892). "I can't make bricks without clay."[148]

What Police Knew

Most important of the commodities traded by the police was information—the content, of course, but equally the flow. Tsar Nicholas's secret police were his best—and surprisingly accurate and useful—source of information on the state of his realm in all respects.[149] Their hierarchical organization, military-style command and communications, and strategically located outposts made the police efficient conveyors. Someone reporting a crime could expect that something might actually happen in response.[150] The early Russian police in cities were spaced at stations within eyesight or earshot of each other. Electronics merely amplified this technique. Already in the 1840s, the New York police connected the chief's office with precincts via telegraph.[151] With telephone and then two-way radio, help could be summoned at greater distances. Motorizing officers separated policing even more from the crime scene. Today, three-digit emergency phone numbers have annoyingly similar but unidentical three-digit codes: 911 (United States), 112 (European Union, but with local variants for landlines: 110 in Germany, 999 in Britain), 100 (India), 110 (China and Japan), 190 (Brazil), 102 (Russia). Once mastered, they make official emergency responders the first and best source of help. Americans know officers swooping in via car or helicopter as "911 policing." Having once been a duty for all citizens, rescue became yet another state service, much like the government disaster relief that has mushroomed to cover most uninsured losses.[152] The paparazzi who tailed Princess Diana's car in Paris and then did nothing to save her after the crash were not prosecuted since, as the court noted, one had phoned in the accident. With that, their legal duties had been fulfilled.[153]

The content of what the police knew or could discover was even more important. So long as most crimes pursued were tangible ones committed by offenders tied into networks of kin and community—known people deliverable for revenge or restitution—police were largely superfluous. But a private prosecutory system could scarcely deal with occult crimes that were not evidently known to others or with crimes that had been committed by people who were not members of groups that were willing to prosecute or defend.[154] For the anomic criminal, for offenses requiring investigation, or for crimes knowable only by probing, kin or other informal arrangements did not suffice.

The state had tackled occult crime from the start. Ordeals—God's testimony—were intended to solve crimes that might not have witnesses (individual heresy, infanticide) or where witnesses were party to the offense (simony, adultery, incest, sodomy, concubinage, bribery) or could not testify (bestiality).[155] Torture, too, was meant to uncover hidden evidence. But over time, the judiciary's verdicts came to depend not on supernatural and forced testimony but on circumstantial evidence and other simply empirical and scientific data. As oaths, ordeals, and torture were replaced by observational, scrutinized evidence, policing as an epistemological tool came into its own.

The judiciary found and punished ever more offenders as it grew better able to marshal evidence, constructing convincing cases. And as more merciful sanctions set in, ending popular resistance to how offenders were penalized, only faulty evidence impeded the state in prosecuting criminals. The civil law's inquisitorial system was more targeted than the common law, with its adversarial confrontation before a jury. Prosecutors' discretion whether to pursue cases varied, from largely none in nations such as Finland, Italy, and Germany to a great deal in the Netherlands and Norway.[156] But after preliminary investigation, all civil law prosecutors brought forth those cases they considered winnable, thus increasing their hit rate. The common law states attorneys, in contrast, had to decide whether to proceed while armed with less information. And they were at the jury's mercy, however watertight their arguments.[157]

The jury in turn evolved into a mechanism for evaluating evidence. Having been a group of self-informing peers, picked largely because they already knew the circumstances, the jury turned into a forum for weighing evidence of thirdhand events. In the Middle Ages, they had been selected for their personal knowledge of the case. But such contact eventually disqualified jurors as nonimpartial.[158]

Once the oath, with its appeal to supernatural intervention, no longer promised certainty and a verdict, jurors had to evaluate the evidence.[159] Sealed in the black box of the jury room, they judged witnesses' credibility, their testimony's verifiability. "Beyond a reasonable doubt" evolved as the evidentiary legal standard at about the same time as the seventeenth century's scientific revolution made testimony of the senses and empiricism more generally the most trusted form of knowledge.[160]

The state won cases largely on the evidence supplied from citizens and rounded up by police legwork. Before technology helped them much, the police turned to an unsavory ecosystem of spies, snitches, snoops, stooges, and informers who passed on gossip, denunciations, and hints, all prompted by an array of mixed motives: pay, reward, exemption from punishment, and sometimes even public-spiritedness. Napoleon's concierges or the *dvornik*s of St. Petersburg were only the most regularized of the bunch.[161] Plato required citizens to report impieties they came across.[162] In early modern England, those who turned in criminals had their own crimes pardoned. Informers ratted on tariff and customs violators and religious dissenters in the seventeenth century and then on violators of Sabbatarian laws and public cursers in the eighteenth. Lutheran pastors in sixteenth-century Württemberg were required to inform on each other.[163] Informants often made serious money from rewards paid for leads. In the Victorian era, this use of rewards led to scandal and parliamentary inquiries.[164]

Old-regime France required brothel madams to file reports on their clients. Prostitutes were handy sources of information in the nineteenth century. French detectives believed that *mouchards* (informants) were as useful to tracking down crime as smoke was to locating fire. Chinese Communists took a similar approach in the late 1940s.[165] The tsarist police enlisted house porters and night watchmen.[166] The Soviet and Nazi secret police relied heavily on denunciations, and no system has ever roped in proportionately as many snitches as the East German Stasi. Former criminals in China today provide the bulk of informants and information.[167] In modern liberal democracies, too, informers pull their weight, encouraging religious extremists to become terrorists, for example, and thus leading to their arrest.[168] The recent lavish development of conspiracy law has incentivized criminals to rat on their fellow offenders.[169] But, like entrapment, relying on informers means that the police must encourage crime in order then to solve it.

Bounties made lay citizens collaborators with the police. In ideologized states, whether religious or political, denunciation enforced orthodoxy.[170] But denouncers have been found everywhere. In ancient Greece, sycophants were those who turned in offenders for a share of the spoils. In the Middle Ages, denunciation allowed prosecution even of those whom no one wished to officially accuse.[171] In seventeenth-century England, neighbors denounced each other at extraordinary rates for sexual deviance.[172] In fourteenth-century Venice, carved lions' mouths on the sides of buildings hid letter slots for denunciations. In Florence a century later, residents' *tamburazione*, anonymous denunciations to the police, initiated many prosecutions. Tsar Paul I placed his infamous yellow box to receive denunciations in front of the Winter Palace in St. Petersburg.[173] The French revolutionaries—like later totalitarian regimes—elevated denunciation to a civic virtue. Done publicly, it protected the general good against enemies and was therefore allegedly morally superior to the private gain pursued by the old regime's snitches.[174]

Informers played crucial roles in early modern Europe. Eight percent of Florence's police budget went to paying them, and another 12 percent to reward those who reported violations of peace and treaty agreements. Minor public officials, the *sindaci*, were selected for each neighborhood, tasked with reporting crime and rewarded by the case.[175] In seventeenth-century England, rewards for evidence leading to conviction became a lucrative element of the justice system—apprehending a highway robber paid £40 and the offender's horse, arms, and money. Informants on illegal London gin shops collected half the fine, as did their colleagues in the American colonies who reported shoddy merchandise or retail fraud.[176] More than 90 percent of prosecutions under the Statute of Apprentices (1563) were brought by private informers. Many made a profession of informing. In 1699, the "Tyburn Ticket" was granted to those who helped convict burglars, shoplifters, and horse thieves, exempting them from duties in local offices—such as policing their neighborhood as constables. In 1720, the total reward for the conviction of a robber in London was £140, thrice a journeyman's annual income.[177]

Such incentives continue today. Besides the rewards posted on the most-wanted list, information leading to conviction pays off as immunity from prosecution for those who testify as state's evidence. Bounty hunters are rewarded, as are whistle-blowers—in tax fraud, proportionately to the recouped sums.[178] US state attorney generals' offices keep the fines they impose on banks for malfeasance.[179] Law enforcement agencies retain some of the proceeds of confiscated crime-related property.[180] Prosecution of some crimes relies heavily on covert information, for example, insider trading, where bounties can reach 10 percent of penalties (which can be thrice the illicit profits). Up to a third of cleared-up crime may be thanks to informers.[181]

Other surreptitious means of information gathering have evolved with the technology at hand. For centuries, private letters have been opened by state officials, leading to an arms race of competing techniques of sealing, opening, and resealing them. Eavesdropping in the literal sense has occurred ever since there were eaves to stand under, the edge of the eaves marking the legal limit of the private, domestic space.[182] Electronic devices now make for more convenient listening, wiretapping phones, secretly recording conversations, and audio-surveilling homes and offices. Today, we debate government access to email and social media.

Much more of a revolution and not just amplifying the circuits of witnessing was the growing acceptance of empirical and scientific evidence independent of human testimony. The judicial system's evidentiary base gradually shifted from confession and witnessing to evidence that existed autonomously of anyone involved in the offense. Insisting on eyewitness testimony and confession, Roman law had discounted circumstantial evidence. Interrogation, with torture as its most extreme form, never got beyond witnesses, including possible perpetrators, and their limited and self-interested vantage. Today we forbid torture, not only for humanitarian motives but also for epistemological reasons as likely to produce self-serving and unreliable information. And we understand eyewitness testimony to be inherently unreliable, colored by all manner of influence and but a dim reflection of what happened.[183] The testimony of facts and the traces of our biological and physical trails instead supply the most illuminating evidence. We are spared the forceful extraction of confession from our souls by the betrayal of our bodies. *Indicia*, once spurned as merely epiphenomenal, have returned as the queen of evidence.

The new evidentiary gold standard relied on induction from knowledge of the world to conclude guilt or innocence, entirely independent of whether the acts in question had been witnessed or even perceived. Knowledge could be uncovered regardless of humans encountering it, having it, or testifying to it. One of Roman law's two queen proofs, eyewitness, came to be understood as unreliable and often outright misleading. Indeed, false or mistaken eyewitness accounts have proven to be the preeminent cause of wrongful convictions.[184] The apparently stolid facts presented by the world instead took their place. Forensic investigations have been performed at least since the physician Antistius claimed that only one of Julius Caesar's twenty-three stab wounds had been fatal and even two centuries earlier in China. Sung Tz'u's thirteenth-century Chinese text on forensic investigation, *The Washing Away of Wrongs*, explained how to distinguish between corpses killed before or after being burned or inundated, how to discern the difference between hanging and strangulation or between drowning and being drowned, and how to distinguish murders from suicides committed so as falsely to implicate others. With a deft noirish touch, he recommended checking the anuses of unexpectedly deceased elderly husbands married to young wives—to look for hidden penetration wounds.[185] In early modern Europe, mothers who gave birth while alone and whose child died were often suspected of infanticide. Had the infant been stillborn or killed postpartum? In the absence of an unimplicated eyewitness, the lungs of the infant were submerged in water. If they floated, that was considered proof that the child, born alive, had taken its first gasps to inflate them.[186]

Early modern Russian peasants killed by beating on planks placed on their victims' swaddled stomachs. This technique destroyed the victims' innards without leaving external traces but was rendered obsolete once coroners began their forensic investigations in the late nineteenth century.[187] In 1905, two murderers were hanged on the basis of a thumbprint on a cash box.[188] In the late nineteenth century, crime photography began to reveal evidence obscure to the naked eye. The disturbed dew drops on a park bench next to the body of an apparent suicide, for example, betrayed the presence of someone else at the scene.[189] In such cases—whatever the merits of the science of the day—nature spoke directly, though not unaided, to the court. We now take cross-examining nature on the stand—the dramatis personae of countless courtroom dramas—so much for granted that we are blind to the significance of the change.

Fingerprinting emblematized the justice system's embrace of the new scientific evidence. "Every contact leaves a trace" was the mantra of the investigatory work that underlay forensic science.[190] Fingerprinting was used sporadically in the ancient world and likely developed first in China. It caught on systematically in British India and then in Europe and the Americas in the 1890s. The first trial where fingerprinting provided the main evidence was held in India in 1898. The court accepted that the partial print left behind proved the suspect had touched a box with stolen money and so convicted him of burglary. But it was still unwilling to accept by the implied logic that he had also killed the box's owner.[191]

Subsequent technologies have sharpened our observational lens, often demonstrating that earlier techniques were faulty or unreliable. Crime scenes were photographed to scale, footprints measured and cast in plaster, soles typologized, as were automobile and bicycle tires later.[192] Particulate residue in earwax as well as nail and hair clippings gave evidence of activities undertaken even months earlier. Starting in the 1930s, blood typing began to crudely associate suspects with offenses. DNA testing has since become an exact and reliable science.[193] Together with genetic databases, it now allows criminals to be identified even decades after their offense. Dental records began identifying murder victims. Tooth isotope analysis revealed where victims had grown up and sometimes events of their lives—whether they had been weaned and if they had ever starved. Toxicology pinpointed more wrongful poison deaths. Microscopic examination allowed crime's implements to be identified. Ballistics, the forensic analysis of bullets and firearms, became its own discipline in the late eighteenth century.[194] Chemistry was turned to detecting forgeries—of checks, wills, or artworks.

Over time, some technologies were displaced or discredited. Now supplanted by DNA analysis, the once popular microscopic inspection of hair proved largely worthless.[195] Graphology held the nineteenth-century world in thrall. It still retains adherents but has been largely discredited—indeed, handwriting itself is a technology in steep decline. Alphonse Bertillon—inventor of the mugshot—helped convict Alfred Dreyfus, the Jewish officer accused of treason against France in 1894, with convoluted claims that Dreyfus himself had written incriminating documents using a tracing method as though someone were forging his actual hand, thus giving him deniability.[196] Not that we have freed ourselves of charlatanry. Doubtful technologies of alleged expertise still sway juries, such as blood-spatter analysis, forensic investigation of clothing, and body-language scrutiny.[197] DNA analysis has instead become the gold standard, revisiting and upending past wrongful convictions based on more primitive technologies. "DNA testing is to justice what the telescope is for the stars," one of its early practitioners put it, "a way to see things as they really are. It is a revelation machine."[198] But its precision can and has been overstated, and its seeming accuracy has created problems. A German swab-manufacturing technician (dubbed the "Phantom of Heilbronn") inadvertently spread his own DNA to evidentiary samples and so appeared to be a prolific serial offender. Transplant recipients receive and incorporate the DNA of their donors and can leave it behind as traces. And people may plant misleading DNA at crime scenes.[199] More generally, such evidence supplies evermore ammunition for the common law's adversarial system. Experts duel for both sides, leaving juries to sort out whose testimony deserves credence.[200]

Keeping track of previous offenders has been vital. Mutilation and branding were once both an element of punishment and a convenient indicator of recidivism. Now we use the everyday singularities of the human body.[201] The British compiled a Register of Distinct Marks in the 1870s on the assumption that criminals' bodies were individual enough to allow identification.[202] Bertillon systematized this approach in the 1880s by measuring bodily dimensions for individual identification. This cumbersome anthropometrical method, Bertillonage, was overtaken by the (re)discovery late in the century that fingerprints were unique.[203] Fingerprinting also had the enormous advantage of combining a system of identification—like Bertillonage—with the evaluation of traces left behind at the crime scene. And today fingerprints can even be dated.[204] The more fingerprints, the more useful the database, and so the race was on to expand the files. By 1906, Australian police were routinely collecting fingerprints of known "bad characters under arrest." By the 1950s, the volume had become so large that some jurisdictions discontinued printing minors.[205] In the United States, the FBI amassed some eighty million fingerprints, only some of which belonged to criminals. Reformers pushed for universal or at least broad fingerprinting of all citizens.[206]

From the 1840s, photography, too, was used to identify offenders. The Prevention of Crimes Act of 1871 in England established a national photographic record.[207] In the 1880s, the mugshot was standardized by Bertillon. Unable to send photographs other than by mail, he also developed a system of written portraits to telegraph descriptions of suspects. This foreshadowed the algorithms that contemporary face-recognition technology uses to express images in machine-searchable formats. But, given the technology of the day, in fact most of these late nineteenth-century written portraits were largely identical, and few suspects without identifying marks were arrested on this basis.[208] Like fingerprints, DNA records even of nonconvicts are kept today. In France as of 2003, DNA profiles were collected from suspected offenders, with fines and jail for refusals, and of all inmates serving longer sentences.[209]

Quotidien Policing

As policing joined the state's machinery, many of its functions blended into everyday life. Data gathering hummed along in the background. Secret police and informers did their work covertly, but information was also amassed openly, often with subjects' active help. This was the "long, laborious, repulsive investigation" foreseen by Edwin Chadwick, the great Victorian social reformer, as necessary for preventive policing.[210]

In the Middle Ages, self-governing towns and cities decided who could live there, just as guilds and other corporations chose who exercised the professions. We take freedom of movement and residence, *Freizügigkeit*, for granted, at least within each nation, but it was one of the first civil rights won—in France with the revolution as intermediary organizations were abolished. But the state still wanted to know who lived where and worked as what. Deep into the twentieth century, localities could deny paupers residence.[211] The duty to register home addresses, broadly imposed across the European continent, helped police track suspects. Required to record visitors, hotels, too, were dragooned into the effort.[212] With *livrets* and other work papers, police could monitor apprentices' and journeymen's movements as of the mid-eighteenth century. Passports did the same for border crossings.[213] Their analogues also allowed control domestically in nations such as the Soviet Union and China today that restrict freedom of residence. When in the midst of the Seven Years' War Mr. Yorick in Laurence Sterne's novel *Sentimental Journey* (1768) traveled without any papers from London to Paris, the modern reader is amazed by the sheer haphazardness of it all.

Security cameras and traffic monitoring gather petabytes of data, tamed into intelligibility by face-recognition and other ordering technologies. A city dweller in Britain can expect to be filmed every five minutes. Police have become eager consumers of military and other databases. The satellite photos used by the Los Angeles police to place O. J. Simpson's white Bronco at the site of his wife's murder were supplied by a commercial company.[214] Police speed traps were set up in Britain already with the first speed limits in 1903. Radar and other remote monitoring of driving and random breathalyzer tests have turned all drivers into potential suspects. Even without being considered offenders, we are surveilled.[215] DNA databases allow authorities to identify offenders using family resemblances from samples of relatives, not just to confirm suspicions of guilt based on other evidence. Automated face recognition coupled with blanket closed-circuit television coverage has undermined the anonymity once expected in public.[216] Every year the London police crack some two thousand cases using fingerprints and another two thousand with DNA. But in 2016 they solved twenty-five hundred cases using imagery and face recognition—and more cheaply, too. In 2018, the Chinese police used face recognition to spot a suspect in a concert audience of sixty thousand. The culprit had hoped he would blend in.[217] Durkheim's proverb "One is nowhere so well hidden as in a crowd" no longer held. Virtual policing at a distance had arrived.[218]

Computer-analyzed big data have begun to routinize the constant background surveillance of all citizens, suspects and innocents alike, begun by traffic monitoring. By uncovering patterns indiscernible to the naked eye, digital analysis lays bare what once was secret—criminal or not.[219] Indoor marijuana farms in bland suburbia have been betrayed in the days of incandescent lighting by exorbitant electricity bills. Insider trading has been revealed by analyzing stock sales patterns in the run-up to important corporate announcements. Radiologists are being displaced by computerized detection of clinical anomalies in medical scans, and doctors use pattern-recognition technology to diagnose rare diseases that mark our faces. Algorithms have been able to discern the sexuality of photographed persons better than human observers, and they predict recidivism as well as professionals do.[220] The body continues to betray the soul. Without torture, observers can still penetrate our interiors. More mundanely, big data feed the actuarial calculations that foresee who will reoffend. Algorithms analyze homicide data, identifying subtle similarities among cases and thus indicating serial killers at work.[221] Police forces in Chicago and New Orleans have data trawled through police records, social media, and auto records to identify likely future offenders and crime hot spots. Though the results have been mixed, the trend is undeniable.[222]

Today's data-drenched surveillance technologies arguably reachieve on a global scale the transparency and lack of privacy once characteristic of the village community. Urban anonymity and the policing functions it required may turn out to have been a two-century blip in a longer continuity of panoptic self-policing. As more accurate information is gleaned from freely available observation, strengthened privacy may not suffice to shield citizens. Laws protecting privacy assume that legally enforceable ignorance of what you want to keep to yourself is a goal in itself, worth defending. In fact, privacy is but a crude and indirect means of achieving the real aim: ensuring that we do not suffer from others knowing what were once our secrets. When we no longer can hide information, privacy promises little. Assuming instead that greater transparency is inevitable, whether privacy protections are beefed up or not, it is arguably better to protect against being persecuted by others who now know what once was kept under wraps. We achieve autonomy more effectively by strengthening other rights than by hiding behind an ever less opaque veil of privacy.

Policing has also been baked into everyday life by gradually hardening the environment against crime. Theft, for example, was once a different sort of offense. There were fewer things to steal, and they were more easily identifiable because hand-made and unique. Even coins were once—in medieval Iceland—individually identifiable.[223] With the largely interchangeable artifacts of mass industrialization, however, theft is often not worth the bother of investigating. Women's jewelry, its sentimental value often greater than its market value, is among the last kind of item we seek to retrieve, not just to replace. We have instead socialized theft's cost through compensation or insurance, simply substituting largely fungible goods. Items whose return is worth pursuing we make even more unique by tagging them with serial numbers or other identifiers (and sometimes even by swabbing them with human DNA). Yet even with mass consumption, society seeks to make fungible goods less available. Early modern burglars often tortured their victims to reveal where valuables were hidden.[224] Today safes and bank deposit boxes have the musty air of a declining technology. Muggers might force victims to reveal their ATM pin codes, but the amount and number of withdrawals that can be made are limited, anyway. Credit instruments have reduced the valuables in circulation. In the early nineteenth century, cattle salesmen who once carried cash began using checks, postdating them so that if they were stolen, the funds could be frozen.[225] Stripping cash out of retail transactions has diminished the incentives for theft. In return, crime has gone cashless, too, targeting digital repositories of value—identity theft, internet fraud, and the like.

Theft is now an increasingly socialized risk, yet it has also become more difficult. The early modern thief faced few obstacles. Today, there is more to pilfer, but it is harder to do so. Locks have become evermore intricate, resistant, and cheap—allowing everyone the security of the rich person's strongbox. Lockpicking is a skill in terminal decline. As simple bolts, locks merely impeded intrusion into an occupied space. The development of the key allowed owners privacy and security even when they went out. Homer described an early version of such a contraption, and Christ promised Peter the keys to heaven.[226] Locks were two-faced. They protected people from each other and from the state. As in our own debates over encryption software (a digital lock), the state also demanded access to physical locks for its own authorized purposes. In Plato's republic, the Guardians—with nothing to hide—were forbidden locks on their doors. When that prohibition was no longer possible, the state still demanded entry. Following a bombing of the tsar's train in November 1879, the authorities ordered St. Petersburg students to leave their keys in the door, allowing the police to enter at will. The Nazis required known criminals to leave duplicate house keys with the police.[227] The US Transportation Security Administration–approved luggage lock is the modern version of this pas de deux of citizen and authority. It protects us against each other but not against the state and its authorized intrusion.

Making the environment crime resistant goes back almost as far as the lock itself. The Statute of Winchester in 1285 prescribed what current terminology calls "target hardening" of highways between market towns. They were to be broadened, with woods and hedges pruned back on either side to eliminate hiding places for robbers.[228] In the late seventeenth century, London required house owners to light public spaces by hanging lanterns in front of their homes between nightfall and curfew's onset. Only in the following century did that become a municipal task, centrally organized and paid by taxes. Robberies on highways were down, Edwin Chadwick celebrated in the early nineteenth century, in part because street lighting discouraged thieves.[229] Just as sunlight is the best disinfectant, Supreme Court justice Louis Brandeis agreed, so electric light is the most efficient policeman.[230] Lest we forget how terrifyingly crimogenic darkness was in pre-electric days, recall that committing an offense at night was long considered an aggravating element—as late as in the Napoleonic penal code. Burglary even today, defined as a nocturnal crime in Britain, can be punished more harshly than its daylight pendant, housebreaking.[231]

In our own day, ordinances in Florida hamper robbery by requiring late-night convenience stores to remove window ads, making their interiors visible from the street.[232] Shopping centers broadcast high-pitched sounds audible only to young ears to discourage teenagers from congregating. In the United States, post-9/11 federal buildings were built to resist bombs, while not resembling bunkers.[233] Over the years, coins were made harder to shave, paper currency less easy to counterfeit, checks more difficult to forge.[234] Credit cards once required signatures, then pin codes; phones needed pin codes, then finger prints or face recognition. Safes became harder to crack, cars more theft resistant. Ignition keys stopped thieves from starting cars, and steering-column immobilizers prevented them from being driven even if hotwired. Improved registries of ownership impeded selling stolen vehicles for parts. GPS technology can locate stolen automobiles almost instantly, and kill switches immobilize them. Thefts of cars have plummeted (by 96 percent in New York City since the 1990s), with only older models still targeted.[235] A fully crime-resistant environment will eventually leave little to chance, constantly supervise its residents, instantly monitor outsiders, and never allow offensive situations to arise. In other words, we will one day live in something akin to today's theme parks.[236]

Preventive Policing

Policing has been a preventive enterprise from the start. Making punishment collective gave many a stake in encouraging would-be offenders not to act in the first place. While society was organized in small communities, the state had little choice but to hope for enforcement from families, towns, corporations, and churches. Though the state might make the initial move, last-mile policing fell to civil society. Sureties and bonds required such intermediary groups to vouch for their members' behavior, often punishing everyone if individuals strayed. In China, groups of five to ten households were held responsible for each member's conduct. The *silin* were the immediately proximate households that were duty bound to keep an eye out for illegal or immoral behavior and reform or report it. Failure to report criminal activity could result in bisection at the waist, while those who turned in offenders were rewarded like those returning from battle with an enemy's head. Family members could also sometimes substitute for each other in serving prison sentences. In the 1950s, the Communists saddled work units with similar collective policing duties.[237]

Sureties in pre-Norman England held those who had posted them—sometimes the entire community—liable for the actions of others and subject to the punishment the offenders dodged by failing to appear for trial. Most extremely, those who acted as sureties were required to kill their charges if they continued to offend.[238] The Statute of Winchester continued this system, imposing collective responsibility on the hundreds. Under the frankpledge, every adult male was enrolled in a group of ten (a tithing), and it in turn in a group of one hundred, which guaranteed the appearance of its members in court and paid fines in their absence.[239] Aztecs punished kin for both treason and drunkenness by their family members. In fifteenth- and sixteenth-century Russia, communities were collectively fined or flogged for members' transgressions.[240] Revolutionary France, which otherwise mandated individual liability, held communities collectively responsible for violent crimes and damages, except when offenders were demonstrably from elsewhere. The Soviets and Nazis punished and sometimes executed families of deserters.[241] In the era of community policing, everyone was in effect a vigilante.

As with most other early means of enforcement, even when policing finally fell mainly to the state, sureties and bonds remained—used against labor leaders in the United States in the 1930s and against antiwar demonstrators in the 1960s.[242] Canadians can still demand sureties, obliging each other to keep the peace. Anyone who fears harm to person or property or to spouse or child—for example, sex with a minor or publication of intimate photographs—can ask a court to require the defendant to sign a recognizance, promising to behave, with prison a threat otherwise. In 2014, a Canadian radio broadcaster, fired after allegations of sexual harassment, avoided one charge by agreeing to a peace bond guaranteeing his good behavior for a year.[243] Chinese corporations are expected to police their employees even outside the workplace and are held accountable for their offenses.[244] Bail grew out of the English variant of this approach in the thirteenth century. Prisoners were released into the custody of sureties who vouched for them. No distinction was drawn, legally speaking, between being in jail and being under the guardianship of the surety. This system broadly continues today in the United States, where commercial bondsmen have full custodial rights over bailees, whom they guarantee to bring to trial.[245]

Even more obviously preventive were individual pledges of good behavior. Ulysses famously tied himself to the mast to avoid succumbing to temptation. The Egyptians formalized the precautions individuals imposed on themselves. A man whose family tomb abutted another's was made to swear in court that should he steal from the neighboring grave, he would be impaled, and his nose and ears cut off. Another Egyptian promised in court that if he divorced his wife, he would suffer a hundred blows and forfeit his share of their common property. Medieval Europe's peaces obliged men to abjure violence, punishing them if they violated their word. In fourteenth-century England, the binding-over system gave the authorities—often prompted by private parties—power to require certain behaviors of someone on payment of a bond, which would be forfeited in default.[246] Justices of the peace in Britain could demand sureties of those who threatened to beat or kill others, who brandished unusual weapons, who spoke intemperately, or who were quarrelsome. Indeed, anyone could demand sureties if willing to swear to the truth of the threat. Those of demonstrably bad character were also liable: people who consorted with prostitutes, badmouthed the authorities, slept during the day or were out at night, sired illegitimate children, or were thieves, eavesdroppers, drunkards, cheats, or vagabonds.[247] Released prisoners in France had to post a cash security and could be ordered to live where the authorities designated, which as of 1851 meant outside of Paris or its suburbs.[248] More generally, the institution of the oath was a form of preventive self-policing, the act of committing oneself to a certain standard of conduct.

Policing in the form of Polizei was inherently preventive. It was woven into society's fabric, ordering and regulating almost every aspect of the community. As social engineering, it sought to prevent not only crime but also poverty, disease, hunger, pollution, unemployment, addiction, bad housing, illiteracy, and, indeed, most other social ills. The French revolutionaries designated part of policing as administrative, tasked with maintaining public order and thus with preventing offenses.[249] What the English considered preventive policing—the scarecrow function of men in uniform—was by comparison much narrower: deterring by making police presence obvious. Polizei, in contrast, dealt with the causes of crime by regulating society as a whole. Yet even the continental nations eventually narrowed the police role to solving crimes and maintaining order in the superficial sense of public placidity. Modern policing let society run its course, reacting only in a specific and localized manner to punish transgressions after the fact.

Nonetheless, modern policing also had its preventive aspects. If crime were worth punishing after the fact, all the more reason to sidestep it in the first place. Spies and informers gave the police a head start on offenses. As we have seen, the law began to intervene evermore anticipatorily. Policing followed suit, expanding from a post facto reactive rounding up of miscreants to a preventive throttling of crime in the cradle. Preventive policing had been baked into traditional society's small *gemeinschaftlich* communities where privacy was scant and everyone's business public knowledge. Strangers could not settle there, and no one was unknown. Reputation was part of society's informal information control. But in the anonymity of big cities, the authorities had to grow their own ears and eyes. Surveying the world from the compact urbanity of late eighteenth-century Edinburgh, Adam Smith noted that people in small communities were known, their actions observed. By misbehaving, they forfeited their good character and reputation. But in large cities residents could do as they pleased.[250]

Bereft of help from offenders' kin or community, metropolitan police had less chance to solve old crimes and therefore an incentive to prevent new ones. By surveillance, spying, warnings, and anticipatory arrests, police identified and supervised potential offenders, seeking to forecast what was coming. When the London bobbies were first organized in the 1830s, they were reactive, maintaining a public presence to deter crime and responding when that failed. But police gradually began investigating on their own initiative, gathering data to foresee and solve crimes, and deciding whom to keep tabs on. They even organized or facilitated transgressions to elicit offenses (i.e., soliciting sex, offering bribes or to buy drugs, receiving stolen property, and even paying for murder), thus entrapping the too easily tempted with sting operations.[251]

Like the law, the police were preventive in different ways. Most rudimentarily, they deterred. A constant, uniformed, visible police presence reminded citizens they were under scrutiny. London watchmen occupied their stations throughout the night, while town criers walked the streets.[252] Nighttime curfews kept potential miscreants in bed. Police actively patrolled neighborhoods, seeking out crime and not just waiting for burghers to report offenses. The London and New York forces made such proactive intervention part of metropolitan life.[253] In the words of the instructions issued to its superintendent in 1829, the London police should make "it evident to all such that they are known and strictly watched, and that certain detection will follow any attempt they may make to commit the crime."[254] By their continual presence, Patrick Colquhoun's London river police deterred theft of cargo from boats. The French rural police of the nineteenth century, the *gardes champêtres,* were also said to prevent merely by being there.[255]

Uniformed officers were visible deterrents—at least until they became taken for granted. As in the military, uniforms held their wearers to account. Much as mercenary soldiers in military regalia were dissuaded from melting away in battle, so uniforms hampered the police from repairing to the nearest bar rather than walk their beat in the cold. And it held them responsible. By contrast, plainclothes police occasionally shirked duties or acted unaccountably—as they sometimes do today.[256] Uniforms also kept police from secrecy, stealth, or subterfuge. The English made much of how their bobbies in blue (not red, the military color of the day) were the antithesis of the continent's civilian and therefore secret police. Though not conventionally uniformed, the London police were recognizable in their blue-tailed coats and top hats (which were reinforced so that in a pinch they served as stools to peer over walls). To avoid being confused with autocratic secret police, bobbies wore their uniform even off duty.[257] The Parisian police of the eighteenth century also patrolled in uniform. The *sergents de ville* sported blue uniforms, bicorne hats, and a white cane during the day but a saber by night. By the late nineteenth century, European police were uniformly uniformed, with the most splendid regalia found in Hamburg, the shabbiest in Glasgow.[258]

The issue was more complicated in the United States. Uniforms were initially resisted to avoid suggestions that police were a military-style force but also because they were considered socially degrading. In the 1830s, even servants refused livery, as did railroad conductors and police. They gave in only later in the century as labor-market competition heated up. In 1844, officers in New York trialing new blue uniforms were hissed and stoned. Yet uniforms eventually won out. They enhanced the police's moral authority and also helped civilians avoid picking inadvertent fights with authorities in civvies. In 1853, New York police began wearing them on a regular basis.[259]

To this day, the police deter crime through an ongoing public presence. Zero-tolerance policing, introduced in the 1980s as a constant neighborhood patrolling, deliberately turned away from the hyperreactive 911 style of policing at a distance. Even with the most rapid 911 response times, police nabbed only a tiny fraction of criminals in the act (3 percent in some studies). Tactics were therefore rejiggered. Officers continuously patrolled on foot, exercising a low-level discretionary authority to maintain order. That returned them to the scarecrow function implemented by the London bobbies more than a century earlier.[260] Community policing likewise provided a constant uniformed presence and a willingness to handle disorder and minor offenses, not just intermittently pursue serious crime. This made policing a more persistent, intrusive, and ongoing intervention into communities than the 911 style. Day after day, the police warned and advised, sending drunks home in taxis, shooing juveniles off the street, warning lovers to shun dangerous parks, cautioning the disorderly.[261] Everyday policing approximated the Japanese model, where officers behaved more like postal workers, patiently following quotidian routines, than firefighters, rousted only in emergencies. Most Japanese police work not in patrol cars, but from local mini stations, the Koban, keeping an eye on neighborhoods.[262] Similarly, the Chinese use "grid managers" as a form of community control to keep an informal check on residents.[263]

As we have seen, target hardening, or building crime resistance into everyday infrastructure, also rudimentarily prevented offending by tamping down opportunities and temptations. A variant was the increasing passive knowledge that police collected on citizens. Routine sobriety checkpoints and other forms of suspicionless testing, such as workplace drug probes, identified offenders and encouraged compliance by heightening the risk of being caught.[264] Broad, possibly universal DNA collection will likely soon dampen offending—at least by rational would-be perpetrators. As the traces we leave behind in public reveal evermore information about us (about our diets from a dried drop of sweat via metabolite analysis, for example), our hope of keeping secrets will diminish.[265]

Deterrence and everyday keeping order were just the start of the preventive effort. Deterrence did not demand any deep investigation, though omnipresent authority—its trump card—required resources. Moving beyond deterrence, the authorities also sought to get out ahead of crime. As new crimes were formulated, the police's remit expanded. Thoughts—the motor of potential offenses—had long been under the glass. As the concept of inchoate offenses developed, the authorities had to investigate before or in the absence of the fact. Crimes without victims or witnesses could not await first being reported, nor could offenses where victims might not even know they had been harmed—fraud, say, or toxic-waste dumping.[266]

Some preventive policing was direct and uncomplicated. In the 1930s, US police goon squads targeted violent criminals who enforced business deals or extorted payments. These offenders were known to the authorities, who cruised in patrol cars until they recognized one, beating and disarming him. Decoy units were used to catch robbers, sting operations to nab burglars. Illicit-drug marketplaces were patrolled, and special units kept tabs on repeat offenders.[267] The police sought those most likely to offend. They extrapolated from past behavior and the characteristics of specific groups to anticipate future acts. Certain categories of people were statistically likely to have offended. Belonging to one was therefore often treated as tantamount to having committed a crime. Predictions based on past conduct or on characteristics statistically associated with offending justified laws that targeted certain statuses or behaviors as proxies for others. Being statistically associated with offending often became a crime in itself.

Such guilt by proxy was not new. Those classified as *landschädlich* (harmful to the land) in the twelfth century (mainly robber knights and peasant vagabonds) were not allowed to defend themselves by oath and thus were legally disadvantaged. Nightwalkers were considered inherently suspicious and punished. Scolds were chastised in the early modern era for being just that and so made to wear bridles.[268] In sixteenth-century England, Jesuits were declared ipso facto traitors. In early modern and Victorian Britain and in the Napoleonic penal code, being a vagrant was punished regardless of any specific acts.[269] Loiterers could be arrested for that reason alone in England as of 1824. So in 1829 could loose, idle, and disorderly Londoners as well as anyone lying down or loitering in public between sunset and morning.[270] Loitering with intent to commit a felony was punishable, and after 1869 even the intent was not required for former convicts. The interwar fascist regimes also singled out political opponents and so-called asocial elements, aside from their supposedly racial enemies.[271] Japanese Americans were interred during World War II as enemy sympathizers because of their ethnicity. In 1934, New Jersey outlawed being a gangster, defined—among other ways—as possessing a machine gun while not in the military. A

Chicago ordinance in the 1970s forbade habitual drunkards, addicts, prostitutes, or felons from meeting in public.[272]

Gang membership has often been criminalized.[273] If done in high-crime areas, otherwise legal behaviors have allowed police to stop suspects. British police gained broad powers to temporarily contain suspects, excluding certain categories of people from specific areas, stopping and searching, detaining for questioning, and remanding them to custody.[274] Tax authorities have used algorithms to identify filers worth auditing. Terrorists have been targeted as such, before any act.[275] Airport-security profiles justify pulling aside likely hijackers or drug couriers. Police have employed an array of shorthand descriptions of potential offenders: the car-thief profile, the poacher profile, the serial-killer profile—and, of course, not forgetting the alimentary-canal-smuggler profile. With a touching faith in reverse psychology, one Florida state trooper developed a drug-courier profile that targeted those who hoped to avoid drawing attention by driving through his remote beat precisely at the speed limit.[276]

Though modern policing sought more sophisticated criteria, it relied most heavily on past offenses to calculate the probability of future transgression.[277] However crude, bygone behavior proved to be the most reliable indicator of that to come. Crime came to be seen not just as a one-off, spontaneous fluke but as the outcome of character, habit, or proclivity. Sentencing recidivists more harshly followed logically as a preventive tactic, even though it targeted the person more than the act. Recidivism was a self-fulfilling prophecy. As record keeping improved in the late nineteenth century, the British and French authorities recognized that crimes were disproportionately committed by a small group of hardened roués.[278] In Britain, the Habitual Criminals Act of 1869 imposed seven years of police supervision for second-time felony offenders, with swift summary punishment for subsequent crimes.[279] As of the 1880s, France relegated repeat offenders to penal colonies for life, while Italy used *domicilio coatto*, a form of internal exile.[280]

Louisiana passed a habitual offenders statute in 1870, allowing doubled and tripled prison terms for second and third offenses and a life term for a fourth. Britain's Prevention of Crime Act of 1908 targeted repeat offenders with indefinite preventive detention added to the sentences already imposed. US laws in the 1930s imposed life sentences for fourth felony convictions.[281] American three-strikes (habitual-offender) laws in the 1990s followed a similar logic. Ever-harsher subsequent punishments were not tailored to the crime but assumed that past offenses predicted future ones. They were in effect a form of preventive detention. Unfortunate results followed, such as lifelong prison for petty thefts, which had been haphazardly classified as felonies.[282]

Predicting future behavior on the foregone meant believing that past acts betrayed a quality likely to repeat itself. Based on psychology, as a reading of character or proclivity, this type of prediction might have been plausible. Based on actuarial calculations associating certain citizens with particular behaviors, however, it had at most probability going for it. Two big problems bedeviled such reasoning. First, requiring a history of transgression meant that offenders were identified as recidivists only late in their criminal careers. Yet offending is largely inversely proportional to age, the old obeying the law more than the young. When someone could finally be identified as a dangerous recidivist, chances were that he no longer was.[283]

Second, if recidivism were a proxy for an underlying causal variable, then the problem had only been pushed back one level. To suspect someone on the basis of demographic, economic, social, or other indicators came close to criminalizing a certain status. But if a status were outlawed, how could being in breach of that status ever end? Status based on volitional behaviors was one thing: scolds could perhaps bite their tongues, vagrants find housing and a job. But being born in a poor neighborhood to immigrant ethnic minority parents was a potentially lifelong condition, impossible to overcome. Even so, targeting status rather than act proved a durable policing tactic. In 1962, the logic was challenged in the United States when a law making it illegal to be an alcoholic was struck down.[284] Yet to distinguish legally between status and act proved difficult. Sometimes status made certain acts unavoidable. The homeless had no choice but to sleep and drink in the open. So laws forbidding public drinking, though technically targeting acts, effectively also punished status.[285] Rarely has jurisprudence come so close to Anatole France's trenchant bon mot about the law in its majestic impartiality forbidding both rich and poor from sleeping under bridges.

Despite flaws, actuarial predictions have increasingly been used to target recidivists and thus to prolong their sentences by denying them probation or parole and supervising them after release. The authorities have also moved to prevent future acts by the potentially dangerous. Restraining orders, antistalking orders, antiloitering laws, limits on residence and employment, and restrictions on weapons have been tactics. In Chicago, thousands of young men on a "heat list" of those statistically predicted most likely to die in violent crime are warned by teams of detectives and social workers of their risk in hopes of turning their lives around. In Kansas City, police routinely gather young—often Black and Hispanic—lawbreakers to caution them that if caught again even for minor infractions, they will suffer the severest penalties possible.[286] Extreme risk protection, or "red flag," orders allowed authorities to deny access to weapons for those thought to pose threats. The US "war on drugs" permitted police to serve search-and-arrest warrants on sellers and users preemptively through no-knock raids.[287] The implements of crime were also targeted. As we have seen, possessing the requisite tools has been used as evidence of inchoate crimes such as conspiracy and attempt. Targeting mere possession made it easier to prosecute. Confiscating tools mixed prevention and punishment.[288] Impounding a john's auto might deter prostitution, but it also punished his wife as its co-owner. The same held for the house where drugs were stashed. Confiscating the cash intended for a drug buy became in effect a fine on intent.[289] Together with punitive fines, such civil asset forfeitures built on the logic of deodands—punishing the things that had offended—and added a retributive element to civil cases.[290]

Preventive sentencing, too, has become a large-caliber weapon in the arsenal of anticipatory enforcement. Why, after all, identify likely offenders if not to render them harmless? Subordinating individual rights to the public good, sentencing in anticipation of offending has understandably sparked controversy. Law enforcement here adopted a technique long common in public health, restricting the freedom of those whose travels, contacts, habits, or proclivities made them epidemiological threats. A community danger justified civil rights restrictions.[291] The Old Testament imposed isolation and cleansing on those with unclean bodily discharges.[292] In fourteenth-century Venice, arrivals on ships from infected ports were detained for the forty days that the medicine of the day took to be the plague's incubation period. Suspected prostitutes were compulsorily tested for venereal disease in the nineteenth century. If infected, they were detained and treated. In the 1980s, Swedish and US authorities jailed HIV seropositives who continued to have unsafe sex.[293] Sufferers of drug-resistant tuberculosis have been compulsorily medicated and sometimes detained, epileptics and narcoleptics forbidden to drive.[294] Modern citizens suffer legally imposed bodily violations such as vaccination for the community's good. The motives of such interventions mix concern for the afflicted with the desire to protect society at large, but the results impinge on the rights of individuals. All nations permit drastic interventions in emergencies. Faced with the coronavirus pandemic in early 2020, China imposed mass quarantines on several cities. Even otherwise liberal Denmark enabled its authorities temporarily to compel inspection, isolation, vaccination, and treatment of victims, end public assemblies, blockade neighborhoods, shut down transportation, forbid visits to hospitals and care homes, and close institutions.[295] Thanks to the gravity of the potential consequences for not acquiescing to such public-health legislation, it has been broadly uncontroversial despite its draconian effects.

Preventive sentencing—selective incapacitation—expanded this logic to more people.[296] Those judged to be risks could be detained or restrained even before trial. Already imposed sentences could be extended. To avoid the penal code's due-process restrictions, civil law was mustered to give the authorities more leeway.[297] These impositions—not for offenses committed but for ones that might occur—moved punishment far from its retributive foundations. Not only were predictions unavoidably vague and often inaccurate, but even had they been true, holding potential offenders accountable for crimes not yet committed also amplified the utilitarian logic of subordinating individual rights to community needs.

In principle, an accused is presumptively innocent before being convicted and should therefore not be incarcerated, but detaining arrestees even before trial and conviction has become more common. Many nations make little or no use of bail or other means of pretrial release: most of the European continent and Japan, for example.[298] Half of all prisoners in Italy and France remain jailed on remand, awaiting trial. Suspects in Japan can be jailed for twenty-three days before charges are brought.[299] Even in the Anglo-American systems, the role of bail, which has been used since the early Middle ages, has shrunk. In England, a third of defendants are held in custody before trial, on average for nine weeks, though a quarter of those for up to half a year. In the United States, the bail bond industry allows release for those able to pay (usually 10 percent of bail). Even so, about a third of US arrestees remain jailed until trial.[300]

Not only those accused of crime were jailed before trial. Pretrial detention was the obverse of bail. Rather than assuming innocence before guilt was determined, even those whose offense was merely being potentially dangerous were jailed. Starting in the 1960s, the US and Britain passed laws allowing pretrial preventive detention. These laws made explicit judges' informal ability to detain suspects preventively by setting excessive bail. Judges could then deny bail to or impose other restrictions on defendants considered likely to commit crimes in the interim.[301] After trial, the sentences of those deemed to be risks have also been extended. Most countries allow prolonging the sentences of defendants considered special threats. The Netherlands have "detention at the Government's pleasure," for two years at a time, indefinitely extendable by court decision; the Germans have *Sicherungsverwahrung*. Canada, too, allows preventive detention for indefinite terms of those considered habitual criminals.[302] This tactic is also applied to sex offenders, as discussed in the next section.

To defang objections to this side-stepping of due-process restrictions, the civil law was also roped in. Civil preventive orders were marshaled against offenses that although perhaps not quite criminal were sufficiently noisome to be worth targeting.[303] They imposed punishments similar to the penal code, including jail, while having to meet only the civil law's lower standard of proof. In the United States, such orders began being levied in the 1970s against gangs and juvenile offenders as well as against nuisance and public-order behaviors and drug- and alcohol-related conduct. The Supreme Court allowed civil commitment of the potentially dangerous without the full due-process protection of criminal cases.[304] Britain, too, enthusiastically adopted the technique early in the new millennium. A dozen variants emerged, from Anti-Social Behavior Orders (ASBOs) to Serious Crime Prevention Orders, Risk of Sexual Harm Orders, and Terrorism Prevention and Investigation Measures.[305] Authorities could close noisy or drug-infested premises, pursue parents of chronically truant or misbehaved children, restrict where sex offenders could live or work, restrain people from harassing others, and disperse groups in public. ASBOs could last indeterminately and apply to offenders as young as ten. Breaching them was a criminal offense punishable by prison for up to five years or fines or both.[306] Allowing the authorities broad discretion against low-level behaviors that individually might not have triggered sanctions but that collectively and over time were a nuisance, ASBOs were often eccentrically applied: the pirate DJ who had broadcast from a top floor forbidden ever to set foot in a building taller than four stories; the car thief prohibited from entering any parking lot anywhere for any purpose; the suicidal woman who had to promise not to approach rivers, lakes, or railway bridges; the hip-hop musicians forbidden to mention death, injury, or competing musicians in their songs.[307]

As the definition of crime expanded, the authorities were evermore concerned with risks, not committed offenses. Getting out ahead of crime meant investigating plans drawn up, intents formulated, conspiracies hatched, and dangers posed. Interrogative techniques were developed to ascertain what was being planned. Police noted, for example, that although dissembling about past events was often less detailed than truthful recounting of what had happened, for future plans the level of detail—with no actual experience to narrate—between false and true accounts was largely similar.[308] Once the authorities began trying to prevent risk, few behaviors were indifferent, and almost all citizens potentially posed a threat.[309] Preventive detention inevitably affected many false positives, people who were locked up even though they would have committed no crime. But falsely jailed innocents were less conspicuous in the media and political debate than the guilty set free to offend. Once established, a preventive system thus invariably generated data in favor of its expansion.[310] The logical extreme was universal preventive detention, the ability to detain anyone considered a possible threat. In effect, all citizens began to be treated as parolees.[311]

Catholic inquisitors rooting out Cathar heretics in thirteenth-century Languedoc had taken this approach. All sentences were for life, in principle. Even after the sinner had been released, the issue could be revisited at any moment, adding new penalties for relapses or extending existing ones.[312] Indeterminate sentencing and conditional release, practiced increasingly in most Western nations as of the late nineteenth century, applied a similar logic. Whether in or out of prison, offenders remained within the carceral loop. Laws on habitual criminality in the English colonies, modeled on the homeland, permitted police to keep discharged prisoners under surveillance and to search the dwellings of those suspected of receiving stolen goods. The Prussian penal code allowed indefinite detention of thieves and other dangerous offenders until they showed they could provide for themselves honestly on release. Napoleon imposed postrelease surveillance on former prisoners that lasted from two years to life, depending on the offense, with the authorities allowed to decide where they could live.[313]

In 1877, the prison administrator Zebulon Brockway proposed a law in New York to make all sentences indeterminate, releasing only the compliant. This law was adopted only partly, and parole and probation have fallen out of favor in the United States since the 1970s. But something like indefinite sentencing is now imposed, as we will see, on sex offenders.[314] In New York City, a common outcome of misdemeanor arrests is to adjourn the case for some specified time, then dismiss it if the defendant has not been rearrested in the meantime. The British Criminal Justice Act of 2003 allowed mandatory life sentences. Prisoners could be released at the discretion of the parole board but remained on license for life, reincarcerated if judged a risk.[315]

Universal preventive detention, where all citizens are treated as parolees, differs from our own state by degree, not kind. We are all on notice. At the end of Franz Kafka's novel *The Trial*, the court artist tells Joseph K. that final acquittals are elusive, the court forgets nothing, and he can be hauled before it again on renewed charges. Any citizen who offends is naturally subject to official attention. Yet as the definition of crime has expanded to new acts and to ever-earlier preparatory stages of potential offenses, the chances of being investigated have expanded, too. In no case is that truer than with sex offenders.

Sex Crimes

Though homicide is the oldest crime, rape must have been a close second.[316] As long as there has been law, it has been punished—though motivated at first more by the damage done the property interests of father, lord, or husband than by consideration for the woman. Male-on-male rape has long been punished, too—primarily as a violation of strictures on sodomy.[317] Statutory rape expanded the offense as the age of consent was raised. That change required adjusting for the relative ages of the parties involved, distinguishing between older predators and young lovers. What counted as consent has been debated, too, as reformers sought to ensure that rape was treated as a real crime, not merely an indiscretion. Allowing adultery to be punished within the family was long tolerated. Today, sexual betrayal is no longer considered a crime and excuses neither battery nor murder.

Sex crimes became the object of particular attention at the turn of the millennium, especially pedophilia. Even while the incidence of rape and sexual assault was falling, convictions for sex offenses quadrupled in the 1990s. Between 10 percent and 20 percent of state prisoners in the US are now locked up for such reasons. Incarceration for child porn and other sexually explicit material increased more than sixtyfold between 1996 and 2010.

Because pedophilia—along with incest and cannibalism—is universally regarded as viscerally repugnant, few objected as punishments grew more severe. Sentences for pedophilia and child pornography lengthened. The PROTECT (Prosecutorial Remedies and Other Tools to End the Exploitation of Children Today) Act of 2003 in the United States imposed mandatory life on those convicted of child sexual abuse for a second time. Arizona required ten-year sentences for each illegal porn image possessed, thus life in most instances. The average federal child porn sentence became longer than for all other crimes except murder and kidnapping.[318] Long criminal sentences for pedophilia are now often supplemented by extensions under civil law, allowing offenders believed likely to recommit to be held beyond their initial verdicts—sometimes indefinitely.[319] In 1997, the Supreme Court upheld an instance of someone civilly committed for life in anticipation of crimes he might commit.[320] The Adam Walsh Act in 2006 allowed sex offenders to be detained indefinitely after their sentences were complete if they were considered dangerous. Nor did such civil detentions count as a double-jeopardy bar to criminal prosecution for the same action.[321]

Sexual harm against children, including real-life pornography, is indisputably evil. Virtual pornography—comics, anime, drawings, and the like—poses the question of what precisely is being prohibited. If no actual child has been harmed in making it, how and why are viewers of it culpable? For their thoughts? For the corruption of social morality that follows when some are depraved in private (much as Devlin had insisted that private immorality is as impossible as private subversive activity)? What is the underlying crime? Is it enhanced when technologies go beyond two-dimensional porn, allowing viewers to participate actively in on-screen or soon-to-be fully immersive virtual-reality experiences of seducing, raping, or worse? Should it be a crime to sexually violate in cyberspace? Or to do things to pretend minors (virtual ageplay) that would be illegal in the wetware world? *Second World*, a virtual ecosystem, for example, allows sex with minor avatars.[322] No doubt it is but a pale simulacrum of what fully developed virtual reality will soon deliver. The burgeoning sex-robot industry also stands ready to tailor product to any taste—including devices resembling specific identifiable children.[323] Should virtual rape of a facsimile of an actual human be treated as similar to inflicting emotional distress?[324] Would we then be outlawing ideas or fantasies outside of actual harm?

Those who advocate forbidding even virtual pornography have marshaled a Devlian logic on the collateral social damage that follows in immorality's wake. First, much virtual porn still manipulates images of existing children, thus harming actual victims. Arguing that their materials were virtual, pornographers have in fact sometimes been exonerated.[325] But even born-digital images, with no real-world referent, might have noxious knock-on effects. Pedophiles could harness virtual porn to convince actual children that joining in was normal and fun. Perhaps they thus whetted their own sexual appetites, raising the chances of an actual sexual encounter.[326] But perhaps by having such material—as is also argued for pornography in general—they thus satiated their desires harmlessly, lessening the chances of real-world offenses.[327] Did virtual porn encourage the idea of children as sexual objects and therefore put them at risk?[328] Arguments at this level of generality cut both ways. Attempts to prosecute child porn also kept the topic in the limelight, helping sexualize children. A case in 1993 determined that even images of clothed children (videos of young girls striking poses in bathing suits) could be pornographic. Cases involving mainstream advertising (Calvin Klein) parsed seemingly innocent photos of children and adolescents in terms of whether their genitals were discernable beneath the underwear, whether they thrust forth their pelvic regions, and the like. Some pedophiles find innocent images the most alluring, thus impeding hopes of policing, forbidding, or even defining child porn except in the most expansive of terms.[329] Since even innocuous images can prompt outlawed thoughts, what is not illegal?

Undaunted by these conundrums, the law plowed ahead. Britain outlawed "pseudophotographs" in 1994, apparently aiming at computer-generated composite photographs of real people.[330] In 2001, article 9 of the European Convention on Cybercrime defined child porn to include both the virtual and the real.[331] In 1996, the United States banned virtual child pornography, including any image that "is, or appears to be, of a minor engaging in sexually explicit conduct," whether a computer-generated minor or an adult who looks underage. It was forbidden to possess, produce, sell, transport, ship, receive, mail, and distribute such images in interstate or foreign commerce and by any means, including electronic. Also forbidden were all pornographic images of children, whether of actual or computer-generated or morphed children or of youthful-looking adults.[332] Aspects of this law were struck down by the Supreme Court in 2002 as overbroad violations of free speech. A compromise in 2003 protected realistic virtual images and nonrealistic ones (drawings, cartoons and the like) unless they were deemed obscene (lacking serious literary, artistic, political, or scientific value). Pornographic images of actual children remained illegal.[333] The code now specifically stated that it was not a requirement that the child portrayed actually existed.[334] And it defined child pornography to include computer images "indistinguishable from" images of real minors having sex.[335] But it explicitly excluded drawings, cartoons, sculptures, and paintings.[336] And it allowed as an affirmative defense that the child pornography in question had been produced with adult actors or that it had been created entirely virtually.[337]

One case under the rewritten law was of a teacher whose computer stored images of the *Simpsons* cartoon children having sex with adults and animals. In theory, that should not have been actionable. But the defendant pled guilty and the case never went to trial. His computer also held other images depicting actual children in suggestive and clothed poses.[338] Another case convicted someone of having anime-style child pornography. No actual minors had been involved, but the material was deemed obscene and thus without free-speech protections. He was also punished for emails describing sexual fantasies with minors—pure speech with no representational qualities.[339] Though the legal subtleties of these and similar laws are difficult to parse, the law here came close to prosecuting desires, thoughts, and other mental states. Aiming at the offense of child molestation, an overt and tangible crime, the law in fact ended up targeting pedophilia, a state of mind that is not always acted on.

Conclusion: Still Present after All These Years

Dominated by Anglophone scholars interested in their own nations and engaged by an important political issue, criminology is focused largely on the present. Much of the recent historiography reflects the American situation—its crime wave of the 1960s and 1970s and the attendant incarceration boom. It is preoccupied by the turn to retributive justice in the late twentieth century, with its adoption of long and harsh jail sentences and abandonment of earlier rehabilitative ideals.[1] Only recently has the literature begun to address the decline of urban crime since the 1980s as many big cities have become safer.[2]

We gain perspective by stepping back from the ripples of immediate events to consider long-term currents. The retributive turn of the late twentieth century had most impact on the Anglo-Saxon nations, and even there it may be in the process of stabilizing. Letting this tail do the wagging obscures our view of the dog. In Europe, a tempered rehabilitationism lived on.[3] Though rising in the Anglophone nations, most extremely in the US, rates of imprisonment remained flat in Scandinavia, Germany, and Japan and only moderately increased elsewhere.[4] Britain and France are the European nations that most closely followed the neoretributionist path.[5] In Saudi Arabia, Singapore, and China, harsh punishments have continued to go hand in hand—whatever the causality—with low crime rates and even lower recidivism.[6]

If we instead examine how the state has grappled with crime over the *longue durée* of three millennia, recent events appear in a broad historical context, revealing some unexpected aspects. Two general observations on the deep history of crime merit mention. History deals with both ruptures and continuities. Taken over three thousand years, as here, both will inevitably figure. Almost every era has debated whether punishment's justification is retributive (delivering what offenders deserve) or utilitarian (aiming to diminish crime). The emphasis has tipped one way, then another. But elements of both have invariably left traces—as indeed today when retributivists pander to public sentiment to be tough on crime at the same time as utilitarians seek to reduce offending by ignoring desert to focus on result.

Equally notable from a long perspective is how development proceeds by accretion, not just by substitution. Layers of the old remain, a palimpsest of policies. The old is present though partly shunted aside, never fully obscured or covered by the new. Much of the old privatized approach to crime remains even now when the state pretends to have assumed this task wholly. Pardons remind us of our feudal past, when the king kindly dispensed justice regardless of what the law actually said. Churches remain refuges, an exception by courtesy to the state's allegedly all-encompassing territorial domination. Parole is a modernized form of surety as the community to which the inmate is released fulfills a similar role to compurgators. Bail is the obverse of the frankpledge, a guarantee given before rather than after the crime.[7] Civil asset forfeitures continue the medieval idea of deodands, the state confiscating the tools of crime. The persistent acceptance of the concept of justifiable homicide suggests that the state cannot be bothered to—or perhaps just cannot—impose its will on all our actions, even extreme ones. So do the remnants of vigilante justice the state still tolerates, as does the private assistance it accepts (and indeed relies on) from civil society, whether in the form of vast nonofficial police forces or the cooperation of citizens in investigating crime. Also to be included here is the barely polite fiction that the state has imposed a thoroughgoing monopoly on violence and its means. In the United States, Second Amendment discussions continually raise the primal heresy—sedition, really—of civil society's possible armed revolt against its own state, not just against outside enemies. But nations defended by citizen armies, such as Switzerland and Israel, face the same prospect should major political disagreement erupt. So do countries with heavily armed citizenries and living memories of partisan strife and civil war, such as Finland and Greece.

That brings us to more specific conclusions about the state's role in dealing with crime over the past several millennia. The first is how late the idea of crime as an offense against society emerged as distinct from the more immediate sense of wrongs committed between private parties and resolved among them independently. That broader idea of crime, in turn, was a function of how late the state came to what now seems one of its core competencies—enforcing law and punishing its violation. As treason's immediate victim, the state did, of course, punish it from the outset. But for centuries other offenses were left to be sorted by the implicated parties themselves. The ancient Greeks and Romans established rudimentary judicial and policing systems, taking some matters out of private hands. But not until the early modern era did the state once again penalize crime. That holds even for the world's oldest continuous statutory authority, in China. Across the world, most judicial and police work was outsourced to civil society, with kin groups and other intermediary organizations accountable for their members' transgressions. Today we think of law enforcement as one of the state's primary functions. But policing in the modern sense is in fact a very recent activity—arising long after defense, taxation, economic regulation, social services, and often even public education.[8]

Starting in the seventeenth century, as the European state became directly involved in enforcing law and penalizing crime, it moved to consolidate its power. Monopolizing violence, confiscating and regulating weaponry, subordinating private military troops to its own armies, running one universally recognized judicial system, the state took in hand the business of formulating, promulgating, and enforcing law. To assert its preeminence despite its limited capacities, it acted harshly and publicly. Bloody town-square executions under emperors in China and monarchs in Europe testified both to the state's claims to obedience and to the patchiness of its enforcement. The state's imperfect knowledge led to only occasional capture of offenders and even rarer conviction. Public torturing was needed to deter. The miserable bird in the hand suffered for all its compatriots in the bush.

From a long historical perspective, the state's need to demonstrate its power diminished as its actual strength grew. As the state multiplied its capabilities, it could better detect, deter, and punish transgression. It no longer had to strong-arm and terrorize its subjects. The more powerful and self-confident a community, the more moderate its penal law, Friedrich Nietzsche pointed out.[9] The Enlightenment philosophes were right: predictability deterred more than ferocity. Torture was the weak state's route to evidence. Better surveillance and detective work made torture redundant. Recalibrating the correspondence between offense and punishment also changed the nature of the evidence required. In the early Middle Ages, confession or two eyewitnesses were needed for capital crimes. Later, when lesser but factual evidence was admitted, in return punishments were moderated.[10]

With the admittedly gaping exception of Europe's twentieth-century totalitarian regimes and arguably today in China, the state's power and its harshness have been inversely correlated. A stronger and more pervasive state could police more effectively and therefore benignly. With data flowing evermore freely, the reciprocal transparency between authority and citizenry reduced the need for drastic interventions and in any case limited the extent to which they were tolerated. That historical trend continues today. DNA analysis has retrospectively spared innocents convicted on faulty testimony, electronic automobile tracking has dramatically reduced thefts, and closed-circuit TV evidence has raised detection and conviction rates. Riots in Los Angeles followed the acquittal in 1992 of the police who had beaten Rodney King while being filmed with one of the then-new digital cameras. Today, nearly thirty years later, we all inhabit a digital panopticon. Our insistence that police now film their encounters with the public demonstrates how transparency holds both authorities and citizens accountable. The killing in broad daylight of George Floyd by Minneapolis police in May 2020 demonstrated how little some things had changed in three decades. That the encounter was filmed from half a dozen vantages and the officers quickly arrested and charged suggested that others had.

This inverse correlation between the state's power and its harshness leaves a conceptual conundrum. Is the state becoming nicer, less intrusive, less draconian? Or is it becoming more pervasive, possibly less visible, but simultaneously more widespread and embedded in its subjects' lives? In the early nineteenth century, prison reformers heralded solitary confinement as a sea change in punitive techniques. Hoping to resocialize offenders' souls, its proponents knew they were inflicting a different but no less drastic form of pain: "no longer mere animal pain, but a pain that affects the whole spirit" or a "slow and daily tampering with the mysteries of the brain" that was "immeasurably worse than any torture of the body."[11] Was a lesser force being exerted? Or did solitary confinement herald something different but equally imposing? The new, apparently more moderate state might simply be more subtle, not less strong.

Legions of social control theorists have sought to rip the mask from the face of modern state power, revealing how the authorities—though more surreptitious—dominate citizens' lives more than ever. Herbert Marcuse's seeming paradox of "repressive tolerance" emblematized this approach. Even the exercise of democratic rights, he argued, merely legitimated suppression.[12] That explanation solved the dilemma by definition, not by empirical analysis. Did the contemporary state's subtle power mean that it remained as absolute as in the era when it pulled no punches and had merely changed tactics? Or did modern moderation indicate that the state had actually retreated from centralized authority and its ability to compel? That was the crux of the matter.

Michel Foucault famously argued that as the modern state evolved from absolutism, it aimed to punish better, not less. That was a fence straddle. On the one hand, he spurned the whiggish view that growing enlightenment made the democratic state friendlier, exerting less immediate sway over its subjects. On the other, prison certainly seems preferable to drawing and quartering. His solution was to reframe the concept of power, moving from the absolutist authorities' centralized somatic brutality to modernity's "discipline," a form of coercion that was exerted from multiple sources, that was often self-imposed, and that held sway over both elites and subordinates. In this reframing, he was following the torch brandished by Norbert Elias in his concept of the civilizing process. Foucault and Elias share more in common than often realized. Elias focused on individuals learning to control themselves, the demand side. This they were spurred to accomplish by a mutual dependence arising from society's growing complexity and interflection as well as by states that encouraged such reciprocal self-limitation, as among the French nobles corralled at Versailles before the revolution.

Foucault focused more on the supply side, looking at the all-pervasive disciplining imposed on subjects in countless ways through networks of power.[13] Yet Foucault's only incipiently formulated concept of governmentality followed Elias in looking at civil society's self-disciplining and the mutually reinforcing effects of internal and external constraints. Late in his life, he turned away from his earlier preoccupation with state power to examine how individuals took care of and cultivated themselves, a task more akin to Elias's concerns.[14] His interest became "to show how the government of self is integrated with the government of others."[15] The concept of governmentality was also a move beyond his early concern with social discipline. Though dispersed, power was still at the heart of discipline, exerted over citizens to mold their behavior to align with prevailing norms. Elias focused on individual self-discipline, and Foucault on the disciplining exerted through institutions, but both were concerned with the shaping of the individual psyche and its habits.

Governmentality was the strategy of managing risk by using nondisciplinary techniques. And that, in turn, was but one aspect of a broader governance approach to the state that saw it less as imposing top-down power and more as coordinating multiple ways of regulating independent social actors.[16] The averaging of risk through insurance, for example, has long been put to use by individuals, but in the past two centuries it has come to pervade society as one of the main technologies imposed by the modern welfare state. Businesspeople have shared risk almost as long as humans have traded.[17] The broader state strategy of averaging the risk of social problems threw up issues of free riding and underinsurance. Those, in turn, were dealt with once the state marshaled its powers of enforcement, requiring evermore citizens to be insured against risks that could be quantified, averaged, predicted, and priced. In the late nineteenth century, the German social reformer Lujo Brentano advised workers to maintain at least six different insurance policies: life insurance for their children, pension insurance for old age, burial insurance to pay for their funerals, and coverage for disability, illness, and unemployment.[18] Not all of these risks were privately insurable, however, and over time the welfare state socialized the cost of such eventualities.

The modern state has also effectively mandated public health, thus socializing individually beneficial behaviors. It prophylactically vaccinates infants, screens schoolchildren and army recruits, forbids noxious habits, quarantines the infected, and determines what happens to our bodies after death. In its benign form, such risk management became the liberal welfare state, but similar impulses prompted other states to assess, categorize, manage, improve, mold, and ultimately to deport or kill unwanted subjects. These impulses, some scholars have argued, lay at the heart of Stalin's supposedly improving ambitions and even—formulated in racial terms—of Nazism.[19] Those terror regimes take us beyond our concern with crime and its punishment. In nontotalitarian countries, the shift from social disciplining to governmentality was not just from meddling with the individual psyche to mustering citizens. Managing risks meant combining individual self-discipline and social engineering. Citizens were increasingly expected to anticipate what needed to be done—adopting healthy habits, curbing excesses, training for the work to be done, insuring themselves. Only in the absence of or in addition to such individual prudentialist approaches did the state then step in.[20]

Both Elias and Foucault realized that a binary approach to power led astray. Both rejected the nineteenth century's philosophical dead end of viewing the state as unilaterally all-powerful. Hegel defined the state as a transcendent force above civil society. Marx thought he was exposing the state's faux neutrality by unmasking its role as the tool of the dominant classes. But both agreed in regarding the state as being the dominant force in the relationship between the two. A century later Elias and Foucault parted with this tradition, insisting instead on the interaction between state and civil society and on how the state's role was shaped by the tasks presented to it by civil society. The modern democratic state could not impose itself unbidden on its citizens. Without at least some cooperation of the masses, for whom all modern states claimed to rule, it would fail. Even Hitler was in no position to force his subjects to obey when they refused outright.[21] Stalin, governing a much less industrialized and urbanized—thus less self-controlled—population than the Germans, used more overt violence against so-called antisocial elements (the unemployed, petty criminals, drifters, and the like) than did the Nazis.[22]

Democracy required the state to work in tandem with its subjects. They in turn were expected to meet authority halfway, disciplining themselves and thus requiring less attention from on high. The state's authority was no longer unilateral. It interacted with civil society. That citizens imposed limitations on themselves did not necessarily mean that these were self-willed or self-chosen—anymore than are the details of our childhood socialization.[23] Yet, by accomplishing much of what it would otherwise have had to do, self-discipline did reduce the state's remit. The psychic, emotional, and instinctual limitations citizens imposed on themselves were rewarded with physical freedom from statutory attention.

Both Foucauldian governmentality and Elias's civilizing process thus displaced attention from the unilateral imposition of state power to the interaction of authority and civil society.[24] Humans are hypersocial creatures, our communal existence wholly dependent on the culture that we learn from each other, passed down from our ancestors.[25] But we are not massified by instinct, like ants or bees, blindly slotting into our appointed social roles. Culture, not biology, socializes us. How then to ensure human behavior that is compatible with organized society?

Social contract theorists have imagined humans discussing the terms they would unite under, trading nature's autonomy—whether the bliss of noble savages or a war of all against all—for protection in organized society. But that reversed cart and horse. These allegedly presocial negotiators, adeptly parsing the fine points of contract law, had somehow already achieved what they were supposed to be accomplishing. Historically, no such ur-constitutional convention of Robinson Crusoes ever assembled. Humans first organized themselves in small bands. Some of these bands eventually joined together in larger associations with incipient social stratification and some semblance of durable authority. Finally, some five millennia ago they formed the first recognizable states.

Before states emerged, and in the societies that remain without them, small and homogenous groups have governed themselves without much formal rule making or vesting of authority beyond their clan head.[26] Kin alliances forged largely through marriage helped create broader unity among disparate members as a matter of (sometimes made-up) descent. Polite fictions allowed new family members to be incorporated—adoption among the Romans, for example—alongside other means of artificially extending consanguinity.[27] Existing and historically documented tribes typically used such devices.[28] Chiefdoms, in turn, represented a halfway step between tribes and formalized state structures. They were still based on descent from a common ancestor but now had some social stratification. Hereditary leaders ruled, but there was still no formal legislation or enforcement.[29]

How tribal societies kept the peace by punishing aggressive or asocial members with the cold shoulder or worse is a leitmotiv of the anthropological literature.[30] With the hyperdense sociability of the igloo as their norm, Inuits regarded the Western anthropologists who visited them as emotionally incontinent in their petty outbursts and everyday irritable flare-ups. Having violated precept, offenders were ostracized into the cold. Shunning and exclusion were the most widespread sanctions, formalized in larger-scale societies as excommunication. Habitual bullies or other intolerables who violated the egalitarian premises of hunter-gatherer societies were killed by delegated executioners, the victim's immediate kin standing aside.[31] Extrapolating backward from such anthropological findings, historians agree that prehistoric societies of hunter-gatherers and early agricultural settlements were likely similar.[32]

Yet such theories of purely informal regulation have also been questioned. Anthropologists have disputed the relative roles of custom and law to guide behavior in what used to be called primitive society. Bronislaw Malinowski rebelled against the anthropology of his day, which argued that group custom, obeyed unthinkingly, governed tribes and clans, with the individual but a cog in a kinship machine. He claimed to discern both criminal and civil law in such societies, with autonomous individuals tied into to a web of mutual obligation, responding to strictures prescribed for neglecting their duties. Much hinged on definition.[33] Formal mechanisms of adjudication, "codes, courts, and constables," indicating the presence of law, were admittedly absent, but that scarcely meant no regulation. Quite the contrary. Early humans were likely governed by a dense network of stricture, with law being, as Malinowski put it, but one form of custom.[34]

States, in turn, first arose some five millennia ago because they were better able to deal with challenges that stumped smaller, less-organized societies. Their organizational prowess delivered a competitive advantage, allowing them to prosper, grow, and dominate. Early states were adept at marshaling resources. Armies were assembled, economies organized, towering infrastructural projects stamped out of the ground—all by institutions with only basic technology. *Homo sapiens* lived for three hundred thousand years in rudimentary circumstances. Having invented the state, our ancestors took but a few thousand years to build pyramids, aqueducts, palaces, and roads, start to write, and worship universalist gods. The state is arguably the most important invention in human history. It is the ultimate organizing tool of our ultrasociable species, whose main competitive advantage has been its ability to muster itself collectively and to transmit accumulated knowledge over generations.

Historians of Europe are perhaps at a disadvantage in appreciating how ancient states are. After the fall of the western Roman Empire, nearly a millennium passed before European institutions again approximated what had been achieved under the Egyptians and Greeks, not to mention the Romans. Europe's early modern history is largely the story of rebuilding the state. We tend therefore to think of the state as a recent development. Add Hegel's insistence that the state of his era was its culmination and Max Weber's precise, exclusive definitions that made the difference between the modern state and all earlier states one of kind, not just degree. The result has been a historically myopic view of the state as a recent and unprecedented invention.

But states have long been with us. Unlike small, informally governed societies, they imposed the controls required to coordinate their many subjects from the top and from outside. Thanks to painstaking historical work, we now know, for example, how insufficient Weber's idea is that real bureaucracy developed only in the nineteenth century. It may be that the bureaucracy of the Third Dynasty of Ur, two millennia before Christ, answered to individual families and was thus not rational and impersonal in a Weberian sense.[35] But already the Zhou dynasty of China, in power for some eight hundred years starting a millennium before Christ, had developed a bureaucratic apparatus independent of the ruler's person, with meritocratic recruitment and advancement as well as specialized functions.[36]

Such efforts were both cumbersome and costly. States with sufficient resources could police and tame their civil societies. Independent sources of revenue helped, such as state-owned mines, farms, or eventually factories. So did slaves or other forced labor. Early states were mechanisms to tame subject populations and extract resources. Karl Wittfogel's theory of hydraulic despotism argued that ancient Egypt and other early states organized agricultural water by harnessing subjects for public irrigation works. He has been criticized for extending this theory too broadly, but it has the virtue of highlighting how states mustered resources and subjugated populations to solve collective problems. James Scott has also recently argued that early states were predatory, centralizing power to accumulate wealth stored as grain.[37]

We can thus imagine at one extreme autocratic external control over everything and at the other voluntary conformity produced by autonomous self-regulation. At times, states have been overbearing—not just among the Egyptians, Aztecs, or Incas but also in early modern Europe's Polizei regulations, addressing every conceivable behavior, and in the twentieth century's totalitarian autocracies, where the state permeated civil society, though perhaps less thoroughly than historians first imagined.[38] Of the organizational forms that governed through pervasive informal behavioral control, we find only faint echoes from distant and semidocumented societies and from short-lived experiments of the like-minded, withdrawing from established society to unite in voluntarily adopted uniformity: utopian associations, communes, kibbutzim, and religious communities. That is what Christian society was supposed to be like. Christ had only a staff, Luther explained, because Christians were sheep and he their shepherd. The wolves and lions of the mundane world, in contrast, required force. In historical fact, a few such communities have been successful, such as the Amish, Mennonites, and the Hasidic town of Kiryas Joel in New York State. Others went spectacularly bad: the Anabaptists in Münster in 1534, the People's Temple in Jonestown in 1978, and the Branch Davidians in Waco in 1993.[39]

Complex societies have traded off between these two techniques of behavioral control—outside imposition and internal informal self-regulation. At times, civil society has functioned efficiently as the engine of socialization, with family and church acculturating community members. If someone who had violated a deeply felt point of honor was shunned and ostracized or left to commit suicide—thus sparing the law the unpleasant necessity of an execution—that indicated that custom and code still reinforced each other.[40] In ancient Egypt, defendants condemned to death were sometimes allowed to kill themselves, as was Socrates in Athens. Convicted Japanese Samurai, too, were permitted to commit seppuku, or harakiri.[41] Early twentieth-century Melanesia considered it a sign of cultural decline that those who had seriously violated norms were now jailed rather than, as earlier, committing suicide.[42]

Yet at some point more was needed. Most states began formalizing rules that had earlier been implicit. Whom one married, how one dressed, what one believed about the supernatural—all became matters of law. The state moved into new arenas of behavioral regulation, taking as its remit education, large swaths of childrearing, and more generally the socialization of citizens. Laws replaced or supplemented informal behavioral molding. Raising the next generation became evermore a task for institutions beyond the family. As the church lost influence, religion ceded pride of place to secular morality and etiquette, the last-mile guide to appropriate behavior. And as the informal socialization into correct conduct that had been religion and morality's task dissolved in modernity's anomic acid bath, it was displaced in turn by the law as an immediate guide to behavior. Village communities once prodded, scolded, exhorted, and shamed their members to toe the line. In urban society, matters became formalized. In the eighteenth century, laws were passed against vagrancy, prostitution, public drunkenness, sloth, and other behaviors that had earlier been only informally discouraged. Expanding its policing function, the state minutely regulated every conceivable behavior: from how children should address their parents to locking doors in the evenings. The state replaced kin as the enforcer.

The Civilizing Process

State and civil society thus engaged in a pas de deux. Over the past four millennia, the state's role has expanded enormously—as we have seen here in the single sphere of crime control. Yet, despite absolutism's or even totalitarianism's pretensions, the state never acted alone. First of all, starting some five thousand years ago, the state could rely on humans' own evolutionary history. Compared to our surviving primate cousins, humans are generally less violent within our own communities. We slaughter others in planned and organized raids, skirmishes, and wars, but to those we live with we are roughly a hundred times less violent than chimpanzees. Even more so than the fairly pacific bonobos, humans are self-domesticated. Like dogs and other domesticated animals, but unlike other human or near-human species such as Neanderthals, we have developed smaller brains and teeth, more gracile limbs, and shorter faces, males becoming more like women and adults like children. Such attributes of the domestication syndrome go hand in hand with the most basic change, the taming of our propensity for violence, allowing us to associate peacefully and cooperatively to solve problems collectively. Humans' evolutionary advantage lay in our ability to learn from each other, including elders and ancestors, profiting from accumulated wisdom and experience. From deep time to the present, the most successful groups have arguably been those that self-selected for cooperation, cultural accretion, and collective problem solving.[43]

Though they are strikingly clever, no other primates could cooperate sufficiently to form a state. Humans are not happy cheek by jowl on long-haul flights, but three hundred chimps crowded together in similar circumstances would tear each other apart.[44] Elias's civilizing process is arguably but the tip of a massive evolutionary iceberg of behavioral adjustment that has brought forth today's ultrasociable humans. Elias described behavioral changes that were culturally driven as pacification was rewarded in increasingly complex and interdependent human societies. But those changes built on a broader evolutionary logic of how humanity has housetrained itself into sociability. The state relies both on this evolutionary self-domestication and on society's informal self-regulation.

This has not been a simple trade-off across the board. From the state's perspective, some forms of antisocial behavior were best tackled through voluntary means. Others required a bit of steel. One could in theory mandate healthy living to achieve public-health goals, and to some extent we still do. Public smoking is banned today in the most liberal societies, as it once was in autocratic eighteenth-century Prussia. But on the whole states seek to convince citizens to adopt healthy habits. They do not mandate daily push-ups or muesli for breakfast.

Yet not every public good can be achieved by jollying along worthy habits. Vaccination has to be required and enforced, lest free riders undermine herd immunity. Even the most law-abiding societies, with few citizens in jail, have kept their police departments. The better its policing, the less the state has to rely on prison. Yet on the whole the relationship between authority and citizen has become less enforced and more voluntarily compliant. Today, taxes are deducted at source or via bank transfer and not wrested in kind from barns and lofts by collectors' thugs. Military recruits muster up; they are no longer dragged off at bayonet point.[45] The triumph of informal behavioral molding is confirmed more than one hundred thousand times daily in each airplane safety briefing. Passengers politely ignore the stewards' demonstrations, idly wondering, "Where be this mythical creature who in this day boards a plane actually ignorant of how to buckle a safety belt?"

Today we are nearly all socialized into the conduct that makes dense metropolitan life tolerable and safe. Behaviors we now regard as innate have in fact often been only recently learned. The basic politeness and civility analyzed by Elias dated mostly from the sixteenth century.[46] Yet, like human evolution, the civilizing process continues to socialize us into behaviors that we quickly come to regard as necessary or even natural, not recognizing how recent is their pedigree. Behaviors as functionally imperative as toilet training developed only gradually and recently and still vary widely. In many earlier societies, sphincters did not require strict control. Nor was privacy in the act prized. The Spaniards conquering Mexico in 1519 were amazed that the locals had set up shelters of reed or straw along roads to allow discreet excretion and to save the results, which they used to tan hides.[47] In most agrarian societies as late as the 1950s, scheduling and timing toilet use was not pressing. In cities, such controls are now being extended from humans also to their pets. Already in the 1890s, a quarter of all fines imposed by French auxiliary police were for public excretion—human and canine.[48] It even rose to become a labor issue: How frequent and lengthy bathroom breaks did workers need?[49] The Indian government has recently unrolled a massive campaign to discourage outdoor excretion, which spreads disease and allows rapists to prey on women. Even among industrialized nations, toilet training has varied dramatically—early, communal, and draconian in East Germany, for example, but more prolonged and forgiving elsewhere.[50] Mainland Chinese still often permit toddlers to relieve themselves in the street, while Hong Kong frowns on such crudity.[51]

Spitting, too, was once regarded as an irrepressible natural instinct, like breathing or urinating. In the 1890s, Chicago streets could be walked only gingerly, picking one's way among the expectorations. The trams were even worse.[52] Nineteenth-century public-health officials, rightly fearing that public spitting spread tuberculosis, campaigned against it. Spittoons became a fixture of urban life. During the Spanish flu epidemic of 1918, New York City punished open coughing or sneezing in public by a $500 fine, close to an average annual wage.[53] Largely involuntary, coughing and sneezing remain beyond the law's reach, but public spitting has generally been socialized out of everyday behavior. Spittoons are but curiosities. Today we judge it much as our grandchildren will regard smoking: a nasty habit worthy at best of country bumpkins—or the occasional baseball pitcher.

In other aspects of personal hygiene, we have come far from even our recent forbears. Asians have long adopted modern habits, but among Europeans washing and cleanliness were until recently considered enervating and debilitating.[54] Oral hygiene today is a $40 billion industry. But cleansing teeth—except perhaps using urine, as the Dutch thought was practiced among the Spanish in the 1500s—was uncommon before the twentieth century.[55] Today, anyone as dirty as many Europeans were even in the 1950s would be ostracized. In those days, an English landlady could eject an American tenant who bathed daily—not so much for wasting water but for the contagious dermatological disease self-evidently betrayed by such peculiar behavior. Even English toffs, who self-identify by scorning bourgeois propriety, are reasonably clean these days. Princess Margaret once humiliated one of her ladies in waiting by giving her a loo brush for Christmas, having noticed the absence of one while visiting her home.[56] In fact, the mortified lady—as posh of course as the princess herself—had merely hidden it while Margaret was staying, too embarrassed to leave it out in the open because of the implied suggestion that a royal might be expected—Gandhi-like—to scrub her own toilet.

To *épater les bourgeois*, hippies of the 1960s made a virtue of being smelly. More recently, habits have become so squeakily clean that our children's asthmas and allergies are likely aggravated because their immune systems simply lack practice on now banished microorganisms. In the Korean movie *Parasite* (2019), a chauffeur murders his employer for humiliating him by complaining about his odor—an olfactory class divide now largely unthinkable in the West. Westerners, in turn, still suffer a certain chronic humiliation, knowing that the Japanese consider them smelly.[57] Once extravagances of the rich, mani- and pedicures have become everyday grooming. The depilation craze has made pubic hair exotic, akin to muttonchop sideburns. The Brooklyn hipster beard is admittedly a bit anomalous, yet the sheer variety of product and the specialized implements required for it reveal it to be not a return of untamed nature but stylized hirsute adornment.

Belching, farting, and urinating in public, once commonplace, are now frowned upon or illegal. Kibbutzniks in postwar Israel deliberately upended the dining rituals of the shtetl. To signal rejection of their proper upbringing, they ate communally, unceremoniously, and each at their own pace.[58] While eating habits are informalizing everywhere, the purely bodily aspects have tightened up. We may eat dinner off paper plates, supine on the couch before the television, but we have also coined a word, *misophonia*, for the agony of disgust that others' open-mouthed chewing now inflicts. Something as biologically unremarkable as mouth breathing is today lambasted as uncouth and evolutionarily harmful.[59] Drinking to oblivion on Saturday nights used to be commonplace in the northern and eastern European countryside, accompanied by swaggering and fisticuffs. In those nations that drink, alcohol consumption remains high, but some binge-drinking cultures are shifting to more Mediterranean habits, favoring beer or wine over spirits and consuming more moderately with meals.[60] Seatbelts were installed in cars beginning in the late 1960s, and their use was required globally as of the mid-1980s. Thirty years later, compliance (front-seat use) has become largely universal. A few nations (Cambodia, Italy, Argentina) lag, but most of the developed world arrays itself in serried ranks, from 90 percent compliance up through the most obedient, the French at 99 percent.[61]

Gay sexuality has been normalized over the past several decades. In the 1970s, in the first flush of gay liberation but before the AIDS epidemic of the early 1980s, male homosexuals celebrated their newfound erotic freedoms with festive abandon—their polymorphous hookups and unabashed promiscuity. The gay bathhouse culture of San Francisco and New York, with its pansexual anonymous delights, explicitly challenged the bodily restrictions of monogamous heteronormative society. As a visiting professor at Berkeley, Foucault may have consciously risked a *va banque* wager between prudently avoiding HIV infection and the Dionysian delights of

San Francisco's bathhouses.[62] This was the world of John Rechy and his vision of gays as erotic outlaws, defiantly upending conventionality. Promiscuity was then seen as the core of gay male sexual practice, the "righteous form of revolution."[63]

This revolution was, alas, an ambition cruelly dashed by AIDS and the gradual realization that unprotected promiscuity was epidemiologically risky.[64] Forty years on, the hot topics of debate are no longer glory holes, doors on bathhouse cubicles, or condom use but gay marriage. Safe sex has gone from being regarded as the public-health authorities' attempt to squelch gay self-expression to the price of admission for intercourse. Once resisted as a plot hatched by sexual Quislings to bring homosexuals to heel, gay marriage is now considered a major rights victory for formerly shunned outsiders. By abandoning the riskiest sexual practices, male gays were able to stave off coercive public-health interventions during the AIDS epidemic. They won broad social acceptance as a group distinguished by the object of their sexual desire but no longer meaningfully by their erotic practices. Heteronormatized, gaydom became accepted precisely because it had domesticated itself.

Besides producing ever cleaner and more circumspect citizens, the interaction of law and socialization in the civilizing process also led to behavioral shifts more closely related to our theme here and ultimately more important. We have followed the process by which law's adjudication and enforcement became the state's mandate, removing such functions from the hands of kin and community. For most of history, civil society was crime's primary punisher. Once the state began playing a role, too, civil society did not of course vanish, but the division of labor between the two parties changed. Formal detection, adjudication, and enforcement fell to the authorities. Civil society was relegated to socializing humans into citizenship—in effect ensuring that they would intersect with formal sanctions only rarely. Meeting the state halfway, civil society's ability to regulate itself meant the modern state grew less repressive and interventionist. Political freedom was arguably the reward for self-discipline.

Taming War

Making crime the state's problem also became an element of a larger pacification in human history. Most significant among its effects was the overall decline of pain, cruelty, and violence. Pain is something that we have done our best to banish. Anesthesiologists are among the unsung heroes of civilization, allowing us to endure and not just survive childbirth and surgery. Pain medication has become so sophisticated that, as with food, its provisioning has met needs while creating problems of overconsumption. One fundamental remaining global injustice is the divide setting us apart from those who still face sickness, age, and accident largely bereft of any analgesia.[65] Meanwhile, the developed world chokes on its own excesses as death rates from addiction to pain relief soar.

The taming of violence is probably the state's single most significant accomplishment. But at the same time, the state, like a protection racket, may well also have been the main cause of the violence it then suppressed. As it subdued its subjects at home, it united them in warfare abroad. Domestic peace and outward aggression were flip sides of the state's coin. Yet this was not a hydraulic effect, with pressures reduced in one spot erupting elsewhere. Total violence decreased. Living as we do in the shadow of half a century of world war, it may seem counterintuitive, but violent deaths per capita—including the state's own military acts—have steadily declined over the past five millennia. On that there is scholarly consensus. In dispute remains what the situation looked like ten thousand years ago, in the prestate age of hunter-gatherers. From the behavior of certain primates, from existing human tribes, and from skeletal evidence at prehistoric burial sites, some archaeologists and evolutionary psychologists have concluded that warfare was then sufficiently endemic (killing perhaps a quarter of all males) to have powered the engines of evolution—warlike traits being selected for.[66] Others have questioned this conclusion, pointing out that the evidence for wide-scale warfare in prehistoric times is still scant.

That warfare eventually grew common is undisputed; the question is when. Much also hangs on how warfare is defined. Besides eradicating most of the planet's terrestrial megafauna, *Homo sapiens* may also have had a hand in the extinction of Neanderthals, Denisovans, *Homo floresiensis*, and other archaic near-human peoples. Whether that happened through outright aggression or a subtler outcompetition for resources is unclear. By perhaps thirty thousand years ago, *Homo sapiens* were the lone humanoids on the planet.[67] Given this possible ur-xenocide, the scholarly debate over warfare among hunter-gatherers thus deals largely with our aggression against ourselves, not our near kin.

The *Homo sapien* hunter-gatherers of sparsely populated prehistoric times likely came into contact with each other only sporadically, perhaps meeting up at hunting grounds or for ceremonial purposes. They probably rarely fought over common resources, though this is a guess only. From ten thousand years ago, as with most other aspects of human life then, little evidence of warfare has survived.[68] But as populations densified and settled, social stratification multiplied. With the emergence of complex foraging communities, hereditary leaders arose, and the potential for antagonism between now more proximate groups increased. The beginnings of agriculture and domesticated livestock intensified the territoriality of settlement. At some point, moving in search of new resources put groups in conflict with others who were already occupying what only seemed to be empty and yielding territory.[69] That complex hunter-gatherers were violent seems widely agreed upon. Evidence for warfare increased in the Neolithic (starting ca. 5500 BCE). By the beginning of the Copper Age (ca. 4500 BCE), it was undeniable.[70]

Beyond the hunter-gatherer stage, proto-states began, ordering the affairs of evermore complex, sedentary, agricultural civilizations. Sedentism preceded both widespread grain agriculture and state formation by several millennia. There was no lockstep in which these various aspects of human development marched.[71] Though sedentism did not automatically lead to statehood, states did require sedentary subjects. As Neolithic people densified on fertile lands, chiefdoms likely emerged, besting smaller, disorganized villages.[72]

States produced violence, then, but mostly in the sense that the circumstances they were called on to tame would have led to warfare even in their absence. Proximity, density, and the ability to produce and store valuables that were vulnerable to plunder, such as nuts, grains, textiles, and slaves—all this encouraged raids and wars as a shortcut to wealth without work, though of course not without the cost of armaments, training, and casualties. States, too, fell for this temptation. True, they suppressed violence internally by adjudicating and policing, but they encouraged violence externally by plundering and conquering neighbors. As tribes and villages became chiefdoms, chiefdoms became states, and states eventually empires, the internal pacifying effect spread, reducing the number of entities in competition and expanding what counted as domestic and thus demilitarized territory. States thus both produced and suppressed violence. Had humanity remained foragers, with Malthusian pressures checking their numbers, warfare could perhaps have been sidestepped. But after the shift to agriculture, states and warfare were unavoidable. Having perhaps invented or at least accompanied war, states then also became part of subduing violence.

Those scholars who have most forcefully noted the pacifying effect of states compare today's violent-death rates to the rates supposedly characteristic of hunter-gatherer societies. Among prehistoric societies, an average of 15 percent of skeletons examined give evidence of violent death, some of which may have happened in hunts. Violent deaths in the twentieth century, including even those caused only indirectly, range between 1 and 3 percent.[73] Compared to stateless societies, states thus successfully suppressed violence. The point remains, less forceful but dramatic nonetheless, even if we agree that the portion of violent deaths among hunter-gatherers has been exaggerated. The life of an ancient forager may not have been as violent as supposed, and the state may have helped create the problem it then solved. Yet, overall and in the long run, given that humanity turned to agriculture and violence intensified, states tamed violence.

Living as we do under the state's thumb, it takes an act of historical imagination or perhaps a comparison with the turmoil of contemporary failed states to appreciate the effect on our lives of this peaceful ordering. The level of social chaos considered acceptable even as recently as the eighteenth century would be inconceivable today, absent utter social breakdown. Intent on plunder, thousand-strong crowds savagely attacked the crews and the police trying to protect them of ships wrecked on the English coast in the eighteenth century. During the Gordon riots of 1780, the mob ran unchecked in central London. After the elections in 1819, prominent MPs were pelted with mud in public, and the windows of the rich were broken if they refused the crowd's insistence on candles in them.[74] Rioting was in effect a tolerated form of public expression, and the authorities were largely unable to do anything about it in any case. Today we accept only much lower levels of public disorder. Outdoor marches and assemblies require official approval and all manner of permits and insurances.[75] Universal suffrage has made everyone complicit in governing, dramatically raising the bar for legitimate rioting by providing other means of being heard. Enhanced police power, too, has raised the stakes of unrest.[76] When riots occur, they are often own goals, the poor damaging their own neighborhoods.

Social Control

How do we understand civil society's self-regulation? Is it something undertaken voluntarily in a neo-Kantian spirit of self-willed autonomy and freedom? Or is it a subtle but still outside imposition on unwilling subjects by the state, possibly acting on behalf of powerful interests? Where an initial socialization had failed and citizens were then brought back into the fold, power relations were obvious. Alex's resocialization in Stanley Kubrick's dystopian film *A Clockwork Orange* trained him in conventional behavior, spoiling his pleasure in Beethoven as collateral damage. Unsurprisingly, state-led socialization often legitimized and favored elite habits, activities, and entertainments. Alfred Doolittle, Eliza's dustman father in *My Fair Lady*, resentfully chides "middle-class morality" for spoiling his enjoyment of being one of the undeserving poor. Nineteenth-century social workers scrutinized proletarian families and their habits, vigilantly encouraging them to adopt middle-class mores. Public-health officials forced themselves on often unwilling subjects, requiring them to vaccinate their children, send them to school, not crowd too densely in their dwellings, give up sharing them with animals, and the like. Urban workers resisted antidrink campaigns for undermining accustomed rituals of sociability. Sports and other leisure activities varied by class. Joys of the elite were protected, whereas working-class pleasures were denied. Fox hunting and falconry flourished; ratting, bearbaiting, and cockfighting were banned. Dog racing ceded pride of place to horse racing. Some gambling and often prizefighting were suppressed.[77]

Yet self-control could be liberating, too. Self-discipline was not just a crude class-determined imposition. Social control has often been interpreted as a subtle way to ensure what the state or dominant groups sought. But the civilizing process cannot be boiled down just to class terms. Did elites force controls on their inferiors in order to maintain their dominance? If so, then, as Elias has shown, they did it only after imposing this self-discipline on themselves. Historically, certain elites were the first to control themselves. That was the implicit assumption in codes, such as the Islamic, which punished more harshly the further down in the social scale they went. Inspired by his Calvinist faith, the seventeenth-century Great Elector of Prussia, Friedrich Wilhelm, imposed austerity, self-discipline, and rigor on his administration, helping by willpower and effort his small, poor, distant nation punch far above its geopolitical weight.[78] The first cohort of aristocrats could by definition not have been chosen by lineage. Even as the caste solidified, it recognized and folded in outsiders with enviable personal qualities. Having achieved social recognition under feudalism, certain families managed to remain prominent for centuries thereafter, across revolutions, depressions, crashes, and other misfortunes likely to have undermined their unearned social advantage. Was that longevity due to qualities of mind and character they managed to pass on to descendants?[79]

The civilizing process aimed for a self-controlled citizen of moderate, restrained tastes and habits. That selected against the rowdier of lower-class pursuits as well as against paupers, with their alleged tendency to be insubordinate, footloose, improvident, and unwilling to work.[80] But the civilizing process was equally a rejection of the sexual libertinage, purposeless blood sports, and lavish consumption of the wealthy. In countless ways, markets, societies, and states have socialized modern people into prudent, regular habits, bringing forth the disciplined, punctual, reliable, and predictable citizens required by complex economies. The meritocracy debate of our own era indicates the extent to which the allegedly bourgeois virtues of thrift, hard work, tamed instincts, and the cultivation of talent and intellect have come to define us all.[81] Hedge-fund managers, quants, and technonerds are the new exemplars; landowners have lost their allure.

The discipline that drove the civilizing process could be democratic and liberating in a neo-Kantian way. Much as Kant and Hegel thought that freedom was achieved by following just law, so citizens came to see self-discipline and self-control as means to avoid authority's outside impositions by submitting voluntarily to the dictates of civilized cohabitation. The point of socialization was to sidestep the need for external interventions. The more self-control and self-policing, the fewer the state's impositions. Nikolas Rose has expanded Elias's theory to argue that self-government is true government and self-discipline not the state's psychic imposition but the means of achieving freedom.[82]

Social control has been a conceptual black box, concealing various approaches to the question "Who wields power?" Social control has been innocently interpreted as the means of assuring the behavioral calibration required by life in interdependent industrialized society. The nineteenth-century sociologists who first formulated the concept meant the way in which necessary behavioral modifications were achieved through a consensual mutual adjustment by everyone.[83] Socialization, informal social pressure, and then, only if these had failed, the state's formal apparatus—those were the tools to keep citizens in line. The American jurist Roscoe Pound defined social control as "the pressure upon each man brought to bear by his fellow men in order to constrain him to do his part in upholding civilized society."[84] Seen thus, social control was necessary and benign.

Social control is also more cynically seen as how elites ensure their predominance, merely disguising the exertion of power and coercion. Precisely by whom and why were the issues. Prisons were unmasked as means of turning recalcitrant proletarians into a docile reserve army of workers. Mental hospitals made differently thinking patients conform. Even welfare or charitable policies or organized leisure pursuits—sports and the like—might be means of keeping a possibly unruly lower class placid by supplying bread and circuses. Exerted as indoctrination, such power left even people who felt free toeing a line drawn by someone else—led astray by the ever-malleable false consciousness.[85] With some imagination, everything short of outright revolution could be interpreted as socially stabilizing and functionally coercive.

Self-abnegation, thrift, industriousness, and temperance could be taken at face value as habits that helped their practitioners make something of themselves. Or they could be interpreted cynically as what capitalism required of its workers. Without a clear steer as to whose interests governed society, social control arguments easily tied themselves in knots. If docility were the goal, why inculcate habits of self-discipline that might lead workers to expect a better future for themselves?[86] Religion, the opium of the masses, might be a better ideological control, as it in fact remained in those states that recognized the inherent danger of allowing subordinates, whether the poor, ethnic minorities, or women, to learn to read or otherwise better themselves.

And all this assumed that the institutions of social control actually performed as planned. But did they? Victorian prisons, for example, were rarely the engines of social discipline imagined by Foucauldians. More often, they treated their inmates better than they were accustomed to in the outside world, imposing little discipline and scarcely any control. In any case, the prisons were too understaffed and kept their charges too briefly to have much influence one way or the other.[87] Ironically, the theorists of disciplinary institutions—Erving Goffman, Michel Foucault, and David Rothman—wrote at just that twentieth-century moment when they witnessed these institutions' trajectory reverse.[88] Convincing anyone that universities and hospitals were institutions of covert coercion had always been a long shot. Workhouses and poorhouses were long gone. Asylums and orphanages, in turn, emptied out precisely at the moment their affinity to prisons was being trumpeted. Starting in the 1960s, the mentally ill were radically deinstitutionalized.[89] Like the blind, orphans and their institutions have largely vanished thanks to a combination of demographic, medical, and social changes. Only the prison—the most obviously disciplinary of the institutions—remained and has expanded. The insight into these institutions' supposed carceral commonality that then seemed so trenchant has been considerably blunted since.

Conversely, if social control actually did what was claimed on its behalf, why so ineffectually? If modern prisons were supposed to keep a reserve labor force off the streets when unemployment was high, why should incarceration cost more than the dole? If state schools were intended to train the rising generation of worker bees, why not do so more effectively? Who were these Machiavellians covertly running things? If they were so clever, why did they usually fail? Like all conspiracy theories, the view of social control as an effective force stumbled over the fatal contradiction between an allegedly omniscient and omnipotent group of manipulators and the hash they were in fact making of things. Nor, in this view, was there any room for discipline that individuals underwent for their own betterment—abstinence, self-improvement, or even any form of training or education.

Whatever their precise formulation, social control arguments still approached power as a bilateral encounter: the powerful exerted force over the dispossessed, either directly or indirectly, covertly or overtly, and the dispossessed in turn resisted as best they could. But this view was rife with ambiguities. Who controlled whom, and for what purpose? If the powerful were the first to self-discipline, if self-control were broadly speaking good for those undertaking it and not just something forced on them, then who was to say that power was being exerted in only one direction? Hospitals sought to cure, schools to educate, factories to produce, and even prisons sometimes to rehabilitate. Could all these activities be unmasked as somehow serving the dominance of the powerful? Unless one were willing to argue that they were ultimately motivated less by what they did for their immediate clients than by how they maintained the system for elites, then power described only as an act of domination was insufficient. Yes, prisons, factories, hospitals, and schools resembled each other in being disciplinary institutions. Inmates, pupils, and workers may have resented the control imposed. Patients did not, so long as physicians cured them. Nor did the civil servants, managers, scholars, and other professionals who spent long years in training to achieve their coveted positions.

Elias willingly accepted the socially ameliorative aspects of self-discipline. Rose expanded on that notion, harnessing it to a broader Kantian project of freedom achieved through law. Foucault shunned the crude Marxism of locating power reductively in the hands of dominant classes, with the state but their handmaiden. His escape from the dilemma that remained was to obfuscate the very idea of power. No longer something exerted by one actor over another, power became decentered, a multitude of forces cascading hither and yon, controlling elites and subordinates equally. Discipline, not power, became the overarching concept, able to reconcile the apparent moderation of the modern state with an insistence that the velvet glove still harbored iron. Power, quoth Foucault, is "a machine in which everyone is caught, those who exercise power just as much as those over whom it is exercised."[90]

L'état continue

Whether the state really has become more moderate therefore depends on the extent civil society regulates itself. If civil society's (self-)disciplinary efforts in fact have left the state with less enforcing to do, then perhaps it really has been rolled back. The overall social control effort may have remained constant but is now apportioned differently—more for civil society, less for the state. Yet there lies the rub. "Law varies inversely with other social control," scholars have assured us.[91] If Elias, Foucault, and Rose were right, if the disciplinary and normalizing effort was working and controls were increasingly internalized and informalized, we would expect ever fewer new laws and less enforcement of existing ones. Indeed, law would have been superseded. But has it been?

Cultures have made use of formal and informal controls to different extents. To sting, shame punishments require buy-in to shared standards. A communitarian society can enforce norms by threatening to ostracize offenders. An individualistic one relies more heavily on the state and its coercive apparatus.[92] Nor has every society been able to impose the same degree of informal social control. Immigrant societies, with few shared values or traditions, have struggled to institute broad risk- and cost-sharing social policies, compared to the more easily achieved solidarities of nations that—at the moment of forming their welfare states—were more ethnically and religiously homogenous.[93] The citizens of multicultural, immigrant nations, especially if their welfare policies do not shore up the traditional institutions of socialization, are less likely to agree on common social norms than the inhabitants of countries governed by what the Germans call a *Leitkultur*, a dominant cultural ethos.[94] Multiculturalism's fissures have come to strain countries whose policies once could assume a certain behavioral uniformity. Even something as mundane as ticketing on mass transit spans a range, from relying on citizen honesty to up-front uniformed control.[95]

Within any given culture, the balance between formal and informal control has also shifted back and forth historically. Inculcated behavioral norms sometimes weaken or reverse. Increasing urbanization has drained small, tight-knit communities with their everyday mechanisms of socialization. The recent rise of antivaccination movements has undermined once widely adopted, socially beneficial conduct, prompting authorities to reinforce formal obligations—subjecting children to the needle before enrolling them in school.[96] For a brief moment in the 1960s, the West seemed to relax informal control, lessening behavioral regulation.[97] Individual civil rights were enhanced, conventional proprieties disregarded. Hedonistic behavior—sexual, emotional, drug-related—spread into even the middle classes. Were an older work ethic and norms of social control more generally unwinding?

Perhaps behavioral control did briefly relax during the 1960s and 1970s. Nonetheless, looking back half a century later, the continuities impress more than the ruptures. Despite some loosening in matters sexual and possibly also on inebriation, social self-regulation seems as strict today as ever. The shift from blue- to white-collar jobs, from production to service, demands ever firmer self-discipline. Ill-educated working-class men, smarting at their inability to master new jobs, supply the shock troops of today's populist movements. Educational requirements and demands have ratcheted steadily skyward. The universities where the sixty-eighters lazily turned on, tuned in, and dropped out now expect Stakhanovite hyperaccomplishment. Even adolescents have lengthy CVs. Far from relaxing, informal controls have arguably strengthened in the past half century. Jerry Rubin, for example, went from Yippie to yuppie. He led Berkeley protests in the 1960s, taunted brokers by throwing dollar bills onto the New York Stock Exchange floor, and was tried as part of the Chicago Seven after riots at the Democratic National Convention in 1968. In the 1970s, however, he became a businessman and multimillionaire before being killed while jaywalking across Wilshire Avenue in Los Angeles. Jane Fonda trod a similar path toward self-discipline, from the sex-kitten Barbarella to antiwar protester to the queen of the autoregulating rigor of fitness and diet.

Informal social control and formal law have counterintuitively increased in tandem. As society has become more complicated and less homogeneous, increasingly rift by social, religious, ethnic, and other multicultural divides, control has shifted. Formal imposition has arguably made a comeback, supplementing informal socialization. A neoretributionist wave of penal policy has hit some nations, with more people imprisoned. And police numbers have grown across the world, with vast private forces now enhancing the official.

But, more important and less expected, new laws and novel kinds of regulations have expanded the state's reach into our lives, indeed our minds. Even as we exert more self-control, and even as the engines of informal socialization turn more swiftly, we also have more overt law—not just regulatory but penal too. More and different behaviors have been criminalized. Thoughts and intentions have increasingly become actionable. Even when multiple laws merely duplicate prohibitions, the state has arrogated to itself unprecedented powers through charge stacking—that is, targeting the same behavior via multiple avenues of prosecution.[98] Prosecutors have gained greater leverage to insist on plea bargains—effectively coercing defendants into pleading guilty, increasing the court system's throughput, and sparing themselves work. The charge that overcriminalization is now a problem has come from both Left and Right.[99]

Following Tocqueville, Foucault argued that modern regimes sought to change citizens' souls and did not just require correct outward behavior. These two thinkers focused on prisoners and mental patients, those pitiful, deviant marginals who bore the brunt of society's disapproval and discipline. Yet, as we have seen, the state's ambitions went even further. It aimed not only to criminalize more behaviors but also to apply formal statute ever deeper into citizens' psyches, holding them accountable for a wider palette of offenses at ever earlier stages of planning or even just consciousness. As the state sought to prevent—and not just punish—crimes, simple retributionist verities dissipated. It was no longer clear precisely what was forbidden, nor was the punishment for each offense set. Even the fundamental principle of no punishment without law seemed up for grabs. Expanding into inchoate offenses and crimes of omission, the law pushed past our actions to peer into our thoughts, holding us responsible for what went on in our minds, too.

Setting itself ever more tasks and motivated by the best of intentions, the modern state willy-nilly became a bigger part of the everyday. Modern life, it seemed, required more law. New technologies of course demanded new regulation, but the state was also asked to do more. We have more immigration law than ever before, not because we have more immigration than in, say, the late nineteenth century but because citizens expect the state to regulate it. Preserving the environment, ensuring workplace health and safety, protecting women from abuse, minorities from discrimination, children from predation, and consumers from fraud: all have become state tasks. Environmental legislation alone now makes up 15 percent of US federal regulations.[100] That would have surprised the early modern state. And the development of inchoate law in effect quadrupled the range of possible offenses, as planning, conspiring, and intending crimes were added to the acts themselves.

As the law expanded to an ever broader array of both overt and covert behaviors, more citizens became potential offenders—defendants who had just not yet been caught, the sword of Damocles ever pendant over them. As more actions became crimes, more citizens became criminals. Wanting to preserve First Nation artifacts, the state prosecuted campers on federal land who dug for arrowheads. Hoping to corral toxic poisons, it jailed entrepreneurs who shipped chemicals in nonregulated containers. Intending to preserve marine life, authorities went after food wholesalers who imported undersize lobsters. Worried at growing drug use, the state punished as complicit not just narcotics dealers but also the realtors who sold them houses and the interior decorators who chose their carpets.[101] Indeed, as one wag has pointed out, legal codes "are full of ingenious suggestions for committing crimes."[102]

Seeking to make life safer, healthier, and happier, US lawmakers have at one time or another prohibited hat pins of certain lengths, the public eating of reptiles, masked balls, hats at theatrical performances, and hotel sheets less than nine feet in length. In the 1880s, James Bryce, British ambassador to the United States, followed in the footsteps of Tocqueville's earlier travels throughout the country and reported wryly on the state-level regulations governing every conceivable topic. His irony extended not just to how it was forbidden to send annoying letters or employ the color-blind on trains but also to what we might consider sensible, indeed prescient, measures: requiring doctors and dentists to be licensed, obliging buildings taller than a certain height to have fireproof staircases, and prohibiting hotels and insurance companies from discriminating against Blacks and Jews. All such measures, he seemed to think, were wildly beyond anything at home in Britain.[103] Already in 1900, long before our own era's tsunami of new legislation, an observer imagined Dracon and Solon, the Greek legislators whose names live on in their codes, shaking their heads in bemusement at the panoply of laws governing the lives of modern Americans: punished for jumping off trains in motion, sleeping in bakeries, killing partridges out of season, failing to report infants' infected eyes, serving margarine in prisons, riding horses on the sidewalks of unincorporated villages, and so forth in all their eccentric glory.[104]

In sum, across the past several centuries, civil society has grown evermore orderly and regulated, but the state has also continued to expand in parallel. The retributive turn of the 1980s, with harsher punishments and more incarceration, was an Anglo-Saxon blip on larger secular developments. The state's interventions here were naked and undeniable. But more subtle states expanded their role, too, even as civil society's self-regulation continued apace. Insofar as sexual relations were governed at all, for example, they used to be regulated by morality, propriety, deference, and some local police powers. Only in extremis did law and employment regulation enter the picture, which left a wide field for sexual predators, ranging from workplace pests to flashers, molesters, and rapists. Today, protection from predation in homes, schools, workplaces, and public spaces has been legalified. Much mocked at the time, the Antioch College rules from the early 1990s were a harbinger, setting out procedures to ensure explicit verbal consent at each stage of the courtship ritual.[105] Similar formalization has spread from universities to the workplace. Men patting or pinching waitresses' or secretaries' bottoms, framed as harmless fun half a century ago, is now an offense. Domestic violence has been dealt with evermore formally. Injury to wives and children was specifically forbidden, as in England in 1853, and marital rape was finally explicitly outlawed there in 2003. In the past, police came only when domestic disputes spilled into public view, prompting someone to summon help. The authorities often sought to calm matters, resolving them without arrest. Today, this approach is seen as tolerating abuse. Police are now often required to arrest, turning what was once husbands' legal right to attack and batter their wives into a public offense. Abusive partners can be banished from the common home, imposing a de facto divorce.[106]

Once-tolerated behaviors have evermore become law's object. Although we might smile at the painstakingly officious and meticulous Polizei regulations of the eighteenth century, much of their intent remains in effect. Modern microregulation is often administered through regulatory law rather than through the penal code, but it is enforced more effectively. Use of inebriants is subject to law, even as some are exempted from statute's attention—as most recently with marijuana. Of course, states have regulated consumption for centuries, but rarely on today's scale. America's war on drugs—heir to similar battles against alcohol—has formalized behavioral control as it massively applies semi-militarized state force against deeply engrained and widespread behaviors. Drug-using Americans, especially ethnic minorities, were sent to prison ten times as often in the late 1990s as a decade earlier.[107]

Even sartorial regulations—seemingly pointless in the era of spandex worn in public—remain with us. East Germany outlawed long hair on men and short skirts on women. The Chinese use their digital panopticon surveillance to harass old folks who wear pajamas in public. But liberal democracies, too, intervene. Until 1937, a Yonkers ordinance prohibited appearing in public in "other than customary street attire." More recently, municipalities have forbidden baggy pants, the wearing of baseball caps backward, certain colors associated with gang membership, as well as ceremonial daggers borne by Sikhs. Japanese schools have required brown-haired pupils to dye their hair black to fit in. France and Denmark have banned burqas and other face coverings.[108] And the quickest way to end up in detention almost anywhere is to strip in public—or even in private if one is publicly visible.[109]

At the same time, as noted, citizens are more self-controlled than in the past. Cultural conservatives often lament that we are losing our sense of humor, by which they mean that we are no longer permitted to mock or sneer at the downtrodden and vulnerable. This change testifies to the success of shifting informal standards: "Mean jokes go out of style because civilization moves on."[110] Old coots may lament being reprimanded for telling Polish or mother-in-law jokes. But few would desire a return to the early twentieth century, when victims of discrimination often turned to libel or defamation law to protect themselves against "accusations" that we no longer regard as calumnious. In those days, it was considered a libel or slander per se (one that was actionable even without causing harm) to be called Black and, later, Communist or homosexual.[111] Similarly those called Jewish who did not consider themselves such could and did sue for having been vilified.[112]

Society exerts all manner of restraint on us. Foucauldians are right to have emphasized that. But the expected corollary—that overt, formal, statutory control ceded pride of place to the new disciplinary regime—rings false. As we have seen, along with the growth of informal social discipline, the state has also vastly expanded its formal regulatory powers. It passes new laws on a massive scale, sharpens existing ones, and intervenes ever deeper into civil society. As has often been pointed out, new laws proliferate, while old ones remain. Accretion of old and disused statutes explains only in part the mushrooming quantity of law. The US Congress has created fifty new crimes annually for the past several decades, the US states some forty.[113] Of the federal criminal provisions put on the books since the American Civil War, a calculation in 1998 put the figure enacted since 1970 at an astonishing 40 percent.[114] Britain instituted seventy immigration offenses over the entire twentieth century. A further eighty-four arrived in the first decade of the following millennium. The twelve years after 1979 saw half of all Chinese laws on public security enacted.[115] Add to this the way courts have expansively interpreted these burgeoning laws, further extending the state's reach.[116]

Policing has also expanded accordingly. The state once took as its primary function the protection against external enemies. Today, internal adversaries are considered equally important. The manpower allotted to policing once paled in comparison to the armed forces. Today it has largely pulled even, and that counts just official police. Add in private policing, and the point is hammered home. The first national police force, the French *maréchaussée* from the 1760s, had 3,000 men, the French army 400,000.[117] Today the US military has more than a million active personnel. Official policing institutions have somewhat less than a million, and there are about a million and a half police if the private forces are added in.[118] In Britain, the military has 192,000 personnel, and the official police force has 150,000 or 381,000 if private security forces are counted, too, bringing it to twice the size of the military.[119]

As the number of laws and potential crimes increased, the theoretical chances of the average citizen crossing the line has also multiplied. "The vehicle code gives me fifteen hundred reasons to pull you over," as one California highway patrolman put it.[120] No one disputes that the poor are punished disproportionately or that white-collar offenses are often treated lightly.[121] But the law has also taken aim at behaviors that were once not criminal at all. Today's good burghers, whose forebears might rarely have encountered the police, now often will—at least in theory. Citizens did not become more evil, but as the arena of illegality extended, they were likelier than ever to offend. We thus face an apparent paradox. Did expanding and deepening the law's reach mean that more citizens became potential criminals? The expansion of drug laws has fueled America's jail boom. Many current white-collar crimes were once legal or at least ignored. Bankers are now perp-walked to prison. Could it be that the civilizing process actually increased criminality?

Writing in 1902, Arthur Cleveland Hall welcomed the growth of convictions and imprisonment as signs of civilization and progress. As society became more complex and sophisticated, he thought, it required more laws. Since that, in turn, forbade more actions, society necessarily pushed more people beyond the pale. But the nature of crime changed. The number of archaic, primitive crimes committed—assault, mayhem, homicide—declined. The number of new, more genteel offenses—fraud, forgery—increased.[122]

How true that may be is hard to measure. Conviction rates have increased, though not in all nations.[123] Today, proportionately twice as many Americans have spent time in jail than half a century ago.[124] Almost twice the percentage of Britons were in jail in 2008 compared to in 1900.[125] Since more citizens have likely violated the law than we can ever pursue, the decision of who is a criminal now rests less with legislators than with the police and prosecutors.[126] Contacts between authorities and citizens that lead neither to arrest nor conviction yet serve a broader sense of enforcement have increased. Being stopped by police has become the most common form of citizen contact with criminal justice. Zero-tolerance policing has consigned a whole new class of petty misdemeanants to a system of official chicanery and invasive social control that stops short of conviction and incarceration.[127]

But to know whether the average citizen is more likely to be arrested and convicted, we need to know about recidivism, too. Are some people being convicted multiple times even as more people avoid entanglement altogether? In the United States, three-quarters of federal state prisoners released in 2005 were arrested again within five years.[128] What we do know is that even though the possibilities of offending have mushroomed, the overwhelming majority of citizens pass their lives without seriously confronting the law. Prison populations have skyrocketed, but over a lifetime "only" 5 percent of Americans will spend time in jail.[129] Given the exceptionally high incarceration rates in the United States, far fewer people go to prison almost anywhere else in the world. Though Hall's extrapolation was logical, more laws would have led to more criminals only if average citizens did not adjust their behavior in tune with the ever-wider web of potential ensnarlments. Exercising even greater self-control, they may have fallen no more afoul of the law than they did earlier—even as the law expanded to dig more potential pitfalls. If so, then the law spurred further efforts at self-control by defining the parameters of the acceptable ever more precisely.

By contrast, those least adept at self-control were likely to have had difficulty navigating the ever-narrower roads of legality. In theory, more citizens could offend since there was more to offend against. But they may not have. A small minority, however, has been caught in the unforgiving forcefield between expanding formal prohibitions and ever-higher demands on personal restraint. Society seems increasingly to have bisected: the majority self-regulated, only rarely encountering the business end of authority. Meanwhile, a smallish group of outsiders, downtrodden, and unfortunates bore the law's full brunt. For them, law became the last remaining engine of socialization. Law enforcement targeted racial and class outsiders, foreigners, the mentally ill, drug addicts, and others who violated society's increasingly numerous and elaborate norms, insufficiently reined in by informal guidance. Even when these outsiders were not convicted or locked up, a persistent barrage of petty violations (subway free-loading, marijuana use, and knife possession) sought to identify and control them.[130]

The world over, prisons are filled with ethnic and national outsiders. The story of America's jails is well known. The prison boom of the late twentieth century has not made inmates more representative of society as a whole. Quite the opposite, most prisoners are Black and Latino men. In Europe, racial minorities are even more overrepresented behind bars. In the United States, Blacks are represented six times disproportionately in the prison population. In Britain, it is seven times. It is twelve times for Aborigines in Australia, and sixteen times for Afro-Caribbeans in Canada.[131] In the US foreign nationals are underrepresented in prison—only 6 percent. Across Western Europe, however, foreigners often make up a large fraction and sometimes the majority of prisoners.[132] In North Rhine Westphalia, Romanians are arrested at forty-four times the rate of Germans and jailed twenty-one times as often.[133] Seventy percent of the Swiss prison population is foreign born, 45 percent in Austria, and 30 percent in Germany.[134] Banishment is added to lockup, and foreign prisoners in Europe are often expelled once their sentences are over—frequently to "homes" they have never actually lived in.[135]

Even as the state has grown relentlessly—with only few setbacks—over the past five thousand years, humans still dream of life without it. That law would eventually become unnecessary has been a fond illusion. The ancient Chinese expected law to vanish—Confucians because right living would become second nature, Legalists because punishments would be so cruel that no one would dare transgress.[136] In the fourth century, Augustine regarded the state as a necessarily coercive relationship between authority and humans, whose evil nature required subjugation, so it would be unnecessary in paradise.[137] Utopians have long hoped for communities held together by common sympathy and purpose, with no need for law.[138] Anarchists definitionally shunned the law when outlining their ideal futures. Like today's neoliberals, Proudhon imagined that contract would substitute for it. Indeed, neoliberals aim to limit the state's task to fighting crime, thus leaving markets free to arrange most other social relations.[139]

Marx and especially Friedrich Engels argued that after a proletarian dictatorship, when new rulers made use of old-regime power, the state would wither away. Absent private property, social contradictions would dissipate, and so, too, would the state. We all recognize the naïveté of this messianic expectation that law and policing would vanish as capitalism's social tensions evaporated under socialism's warm sun. Stalin certainly made short shrift of such yearnings. The illusion of doing without law was condemned, and socialist legality was declared statute's highest form, rigorously enforced.[140] Nonetheless, in the West today a related assumption remains widespread—the Foucauldian conviction that modernity shifts social control from state to society. These theorists insist that despite the illusion of liberalization, power remains, but it has moved from the state's heavy, centralized authority to subtle, diffuse, dispersed forms of discipline within society's institutions. The law has been expelled.[141]

Has no one recognized the continuing importance of the law? History has not been kind to Durkheim's understanding of why offending is sanctioned. He argued that society punishes crime not to revenge itself or to deter future offenses but ritually to express its communal ties, to reaffirm the unity of law-abiders against transgressors. The point of punishment was to influence not the offender but honest citizens, thus rallying the troops. In his early writings, Durkheim defined crime as acts that most people agree are transgressions, ones that offend the "collective consciousness" (society's "psychological type"), which he imagined present everywhere and across generations.[142] This definition presupposed a communal mind, an essentialist cultural unity of a sort now largely rejected by social scientists.[143] At best, it would describe only a small fraction of all statute. Unsurprisingly, however, lawyers have been gratified by the importance Durkheim attributed to the law. Some have arrogated to themselves the role once served by high priests. They argue that in the absence of shared national religions, law expresses our common beliefs of what must be condemned and helps create norms.[144]

Durkheim's later writings, elaborating the development of individualism, more plausibly argued for a collective sense of justice and has influenced thinking on human rights.[145] Restorative justice, returning punishment to its traditional prestate role of making good the damage done, has Durkheimian roots. Though Durkheim had a curiously mystical view of the law as expressing the collective nous, he also made other points of interest here. Early gods were enforcers. Religious transgressions were the first public crimes, affecting the whole community. The state eventually assumed the divine's role in enforcing. The law socializes us, though he understood it as the expression of shared communal values and not—as seems more plausible today—a tool wielded by powerful social groups. Durkheim also thought that punishments moderated as society developed, though not, as argued here, because the state strengthened but because human sympathy extended from victims to criminals.[146]

The argument made here is simple. Seen in the *longue durée* of global history, the state came late to making and enforcing law. But once started, it never looked back. Today, we are governed by more law than ever before. And yet even outside the law we are also increasingly socialized into correct behavior by an array of other means. So powerful is this socializing process that it raises the question: Why do we need the law any longer, especially more of it? Belt and suspenders? Clearly, the law persists. Despite our ever better-mannered and docile citizenry, law remains the workhorse of social control, defining and deepening the parameters of our socialization. Time therefore to bring the law back in, to move beyond Foucault. Today's penal codes are an absolutist ruler's wet dream, bestowing real power such monarchs would have envied. Yet most of us—the codes' subjects—scarcely notice them in our daily lives. In *The Devil's Dictionary,* Ambrose Bierce defined *opiate* as "an unlocked door in the prison of identity. It leads into the jail yard." We might say something similar of the Foucauldian vision of social discipline—the yard where inmates catch a glimpse of sky, run a few laps, and imagine the world beyond the prison walls. It remains in fact wholly under the state's umbrella.[147] To deter and otherwise shape our behavior, the law must exist, and it must be enforced. The rule of law requires laws, indeed ever more of them as matters become complex. A more advanced society may not have more criminals, as Hall thought, but it certainly has more laws, and those statutes require and encourage most citizens to toe the line. Ever new behaviors are forbidden, even as formerly offending conduct is gradually socialized away. To gain more self-control, it seems, we need more law.

Although the state may lay low, in dealing with crime it does not wither away.

Acknowledgments

I am indebted to Michael Kellogg, as always, for invaluable research assistance; to my colleagues Elisheva Carlebach and Martina Steer for help on the fine points of holy sin; to Abram de Swaan for a needed caution on (mis)interpreting Norbert Elias; to Larry Wolff and Stephen Gross, successive heads of the Center for European and Mediterranean Studies at NYU, for the chance to try out the ideas expressed here in classes there; and to Katy Fleming and Lauren Benton for making that possible.

Notes

Introduction

1. Tim Newburn, "'Tough on Crime': Penal Policy in England and Wales," *Crime and Justice* 36, 1 (2007) 457–458.

2. Steven Pinker, *The Better Angels of Our Nature: The Decline of Violence in History and Its Causes* (New York 2011) 47–56. The debates over Pinker's numbers are discussed in the conclusion here. Arriving anecdotally at a similar conclusion is James Sharpe in *A Fiery and Furious People: A History of Violence in England* (London 2016).

3. Max Nordau, *Degeneration* (London 1898) 40; Cesare Lombroso, *Crime* (Boston 1911) 43; Émile Durkheim, *The Division of Labour in Society*, 2nd ed., trans. W. D. Halls (orig. ed. 1893; reprint, Houndmills 2013) 42, page citations referring to the Houndmills edition.

4. Sarah A. Seo, *Policing the Open Road: How Cars Transformed American Freedom* (Cambridge MA 2019) 12–13; Frank R. Baumgartner et al., *Suspect Citizens: What 20 Million Traffic Stops Tell Us about Policing and Race* (Cambridge 2018) 5.

5. US Department of Justice, *Crime and Justice Atlas 2000* (Washington DC 2000) 40. Adding driving under the influence, drunkenness, liquor laws, and drug abuse together for 2017 gives a total of 30.4 percent of total arrests, which is larger than even traffic violations, whose true size is submerged in the category "all other offenses," at 31.2 percent. Percentages calculated from the figures in FBI, "Table 29: Estimated Number of Arrests," Uniform Crime Reporting Program, Crime in the United States 2017, https://ucr.fbi.gov/crime-in-the-u.s/2017/crime-in-the-u.s.-2017/topic-pages/tables/table-29.

6. Cal Winslow, "Sussex Smugglers," in Douglas Hay et al., eds., *Albion's Fatal Tree: Crime and Society in Eighteenth Century England* (New York 1975) 147; Clive Emsley, *Crime and Society in England, 1750–1900,* 4th ed. (Harlow 2010) 29.

7. *The Week*, 13 December 2019.

8. Manuel Eisner, "Long-Term Historical Trends in Violent Crime," *Crime and Justice* 30 (2003) 96–98.

9. Randolph Roth, "Homicide in Early Modern England 1549–1800," *Crime, histoire et sociétés* 5, 2 (2001) 55; Randolph Roth, *American Homicide* (Cambridge MA 2009) 13–14; Robert R. Dykstra, "Body Counts and Murder Rates: The Contested Statistics of Western Violence," *Reviews in American History* 31, 4 (2003) 556.

10. Eisner, "Long-Term Historical Trends in Violent Crime," 107.

11. Starting in the early 1990s, the US murder rate declined from around 6.5/100,000 to 4.4/100,000 in 2014 (FBI, "Table 1: Crime in the United States by Volume and Rate per 100,000 Residents, 1998–2017," Uniform Crime Reporting Program, Crime in the United States 2017, https://ucr.fbi.gov/crime-in-the-u.s/2017/crime-in-the-u.s.-2017/topic-pages/tables/table-1).

12. Norbert Elias, *The Civilizing Process* (London 2000).

13. Peter Baldwin, *Contagion and the State in Europe, 1830–1930* (Cambridge 1999) 410–413.

14. Hubert John Pragnell, *Early British Railway Tunnels: The Implications for Planners, Landowners, and Passengers between 1830 and 1870*, University of York Railway Studies (October 2016) 233–234, http://etheses.whiterose.ac.uk/16826/1/Railway%20tunnels%20recovered%203.pdf; Sonya Sawyer Fritz, "'A Room of Her Very Own': Privacy and Leisure in the Victorian Girl's Bedroom," *Girlhood Studies* 8, 2 (2015) 46–47.

15. Peter Baldwin, "The Return of the Coercive State: Behavioral Control in Multicultural Society," in T. V. Paul et al., eds., *The Nation-State in Question* (Princeton 2003) 114.

Chapter 1

1. Durkheim, *Division of Labour*, 60.

2. The theme of E. Adamson Hoebel, *The Law of Primitive Man* (Cambridge MA 1954).

3. Jan Assmann, *The Price of Monotheism* (Stanford 2010) 54.

4. Alan E. Bernstein, *The Formation of Hell: Death and Retribution in the Ancient and Early Christian Worlds* (Ithaca 1993) 3, 61, 160–161, 200–201.

5. Plato, *Phaedo*, trans. David Gallop (Oxford 1975) 107c.

6. Trevor J. Saunders, *Plato's Penal Code: Tradition, Controversy, and Reform in Greek Penology* (Oxford 1991) 53.

7. Rémi Brague, *The Law of God* (Chicago 2007) 14; Yonglin Jiang, *The Mandate of Heaven and the Great Ming Code* (Seattle 2011) 9; R. P. Peerenboom, *Law and Morality in Ancient China: The Silk Manuscripts of Huang-Lao* (Albany 1993) 5.

8. Derk Bodde, "Basic Concepts of Chinese Law," *Proceedings of the American Philosophical Society* 107, 5 (1963) 378.

9. Hoebel, *Law of Primitive Man*, 260; Henry Maine, *Ancient Law* (London 1861) 218.

10. Helen Silving, "The Oath," *Yale Law Journal* 68 (1959) 1335, 1383; Richard H. Underwood, "False Witness," *Arizona Journal of International and Comparative Law* 10 (1993) 229; Michael D. Gordon, "The Invention of a Common Law Crime: Perjury and the Elizabethan Courts," *American Journal of Legal History* 24, 2 (1980) 148.

11. Kent Flannery and Joyce Marcus, *The Creation of Inequality* (Cambridge MA 2012) 55.

12. Saunders, *Plato's Penal Code*, 34–38.

13. Raffaele Pettazzoni, *The All-Knowing God* (London 1956) 20–21.

14. Leviticus 26:14–18.

15. Genesis 4:9–10.

16. J. Walter Jones, *The Law and Legal Theory of the Greeks* (Oxford 1956) 97.

17. Christine Hayes, *What's Divine about Divine Law?* (Princeton 2015) 2.

18. Paula Fredriksen, *Sin: The Early History of an Idea* (Princeton 2012) 18.

19. Israel Drapkin, *Crime and Punishment in the Ancient World* (Lexington 1989) 276.

20. Frederick Pollock and Frederic William Maitland, *The History of English Law before the Time of Edward I*, 2nd ed. (Cambridge 1898), 1:130.

21. Cynthia Herrup, *The Common Peace: Participation and the Criminal Law in Seventeenth-Century England* (Cambridge 1987) 3.

22. Emsley, *Crime and Society in England*, 188, 196; Craig B. Little and Christopher P. Sheffield, "Frontiers and Criminal Justice: English Private Prosecution Societies and American Vigilantism in the Eighteenth and Nineteenth Centuries," *American Sociological Review* 48, 6 (1983) 797.

23. Daniel Klerman, "Settlement and the Decline of Private Prosecution in Thirteenth-Century England," *Law and History Review* 19 (2001) 8; Prosecution of Offenses Act 1985, c. 23, sec. 6(1); Alec Samuels, "Non-Crown Prosecutions: Prosecutions by Non-police Agencies and by Private Individuals," *Criminal Law Review* (1986) 34; David Friedman, "Making Sense of English Law Enforcement in the Eighteenth Century," *University of Chicago Law School Roundtable* 2 (1995) 476; Bruce P. Smith, "The Emergence of Public Prosecution in London, 1790–1850," *Yale Journal of Law and Humanities* 18 (2006) 29.

24. Michael Cavadino and James Dignan, *Penal Systems: A Comparative Approach* (London 2006) 165, 178–179.

25. Strafgesetzbuch, §123, §247, §183, §§293–294.

26. Gerhard O.W. Mueller, "Tort, Crime, and the Primitive," *Journal of Criminal Law, Criminology, and Police Science* 46 (1955) 312; Jones, *Law and Legal Theory of the Greeks*, 116–117.

27. Montesquieu, *Spirit of the Laws*, 6:9.

28. Immanuel Kant, *The Philosophy of Law*, trans. W. Hastie (Edinburgh 1887) 197; Peter J. Steinberger, "Hegel on Crime and Punishment," *American Political Science Review* 77, 4 (1983) 860.

29. Tom R. Tyler, *Why People Obey the Law* (Princeton 2006) passim.

30. Hence, Marxism, which insisted that behind the democratic facade lay only class oppression, also refused to accept the claim of law to be self-imposition, regarding even democratically decided law as akin to that forced on subject populations.

31. David Philips, "'A New Engine of Power and Authority': The Institutionalization of Law-Enforcement in England 1780–1830," in V. A. C. Gatrell et al., eds., *Crime and the Law* (London 1980) 158; Penry Williams, *The Tudor Regime* (Oxford 1979) 232; Michael R. Weisser, *Crime and Punishment in Early Modern Europe* (Atlantic Highlands 1979) 65; Victor Bailey, "The Shadow of the Gallows: The Death Penalty and the British Labour Government, 1945–51," *Law and History Review* 18, 2 (2000) 306. In Mamers in eighteenth-century France, only 9 percent of criminal trials

eventually resulted in sanctions. Alfred Soman, "Deviance and Criminal Justice in Western Europe," *Criminal Justice History* 1 (1980) 7.

32. Thomas Andrew Green, *Verdict according to Conscience: Perspectives on the English Criminal Trial Jury 1200–1800* (Chicago 1985) 310.

33. Both the punisher, whose energies are sapped by harshness, and the punished must be considered. Jiangnan Zhu, "Do Severe Penalties Deter Corruption? A Game-Theoretic Analysis of the Chinese Case," *China Review* 12, 2 (2012) 12.

34. Albrecht Funk, *Polizei und Rechtsstaat: Die Entwicklung des staatlichen Gewaltmonopols in Preussen 1848–1914* (Frankfurt 1986) 320.

35. Edward Jenks, *A Short History of English Law*, 6th ed. (London 1949) 347.

36. Anna Bindler and Randi Hjalmarsson, *The Fall of Capital Punishment and the Rise of Prisons: How Punishment Severity Affects Jury Verdicts*, University of Gothenburg, School of Business, Economics, and Law, Working Papers in Economics 674 (October 2016) 5, 21.

37. Michel Foucault, *Discipline and Punish* (New York 1977) 82.

38. Leon Radzinowicz, *History of English Criminal Law* (London 1948) 1:93.

39. Thomas A. Green, "Societal Concepts of Criminal Liability for Homicide in Mediaeval England," *Speculum* 47, 4 (1972) 671; Green, *Verdict according to Conscience*, 32.

40. Crown Prosecution Service, *Annual Report and Accounts* (2014–2015) 69, https://www.cps.gov.uk/publications/docs/annual_report_2014_15.pdf. The rate in US state courts in 2006 was 94 percent (US Bureau of Justice Statistics, "Felony Sentences in State Courts, 2006," http://www.bjs.gov/index.cfm?ty=pbdetail&iid=2152). Among federal cases, 91 percent ended in conviction in 2011–2012 US Department of Justice, *Federal Justice Statistics 2012: Statistical Tables* (January 2015) NCJ 248470, table. 4.2

41. The conviction rate was almost 92 percent in 2017: Table D-4. U.S. District Courts–Criminal Defendants Disposed of, by Type of Disposition and Offense, during the 12-Month Period Ending September 30, 2017, http://www.uscourts.gov/sites/default/files/data_tables/jb_d4_0930.2017.pdf; Gábor T. Rittersporn, "Terror and Soviet Legality: Police vs Judiciary, 1933–1940," in James Harris, ed., *The Anatomy of Terror: Political Violence under Stalin* (Oxford 2013) 187.

42. Brian Chapman, *Police State* (New York 1970) 82.

43. Alfred C. Kinsey et al., *Sexual Behavior in the Human Male* (Philadelphia 1948) 392.

44. David A. Harris, "'Driving while Black' and All Other Traffic Offenses: The Supreme Court and Pretextual Traffic Stops," *Journal of Criminal Law and Criminology* 87 (1997) 558; Seo, *Policing the Open Road*, 27.

45. Barton L. Ingraham, *Political Crime in Europe* (Berkeley 1979) 6.

46. John Baker, "Revisiting the Explosive Growth of Federal Crimes," Heritage Foundation, 16 June 2008, https://www.heritage.org/report/revisiting-the-explosive-growth-federal-crimes; *Revised Statutes of the United States* (Washington DC 1875), *US Statutes at Large*, vol. 18, pt. 2, chap. 36, https://www.loc.gov/law/help/statutes-at-large/43rd-congress/c43-DC.pdf; *US Code* (2018 ed.) 12:749–1230, 13:1–407, https://www.govinfo.gov/content/pkg/USCODE-2018-title18/pdf/USCODE-2018-title18.pdf.

47. Mila Sohoni, "The Idea of 'Too Much Law,'" *Fordham Law Review* 80 (2012) 1606; William J. Stuntz, "The Pathological Politics of Criminal Law," *Michigan Law Review* 100 (2001–2002) 513–518.

48. John C. Coffee Jr., "Does 'Unlawful' Mean 'Criminal'? Reflections on the Disappearing Tort/Crime Distinction in American Law," *Boston University Law Review* 71 (1991) 216.

49. Ezekiel 18:13.

50. Chad Baruch, "In the Name of the Father: A Critique of Reliance upon Jewish Law to Support Capital Punishment in the United States," *University of Detroit Mercy Law Review* 78 (2000) 54; F. W. Maitland, "The Deacon and the Jewess: Or Apostasy at Common Law," *Transactions of the Jewish Historical Society of England* 6 (1908–1910) 260; Aibek Ahmedov, "Religious Minorities and Apostasy in Early Islamic States," *Journal of Islamic State Practices in International Law* 2 (2006) 1, 5.

51. Gary A. Anderson, *Sin: A History* (New Haven 2009) 3.

52. Markus Dirk Dubber, *The Police Power: Patriarchy and the Foundations of American Government* (New York 2005) 51–52.

53. Islamic law does not insist very firmly on creditors' rights to repayment. As a result, in some places, such as Egypt and the Gaza Strip, there are no bankruptcy laws, and debtors are still jailed. See "Why Hamas Jails People Who Can't Pay Their Debts," *Economist*, 2 August 2018.

54. Tawny Paul, *The Poverty of Disaster: Debt and Insecurity in Eighteenth-Century Britain* (Cambridge 2019) 33; Caleb Foote, "The Coming Constitutional Crisis in Bail," *University of Pennsylvania Law Review* 113, 7 (1965) 991; Jason J. Kilborn, "Foundations of Forgiveness in Islamic Bankruptcy Law," *American Bankruptcy Law Journal* 85 (2011) 344.

55. Paul H. Haagen, "Eighteenth-Century English Society and the Debt Law," in Stanley Cohen and Andrew Scull, eds., *Social Control and the State* (New York 1983) 225.

56. Gordon Wright, *Between the Guillotine and Liberty: Two Centuries of the Crime Problem in France* (New York 1983) 84.

57. Floyd Seyward Lear, *Treason in Roman and Germanic Law* (Austin 1965) 29; Inga Glendinnen, *Aztecs* (Cambridge 2014) 56; J. A. Sharpe, *Crime in Early Modern England 1550–1750*, 2nd ed. (Harlow 1999) 74.

58. Williams, *Tudor Regime*, 144.

59. William Ian Miller, *Bloodtaking and Peacemaking: Feud, Law, and Society in Saga Iceland* (Chicago 1990) 224; F. L. Attenborough, ed., *The Laws of the Earliest English Kings* (Cambridge 1922) Ine cap 2; *Allgemeines Landrecht für die Preußischen Staaten* (1794) pt. 2, §738.

60. J. M. Beattie, *Policing and Punishment in London, 1660–1750* (Oxford 2001) 169–70; Steve Hindle, "The Keeping of the Public Peace," in Paul Griffiths et al., eds., *The Experience of Authority in Early Modern England* (Basingstoke 1996) 219.

61. Saunders, *Plato's Penal Code*, 245.

62. Pieter Spierenburg, *The Spectacle of Suffering: Executions and the Evolution of Repression* (Cambridge 1984) 137.

63. Strafgesetzbuch, Bavaria, 1813, art. 401.

64. Edward Delman, "When Adultery Is a Crime," *Atlantic*, 2 March 2015.

65. David Nash, "Analyzing the History of Religious Crime: Models of 'Passive' and 'Active' Blasphemy since the Medieval Period," *Journal of Social History* 41, 1 (2007) 14.

66. With organized religion having abandoned the everyday duties of witches, such as exorcism, a market has opened up for others to enter. See "Demand for Exorcists Is Soaring in France," *Economist*, 20 July 2017.

67. Christina Larner, "Crimen Exceptum: The Crime of Witchcraft in Europe," in Gatrell et al., *Crime and the Law*, 50.

68. "Witches Are Still Hunted in India—and Blinded and Beaten and Killed," *Economist*, 21 October 2017.

69. "Vatican Gives Official Backing to Exorcists," *Guardian*, 2 July 2014; Adrita Biswas, "The Vatican to Train Exorcists," *International Business Times*, 26 February 2018; Jason Horowitz, "'Shut Up, Satan': Rome Course Teaches Exorcism, Even by Cellphone," *New York Times*, 19 April 2018.

70. Art. 54; Corinne Treitel, *A Science for the Soul: Occultism and the Genesis of the German Modern* (Baltimore 2004) 201; Robin Levinson-King, "Canada's Last Witch Trials," *BBC News*, 30 October 2018.

71. Sharpe, *Crime in Early Modern England*, 121, 123. The last woman punished as a "scold" in the United States was ducked in Jersey City in 1889. Darius Rejali, *Torture and Democracy* (Princeton 2007) 282.

72. George L. Kelling and Catherine M. Coles, *Fixing Broken Windows: Restoring Order and Reducing Crime in Our Communities* (New York 1996) 47.

73. Kelling and Coles, *Fixing Broken Windows*, chap. 2.

74. Defamation suits made up a large and eventually majority portion of all cases in certain courts in England starting in the late sixteenth century. See J. A. Sharpe, "'Such Disagreement betwyx Neighbors': Litigation and Human Relations in Early Modern England," in John Bossy, ed., *Disputes and Settlements* (Cambridge 1983) 170–171. Examples of defamatory language in this period are given in David Cressy, *Dangerous Talk: Scandalous, Seditious, and Treasonable Speech in Pre-modern England* (Oxford 2010) chap. 2.

75. Ann C. Motto, "'Equity Will Not Enjoin a Libel': Well, Actually, Yes, It Will," *Seventh Circuit Review* 11, 2 (2016) 272; Hannah Rogers Metcalfe, "Libel in the Blogosphere and Social Media," *Charleston Law Review* 5 (2011) 486; Ian Burrell, "Libel Cases Prompted by Social Media Posts Rise 300% in a Year," *Independent*, 19 October 2014; "Online Defamation Cases in England and Wales Double," *BBC News UK*, 26 August 2011, http://www.bbc.com/news/uk-14684620; Leslie Yalof Garfield, "The Death of Slander," *Columbia Journal of Law and the Arts* 35 (2011) 42; James Lasdun, *Give Me Everything You Have: On Being Stalked* (London 2013) 110.

76. Durkheim, *Division of Labour*, 113, 123–127.

77. Clive Emsley, "Repression, 'Terror,' and the Rule of Law in England during the Decade of the French Revolution," *English Historical Review* 100, 397 (1985) 807–808; John J. Merriam, "Natural Law and Self-Defense," *Military Law Review* 206 (2010) 80.

78. Weisser, *Crime and Punishment*, 21; Lawrence M. Friedman, *The Republic of Choice* (Cambridge MA 1990) 142.

79. Amanda Vickery, "An Englishman's Home Is His Castle? Thresholds, Boundaries, and Privacies in the Eighteenth-Century London House," *Past and Present* 199 (2008) 148; Weisser, *Crime and Punishment*, 45.

80. Radzinowicz, *History of English Criminal Law*, 1:709–710.

81. Beattie, *Policing and Punishment*, 125–126; Clive Emsley, *The English Police*, 2nd ed. (Harlow 1996) 76.

82. Stuntz, "Pathological Politics," 556; Steven N. Gofman, "Car Cruising: One Generation's Innocent Fun Becomes the Next Generation's Crime," *Brandeis Law Journal* 32 (2002) 6.

83. Markus Dirk Dubber, "Policing Possession: The War on Crime and the End of Criminal Law," *Journal of Criminal Law and Criminology* 91, 4 (2001) 874.

84. John Braithwaite, *Crime, Shame, and Reintegration* (Cambridge 1989) 40–41.

85. John C. Coffee Jr., "From Tort to Crime: Some Reflections on the Criminalization of Fiduciary Breaches and the Problematic Line between Law and Ethics," *American Criminal Law Review* 19 (1981) 127–128; Coffee, "Does 'Unlawful' Mean 'Criminal'?," 202; Samuel W. Buell, *Capital Offenses: Business Crime and Punishment in America's Corporate Age* (New York 2016) 41–45.

86. French penal code, revision of 13 May 1863, art. 406, §2; Carl Ludwig von Bar, *A History of Continental Criminal Law* (Boston 1916) 340.

87. Coffee, "Does 'Unlawful' Mean 'Criminal'?," 200.

88. Peter W. Huber, *Liability: The Legal Revolution and Its Consequences* (New York 1989).

89. Stephen F. Smith, "Overcoming Overcriminalization," *Journal of Criminal Law and Criminology* 102, 3 (2012) 546.

90. Vern L. Bullough, "Age of Consent: A Historical Overview," *Journal of Psychology & Human Sexuality* 16, 2–3 (2004) 37–38; Kate Sutherland, "From Jailbird to Jailbait: Age of Consent Laws and the Construction of Teenage Sexualities," *William and Mary Journal of Women and the Law* 9 (2003) 314.

91. John Pratt, "Scandinavian Exceptionalism in an Era of Penal Excess," *British Journal of Criminology* 48 (2008) 287; Julian V. Roberts et al., *Penal Populism and Public Opinion: Lessons from Five Countries* (New York 2003) 130.

92. Stuntz, "Pathological Politics," 513; "Violence against Women: Government Bill 1997/98:55," Swedish Government Offices, Fact Sheet, 1999.

93. California penal code, §288a.

94. Bernard E. Harcourt, "The Collapse of the Harm Principle," *Journal of Criminal Law and Criminology* 90, 1 (1999) passim.

95. Act of 26 July 1873; von Bar, *History of Continental Criminal Law*, 340.

96. Alex S. Vitale, *The End of Policing* (London 2017) chap. 5.

97. Julius R. Ruff, *Violence in Early Modern Europe* (Cambridge 2001) 35–39.

98. John Boswell, *The Kindness of Strangers: The Abandonment of Children in Western Europe from Late Antiquity to the Renaissance* (New York 1988) 58–60; Benjamin F. Martin, *Crime and Criminal Justice under the Third Republic* (Baton Rouge 1990) 4.

99. Simon Szreter, "The Right of Registration: Development, Identity Registration, and Social Security," *World Development* 35, 1 (2007) 71.

100. Kim Brooks, *Small Animals: Parenthood in the Age of Fear* (New York 2018).

101. Paul G. Chevigny, "From Betrayal to Violence: Dante's *Inferno* and the Social Construction of Crime," *Law and Social Inquiry* 26, 4 (2001) 804.

102. Peter Baldwin, *The Copyright Wars* (Princeton 2014).

103. John Crook, *Law and Life of Rome* (Ithaca 1967) 253.

104. James Barr Ames, "Law and Morals," *Harvard Law Review* 22, 2 (1908) 103; S. F. C. Milsom, *Historical Foundations of the Common Law*, 2nd ed. (London 1981)

384–385; Huw Beverley-Smith et al., *Privacy, Property, and Personality: Civil Law Perspectives on Commercial Appropriation* (Cambridge 2005).

105. Helen Pringle, "Are We Capable of Offending God?," in Elizabeth Burns Coleman and Kevin White, eds., *Negotiating the Sacred: Blasphemy and Sacrilege in a Multicultural Society* (Canberra 2006) 31; Lorenz Langer, *Religious Offence and Human Rights: The Implications of Defamation of Religions* (Cambridge 2014) 370–377.

106. Jonathan Simon, *Governing through Crime: How the War on Crime Transformed American Democracy and Created a Culture of Fear* (New York 2007) 4.

107. Morris M. Kleiner, "Occupational Licensing," *Journal of Economic Perspectives* 14, 1 (2000) 190.

108. Prosecuting those who hurt animals has thrown up its own issues: Why pets but not farmed animals? Why do reformers who reject reliance on imprisonment for other crimes retain it for animal harm? See Justin Marceau, *Beyond Cages: Animal Law and Criminal Punishment* (Cambridge 2019).

109. The Dangerous Dogs Act of 1991 in Britain determines which kinds of dog are not pets, for example.

110. Christopher D. Stone, "Should Trees Have Standing? Towards Legal Rights to Natural Objects," *Southern California Law Review* 45 (1972). The Whanganui River in New Zealand has been given legal standing. "Innovative Bill Protects Whanganui River with Legal Personhood," New Zealand Parliament, 28 March 2017, https://www.parliament.nz/en/get-involved/features/innovative-bill-protects-whanganui-river-with-legal-personhood/. As has the Amazon forest in Colombia: Anastasia Moloney, "Colombia's Top Court Orders Government to Protect Amazon Forest in Landmark Case," *Reuters,* 6 April 2018, https://www.reuters.com/article/us-colombia-deforestation-amazon/colombias-top-court-orders-government-to-protect-amazon-forest-in-landmark-case-idUSKCN1HD21Y.

111. Michael E. Tigar, "The Right of Property and the Law of Theft," *Texas Law Review* 62, 8 (1984) 1454; George P. Fletcher, "The Metamorphosis of Larceny," *Harvard Law Review* 89, 3 (1976) 471–474.

112. Michael D. Gordon, "The Perjury Statute of 1563," *Proceedings of the American Philosophical Society* 124, 6 (1980) 444.

113. Yannis D. Kotsonis, "Taxes and the Two Faces of the State since the Eighteenth Century," in John L. Brooke et al., eds., *State Formations* (Cambridge 2018) 239; Richard S. Willen, "Religion and the Law: The Secularization of Testimonial Procedures," *Sociological Analysis* 44, 1 (1983) 57–62; Underwood, "False Witness," 248.

114. Coffee, "Does 'Unlawful' Mean 'Criminal'?," 202–204; Fletcher, "Metamorphosis of Larceny," passim; Smith, "Overcoming Overcriminalization," 559–560.

115. R. J. V. Lenman, "Art, Society, and the Law in Wilhelmine Germany: The Lex Heinze," *Oxford German Studies* 8 (1973) 98; *Protokoll über die Verhandlungen des Parteitages der Sozialdemokratischen Partei Deutschlands,* Hannover, 9–14 October 1899 (Berlin 1899) 86–87; Franz v. Liszt, *Lehrbuch des Deutschen Strafrechts,* 16th and 17th ed. (Berlin 1908) 619.

116. Kristen E. Eichensehr, "Treason in the Age of Terrorism: An Explanation and Evaluation of Treason's Return in Democratic States," *Vanderbilt Journal of Transnational Law* 42 (2009) 1496.

117. David S. Ardia, "Freedom of Speech, Defamation, and Injunctions," *William and Mary Law Review* 55, 1 (2013) 12; Yang-Ming Tham, "Honest to Blog: Balancing the Interests of Public Figures and Anonymous Bloggers in Defamation Lawsuits," *Villanova Sports and Entertainment Law Journal* 17 (2010) 231.

118. Tabatha Abu El-Haj, "Defining Peaceably: Policing the Line between Constitutionally Protected Protest and Unlawful Assembly," *Missouri Law Review* 80 (2015) 971.

119. Stuntz, "Pathological Politics," 515; Erik Luna, "The Overcriminalization Phenomenon," *American University Law Review* 54 (2005) 704; Stuart P. Green, "Why It's a Crime to Tear the Tag off a Mattress: Overcriminalization and the Moral Content of Regulatory Offenses," *Emory Law Journal* 46 (1997).

120. Markus D. Dubber, *The Dual Penal State* (New York 2018) chap. 4. A similar theme informs Gary Gerstle, *Liberty and Coercion: The Paradox of American Government from the Founding to the Present* (Princeton 2015).

121. R. A. Duff, "Criminalizing Endangerment," *Louisiana Law Review* 65 (2005) 961.

122. Clive Emsley, "'Mother, What Did Policemen Do When There Weren't Any Motors?' The Law, the Police, and the Regulation of Motor Traffic in England, 1900–1939," *Historical Journal* 36, 2 (1993) 366; Seo, *Policing the Open Road*, 50–51.

123. Sanford H. Kadish, "The Crisis of Overcriminalization," *Annals of the American Academy of Political and Social Science* 374 (1967) 158; James R. Copland and Rafael A. Mangual, *Overcriminalizing America*, Manhattan Institute (August 2018) 7, https://media4.manhattan-institute.org/sites/default/files/R-JC-0818.pdf.

124. Elizabeth E. Joh, "The Paradox of Private Policing," *Journal of Criminal Law and Criminology* 95, 1 (2004) 121–122.

125. Douglas Kim, "Asset Forfeiture: Giving Up Your Constitutional Rights," *Campbell Law Review* 19 (1997) 528–529, 541; Todd Barnet, "Legal Fiction and Forfeiture: An Historical Analysis of the Civil Asset Forfeiture Reform Act," *Duquesne Law Review* 40 (2001) 94. The standard work on asset forfeiture is Leonard W. Levy, *A License to Steal: The Forfeiture of Property* (Chapel Hill 1996). Some reform has now been introduced with the Civil Asset Forfeiture Reform Act of 2000: see Michael Van den Berg, "Proposing a Transactional Approach to Civil Forfeiture Reform," *University of Pennsylvania Law Review* 163 (2015) 875–879. There are similarities in the UK Proceeds of Crime Act of 2002: see Simon Hallsworth and John Lea, "Reconstructing Leviathan: Emerging Contours of the Security State," *Theoretical Criminology* 15, 2 (2011) 148.

126. Didier Fassin, *The Will to Punish* (New York 2018) 40; Azam Ahmed, "Fighting as Masked Vigilantes, Brazil's Police Leave a Trail of Bodies and Fear," *New York Times*, 20 December 2019.

127. Edward Peters, *Torture*, exp. ed. (Philadelphia 1996) 117.

128. Swedish penal code, chap. 23, sect. 6, https://www.government.se/content assets/5315d27076c942019828d6c36521696e/swedish-penal-code.pdf; Andrew Ashworth and Lucia Zedner, *Preventive Justice* (Oxford 2014) 101.

129. Dubber, *Dual Penal State*, 41–42.

130. John H. Langbein, *Torture and the Law of Proof* (Chicago 1976) 47–48.

131. Model Penal Code, 211.2; Douglas N. Husak, "The Nature and Justifiability of Nonconsummate Offenses," *Arizona Law Review* 37 (1995) 162–165.

132. Neal Kumar Kaytal, "Conspiracy Theory," *Yale Law Journal* 112 (2003) 1310.

133. Andrew Ashworth and Lucia Zedner, "Just Prevention: Preventive Rationales and the Limits of the Criminal Law," in R. A. Duff and Stuart P. Green, ed., *Philosophical Foundations of Criminal Law* (Oxford 2011) 283.

134. Ira P. Robbins, "Double Inchoate Crimes," *Harvard Journal on Legislation* 26 (1989) 96.

135. Laura Meli, "Hate Crime and Punishment: Why Typical Punishment Does Not Fit the Crime," *University of Illinois Law Review* 3 (2014) 926; Erik Bleich, "The Rise of Hate Speech and Hate Crime Laws in Liberal Democracies," *Journal of Ethnic and Migration Studies* 37, 6 (2011) 925–926.

136. Dubber, *Dual Penal State*, 25

137. *Regina v. Saunders*, 2 Plowd. 473 (1575), quoted in Francis Bowes Sayre, "Criminal Responsibility for the Acts of Another," *Harvard Law Review* 43, 5 (1930) 696.

138. Richard Mowery Andrews, "Boundaries of Citizenship: The Penal Regulation of Speech in Revolutionary France," *French Politics and Society* 7, 3 (1989) 93; John H. Tate Jr., "Distinctions between Accessory before the Fact and Principal," *Washington and Lee Law Review* 19, 1 (1962) 96.

139. Markus D. Dubber, "Criminalizing Complicity," *Journal of International Criminal Justice* 5 (2007) 979–980.

140. Joshua Dressler, "Reassessing the Theoretical Underpinnings of Accomplice Liability," *Hastings Law Journal* 37 (1985) 102.

141. Marc Morjé Howard, *Unusually Cruel: Prisons, Punishment, and the Real American Exceptionalism* (New York 2017) 47.

142. Dubber, "Policing Possession," 843; Michael Heyman, "Losing All Sense of Just Proportion: The Peculiar Law of Accomplice Liability," *St. John's Law Review* 87 (2013) 142.

143. French penal code, 1810, art. 126; Neil K. Kaytal, "This Conspiracy Theory Should Worry Trump," *New York Times*, 23 August 2018.

144. These debates are occurring in congressional hearings as well: House of Representatives, *Over-criminalization of Conduct/Over-federalization of Criminal Law: Hearing before the Committee on the Judiciary, Subcommittee on Crime, Terrorism, and Homeland Security*, 111th Cong., 1st sess., 22 July 2009, Serial 111-67, https://www.govinfo.gov/content/pkg/CHRG-111hhrg51226/html/CHRG-111hhrg51226.htm; House of Representatives, *Reining in Overcriminalization: Assessing the Problem, Proposing Solutions: Hearing before the Committee on the Judiciary, Subcommittee on Crime, Terrorism, and Homeland Security*, 111th Cong., 2nd sess., 28 September 2010, Serial 111-151, https://www.govinfo.gov/content/pkg/CHRG-111hhrg58476/html/CHRG-111hhrg58476.htm.

145. Paul H. Robinson and Michael T. Cahill, "The Accelerating Degradation of American Criminal Codes," *Hastings Law Journal* 56 (2005) 638. Further references to the overcriminalization literature are in the conclusion.

146. Zephyr Teachout, "The Unenforceable Corrupt Contract: Corruption and Nineteenth Century Contract Law," *N.Y.U. Review of Law and Social Change* 35

(2011) 681; Zephyr Teachout, *Corruption in America* (Cambridge MA 2014) 232; Nick Corasaniti, "Why the 'Bridgegate' Scandal Could Backfire on Prosecutors," *New York Times*, 3 July 2019.

147. Elisabeth K. Friedrich, "Insider Trading after Newman: The Impact on Financial Institutions," *Journal of Taxation and Regulation of Financial Institutions* 29, 4 (2016) 23; Jesse Eisinger, *The Chickenshit Club: Why the Justice Department Fails to Prosecute Executives* (New York 2017) 306.

Chapter 2

1. Durkheim was among the first to note the gods' role as enforcers. *Division of Labour*, 72. Since then, an entire school of social psychology has emerged to pursue this insight. See Harvey Whitehouse et al., "Complex Societies Precede Moralizing Gods throughout World History," *Nature*, 20 March 2019; Lizzie Wade, "Birth of the Moralizing Gods," *Science*, 349, 6251 (2015) 919.

2. Thorkild Jacobsen, "Primitive Democracy in Ancient Mesopotamia," *Journal of Near Eastern Studies* 2, 3 (1943) 169.

3. Dominic D. P. Johnson, "God's Punishment and Public Goods," *Human Nature* 16, 4 (2005) 412; Whitehouse et al., "Complex Societies Precede Moralizing Gods"; Edward James, "'Beati Pacifici': Bishops and the Law in Sixth-Century Gaul," in Bossy, *Disputes and Settlements*, 33.

4. Robert Bartlett, *Trial by Fire and Water: The Medieval Judicial Ordeal* (Oxford 1986) 80; James, "Beati Pacifici," 33.

5. Ara Norenzayan, *Big Gods: How Religion Transformed Cooperation and Conflict* (Princeton 2013) 7.

6. Michael Puett, "Genealogies of Gods, Ghosts, and Humans: The Capriciousness of the Divine in Early Greece and Early China," in G. E. R. Lloyd et al., eds., *Ancient Greece and China Compared* (Cambridge 2018) 168, 171; Jones, *Law and Legal Theory of the Greeks*, 48.

7. Saunders, *Plato's Penal Code*, 51.

8. Matthew 5:21–48.

9. Edward Muir, *Mad Blood Stirring: Vendetta and Factions in Friuli during the Renaissance* (Baltimore 1993) 69–70.

10. Mueller, "Tort, Crime, and the Primitive," 314; Brian E. McKnight, *The Quality of Mercy: Amnesties and Traditional Chinese Justice* (Honolulu 1981) 63–64.

11. Wayne A. Meeks, *The Origins of Christian Morality* (New Haven 1993) 114–115; P. D. King, *Law and Society in the Visigothic Kingdom* (Cambridge 1972) 147–148.

12. Larner, "Crimen Execeptum," 69; Francis Young, *Magic as a Political Crime in Medieval and Early Modern England* (London 2018) 23; Christine Caldwell Ames, *Righteous Persecution: Inquisition, Dominicans, and Christianity in the Middle Ages* (Philadelphia 2009) 182–190.

13. Deuteronomy 30:16–18.

14. Leviticus 26.

15. Mark Gretason, "Crime, Guilt, and Punishment in the Old Testament," *Law and Justice* 147 (2001) 140–141.

16. Exodus 22:22–24.

17. "Capitulary of Charlemagne Issued in the Year 802," in Ernest F. Henderson, ed., *Select Historical Documents of the Middle Ages* (London 1896) 198; Gretason, "Crime, Guilt, and Punishment," 144; Joel F. Harrington, *The Faithful Executioner: Life and Death, Honor and Shame in the Turbulent Sixteenth Century* (New York 2013) 33.

18. Robert Parker, *Miasma: Pollution and Purification in Early Greek Religion* (Oxford 1983) 112–115, 133, 193.

19. Mueller, "Tort, Crime, and the Primitive," 311–312.

20. Tacitus, *Germania*, chap. 7.

21. However, influencing divinities was a motive for human sacrifice only in some cultures. Dean Sheils, "A Comparative Study of Human Sacrifice," *Behavior Science Research* 4 (1980) 246.

22. Burr Cartwright Brundage, *A Rain of Darts: The Mexica Aztecs* (Austin 1972) 97.

23. Philip Williamson, "State Prayers, Fasts, and Thanksgivings: Public Worship in Britain 1830–1897," *Past and Present* 200 (2008) 123; Frank M. Turner, "Rainfall, Plagues, and the Prince of Wales: A Chapter in the Conflict of Religion and Science," *Journal of British Studies* 12, 2 (1974) 50–51.

24. Michael D. Coe, "Religion and the Rise of Mesoamerican States," in Grant D. Jones and Robert R. Kautz, eds., *The Transition to Statehood in the New World* (Cambridge 1981) 164–165.

25. Alan Strathern, *Unearthly Powers: Religious and Political Change in World History* (Cambridge 2019) 35; David F. Greenberg and Valerie West, "Siting the Death Penalty Internationally," *Law and Social Inquiry* 33, 2 (2008) 309.

26. Zhongjiang Wang, *Order in Early Chinese Excavated Texts* (Houndmills 2016) 94, 127.

27. Robert F. Ekelund Jr. et al., "The Economics of Sin and Redemption: Purgatory as a Market-Pull Innovation?," *Journal of Economic Behavior and Organization* 19 (1992) 3–5.

28. Dominic Johnson, *God Is Watching You: How the Fear of God Makes Us Human* (New York 2015) 71–73, 227–229; Christine Caldwell Ames, "Does Inquisition Belong to Religious History?," *American Historical Review* 110, 1 (2005) 24.

29. Attenborough, *Laws of the Earliest Kings*, Wihtred cap 3–4; King, *Law and Society in the Visigothic Kingdom*, 127.

30. Dominic Johnson and Oliver Krüger, "The Good of Wrath: Supernatural Punishment and the Evolution of Cooperation," *Political Theology* 5, 2 (2004) 161–162; Kristin Laurin et al., "Outsourcing Punishment to God: Beliefs in Divine Control Reduce Earthly Punishment," *Proceedings of the Royal Society: Biological Sciences* 279, 1741 (2012) 3278; Dominic Johnson, "Why God Is the Best Punisher," *Religion, Brain, & Behavior* 1, 1 (2011) 79, 82; Azim F. Shariff and Ara Norenzayan, "Mean Gods Make Good People: Different Views of God Predict Cheating Behavior," *International Journal for the Psychology of Religion* 21 (2011) 85, 92; Alan Bernstein, "Thinking about Hell," *Wilson Quarterly* 10, 3 (1986) 78.

31. Von Bar, *History of Continental Criminal Law*, 399; Sharpe, *Crime in Early Modern England*, 8.

32. Martin Lewison, "Conflicts of Interest? The Ethics of Usury," *Journal of Business Ethics* 22, 4 (1999) 329, 333.

33. Pieter Spierenburg, *A History of Murder: Personal Violence in Europe from the Middle Ages to the Present* (Cambridge 2008) 146.

34. Anne-Marie Kilday, "'Monsters of the Vilest Kind': Infanticidal Women and Attitudes to Their Criminality in Eighteenth-Century Scotland," *Family and Community History* 11, 2 (2008) 106.

35. Joel F. Harrington, *The Unwanted Child: The Fate of Foundlings, Orphans, and Juvenile Criminals in Early Modern Germany* (Chicago 2009) 68; Spierenburg, *History of Murder*, 150; Soman, "Deviance and Criminal Justice," 9. Infanticide was reduced from murder to manslaughter in Britain only in 1922, but most women convicted were pardoned, not executed. Bailey, "Shadow of the Gallows," 313.

36. Benoît Garnot, "La législation et la répression des crimes dans la France moderne (XVI–XVIIIe siècle)," *Revue Historique* 293 (1995) 80.

37. Kenneth Pennington, *The Prince and the Law, 1200–1600* (Berkeley 1993) 132.

38. Numbers 5:12–28; Paul R. Hyams, "Trial by Ordeal: The Key to Proof in the Early Common Law," in Morris S. Arnold et al., eds., *On the Laws and Customs of England* (Chapel Hill 1981) 103; Bartlett, *Trial by Fire and Water*, 84; Jones, *Law and Legal Theory of the Greeks*, 136–137.

39. Patrick Wormald, "Charters, Law, and the Settlement of Disputes in Anglo-Saxon England," in Wendy Davies and Paul Fouracre, eds., *The Settlement of Disputes in Early Medieval Europe* (Cambridge 1986) 160.

40. Margaret H. Kerr et al., "Cold Water and Hot Iron: Trial by Ordeal in England," *Journal of Interdisciplinary History* 22, 4 (1979) 574, 580–581.

41. Two pilgrims returned from Jerusalem. One detoured to a shrine; the other, arriving home first, was accused of having murdered his companion. Put to the ordeal, he failed and was executed. When the other eventually arrived, consternation ensued. John W. Baldwin, *Masters, Princes, and Merchants: The Social Views of Peter the Chanter and His Circle* (Princeton 1970) 326–327.

42. Finbarr McAuley, "Canon Law and the End of the Ordeal," *Oxford Journal of Legal Studies* 26, 3 (2006) 476–477, 482–483; Charles M. Radding, "Superstition to Science: Nature, Fortune, and the Passing of the Medieval Order," *American Historical Review* 84, 4 (1979) 960, 965–966.

43. Bartlett, *Trial by Fire and Water*, 88; Deuteronomy 6:16; Matthew 4:7.

44. A. S. Diamond, *Primitive Law Past and Present* (London 1971) 47.

45. Matthew 5:33.

46. Silving, "The *Oath*," 1330; Jones, *Law and Legal Theory of the Greeks*, 139; Hindle, "Keeping of the Public Peace," 221.

47. And yet a malevolent vision of hell has recently again become part of popular culture. See Hanré Janse van Rensburg and Ernest van Eck, "Hell Revisited: A Socio-critical Enquiry into the Roots and Relevance of Hell for the Church Today," *HTS Teologiese Studies* 64, 3 (2008) 1501–1503; and Brooks B. Hull and Frederick Bold, "Hell, Religion, and Cultural Change," *Journal of Institutional and Theoretical Economics* 150, 3 (1994) 451.

48. R. I. Mawby, *Comparative Policing Issues* (London 1990) 16.

49. Norman Yoffee, "Law Courts and the Mediation of Social Conflict in Ancient Mesopotamia," in Janet Richards and Mary van Buren, eds., *Order, Legitimacy, and Wealth in Ancient States* (Cambridge 2000) 48.

50. Michael Gagarin, *Early Greek Law* (Berkeley 1986) 20–22.

51. *Iliad*, 18:497–508; Hans Julius Wolff, "The Origin of Judicial Litigation among the Greeks," *Traditio* 4 (1946) 31–33; Jones, *Law and Legal Theory of the Greeks*, 258.

52. Peters, *Torture*, 12.

53. Hubert J. Treston, *Poine: A Study in Ancient Greek Blood-Vengeance* (London 1923) 85; Drapkin, *Crime and Punishment*, 174–175.

54. Peters, *Torture*, 19; Drapkin, *Crime and Punishment*, 180; Gagarin, *Early Greek Law*, 139.

55. Virginia J. Hunter, *Policing Athens: Social Control in the Attic Lawsuits, 420–320 BC* (Princeton 1994) 62–63.

56. Drapkin, *Crime and Punishment*, 236; Edward Peters, *Inquisition* (New York 1988) 12–17.

57. Michael Gagarin, *Drakon and Early Athenian Homicide Law* (New Haven 1981) 117; Drapkin, *Crime and Punishment*, 238.

58. David J. Seipp, "The Distinction between Crime and Tort in the Early Common Law," *Boston University Law Review* 76 (1996) 63.

59. Plato, *Laws*, bk. 9, chap. 13; Douglas A. MacDowell, *The Law in Classical Athens* (Ithaca 1978) 114; Green, *Verdict according to Conscience*, 30; von Bar, *History of Continental Criminal Law*, 8, 12; Parker, *Miasma*, 112; Attenborough, *Laws of the Earliest English Kings*, Alfred cap 42.

60. Attenborough, *Laws of the Earliest English Kings*, Wihtred cap 25; Green, *Verdict according to Conscience*, 30, 80–81; Thomas A. Green, "The Jury and the English Law of Homicide, 1200–1600," *Michigan Law Review* 74 (1976) 429; Jesse L. Byock, *Viking Age Iceland* (London 2001) 109, 213.

61. Gagarin, *Drakon*, 118; von Bar, *History of Continental Criminal Law*, 12.

62. McKnight, *Quality of Mercy*, 50.

63. Green, *Verdict according to Conscience*, 42; J. M. Kaye, "The Early History of Murder and Manslaughter," *Law Quarterly Review* 83 (1967) 577.

64. Green, "Jury and English Law," 438, 458; von Bar, *History of Continental Criminal Law*, 14; Tigar, "Right of Property," 1447.

65. Kwame Anthony Appiah, *The Honor Code: How Moral Revolutions Happen* (New York 2010) 22.

66. Cynthia Lee, *Murder and the Reasonable Man: Passion and Fear in the Criminal Courtroom* (New York 2003) 20; Donna K. Coker, "Heat of Passion and Wife Killing: Men Who Batter/Men Who Kill," *Southern California Review of Law and Women's Studies* 2, 71 (1992) 1.

67. French penal code, art. 324; Lama Abu-Odeh, "Crimes of Honour and the Construction of Gender in Arab Societies," in Mai Yarman, ed., *Feminism and Islam* (New York 1996) 143; Eliza Earle Ferguson, "Judicial Authority and Popular Justice: Crimes of Passion in Fin-de-Siècle Paris," *Oxford Journal of Social History* 40, 2 (2006) 296; Richard E. Nisbett and Dov Cohen, *Culture of Honor: The Psychology of Violence in the South* (Boulder 1996) 2.

68. Italian penal code, art. 587; Donatella Barazzetti et al., "Gender Violence Effects Indicators. National Report: Italia. Daphne Project 'Proposing New Indicatoors [*sic*]: Measuring Violence's Effects. GVEI,'" (Rende, Italy: University of Calabria, July 2007) 3, http://www.surt.org/gvei/docs/national_report_italy.pdf.

69. In Houston in 1969, 40 percent of those arrested for killing a relative were released without prosecution, compared to 24 percent of those who had killed a stranger. Donald Black, "Crime as Social Control," *American Sociological Review* 48 (1983) 40.

70. Lawrence M. Friedman and William E. Havemann, "The Rise and Fall of the Unwritten Law: Sex, Patriarchy, and Vigilante Justice in the American Courts," *Buffalo Law Review* 61, 5 (2013) 1008–1009; Hendrik Hartog, "Lawyering, Husbands' Rights, and 'the Unwritten Law' in Nineteenth-Century America," *Journal of American History* 84 (1997) 83; Lisa Appignanesi, *Trials of Passion: Crimes in the Name of Love and Madness* (New York 2014) 4, 337.

71. Joyce Lee Malcolm, "Self-Defence in England," *Journal on Firearms and Public Policy* 23 (2011) 63; Richard Maxwell Brown, *No Duty to Retreat: Violence and Values in American History and Society* (Norman 1991) chap 1.

72. Stuntz, "Pathological Politics," 513.

73. *Composition*—that is, making whole or restituting—was the term used in the Middle Ages for values paid for harms done.

74. William Ian Miller, *Eye for an Eye* (Cambridge 2006) 25.

75. The talionic principle is stated emblematically in Exodus 21:23–25.

76. Keith M. Brown, *Bloodfeud in Scotland 1573–1625* (Edinburgh 1986) 242; Jeremy Wormald, "Bloodfeud, Kindred, and Government in Early Modern Scotland," *Past and Present* 87 (1980) 85–86.

77. Bertha Surtees Phillpotts, *Kindred and Clan in the Middle Ages and After* (Cambridge 1913) 253–255; Miller, *Bloodtaking*, 186–187, 198.

78. Christopher Boehm, *Blood Revenge: The Enactment and Management of Conflict in Montenegro and Other Tribal Societies* (Lawrence 1984) 61.

79. Mark Edward Lewis, *Sanctioned Violence in Early China* (Albany 1990) 89–90.

80. Robert H. Lowie, *The Origin of the State* (New York 1927) 54; von Bar, *History of Continental Criminal Law*, 5.

81. J. M. Wallace-Hadrill, "The Bloodfeuds of the Franks," in J. M. Wallace-Hadrill, ed., *The Long-Haired Kings* (London 1962) 129; Drapkin, *Crime and Punishment*, 57.

82. A. Hofmeister, "Die Gerichtsscene im Schild des Achill, Ilias XVIII, 497–508," *Zeitschrift für vergleichende Rechtswissenschaft* 2 (1880) 449; Walter Leaf, "The Trial Scene in *Iliad* XVIII," *Journal of Hellenic Studies* 8 (1887) 124.

83. Von Bar, *History of Continental Criminal Law*, 11–12; Drapkin, *Crime and Punishment*, 281.

84. 2 Samuel 4.

85. Peter Stein, *Legal Institutions: The Development of Dispute Settlement* (London 1984) 21.

86. King, *Law and Society in the Visigothic Kingdom*, 86, 93; Tacitus, *Germania*, chap. 21.

87. Phillpotts, *Kindred and Clan*, 68; Alan Harding, *Medieval Law and the Foundations of the State* (Oxford 2002) 37; "Capitulary of Charlemagne," 198–199.

88. James Buchanan Given, *Society and Homicide in Thirteenth-Century England* (Stanford 1977) 73; Wormald, "Bloodfeud, Kindred, and Government," 55.

89. Harding, *Medieval Law*, 73; David Cohen, *Law, Violence, and Community in Classical Athens* (Cambridge 1995) 70.

90. John K. Brackett, *Criminal Justice and Crime in Late Renaissance Florence, 1537–1609* (Cambridge 1992) 3, 90–91; Mary Elizabeth Perry, *Crime and Society in Early Modern Seville* (Hanover 1980) 2.

91. Roland Axtmann, "'Police' and the Formation of the Modern State: Legal and Ideological Assumptions on State Capacity in the Austrian Lands of the Habsburg Empire, 1500–1800," *German History* 10 (1992) 42; Nancy Shields Kollmann, *Crime and Punishment in Early Modern Russia* (Cambridge 2012) 25.

92. Richard L. Kagan, "A Golden Age of Litigation: Castile 1500–1700," in Bossy, *Disputes and Settlements*, 156. The situation was similar in England: Sharpe, "Such Disagreement," 170–171.

93. Ruff, *Violence*, 81; Miller, *Bloodtaking*, 5, 20–21, 181; Jesse L. Byock, *Feud in the Icelandic Saga* (Berkeley 1982) 27; Brown, *Bloodfeud*, 239–242.

94. Pierre Lascoumes et al., *Au nom de l'ordre: Une histoire politique du Code Pénal* (Paris 1989) 138.

95. D. E. Mills, "Kataki-Uchi: The Practice of Blood-Revenge in Pre-modern Japan," *Modern Asian Studies* 10, 4 (1976) 525–526.

96. Treston, *Poine*, 5; Stephen Wilson, *Feuding, Conflict, and Banditry in Nineteenth Century Corsica* (Cambridge 1988) 53; Boehm, *Blood Revenge*, 66, 114.

97. Dan Bilefsky, "In Albanian Feuds, Isolation Engulfs Families," *New York Times*, 10 July 2008; Mark S. Weiner, *The Rule of the Clan* (New York 2013) 85.

98. Von Bar, *History of Continental Criminal Law*, 13; Drapkin, *Crime and Punishment*, 282.

99. Byock, *Viking Age Iceland*, 313; Otto Brunner, *Land and Lordship: Structures of Governance in Medieval Austria* (Philadelphia 1984) chap. 1; Hillay Zmora, *State and Nobility in Early Modern Germany: The Knightly Feud in Franconia, 1440–1567* (Cambridge 1997) 6–9.

100. Miller, *Bloodtaking*, 192, 280; Byock, *Viking Age Iceland*, 79, 207–210.

101. Spierenburg, *History of Murder*, 29; Boehm, *Blood Revenge*, 108; Max Gluckman, "The Peace in the Feud," *Past and Present* 8 (1955).

102. Exodus 21:30.

103. Drapkin, *Crime and Punishment*, 18, 23, 234; Paul Friedland, *Seeing Justice Done: The Age of Spectacular Capital Punishment in France* (Oxford 2012) 29.

104. Henry of Bracton, *On the Laws and Customs of England*, ed. Samuel E. Thorne and George E. Woodbine (Cambridge MA 1977) 2:410; Attenborough, *Laws of the Earliest English Kings*, Æthelberht cap 34–55, 64, Alfred cap 44–77.

105. J. M. Wallace-Hadrill, *Early Germanic Kingship in England and on the Continent* (Oxford 1971) 41.

106. Numbers 35:31–32.

107. Walter Ullmann, *The Medieval Idea of Law as Represented by Lucas de Penna* (London 1946) 144.

108. Mueller, "Tort, Crime, and the Primitive," 311.

109. Treston, *Poine*, 3–4; von Bar, *History of Continental Criminal Law*, 123; Klerman, "Settlement and Decline of Private Prosecution," 6.

110. Perry, *Crime and Society in Early Modern Seville*, 68; Phillpotts, *Kindred and Clan*, 96, 123–124.

111. Randy E. Barnett, "Restitution: A New Paradigm of Criminal Justice," *Ethics* 87, 4 (1977) 285–287; Randy E. Barnett, "Getting Even: Restitution, Preventive Detention, and the Tort/Crime Distinction," *Boston University Law Review* 76 (1996) 159; Pratt, "Scandinavian Exceptionalism," 134.

112. Stephen Schafer, "Restitution to Victims of Crime: An Old Correctional Aim Modernized," *Minnesota Law Review* 50 (1965) 249.

113. Samuels, "Non-Crown Prosecutions," 37; Thomas Erdbrink, "Mercy and Social Media Slow the Noose in Iran," *New York Times*, 9 March 2014.

Chapter 3

1. A. Esmein, *A History of Continental Criminal Procedure* (Boston 1913) 62.

2. Émile Durkheim, "Two Laws of Penal Evolution," in Steven Lukes and Andrew Scull, eds., *Durkheim and the Law* (Basingstoke 2013) 95.

3. Paul Grimley Kuntz, *The Ten Commandments in History* (Grand Rapids 2004) 18.

4. Émile Durkheim, *Suicide*, ed. George Simpson, trans. John A. Spaulding and George Simpson (orig. French ed. 1897; Glencoe 1951) 337.

5. Carl Wennerlind, *Casualties of Credit: The English Financial Revolution, 1620–1720* (Cambridge MA 2011) 131; Jonathan R. T. Hughes, *The Governmental Habit Redux: Economic Controls from Colonial Times to the Present* (Princeton 1991) 49.

6. Chevigny, "From Betrayal to Violence," 788.

7. Ullmann, *Medieval Idea of Law*, 148.

8. Matthew 5:38–48.

9. Durkheim, *Division of Labour*, 72. Durkheim goes further to argue that punishment continues to be inspired by broadly theological concerns, protecting something higher, even as it becomes secular. *Division of Labour*, 77, 110.

10. Drapkin, *Crime and Punishment*, 55–56.

11. Genesis 9:5–6.

12. Plato, *Laws*, 768a; David Cohen, *Law, Sexuality, and Society: The Enforcement of Morals in Classical Athens* (Cambridge 1991) 227–228.

13. Treston, *Poine*, 144. The Cheyenne, too, regarded murder as a sin, afflicting the whole tribe with supernatural consequences. Hoebel, *Law of Primitive Man*, 157.

14. Scott Gordon, *Controlling the State: Constitutionalism from Ancient Athens to Today* (Cambridge MA 1999) 70.

15. Deuteronomy 21:1–9.

16. Andrew Lintott, *Violence in Republican Rome* (Oxford 1999) 41; Tacitus, *Germania*, chap. 12.

17. Arthur P. Wolf, *Incest Avoidance and the Incest Taboos* (Stanford 2014) 98; Diamond, *Primitive Law*, 62.

18. Daniel Schiff, *Abortion in Judaism* (Cambridge 2002) 16.

19. *R v. Brown* [1993] 2 All ER 75, 4, 37, http://www.bailii.org/uk/cases/UKHL/1993/19.html. A similar logic can be found in Plato's *Laws* and among the Bantu monarchies of Africa (Saunders, *Plato's Penal Code*, 263; Lowie, *Origin of the State*, 93).

20. John Baker, *An Introduction to English Legal History*, 5th ed. (Oxford 2019) 571.

21. Immanuel Kant, *Metaphysics of Morals*, trans. Mary Gregor (Cambridge 1996) 6:333.

22. David Friedman, "Beyond the Tort/Crime Distinction," *Boston University Law Review* 76 (1996) 110; Seipp, "Distinction between Crime and Tort," 78–79.

23. Von Bar, *History of Continental Criminal Law*, 71, 115–116. A similar argument has been made for Anglo-Saxon tenth-century law in Wormald, "Charters," 165.

24. Seipp, "Distinction between Crime and Tort," 74; Richard E. Laster, "Criminal Restitution," *University of Richmond Law Review* 5 (1970) 76.

25. J. M. Beattie, *Crime and the Courts in England 1660–1800* (Princeton 1986) 39; Friedman, "Making Sense of English Law Enforcement," 486–487.

26. James Q. Wilson, *Varieties of Police Behavior* (Cambridge MA 1968) 176.

27. Laster, "Criminal Restitution," 76, 86–87. An exception is that marriage to the victim of seduction can prevent prosecution for that crime—but not for statutory rape.

28. Numbers 35:31. "For blood it defileth the land: and the land cannot be cleansed ... , but by the blood of him that shed it," it continued (35:33).

29. Miller, *Bloodtaking*, 190.

30. Robert Nozick, *Anarchy, State, and Utopia* (New York 1974) 65–68.

31. Friedland, *Seeing Justice Done*, 32; King, *Law and Society in the Visigothic Kingdom*, 91.

32. Coffee, "Does 'Unlawful' Mean 'Criminal'?," 222; George Kateb, "Punishment and the Spirit of Democracy," *Social Research* 74, 2 (2007) 303.

33. Josef Pieper, *The Concept of Sin* (South Bend 2001) 51–52.

34. Deuteronomy 17:12; Joshua 7:1–15.

35. J. B. Bury, *History of Greece*, 2nd ed. (London 1922) 172; Treston, *Poine*, 78–79.

36. Tim Whitmarsh, *Battling the Gods: Atheism in the Ancient World* (New York 2015) 237; Pollock and Maitland, *History of English Law*, 1:3; Leonard W. Levy, *Treason against God: A History of the Offense of Blasphemy* (New York 1981) 110.

37. Glendinnen, *Aztecs*, 70–72; Garcilaso de la Vega, *Royal Commentaries of the Incas and General History of Peru* (Austin 1966) 97.

38. Paolo L. Rossi, "The Writer and the Man," in Trevor Dean and K. J. P. Lowe, eds., *Crime, Society, and the Law in Renaissance Italy* (Cambridge 1994) 175.

39. Nash, "Analyzing the History of Religious Crime," 8; Garnot, "La législation et la répression des crimes," 78; Philip S. Gorski, "The Protestant Ethic Revisited: Disciplinary Revolution and State Formation in Holland and Prussia," *American Journal of Sociology* 99, 2 (1993) 279.

40. Sharpe, *Crime in Early Modern England*, 215; Axtmann, "'Police' and the Formation of the Modern State," 42; Stuart Banner, *The Death Penalty* (Cambridge MA 2002) 14.

41. In June 2015, a group of Western tourists on Mount Kinabalu in Malaysia caused outrage by stripping, and a subsequent deadly earthquake was blamed on their disrespect. Andreas Illmer, "Playboy Model Angers Maori with Nude Shoot on Sacred Mountain," *BBC News*, 3 May 2017, http://www.bbc.co.uk/news/world-asia-39789508.

42. Drapkin, *Crime and Punishment*, 64, 69, 71; Baruch, "In the Name of the Father," 56; Leviticus 24:16.

43. Gagarin, *Drakon*, 164; Tacitus, *Germania*, chap. 12; von Bar, *History of Continental Criminal Law*, 72; Laster, "Criminal Restitution," 73.

44. Michael Ignatieff, *A Just Measure of Pain: The Penitentiary in the Industrial Revolution, 1750–1850* (New York 1978) 17.

45. Leon R. Yankwich, "Law and Order under the Incas," *Southern California Law Review* 22 (1949) 149; Mueller, "Tort, Crime, and the Primitive," 321.

46. Drapkin, *Crime and Punishment*, 237.

47. Drapkin, *Crime and Punishment*, 69.

48. George M. Calhoun, *The Growth of Criminal Law in Ancient Greece* (Berkeley 1927) 16–17, 85; Treston, *Poine*, 23, 146, 93.

49. Theodor Mommsen, *Römisches Strafrecht* (Leipzig 1899) 614; von Bar, *History of Continental Criminal Law*, 16; Treston, *Poine*, 4.

50. Green, *Verdict according to Conscience*, 5; Given, *Society and Homicide*, 5; Diamond, *Primitive Law*, 74; Green, "Societal Concepts," 669–670.

51. MacDowell, *Law in Classical Athens*, 53; Jones, *Law and Legal Theory of the Greeks*, 253.

52. Danielle S. Allen, *The World of Prometheus: The Politics of Punishing in Democratic Athens* (Princeton 2000) 39; Calhoun, *Growth of Criminal Law*, 78.

53. Von Bar, *History of Continental Criminal Law*, 39.

54. King, *Law and Society in the Visigothic Kingdom*, 88, 92; "Capitulary of Charlemagne," 199.

55. Mommsen, *Römisches Strafrecht*, 1043; Jones, *Law and Legal Theory of the Greeks*, 183.

56. Richard M. Fraher, "The Theoretical Justification for the New Criminal Law of the High Middle Ages," *University of Illinois Law Review* 3 (1984) 578; McAuley, "Canon Law and the End of the Ordeal," 495.

57. Julius Goebel Jr., *Felony and Misdemeanor: A Study in the History of Criminal Law* (Philadelphia 1976) 36; Harding, *Medieval Law*, 75.

58. Friedland, *Seeing Justice Done*, 36.

59. W. Ullmann, "Some Medieval Principles of Criminal Procedure," *Juridical Review* 59, 1 (1947) 7–9.

60. McAuley, "Canon Law and the End of the Ordeal," 495; Fraher, "Theoretical Justification," 582.

61. John H. Langbein, *Prosecuting Crime in the Renaissance: England, Germany, France* (Cambridge MA 1974) 144.

62. Jean Michel Antoine de Servan, quoted in Lascoumes et al., *Au nom de l'ordre*, 25.

63. Maine, *Ancient Law*, 217; Gagarin, *Early Greek Law*, 63; MacDowell, *Law in Classical Athens*, 57.

64. Martin Ostwald, *From Popular Sovereignty to the Sovereignty of Law: Law, Society, and Politics in Fifth-Century Athens* (Berkeley 1986) 15; MacDowell, *Law in Classical Athens*, 129–131.

65. Mueller, "Tort, Crime, and the Primitive," 309.

66. Goebel, *Felony and Misdemeanor*, 64–68, discussing Frankish law of the sixth century. Yet seventh-century Visigothic law is said not to distinguish clearly between crimes and torts. King, *Law and Society in the Visigothic Kingdom*, 87.

67. Esmein, *History of Continental Criminal Procedure*, 336.

68. Fletcher, "Metamorphosis of Larceny," 479–480; Goebel, *Felony and Misdemeanor*, 66.

69. Spierenburg, *Spectacle of Suffering*, 2–3; Langbein, *Prosecuting Crime*, 211–212; Harding, *Medieval Law*, 19.

70. Pollock and Maitland, *History of English Law*, 1:37; James B. Given, *Inquisition and Medieval Society: Power, Discipline, and Resistance in Languedoc* (Ithaca 1997) 21.

71. Bartlett, *Trial by Fire and Water*, 132; Harding, *Medieval Law*, 33.

72. Max Weber, *Economy and Society* (Berkeley 1978) 762.

73. Genesis 18:21; Luke 16:1–2.

74. Langbein, *Prosecuting Crime*, 130–131; Esmein, *History of Continental Criminal Procedure*, 114–115.

75. Fraher, "Theoretical Justification," 582.

76. Green, *Verdict according to Conscience*, 97.

77. Langbein, *Prosecuting Crime*, 216–217, 177, 198–199; Weisser, *Crime and Punishment*, 94–95.

78. Weisser, *Crime and Punishment*, 96–97; Herrup, *Common Peace*, 68; Kollmann, *Crime and Punishment*, 205.

79. Bruce Lenman and Geoffrey Parker, "The State, the Community, and the Criminal Law in Early Modern Europe," in Gatrell et al., *Crime and the Law*, 26–27; Diamond, *Primitive Law*, 92; Green, "Jury and the English Law," 416.

80. R. van Caenegem, "The Law of Evidence in the Twelfth Century," in Stephan Kuttner and J. Joseph Ryan, eds., *Proceedings of the Second International Congress of Medieval Canon Law* (Vatican City 1965) 297–298.

81. Goebel, *Felony and Misdemeanor*, 76–77; van Caenegem, "Law of Evidence," 300.

82. Klerman, "Settlement and Decline of Private Prosecution," 5–6; Given, *Society and Homicide*, 98–99.

83. Green, *Verdict according to Conscience*, 105–106.

84. Langbein, *Prosecuting Crime*, 22–24, 35.

85. Beattie, *Crime and the Courts*, 35.

86. Ullmann, "Some Medieval Principles," 23–24; Richard M. Fraher, "IV Lateran's Revolution in Criminal Procedure," in Rosalio Castillo Lara, ed., *Studia in honorem Eminentissimi Cardinalis Alphonsi M. Stickle* (Rome 1992) 103; W. Ullmann, "Reflections on Medieval Torture," *Juridical Review* 56, 3 (1944) 130; Goebel, *Felony and Misdemeanor*, 70–75.

87. Ullmann, "Some Medieval Principles," 4; Given, *Inquisition and Medieval Society*, 21–22; Esmein, *History of Continental Criminal Procedure*, 19–20.

88. Treston, *Poine*, 226; Gagarin, *Drakon*, 119; King, *Law and Society in the Visigothic Kingdom*, 113.

89. Leviticus 24:16.
90. Plato, *Laws*, bk. 9, chap. 12.
91. MacDowell, *Law in Classical Athens*, 254; Treston, *Poine*, 423.
92. Lewis, *Sanctioned Violence*, 92.

Chapter 4

1. Exodus 22:28.
2. Pandias M. Schisas, *Offences against the State in Roman Law* (London 1926) 3, 20.
3. Ingraham, *Political Crime in Europe*, 30–31.
4. Derek Bodde and Clarence Morris, *Law in Imperial China* (Cambridge MA 1967) 41; Bodde, "Basic Concepts," 392. However, in the Ming treason was punished only by beheading, not by slow slicing of the body. Jiang, *Mandate of Heaven*, 96.
5. Pollock and Maitland, *History of English Law*, 1:300.
6. David Lorton, "The Treatment of Criminals in Ancient Egypt: Through the New Kingdom," *Journal of the Economic and Social History of the Orient* 20, 1 (1977) 14; Lewis, *Sanctioned Violence*, 28.
7. John Bellamy, *The Tudor Law of Treason* (London 1979) 202–205; "Historical Concept of Treason: English, American," *Indiana Law Journal* 35, 1 (1959) 71.
8. Treason Act 1814, 54 George III, c. 146. But by 1820 decapitation and the other dismemberments were no longer inflicted. V. A. C. Gatrell, *The Hanging Tree: Execution and the English People 1770–1868* (Oxford 1994) 298–299.
9. In the United States, treason remains punishable by death. Eichensehr, "Treason in the Age of Terrorism," 1500.
10. John Bellamy, *The Law of Treason in England in the Later Middle Ages* (Cambridge 1970) 13; Treston, *Poine*, 220; Lex Quisquis, 397, quoted in S. H. Cuttler, *The Law of Treason and Treason Trials in Later Medieval France* (Cambridge 1981) 8.
11. Bruce G. Trigger, *Understanding Early Civilizations* (Cambridge 2003) 237.
12. Allgemeines Landrecht für die Preußischen Staaten, Part 2, chap. 20, pt. 2, §95; Strafgesetzbuch für das Königreich Baiern (Munich 1813), art. 118.
13. Stephen C. Thaman, "Marxist and Soviet Law," in Markus D. Dubber and Tatjana Hornle, eds., *Oxford Handbook of Criminal Law* (Oxford 2014) 317; Mark Edele and Michael Geyer, "States of Exception: The Nazi–Soviet War as a System of Violence, 1939–1945," in Michael Geyer and Sheila Fitzpatrick, eds., *Beyond Totalitarianism: Stalinism and Nazism Compared* (Cambridge 2009) 385.
14. Manuel Eisner, "Killing Kings: Patterns of Regicide in Europe, AD 600–1800," *British Journal of Criminology* 51 (2011) 563–564.
15. Goebel, *Felony and Misdemeanor*, 45; Jiang, *Mandate of Heaven*, 155.
16. Eisner, "Killing Kings," 568–569.
17. G. R. Elton, *Policy and Police: The Enforcement of the Reformation in the Age of Thomas Cromwell* (Cambridge 1972) 387–391.
18. "Historical Concept of Treason," 74; Walter G. Simon, "The Evolution of Treason," *Tulane Law Review* 35, 4 (1961) 687.

19. 33 Henry VIII, c. 23; Bellamy, *Tudor Law of Treason*, 38.

20. Jonathan K. van Patten, "Magic, Prophecy, and the Law of Treason in Reformation England," *American Journal of Legal History* 27 (1983) 10–11.

21. George P. Fletcher, "Ambivalence about Treason," *North Carolina Law Review* 82 (2003–2004) 1614; J. Richard Broughton, "The Snowden Affair and the Limits of American Treason," *Lincoln Memorial University Law Review* 3 (2015) 15.

22. Thomas Jefferson wrote of treason codes that "they do not distinguish between acts against the government and acts against the oppressions of the government; the latter are virtues; yet they have furnished more victims to the executioner than the former." Quoted in *Cramer v. United States*, 325 US 1 (1945) n. 28.

23. Stuart E. Abrams, "Threats to the President and the Constitutionality of Constructive Treason," *Columbia Journal of Law and Social Problems* 12 (1975–1976) 379–380. In the various colonial laws, treason included only levying war and aiding and adhering to the enemy. Richard Z. Steinhaus, "Treason: A Brief History with Some Modern Applications," *Brooklyn Law Review* 22 (1955–1956) 256.

24. James Willard Hurst, *Law of Treason in the United States* (Westport 1971) chap. 4; Herbert L. Packer, "Offenses against the State," *Annals of the American Academy of Political and Social Science* 339 (1962) 78.

25. Hurst, *Law of Treason*, 5–6, 144.

26. US Constitution, art. 3, §3; Steinhaus, "Treason," 258.

27. "The History of Treason," *Law Coach* 2 (1921–1922) 147.

28. Broughton, "Snowden Affair," 17–18; J. H. Leek, "Treason and the Constitution," *Journal of Politics* 13, 4 (1951) 609; Hurst, *Law of Treason*, 195. The Sedition Act of 1798 (allowed to expire in the years immediately following Jefferson's election in 1800), which charged as misdemeanors the uttering, publishing, or printing of false and malicious writings against the government, was a spasm in the other direction, as was the Sedition Act of 1918 and the Wilson Act of 1940. Leek, "Treason and the Constitution," 618–619.

29. Hurst, *Law of Treason*, 7, 198–201; Carlton F. W. Larson, "The Forgotten Constitutional Law of Treason and the Enemy Combatant Problem," *University of Pennsylvania Law Review* 154 (2005–2006) 901–902.

30. The numbers vary: see Mary Connery, "Hung, Drawn and Quartered? The Future of the Constitutional Reference to Treason," *Trinity College Law Review* 5 (2002) 73; Leek, "Treason and the Constitution," 616.

31. John N. Hazard and William B. Stern, "'Exterior Treason': A Study in Comparative Criminal Law," *University of Chicago Law Review* 6, 1 (1938) 78; Leek, "Treason and the Constitution," 617.

32. George Washington pardoned the insurrectionaries of the Whiskey Rebellion of 1794 to undercut hardcore dissent from the new republic. Erin Creegan, "National Security Crime," *Harvard National Security Journal* 3 (2011–2012) 380. But some Southern residents were prosecuted for treason consisting of adherence to the North. *Cramer v. United States*, 325 US 1 (1945), n. 14.

33. *Cramer v. United States*, 325 US 1 (1945) 26.

34. Bruno S. Frey, "Why Kill Politicians? A Rational Choice Analysis of Political Assassinations," *Working Paper Series*, Institute for Empirical Research in Economics, University of Zurich (2007) 3; Abdelilah Bouasria, "Elián Gonzalez: The Messiah of

Fidel Castro," *Journal of the International Relations and Affairs Group* 1, 1 (2011) 107. Attempts on Castro's life are documented in the film *638 Ways to Kill Castro* (2006).

35. Zaryab Iqbal and Christopher Zorn, "Sic semper tyrannis? Power, Repression, and Assassination since the Second World War," *Journal of Politics* 68, 3 (2006) passim.

36. Otto Kirchheimer, *Political Justice* (Princeton 1961) 34–35.

37. Connery, "Hung, Drawn, and Quartered?," 65.

38. A. H. J. Greenidge, "The Conception of Treason in Roman Law," *Juridical Review* 7 (1895) 230.

39. Van Patten, "Magic, Prophecy, and the Law of Treason," 4. To be precise, traitors forfeited their lands to the king, but felons' land escheated. Pollock and Maitland, *History of English Law*, 1:351. This was one of the motives that prompted the development of trusts in English common law—to prevent land of those declared enemies by the king from escheating to him. G. R. Elton, "The Law of Treason in the Early Reformation," *Historical Journal* 11, 2 (1968) 216; Bellamy, *Tudor Law of Treason*, 10.

40. Kathleen A. Parrow, "Neither Treason nor Heresy: Use of Defense Arguments to Avoid Forfeiture during the French Wars of Religion," *Sixteenth Century Journal* 22, 4 (1991) 706.

41. Montesquieu, *Spirit of the Laws*, 12:7.

42. Lear, *Treason*, 152; Samuel Rezneck, "The Early History of the Parliamentary Declaration of Treason," *English Historical Review* 42, 168 (1927) 504; Bellamy, *Tudor Law of Treason*, 42–43; Carla Hesse, "The Law of the Terror," *Modern Language Notes* 114, 4 (1999) 717; 27 Elizabeth I, c. 2.

43. Admittedly charged with defamation, not treason. Thomas Fuller, "Thai Man May Go to Prison for Insulting King's Dog," *New York Times*, 14 December 2015; Austin Ramzy and Wai Moe, "Myanmar Poet Who Wrote of Penis Tattoo Is Convicted of Defaming Ex-Leader," *New York Times*, 24 May 2016.

44. Simon, "Evolution of Treason," 699; Connery, "Hung, Drawn, and Quartered," 68–69; Paul T. Crane, "Did the Court Kill the Treason Charge? Reassessing *Cramer v. United States* and Its Significance," *Florida State University Law Review* 36 (2008–2009) 636–639; Eichensehr, "Treason in the Age of Terrorism," 1457.

45. G. A. Kelly, "From Lèse-Majesté to Lèse-Nation: Treason in Eighteenth-Century France," *Journal of the History of Ideas* 42, 2 (1981) 269–270.

46. MacDowell, *Law in Classical Athens*, 176; Lear, *Treason*, xix, 28; Barrington Moore Jr., "Cruel and Unusual Punishment in the Roman Empire and Dynastic China," *International Journal of Politics, Culture, and Society* 14, 4 (2001) 734.

47. Gretason, "Crime, Guilt, and Punishment," 142; Romans 13:1. Early colonial statutes in North America cited more elliptically relevant sources, from Samuel and Numbers. Hurst, *Law of Treason*, 69–70.

48. Innocent III, *Vergentis in senium*, decretal letter, 25 March 1199. See Helga Schnabel-Schüle, "Das Majestätsverbrechen als Herrschaftsschutz und Herrschaftskritik," *Aufklärung* 7, 2 (1994) 35; Peters, *Torture*, 53; Kenneth Pennington, "'Pro peccatis patrum puniri': A Moral and Legal Problem of the Inquisition," *Church History* 47, 2 (1978) 137.

49. Levy, *Treason against God*, 169; Parrow, "Neither Treason nor Heresy," 707; Garnot, "La législation et la répression des crimes," 78.

50. W. H. Greenleaf, "James I and the Divine Right of Kings," *Political Studies* 5, 1 (1957) 47; Schnabel-Schüle, "Majestätsverbrechen," 36.

51. Hesse, "Law of the Terror," 708; von Bar, *History of Continental Criminal Law*, 279–281. *Lèse-majesté divine* was abolished in the new penal code of 1791. This term was used also by Calvin. Levy, *Treason against God*, 131.

52. Florike Egmond, "The Cock, the Dog, the Serpent, and the Monkey: Reception and Transmission of a Roman Punishment, or Historiography as History," *International Journal of the Classical Tradition* 2, 2 (1995) 167, passim; Mary Nagle Wessling, "Infanticide Trials and Forensic Medicine: Württemberg 1757–93," in Michael Clark and Catherine Crawford, eds., *Legal Medicine in History* (Cambridge 1994) 118.

53. Moore, "Cruel and Unusual Punishment," 747.

54. James Fitzjames Stephen, *A History of the Criminal Law of England* (London 1883) 3:95.

55. Art 13. Attempts on the emperor were punished as parricide. Art 86. Amputation was abolished in 1832 and parricide was no longer singled out in the penal code of 1994.

56. Shigenori Matsui, "Constitutional Precedents in Japan: A Comment on the Role of Precedent," *Washington University Law Review* 88, 6 (2011) 1674.

57. In the Roman Empire and in the English statute of 1351. Lear, *Treason*, xiv–xv, 30.

58. Cuttler, *Law of Treason*, 29.

59. 28 Henry VIII, c. 24; Bellamy, *Tudor Law of Treason*, 36.

60. "Editor Defends Diana over Mirror Letters," *BBC News*, 31 August 2000, http://news.bbc.co.uk/1/hi/uk/905239.stm.

61. Lear, *Treason*, xvi.

62. Greenidge, "Conception of Treason," 229.

63. Elmer Truesdell Merrill, "Some Remarks on Cases of Treason in the Roman Commonwealth," *Classical Philology* 13, 1 (1918) 35.

64. Schisas, *Offenses against the State*, 6.

65. Isaac J. Colunga, "Untangling a Historian's Misinterpretation of Ancient Rome's Treason Laws," *Journal Jurisprudence* 9 (2011) 11–15, 17; C. W. Chilton, "The Roman Law of Treason under the Early Principate," *Journal of Roman Studies* 45 (1955) 74–75; von Bar, *History of Continental Criminal Law*, 42.

66. As an aside, until 2003 the US Secret Service was the police arm of the Treasury and had as its main functions investigating counterfeiting and other violations of money as well as protecting the president.

67. Lear, *Treason*, 29.

68. Adalbert Erler and Ekkehard Kaufmann, eds., *Handwörterbuch zur Deutschen Rechtsgeschichte* (Berlin 1971) 1:649.

69. Lear, *Treason*, chaps. 5 and 6. The Nazis used the same terminology. Georg Dahm, "Verrat und Verbrechen," *Zeitschrift für die gesammte Staatswissenschaft* 95, 2 (1935) 291–292.

70. Brunner, *Land and Lordship*, 222–223.

71. The English Treason Act 1351 (25 Edward III, st. 5, c. 2) codified this. Petty treason involved a servant killing his master or a wife her husband. The penalties were slightly milder than for high treason—no quartering, but still drawing and hanging. Lear, *Treason*, 241–242.

72. As distinguished from *Landesverrat*, which includes acts of outright collaboration and aid to an enemy, as opposed to internal sedition.

73. Simon, "Evolution of Treason," 685; Foster, quoted in Hurst, *Law of Treason*, 43.

74. King, *Law and Society in the Visigothic Kingdom*, 40–41; Harding, *Medieval Law*, 38, 44.

75. Treason Act 1351, 25 Edward III, st. 5, c. 2.

76. Greenleaf, "James I," 45.

77. Quentin Skinner, "The State," in Terence Ball et al., eds., *Political Innovation and Conceptual Change* (Cambridge 1989) 124.

78. Lewis, *Sanctioned Violence*, 205.

79. Lear, *Treason*, 14.

80. Simon, "Evolution of Treason," 681; Elton, "Law of Treason," 211.

81. Ralph E. Giesey et al., "Cardin Le Bret and Lese Majesty," *Law and History Review* 4, 1 (1986) 28–29.

82. Lear, *Treason*, 40: Brian Z. Tamanaha, *On the Rule of Law* (Cambridge 2004) 24.

83. Ann Lyon, "From Dafydd ap Gruffydd to Lord Haw-Haw: The Concept of Allegiance in the Law of Treason," *Cambrian Law Review* 33 (2002) 37; Bellamy, *Law of Treason*, 10; Cuttler, *Law of Treason*, 5.

84. That rebellion against a tyrant is not treason was also identified in the Golden Bull of Hungary in 1222, the Peace of Fexhe of the Principality of Liege, and the Joyeuses entreés of Brabant in 1356. M. Denis Szabo, "Political Crimes," *Denver Journal of International Law and Policy* 2 (1972) 13.

85. Richard L. Greaves, "Concepts of Political Obedience in Late Tudor England," *Journal of British Studies* 22, 1 (1982) 25; Gordon, *Controlling the State*, 125–126.

86. D. Alan Orr, *Treason and the State: Law, Politics, and Ideology in the English Civil War* (Cambridge 2002) 4, 176.

87. Thomas Hobbes, *Leviathan*, chap. 21.

88. Szabo, "Political Crimes," 8–10.

89. Bellamy, *Law of Treason*, 64.

90. Michael Jones, "'Bons Bretons et bons Francoys': The Language and Meaning of Treason in Later Medieval France," *Transactions of the Royal Historical Society* 32 (1982) 96.

91. Orr, *Treason and the State*, 19.

92. Bellamy, *Law of Treason*, 206–207; Brackett, *Criminal Justice and Crime in Late Renaissance Florence*, 127–128.

93. Conrad Russell, "The Theory of Treason in the Trial of Strafford," *English Historical Review* 80, 314 (1965) 37, 46; Orr, *Treason and the State*, 183, 4.

94. *Every Man His Own Lawyer* (New York 1768) 266, quoted in Larson, "Forgotten Constitutional Law," 901.

95. Strafgesetzbuch für das Königreich Baiern, *art. 300*. Articles 309 and following include detailed accounts of libel and other trespasses against the sovereign, his wife, and heir.

96. French penal code, 1810, art. 86.

97. Fritz van Calker et al., *Verbrechen und Vergehen gegen den Staat und die Staatsgewalt* (Berlin 1906) 26, 103–104, 111. However, insulting and defaming the monarch were crimes much less regulated and prosecuted in England than in most other European nations.

98. Treason Act of 1695, 7 & 8 William III, c. 3, s. 6.

99. Treason Act of 1795, 36 George III, c. 7.

100. Treason Act of 1800, 39 & 40 George III, c. 93. The Treason Act of 1817 also removed other protections from the statute of 1695 for those who assaulted the monarch. 57 George III, c. 6 s. 4, repealed by Crime and Disorder Act 1998, c. 37.

101. Giles St. Aubyn, *Queen Victoria* (London 1991) 161–163.

102. Treason Act of 1842, 5 & 6 Vict., c. 51. Until the Security from Violence Act 1863, which punished robbery with violence, the firearms violation was the only crime punished by whipping. Jennifer Davis, "The London Garotting Panic of 1862," in Gatrell et al., *Crime and the Law*, 208.

103. Crime and Disorder Act 1998, c. 37.

104. Eichensehr, "Treason in the Age of Terrorism," 1450–1451.

105. Kelly, "From Lèse-Majesté to Lèse-Nation," 272–273, 283–284.

106. French penal code, art. 86.

107. Thomas R. Robinson, "Treason in Modern Foreign Law," *Boston University Law Review* 2 (1922) 102.

108. Ernst J. Schuster, "'Lèse-Majesté' in Germany," *Journal of the Society of Comparative Legislation*, n.s. 41 (1901) 43; Reichsstrafgesetzbuch (1871), §§94–104; Robinson, "Treason in Modern Foreign Law," 108. Thirteen European nations still make insulting the head of state a crime. *Economist*, 4 June 2016.

109. Reichsstrafgesetzbuch (1871), §80.

110. Robinson, "Treason in Modern Foreign Law," 99. The Prussian Code of 1794 made similar distinctions: *Hoch* and *Landesverrat* and then *Majestätsbeleidigung*, pt. 2, chap. 20, sect. 5, §196.

111. Robinson, "Treason in Modern Foreign Law," 98; Calker et al., *Verbrechen und Vergehen*, 28–29; Thomas Vormbaum, *A Modern History of German Criminal Law* (Berlin 2014) 153.

112. Law of 21 July 1922; Richard J. Evans, *Rituals of Retribution: Capital Punishment in Germany, 1600–1987* (London 1996) 505–506.

113. Strafgesetzbuch, §81.

114. French penal code, 1994, art. 410–411. Other aspects of these fundamental interests are "the balance of its natural surroundings and environment, and the essential elements of its scientific and economic potential and cultural heritage."

115. George P. Fletcher, "The Case for Treason," *Maryland Law Review* 41, 2 (1982) 199.

116. 18 USC §871; Abrams, "Threats to the President," 351.

117. The killing of John F. Kennedy's assassin, Lee Harvey Oswald, by Jack Ruby was blamed on the federal authorities' inability to take the case out of local hands. US Senate, *Judiciary Committee Report 89-498*, 21 July 1965, 2, 6.

118. 18 USC §1751; Abrams, "Threats to the President," 379.

119. Simon, "Evolution of Treason," 687; Bellamy, *Tudor Law of Treason*, 16–17; "History of Treason," 147.

120. "Historical Concept of Treason," 73.

121. Bellamy, *Law of Treason*, 207–208.

122. Penal ordinance of 1532, Emperor Charles V, art. 127; Peter Blickle, "The Criminalization of Peasant Resistance in the Holy Roman Empire," *Journal of Modern History* 58 (1986) S88.

123. Blickle, "Criminalization of Peasant Resistance," S91–93.

124. Orr, *Treason and the State*, 173.

125. *Cramer v. United States*, 325 US 1 (1945) 21.

126. Ernst Fraenkel, *The Dual State: A Contribution to the Theory of Dictatorship* (orig. ed. 1941; reprint, Oxford 2017) 49.

127. Angela K. Bourne and Fernando Casal Bértoa, "Mapping 'Militant Democracy': Variation in Party Ban Practices in European Democracies (1945–2015)," *European Constitutional Law Review* 13 (2017) 230.

128. Thomas R. Robinson, "Treason in Roman Law," *Georgetown Law Journal* 8 (1919–1920) 20.

129. Hurst, *Law of Treason*, 70.

130. US Constitution, art. 4, §4.

131. Andrews, "Boundaries of Citizenship," 93.

132. Decree of 4 December 1792, http://artflsrv02.uchicago.edu/cgi-bin/philologic/getobject.pl?c.32:43.baudouin0314.

133. French penal code, 1810, art. 87. The Belgian penal code of 1867 gave much the same definition of treason.

134. Hurst, *Law of Treason*, 49; Calker et al., *Verbrechen und Vergehen*, 4.

135. These are the themes of Ingraham, *Political Crime in Europe*, chapters 13–15. But Ingraham makes of this trend a return to the old importance of treason rather than the historical anomaly it seems in retrospect to have been. Similar themes are found in Margaret Boveri, *Treason in the Twentieth Century* (New York 1963) 6–8 and passim.

136. Packer, "Offenses against the State," 83; Abrams, "Threats to the President," 358; Szabo, "Political Crimes," 16.

137. The English concept of high treason is confusingly closer to the German *Landesverrat* than to *Hochverrat*. *Landesverrat* is giving away state secrets to foreign powers. *Hochverrat* is violently undermining the constitutional order. Strafgesetzbuch, §§94, 81. In the US Constitution, treason is defined as levying war against the states or aiding and giving comfort to their enemies. Only in the penal code is sedition mentioned as internal attempts to overthrow the government. Sedition is rebellion against the authority of the United States or its laws. 18 USC §2383. And there is a crime of advocating the overthrow or destruction of the government. 18 USC §2385.

138. Williams, *Tudor Regime*, 376; Elton, "Law of Treason," 222, 231–232; Orr, *Treason and the State*, 18. Earlier examples are given in in I. D. Thornley, "The Treason Legislation of Henry VIII," *Transactions of the Royal Historical Society* 11 (1917) 107–109. An overview is given in Cressy, *Dangerous Talk*, chap. 3. The Treason Act 1534 was repealed in 1547 under Edward VI.

139. Abrams, "Threats to the President," 374–376; Cuttler, *Law of Treason*, 47. By the seventeenth century, spoken words alone were no longer thought to constitute treason.

140. Andrews, "Boundaries of Citizenship," 92–93.

141. New York Act, 30 March 1781, cited in *Cramer v. United States*, 325 US 1 (1945) n. 13.

142. Robert Higgs, *Crisis and Leviathan: Critical Episodes in the Growth of American Government* (New York 1987) 149; Tom W. Bell, "Treason, Technology, and Freedom of Expression," *Arizona State Law Journal* 37 (2005) 1028–1029.

143. Abrams, "Threats to the President," 352, 355–356.

144. Michael Lobban, "From Seditious Libel to Unlawful Assembly: Peterloo and the Changing Face of Political Crime c1770–1820," *Oxford Journal of Legal Studies* 10 (1990) 307–309; El-Haj, "Defining Peaceably," 967.

145. 18 USC §§2383–2384. But anyone convicted of insurrection was punished with only up to ten years in prison and forbidden to hold office. These paragraphs were based on laws of 17 July 1862 and 31 July 1861, respectively. *Revised Statutes of the United States,* 2nd ed. (Washington DC 1878) §§5334, 1036; 5336, 1037.

146. Creegan, "National Security Crime," 381–382.

147. 18 USC §§2385–2386.

148. Crane, "Did the Court Kill the Treason Charge?" 684; Hazard and Stern, "'Exterior Treason,'" 81; Broughton, "Snowden Affair," 10; Eichensehr, "Treason in the Age of Terrorism," 1472.

149. The Rosenbergs were convicted only of conspiring to spy because the statute of limitations on espionage had run out. Packer, "Offenses against the State," 87.

150. Treason Felony Act 1848, 11 & 12 Vict., c. 12; Radzinowicz, *History of English Criminal Law,* 5:461.

151. Treachery Act 1940, 3 & 4 George VI, c. 40.

152. French penal code, 1994, arts. 411-2 to 411-11, 412-1 to 450-5.

153. Hazard and Stern, "Exterior Treason" 85–86.

154. Harry Söderman and John J. O'Connell, *Modern Criminal Investigation,* 5th ed. (New York 1962) 499.

155. Martin van Creveld, *The Rise and Decline of the State* (Cambridge 1999) 401–402.

156. Richard Moran, "The Origin of Insanity as a Special Verdict: The Trial for Treason of James Hadfield (1800)," *Law and Society Review* 19, 3 (1984) 493, 495.

157. Eric H. Monkkonen, *Police in Urban America, 1860–1920* (Cambridge 1981) 63.

158. *United States v. Lawrence,* 26 F. Cas. 887 (C.C.D.C. 1835) (No. 15,557), cited in William F. Duker, "The Right to Bail," *Albany Law Review* 42 (1977) 90; Foote, "Coming Constitutional Crisis," 992.

159. Ingraham, *Political Crime in Europe,* 128.

160. Robert Aitken and Marilyn Aitken, "The M'Naghten Case: The Queen Was Not Amused," *Litigation* 36, 4 (2010) 55.

161. Though Napoleon III was perhaps suspected of this fabrication unfairly: see Howard C. Payne, *The Police State of Louis Napoleon Bonaparte 1851–1860* (Seattle 1966) 268–269.

Chapter 5

1. Mommsen, *Römisches Strafrecht,* 24; Maine, *Ancient Law,* 81.

2. Weisser, *Crime and Punishment,* 21.

3. Figures are surprisingly hard to come by. This paywalled site claims to have some: https://www.statisticbrain.com/arranged-marriage-statistics/.

4. Lintott, *Violence in Republican Rome,* 7.

5. Vigilantism is "unreasonable self-help action by citizens that tends to disrupt the administration of the criminal justice system." *State v. Johnson*, 122 N.M. 696, 930 P.2d 1148 (1996), quoted in Jane Boyd Ohlin and Alvin Stauber, "The Applicability of Citizen's Arrest Powers to the Hospitality Industry," *Journal of Hospitality and Tourism Research* 27, 3 (2003) 345.

6. *R v. Brown* [1993] 2 All ER 75, 4, http://www.bailii.org/uk/cases/UKHL/1993/19.html; Barbara Falsetto, "Crossing the Line: Morality, Society, and the Criminal Law," *Cambridge Student Law Review* 5 (2009) 186–187.

7. Thomas C. Grey, *The Legal Enforcement of Morality* (New York 1983) 145–146.

8. Patrick Devlin, *The Enforcement of Morals* (London 1965) 6.

9. Robert J. Steinfeld, *The Invention of Free Labor: The Employment Relation in English and American Law and Culture, 1350–1870* (Chapel Hill 1991) 13.

10. Muir, *Mad Blood Stirring*, chap. 8.

11. Markku Peltonen, *The Duel in Early Modern England* (Cambridge 2003) 67, 110.

12. Bartlett, *Trial by Fire and Water*, chap. 6.

13. John W. Baldwin, "The Intellectual Preparation for the Canon of 1215 against Ordeals," *Speculum* 36, 4 (1961) 616.

14. *Grettir's Saga*, trans. Denton Fox and Hermann Pálsson (Toronto 1974) 39.

15. Bartlett, *Trial by Fire and Water*, 104–105, 120–122.

16. Bartlett, *Trial by Fire and Water*, 114.

17. Austrian Aryans did not accept challenges from Jews, for example, unless they were especially persistent. George Weidenfeld, *Remembering My Good Friends* (London 1994) 60–61.

18. Boehm, *Blood Revenge*, 87.

19. Ute Frevert, "Honour and Middle-Class Culture: The History of the Duel in England and Germany," in Jürgen Kocka and Allen Mitchell, eds., *Bourgeois Society in Nineteenth-Century Europe* (Oxford 1993). The Dutch, in contrast, were unimpressed. Pieter Spierenburg, *Violence and Punishment: Civilizing the Body through Time* (Cambridge 2013) 44–45.

20. Beattie, *Crime and the Courts*, 92.

21. Joanne B. Freeman, *Affairs of Honor: National Politics in the New Republic* (New Haven 2001) chap. 4.

22. Spierenburg, *History of Murder*, 73–78.

23. Appiah, *Honor Code*, 30; Spierenburg, *History of Murder*, 182.

24. Banner, *Death Penalty*, 78; Kollmann, *Crime and Punishment*, 406.

25. R. H. Helmholz, *Natural Law in Court: A History of Legal Theory in Practice* (Cambridge MA 2015) 152; Ryan P. Brown, *Honor Bound: How a Cultural Ideal Has Shaped the American Psyche* (New York 2016) 16.

26. This is the spirit in which economists have approached vigilantism. Kelly D. Hine, "Vigilantism Revisited," *American University Law Review* 47 (1998) 1241.

27. Stephen P. Frank, "Popular Justice, Community, and Culture among the Russian Peasantry, 1870–1900," *Russian Review* 46, 3 (1987) 240–241; Spierenburg, *Spectacle of Suffering*, 11.

28. Samuel Walker, *Popular Justice: A History of American Criminal Justice* (New York 1980) 31–32; William C. Culberson, *Vigilantism: Political History of Private Power in America* (New York 1990) 37.

29. France, Code de procédure pénale, art. 73; Germany, Strafprozeßordnung, §127; Malaysia, Criminal Procedure Code, sect. 27.

30. Culberson, *Vigilantism*, 11.

31. Alan Hunt, *Governing Morals: A Social History of Moral Regulation* (Cambridge 1999) 60; Roth, *American Homicide*, 193–194, 266–267; Frederick Allen, "Montana Vigilantes and the Origins of 3-7-77," *Montana: The Magazine of Western History* 51, 1 (2001) 4–6; Friedman and Havemann, "Rise and Fall of Unwritten Law," 1021; Culberson, *Vigilantism*, 47; Ira P. Robbins, "Vilifying the Vigilante: A Narrowed Scope of Citizen's Arrest," *Cornell Journal of Law and Public Policy* 25 (2016) 560, 580. In Montana, schools and businesses are still named "Vigilante" as a mark of approval.

32. Stephanie Juliano, "Superheroes, Bandits, and Cyber-nerds: Exploring the History and Contemporary Development of the Vigilante," *Journal of International Commercial Law and Technology* 7, 1 (2012) 44–45.

33. Culberson, *Vigilantism*, 5; Elizabeth Dale, *Criminal Justice in the United States, 1789–1939* (Cambridge 2011) 47.

34. Sylvia D. Hoffert, "Gender and Vigilantism on the Minnesota Frontier: Jane Grey Swisshelm and the U.S.–Dakota Conflict of 1862," *Western Historical Quarterly* 29, 3 (1998) 357–359; Walter T. Howard, "Vigilante Justice and National Reaction: The 1937 Tallahassee Double Lynching," *Florida Historical Quarterly* 67, 1 (1988) 42.

35. One such orgy of lynch violence was the case of George Hughes in Texas in 1930. Beth Crabb, "White Man's Justice for a Black Man's Crime," *Journal of Negro History* 75 (1990).

36. Tsuyoshi Hasegawa, *Crime and Punishment in the Russian Revolution: Mob Justice and the Police in Petrograd* (Cambridge MA 2017) chap. 5.

37. Loïc Wacquant, *Punishing the Poor: The Neoliberal Government of Social Insecurity* (Durham NC 2009) 217–218; Juliano, "Superheroes," 58.

38. Franklin E. Zimring, *The Contradictions of American Capital Punishment* (New York 2003) 90.

39. David Garland, *Peculiar Institution: America's Death Penalty in an Age of Abolition* (Cambridge MA 2010) 31.

40. Michael J. Pfeifer, *Rough Justice: Lynching and American Society, 1874–1947* (Urbana 2004) 29, chap. 4.

41. There were 1,540 lynchings versus 1,215 executions. Terance D. Miethe and Hong Lu, *Punishment: A Comparative Historical Perspective* (Cambridge 2005) 98.

42. Calculated from figures at Tuskegee University. Tuskegee University Archives Repository, 022 Lynching Information, Monroe Work's Compilation, "Lynching, Whites & Negroes, 1882–1968."

43. Zimring, *Contradictions of American Capital Punishment*, 89–90.

44. Børge Bakken, "China, a Punitive Society?" *Asian Criminology* 6 (2011) 40–41.

Chapter 6

1. Ugo Mattei, *Basic Principles of Property Law* (Westport 2000) 65–67; Barry Nicholas, *An Introduction to Roman Law* (Oxford 1962) 129–130.

2. Although for many offenses the talionic logic was not in fact eye for eye but an infliction that preventively rendered the offender harmless—thus, castration for rape, not counterrape—except in Assyria. Diamond, *Primitive Law*, 98, 102.

3. This description comes from the second-century Christian text *Apocalypse of Peter*. Meeks, *Origins of Christian Morality*, 176; Bernstein, *Formation of Hell*, 285.

4. Beccaria, *On Crimes and Punishments*, chap. 7.

5. Gerald Dworkin and David Blumenfeld, "Punishment for Intentions," *Mind* 75, 299 (1966) 396–399.

6. David Boonin, *The Problem of Punishment* (Cambridge 2008) 57; Paul H. Robinson, "Punishing Dangerousness: Cloaking Preventive Detention as Criminal Justice," *Harvard Law Review* 114, 5 (2001) 1438.

7. Jeremy Bentham, *Principles of Penal Law*, in John Bowring, ed., *Works of Jeremy Bentham* (Edinburgh 1838) 1:396.

8. Bentham, *Principles of Penal Law*, 398.

9. Drapkin, *Crime and Punishment*, 211; von Bar, *History of Continental Criminal Law*, 337, 381.

10. Although Kant was not interested in deterrence, his concern with the bloodguilt that would adhere to that community's members even as they dispersed if they failed to carry out the sentence arguably suggested a worry with supernatural anger that introduced a preventive note—prevention against divine retribution. Kant, *Philosophy of Law*, 198.

11. Robinson, "Punishing Dangerousness," 1439–1440.

12. Punishing attempted murder less than actual murder made no sense unless the hope was to encourage accomplice behavior as a preferable alternative to primary perpetrator behavior. Dressler, "Reassessing the Theoretical Underpinnings," 114.

13. Such branding was therefore ended after seven years. Beattie, *Crime and the Courts*, 491.

14. Esmein, *History of Continental Criminal Procedure*, 235; Radzinowicz, *History of English Criminal Law*, 1:730; Meghan A. Novisky and Robert L. Peralta, "When Women Tell: Intimate Partner Violence and the Factors Related to Police Notification," *Violence against Women* 21, 1 (2015) 67.

15. Montesquieu, *Spirit of the Laws*, 6:16. The marginal deterrence, as modern economists would put it, was askew. George J. Stigler, "The Optimum Enforcement of Laws," *Journal of Political Economy* 78 (1970) 527.

16. Francis Fukuyama, *The Origins of Political Order* (New York 2011) 130.

17. Amy Adler, "The Perverse Law of Child Pornography," *Columbia Law Review* 101, 2 (2001) 254–256, 262–265.

18. *The Digest of Justinian*, trans. Alan Watson (Philadelphia 1985) 1.1.10.

19. Kant, *Metaphysics of Morals*, 6:332.

20. J. M. Kelly, *A Short History of Western Legal Theory* (Oxford 1992) 448–449; Larry Alexander and Kimberly Kessler Ferzan, *Crime and Culpability* (Cambridge 2009) 192–196.

21. Hobbes, *Leviathan*, chap. 28.

22. John Locke, *Second Treatise*, chap. 2, sec. 8.

23. Jeremy Bentham, *An Introduction to the Principles of Morals and Legislation* (Oxford 1907) 170.

24. Von Bar, *History of Continental Criminal Law*, 4–5; Nicola Lacey, *State Punishment* (London 1988) chap. 2.

25. The logic spelled out by Socrates in Plato, *Gorgias*, 525A–B.

26. Plato, *Protagoras*, 324.

27. Walker, *Popular Justice*, 247.

28. William Blackstone, *Commentaries on the Laws of England* (Oxford 1765–1769) 4:249.

29. Hugo Adam Bedau, "Capital Punishment," in Tom Regan, ed., *Matters of Life and Death* (New York 1993) 182; Arne Jansson, *From Swords to Sorrow: Homicide and Suicide in Early Modern Stockholm* (Stockholm 1998) 19, chap. 3; Karin Andriolo, "Murder by Suicide: Episodes from Muslim History," *American Anthropologist* 104, 3 (2002) 739; Vitale, *End of Policing*, 79.

30. Dubber, *Dual Penal State*, 149.

31. That was Alex's objection to hearing Beethoven while being reprogrammed in Stanley Kubrick's film *A Clockwork Orange*.

32. Friedland, *Seeing Justice Done*, 62; Drapkin, *Crime and Punishment*, 27–28; Spierenburg, *Spectacle of Suffering*, 76. The deterrent effect of banishment was undercut, however, as Bentham pointed out, by the punishment being inflicted far away from those to be deterred. Also it incapacitated only as far as the source community was concerned, not necessarily the destination society. John Hirst, "The Australian Experience," in Norval Morris and David J. Rothman, eds., *Oxford History of the Prison* (New York 1995) 274.

33. Hence, the Soviet Union never imposed life sentences, thinking that all prisoners could be rehabilitated. Thaman, "Marxist and Soviet Law," 314.

34. John C. Coffee Jr, "Paradigms Lost: The Blurring of the Criminal and Civil Law Models. And What Can Be Done about It," *Yale Law Journal* 101, 8 (1992) 1882.

35. Friedland, *Seeing Justice Done*, 207.

36. Parker, *Miasma*, 118; Treston, *Poine*, 140; Hirst, "Australian Experience," 274–275.

37. Herbert L. Packer, *The Limits of the Criminal Sanction* (Stanford 1968) 44–45; Paul H. Robinson and John M. Darley, "The Utility of Desert," *Northwestern University Law Review* 91 (1996–1997) 454.

38. Williams, *Tudor Regime*, 235.

39. David J. Rothman, "Perfecting the Prison," in Morris and Rothman, *Oxford History of the Prison*, 125; Norval Morris, "The Contemporary Prison," in Morris and Rothman, *Oxford History of the Prison*, 247; Edgardo Rotman, "The Failure of Reform," in Morris and Rothman, *Oxford History of the Prison*, 172, 189–190; Robinson and Darley, "Utility of Desert," 464; Bernard E. Harcourt, "The Shaping of Chance: Actuarial Models and Criminal Profiling at the Turn of the Twenty-First Century," *University of Chicago Law Review* 70, 1 (2003) 105–109.

40. Anthony Bottoms, "The Philosophy and Politics of Punishment and Sentencing," in Chris Clarkson and Rod Morgan, eds., *The Politics of Sentencing Reform* (Oxford 1995) 19–21; Harcourt, "Shaping of Chance," 105.

41. Miethe and Lu, *Punishment*, 211.

42. Andrew Ashworth, "Social Control and 'Anti-social Behaviour': The Subversion of Human Rights," *Law Quarterly Review* 120 (2004) 270–271; Roberts et al., *Penal Populism*, 127; Barnett, "Restitution," 288–298; Lacey, *State Punishment*, 11.

Chapter 7

1. Vega, *Royal Commentaries of the Incas*, 96.

2. Plato, *Laws*, bk.10, 908a; Jones, *Law and Legal Theory of the Greeks*, 119.

3. Danielle S. Allen, *The World of Prometheus: The Politics of Punishing in Democratic Athens* (Princeton 2000) 202; Crook, *Law and Life of Rome*, 272.

4. Parker, *Miasma*, 118; Salima Ikram, *Ancient Egypt* (Cambridge 2010) 230; Lorton, "Treatment of Criminals," 7, 30. Similar attempts were made in Rome to eradicate the names of traitors altogether. Chilton, "Roman Law of Treason," 80.

5. Plato, *Laws*, bk. 9, chap. 12, 873a–c.

6. Michael R. Dutton, *Policing and Punishment in China* (Cambridge 1992) 78–79; Pollock and Maitland, *History of English Law*, 1:478.

7. Jakub J. Grygiel, *Return of the Barbarians: Confronting Non-state Actors from Ancient Rome to the Present* (Cambridge 2018) 35–41.

8. Anthony Giddens, *The Nation-State and Violence* (Berkeley 1987) 51, 79.

9. Leviticus 18:28–29, 20:3–5.

10. Gagarin, *Drakon*, 123.

11. MacDowell, *Law in Classical Athens*, 73; Seipp, "Distinction between Crime and Tort," 64.

12. Treston, *Poine*, 257; MacDowell, *Law in Classical Athens*, 117; Jones, *Law and Legal Theory of the Greeks*, 256.

13. Drapkin, *Crime and Punishment*, 77–79.

14. Genesis 4:12–21.

15. Bodde and Morris, *Law in Imperial China*, 78; Byock, *Viking Age Iceland*, 315.

16. Ames, *Righteous Persecution*, 150.

17. James Casey, "Household Dispute and the Law in Early Modern Andalusia," in Bossy, *Disputes and Settlements*, 210; Alan Williams, *The Police of Paris 1718–1789* (Baton Rouge 1979) 235.

18. Pieter Spierenburg, "The Body and the State," in Morris and Norval, *Oxford History of the Prison*, 62; von Bar, *History of Continental Criminal Law*, 32–33; Chilton, "Roman Law of Treason," 74–76.

19. Law of 28 March 1793; Lascoumes et al., *Au nom de l'ordre,* 160; Julian Swann, *Exile, Imprisonment, or Death: The Politics of Disgrace in Bourbon France, 1610–1789* (Oxford 2017) 62, 185–188; Patricia O'Brien, *The Promise of Punishment: Prisons in Nineteenth-Century France* (Princeton 1982) 260.

20. Hirst, "Australian Experience," 264.

21. Given, *Society and Homicide*, 93; Pollock and Maitland, *History of English Law*, 1:478; Spierenburg, "Body and the State," 62–63; Williams, *Police of Paris*, 235.

22. Alice Bullard, *Exile to Paradise: Savagery and Civilization in Paris and the South Pacific, 1790–1900* (Stanford 2000) chap. 5; Patricia O'Brien, "The Prison on the Continent," in Morris and Norval, *Oxford History of the Prison*, 212; Andrews, "Boundaries of Citizenship," 94; Wright, *Between the Guillotine and Liberty*, 93, 130, 138, 184.

23. Spierenburg, "Body and the State," 76; Miethe and Lu, *Punishment*, 31.

24. Hirst, "Australian Experience," 293.

25. Hans Mommsen, "The Realization of the Unthinkable: The Final Solution of the Jewish Question in the Third Reich," in Gerhard Hirschfeld, ed., *The Policies of Genocide* (London 1986).

26. David L. Hoffmann, "The Conceptual and Practical Origins of Soviet State Violence," in Harris, *Anatomy of Terror*, 89; Philip Ther, *The Dark Side of Nation-States: Ethnic Cleansing in Modern Europe* (New York 2014) 180–196.

27. Brackett, *Criminal Justice and Crime in Late Renaissance Florence*, 69; John A. Davis, *Conflict and Control: Law and Order in Nineteenth-Century Italy* (Atlantic Highlands 1988) 131, 223–226.

28. Kollmann, *Crime and Punishment*, 243–245; Thaman, "Marxist and Soviet Law," 314–315.

29. Bodde and Morris, *Law in Imperial China*, 82–84; Frank Dikötter, *Crime, Punishment, and the Prison in Modern China* (New York 2002) 53.

30. Dutton, *Policing and Punishment in China*, 82.

31. Though do not forget how many are still assassinated abroad by operatives from the regimes they have fled, such as Russians in London and Rwandan opposition members abroad.

32. Plato, *Apology*, 37c.

33. "Australia Plans to Deny Passports to Convicted Paedophiles," *BBC News*, 30 May 2017, http://www.bbc.co.uk/news/world-australia-40089351.

34. The United States has the most elaborate such rules. Britain and France also have sex-offender registries, but they are not made public. Keith Soothill, "Sex Offender Recidivism," *Crime and Justice* 39, 1 (2010) 151, 189, 191; Roberts et al., *Penal Populism*, 140; Corey Rayburn Yung, "The Emerging Criminal War on Sex Offenders," *Harvard Civil Rights–Civil Liberties Law Review* 45 (2010) 448–450; *New York Times*, 2 October 2005, A20.

35. Joseph Goldstein, "Housing Restrictions Keep Sex Offenders in Prison beyond Release Dates," *New York Times*, 21 August 2014.

36. Automatic alarms go off if sex offenders approach: *Spiegel* 32 (2005) 56.

37. Mandatory life sentences are now also possible in Britain. Ashworth and Zedner, *Preventive Justice*, 156–157; Howard, *Unusually Cruel*, 44.

38. Dubber, "Policing Possession," 855.

39. Diane Taylor, "Former UBS Trader Kweku Adoboli Vows to Fight Deportation," *Guardian*, 18 August 2018; Vanessa Barker, *Nordic Nationalism and Penal Order: Walling the Welfare State* (Milton Park 2017) 92.

40. Peter John Young, "Punishment, Money, and Legal Order: An Analysis of the Emergence of Monetary Sanctions with Special Reference to Scotland," PhD diss., Edinburgh University, 1987, passim, especially chap. 3.

41. Pat O'Malley, *The Currency of Justice: Fines and Damages in Consumer Societies* (Abingdon 2009) 58–60, 77–79.

42. And the majority of sentences for antitrust, food and drug, and environmental offenses. Newburn, "'Tough on Crime,'" 446–447; US Sentencing Commission, *Overview of Federal Criminal Cases: Fiscal Year 2018* (June 2019) 1, 9, 10, https://www.ussc.gov/sites/default/files/pdf/research-and-publications/research-publications/2019/FY18_Overview_Federal_Criminal_Cases.pdf.

43. Drapkin, *Crime and Punishment*, 22–26.

44. Charles H. Miller, "The Place of the Fine in Modern Penology," *Proceedings of the American Prison Association* (1951) 209–210.

45. Derek A. Westen, "Fines, Imprisonment, and the Poor," *California Law Review* 57 (1969) 783–785.

46. Green, *Verdict according to Conscience*, 15, 100–101.

47. Calvin R. Massey, "The Excessive Fines Clause and Punitive Damages," *Vanderbilt Law Review* 40, 6 (1987) 1253.

48. Tacitus, *Germania*, chap. 12; Phillpotts, *Kindred and Clan*, 70.

49. Beth A. Colgan, "Reviving the Excessive Fines Clause," *California Law Review* 102, 2 (2014) 307.

50. Hence, civil fines are often much larger than criminal fines since civil fines price the behavior that requires restitution. Ashworth, "Social Control," 273.

51. Michael K. Glenn, "The Crime of 'Pollution': The Role of Federal Water Pollution Criminal Sanctions," *American Criminal Law Review* 11 (1973) 845–847.

52. Julia Moses, *The First Modern Risk: Workplace Accidents and the Origins of European Social States* (Cambridge 2018) 30.

53. Georg Rusche and Otto Kirchheimer, *Punishment and Social Structure* (New York 1939) 174–175.

54. Beattie, *Policing and Punishment*, 215; Douglas Greenberg, *Crime and Law Enforcement in the Colony of New York 1691–1776* (Ithaca 1974) 162–163; Young, "Punishment, Money, and Legal Order," 40.

55. Coffee, "Paradigms Lost," 1882.

56. John P. Dawson, "Specific Performance in France and Germany," *Michigan Law Review* 57, 4 (1959) 498.

57. Williams, *Tudor Regime*, 394; Simon, "Evolution of Treason," 694; Levy, *Treason against God*, 314; Beattie, *Crime and the Courts*, 459.

58. Alex Harris et al., "Drawing Blood from Stones: Legal Debt and Social Inequality in the Contemporary United States," *American Journal of Sociology* 115, 6 (2010) 1758.

59. "Fighting for Identity," *Economist*, 17 May 2014.

60. Glenn, "Crime of 'Pollution,'" 836–838; O'Malley, *Currency of Justice*, 69.

61. Panos D. Bardis, "Main Features of the Ancient Roman Family," *Social Science* 38, 4 (1963) 237.

62. Lenman and Parker, "State, Community, and Criminal Law," 20; Pollock and Maitland, *History of English Law*, 1:56.

63. Wilson, *Varieties of Police Behavior*, 95; *Times* (London), 5 July 2019, 8.

64. Michael Dutton, *Policing Chinese Politics* (Durham NC 2005) 280–281; Jonathan R. Zatlin, *The Currency of Socialism: Money and Political Culture in East Germany* (Cambridge 2007) 121.

65. Mommsen, *Römisches Strafrecht*, 50; von Bar, *History of Continental Criminal Law*, 271.

66. Blackstone, *Commentaries on the Laws of England*, 4:373.

67. Beattie, *Crime and the Courts*, 456–457; Massey, "Excessive Fines Clause," 1249–1250.

68. Diamond, *Primitive Law*, 67; Edward M. Peters, "Prison before the Prison," in Morris and Rothman, *Oxford History of the Prison*, 6; King, *Law and Society in the Visigothic Kingdom*, 191.

69. Seipp, "Distinction between Crime and Tort," 83–84; Colgan, "Reviving Excessive Fines Clause," 334.

70. Robert J. Steinfeld, *Coercion, Contract, and Free Labor in the Nineteenth Century* (Cambridge 2001) 212, passim.

71. Kant, *Philosophy of Law*, 197.

72. Allen, *World of Prometheus*, 226.

73. Miller, *Eye for an Eye*, 22; Johnson and Krüger, "Good of Wrath," 167. This was Beccaria's argument, too. *On Crimes and Punishment*, chap. 20.

74. Brackett, *Criminal Justice and Crime in Late Renaissance Florence*, 5; von Bar, *History of Continental Criminal Law*, 274–275.

75. Rothman, "Perfecting the Prison," 112; O'Brien, "Prison on the Continent," 212–214; Emsley, *English Police*, 219.

76. Rusche and Kirchheimer, *Punishment and Social Structure*, 172–173.

77. Baldwin, *Contagion and the State in Europe*, 266–273. Similar dilemmas, fines or jail, were weighed for transmitting venereal diseases. *Zeitschrift für die Bekämpfung der Geschlechtskrankheiten* 11 (1910) 219; 15, 3 (1914) 94.

78. Crook, *Law and Life of Rome*, 250.

79. Mommsen, *Römisches Strafrecht*, 23.

80. O'Malley, *Currency of Justice*, 33, 40–41; Pollock and Maitland, *History of English Law*, 1:36, 56.

81. Miethe and Lu, *Punishment*, 135–136.

82. Emsley, "'Mother, What Did Policemen Do,'" 363; Seo, *Policing the Open Road*, 54.

83. The reengineering of fines was unfair in one way but fair in another—that the fine be proportional to the harm caused for everyone, however rich or poor they were. Restitution ran into the same problems, that some could afford it better than others, in which case did one stagger the payments according to wealth? Barnett, "Restitution," 288–298.

84. Saunders, *Plato's Penal Code*, 347.

85. Miller, "Place of the Fine," 213; Westen, "Fines, Imprisonment, and the Poor," 813; Miethe and Lu, *Punishment*, 26; Schafer, "Restitution to Victims," 253.

86. Suzanne Daley, "Speeding in Finland Can Cost You a Fortune, If You Already Have One," *New York Times*, 25 April 2015; *Economist*, 7 November 2019.

87. Han Shen, "A Comparative Study of Insider Trading Regulation Enforcement in the US and China," *Journal of Business and Securities Law* 9 (2009) 71.

88. T. F. T. Plucknett, *Edward I and Criminal Law* (Cambridge 1960) 10.

89. Evgeny Bronislavovich Pashukanis, *The General Theory of Law and Marxism* (New Brunswick 2003) 176; Lon L. Fuller, "Pashukanis and Vyshinsky: A Study in the Development of Marxian Legal Theory," *Michigan Law Review* 47, 8 (1949) 1161–1162.

90. Dawson, "Specific Performance," 496–497.

91. J. Berryman, "The Specific Performance Damages Continuum: An Historical Perspective," *Ottawa Law Review* 17 (1985) 311–312; Charles Szladits, "The Concept of Specific Performance in Civil Law," *American Journal of Comparative Law* 4, 2 (1955) 209–210, 212–213; Robert Bejesky, "The Evolution in and International Convergence of the Doctrine of Specific Performance in Three Types of States," *Indiana International and Comparative Law Review* 13 (2003) 393.

92. Klaus Mühlhahn, *Criminal Justice in China* (Cambridge MA 2009) 186.

93. The Old Testament numbers are disputed. See Gretason, "Crime, Guilt, and Punishment," 143; Baruch, "In the Name of the Father," 54; William A. Schabas, "Islam and the Death Penalty," *William & Mary Bill of Rights Journal* 9, 1 (2000) 231.

94. Li Feng, *Early China* (Cambridge 2013) 289.

95. MacDowell, *Law in Classical Athens*, 42; Parker, *Miasma*, 113.

96. Durkheim, "Two Laws of Penal Evolution," 84; Dubber, *Police Power*, 20; Plucknett, *Edward I and Criminal Law*, 79.

97. Jens David Ohlin, "Applying the Death Penalty to Crimes of Genocide," *American Journal of International Law* 99, 4 (2005) 767–768.

98. Beccaria, *On Crimes and Punishment*, chap. 27.

99. Von Bar, *History of Continental Criminal Law*, 34.

100. Kollmann, *Crime and Punishment*, 28; Phillpotts, *Kindred and Clan*, 82, 165.

101. Quoted in Evans, *Rituals of Retribution*, 464.

102. Egmond, "The Cock, the Dog, the Serpent," 181; Mommsen, *Römisches Strafrecht*, 4, 918; James Leigh Strachan-Davidson, *Problems of the Roman Criminal Law* (Oxford 1912) 1:1; Gretason, "Crime, Guilt, and Punishment," 141.

103. Kateb, "Punishment and the Spirit of Democracy," 280; Evans, *Rituals of Retribution*, 332.

104. Mommsen, *Römisches Strafrecht*, 41.

105. Evans, *Rituals of Retribution*, 495; Lascoumes et al., *Au nom de l'ordre*, 124; Wright, *Between the Guillotine and Liberty*, 171, 216.

106. Banner, *Death Penalty*, 268–270, 282; Zimring, *Contradictions of American Capital Punishment*, 52, passim; Garland, *Peculiar Institution*, 26, 47–50, 277.

107. Børge Bakken, "Moral Panics, Crime Rates, and Harsh Punishment in China," *Australian and New Zealand Journal of Criminology* 37 (2004) 83–84; Evans, *Rituals of Retribution*, 624–625, 780–783.

108. Zimring, *Contradictions of American Capital Punishment*, 30–31; Evans, *Rituals of Retribution*, 780–783; Ohlin, "Applying the Death Penalty," 760.

109. Niklas Frank, *In the Shadow of the Reich* (New York 1991) 3; Philippe Sands, "'This Our Fathers Did': A Nazi Legacy," *Financial Times Magazine*, 22 September 2015.

110. Bailey, "Shadow of the Gallows," 309, 333.

111. Randall McGowen, "History, Culture, and the Death Penalty: The British Debates, 1840–70," *Historical Reflections* 20, 2 (2003) 238.

112. Quoted in Zhang Ning, "Public Opinion and the Death Penalty Debate in China," *China Perspectives* 81, 1 (2010) 87.

113. Lars-Erik Vaale, *Dommen til Døden: Dødsstraffen i Norge 1945–50* (Oslo 2004) 48–52, 58–59, 72; Ohlin, "Applying the Death Penalty," 747–749.

114. Dutton, *Policing and Punishment in China*, 120; McKnight, *Quality of Mercy*, 116; Mühlhahn, *Criminal Justice in China*, 30.

115. Langbein, *Prosecuting Crime*, 195; Peters, "Prison before the Prison," 24; MacDowell, *Law in Classical Athens*, 75.

116. Plato, *Laws*, bk. 10, 908a; Allen, *World of Prometheus*, 226–227; Mommsen, *Römisches Strafrecht*, 961; Attenborough, *Laws of the English Kings*, Alfred cap 1.2, Æthelstan cap 1.3; Given, *Inquisition and Medieval Society*, 52–53; Trevor Dean, "Criminal

Justice in Mid Fifteenth-Century Bologna," in Trevor Dean and K. J. P. Lowe., eds., *Crime, Society, and the Law in Renaissance Italy* (Cambridge 1994) 26.

117. Ames, *Righteous Persecution*, 157.

118. Peters, "Prison before the Prison," 12, 15; Jay Cohen, "The History of Imprisonment for Debt and Its Relation to the Development of Discharge in Bankruptcy," *Journal of Legal History* 3, 2 (2007) 154–155; Randall McGowen, "The Well-Ordered Prison," in Morris and Rothman, *Oxford History of the Prison*, 81.

119. Peters, "Prison before the Prison," 32.

120. Langbein, *Torture*, 28; Peters, "Prison before the Prison," 22, 35; Brackett, *Criminal Justice and Crime in Late Renaissance Florence*, 51; Beattie, *Crime and the Courts*, 289–290.

121. Radzinowicz, *History of English Criminal Law*, 5:441; Ian Christopher Fletcher, "'A Star Chamber of the Twentieth Century': Suffragettes, Liberals, and the 1908 'Rush the Commons' Case," *Journal of British Studies* 35, 4 (1996) 510.

122. Martin, *Crime and Criminal Justice under the Third Republic*, 259.

123. Bodde and Morris, *Law in Imperial China*, 87–88.

124. Beattie, *Policing and Punishment*, 366–367; Langbein, *Torture*, 30–31, 44; Beattie, *Crime and the Courts*, 565–569.

125. Langbein, *Torture*, 38; Beattie, *Crime and the Courts*, 492–493, 88.

126. Jenks, *Short History of English Law*, 346–347; Ignatieff, *Just Measure of Pain*, 15.

127. Weisser, *Crime and Punishment*, 163; Martin J. Wiener, *Reconstructing the Criminal: Culture, Law, and Policy in England, 1830–1914* (Cambridge 1990) 308; Lascoumes et al., *Au nom de l'ordre*, 111; Evans, *Rituals of Retribution*, 240.

128. Von Bar, *History of Continental Criminal Law*, 36.

129. Rotman, "Failure of Reform," 176; Mühlhahn, *Criminal Justice in China*, 231–232.

130. Marie Gottschalk, *Caught: The Prison State and the Lockdown of American Politics* (Princeton 2015) chap. 3; Heather Ann Thompson, "The Prison Industrial Complex," *New Labor Forum* 21, 3 (2012) 42.

131. A possible exception to prison labor not paying for itself was galley labor. Friedman, "Making Sense of English Law Enforcement," 493–495.

132. Michael Poyker, "Economic Consequences of the U.S. Convict Labor System," 7 April 2018, https://www.dropbox.com/s/4fwmbgbzatexc03/CL_Poyker.pdf?dl=0; Thompson, "Prison Industrial Complex," 44.

133. Marco H. D. van Leeuwen, *The Logic of Charity: Amsterdam, 1800–1850* (Houndmills 2000) 157; Walker, *Popular Justice*, 154.

134. Robert Mintz, "Federal Prison Industry: The 'Green Monster,'" *Crime and Social Justice* 6 (1976) 46; O'Brien, "Prison on the Continent," 204; Morris, "Contemporary Prison," 246–247; Wright, *Between the Guillotine and Liberty*, 85–88.

135. Debtors Act of 1869, 32 & 33 Vict., c. 62, s. 5; Cohen, "History of Imprisonment for Debt," 159; Haagen, "Eighteenth-Century English Society," 227.

136. Abed Awad and Robert E. Michael, "Iflas and Chapter 11: Classical Islamic Law and Modern Bankruptcy," *International Lawyer* 44, 3 (2010) 997–998; Irene Schneider, "Imprisonment in Pre-classical and Classical Islamic Law," *Islamic Law and Society* 2, 2 (1995) 158–159; Richard E. James, "Putting Fear Back into the Law

and Debtors Back into Prison: Reforming the Debtors' Prison System," *Washburn Law Journal* 42 (2002) 143–144.

137. Westen, "Fines, Imprisonment, and the Poor," 779; Young, "Punishment, Money, and Legal Order," 259.

138. Spierenburg, "Body and the State," 64.

139. McGowen, "Well-Ordered Prison," 83; Beattie, *Crime and the Courts*, 571; Michael Meranze, *Laboratories of Virtue: Punishment, Revolution, and Authority in Philadelphia, 1760–1835* (Chapel Hill 1996) 168–169.

140. McGowen, "Well-Ordered Prison," 86, 91, 101; Rothman, "Perfecting the Prison," 118; Thomas L. Dumm, *Democracy and Punishment: Disciplinary Origins of the United States* (Madison 1987) 108.

141. O'Brien, *Promise of Punishment*, 26–29; Ignatieff, *Just Measure of Pain*, 194–196.

Chapter 8

1. Durkheim, *Division of Labour*, 44.

2. Mühlhahn, *Criminal Justice in China*, 30.

3. Radzinowicz, *History of English Criminal Law*, 1:3–4.

4. In China during the Spring and Autumn periods, 770–476 BCE, public punishments were, if anything, even worse than in Europe in the 1700s. Dutton, *Policing and Punishment in China*, 109.

5. Dean, "Criminal Justice in Mid Fifteenth-Century Bologna," 27.

6. Gatrell, *Hanging Tree*, 15. Masterfully surveyed in Garland, *Peculiar Institution*, chap. 3.

7. Langbein, *Torture*, 11–12.

8. Similar exemptions for the literate were found widely in ancient law codes. Diamond, *Primitive Law*, 96–97.

9. Williams, *Tudor Regime*, 226; Beattie, *Crime and the Courts*, 141–145, 452.

10. Sharpe, *Crime in Early Modern England*, 90–91, 97, 99; Weisser, *Crime and Punishment*, 140.

11. Herrup, *Common Peace*, 165.

12. Spierenburg, "Body and the State," 60; F. W. Maitland, *Constitutional History of England* (Cambridge 1926) 478.

13. Garland, *Peculiar Institution*, 115, 105; Philips, "New Engine of Power," 156.

14. Gatrell, *Hanging Tree*, 8. Russia did something similar in 1767, as did Austria in 1787.

15. Rothman, "Perfecting the Prison," 114. In 2008, the US Supreme Court reserved death for crimes involving a loss of life, with treason as a possible exception. Eichensehr, "Treason in the Age of Terrorism," 1450, 1500; Creegan, "National Security Crime," 429.

16. Evans, *Rituals of Retribution*, 142.

17. Miethe and Lu, *Punishment*, 127; Bin Liang et al., "Sources of Variation in Pro-Death Penalty Attitudes in China," *British Journal of Criminology* 46 (2006) 130; Dikötter, *Crime, Punishment, and the Prison in Modern China*, 46–47.

18. Susan Trevaskes, "The Death Penalty in China Today: Kill Fewer, Kill Cautiously," *Asian Survey* 48, 3 (2008) 398; Bakken, "Moral Panics," 79; Banner, *Death Penalty*, 284.

19. Miethe and Lu, *Punishment*, 92; Trevaskes, "Death Penalty in China," 400 and passim.

20. Eichensehr, "Treason in the Age of Terrorism," 1450.

21. Garland, *Peculiar Institution*, chap. 4.

22. The term for such punishment was *poena capitis*. Mommsen, *Römisches Strafrecht*, 916. British law did not formally abolish beheading until 1973. Treason Act 1814, sect. 2, repealed by Statute Law (Repeals) Act 1973, c. 39, sch. 1, pt. V.

23. Bodde and Morris, *Law in Imperial China*, 92.

24. James Q. Whitman, *Harsh Justice: Criminal Punishment and the Widening Divide between America and Europe* (New York 2003) 109–110.

25. A US poll. *New Scientist*, 6 May 2017, 24.

26. S. E. Finer, *The History of Government from the Earliest Times* (Oxford 1997) 650; Langbein, *Prosecuting Crime in the Renaissance*, 144; Feng Li, *Early China* (Cambridge 2013) 289.

27. Friedland, *Seeing Justice Done*, 100; Bodde and Morris, *Law in Imperial China*, 97; Mühlhahn, *Criminal Justice in China*, 29; Spierenburg, "Body and the State," 59.

28. Peters, *Torture*, 83; Sharpe, *Crime in Early Modern England*, 95; Dale, *Criminal Justice in the United States*, 38; Beattie, *Crime and the Courts*, 471.

29. Beattie, *Crime and the Courts*, 541; Wright, *Between the Guillotine and Liberty*, 140.

30. Rotman, "Failure of Reform," 184; Whitman, *Harsh Justice*, 152.

31. Gatrell, *Hanging Tree*, 15–16; Radzinowicz, *History of English Criminal Law*, 1:268.

32. This story is told well in Friedland, *Seeing Justice Done*, chaps. 5–7, and Spierenburg, *Spectacle of Suffering*, chap. 6.

33. Evans, *Rituals of Retribution*, 241–246.

34. Beattie, *Crime and the Courts*, 614.

35. Vormbaum, *Modern History of German Criminal Law*, 104; Strafgesetz 1852 (Österreich) §16.

36. Sean McConville, "The Victorian Prison," in Morris and Rothman, *Oxford History of the Prison*, 147.

37. A smidgen of incapacitative motivation continues to salve our consciences, as in the arguments that terrorists must be held incommunicado to prevent contact with outside coconspirators. Terry Allen Kupers, *Solitary: The Inside Story of Supermax Isolation and How We Can Abolish It* (Oakland 2017) 20–23.

38. V. A. C. Gatrell, "The Decline of Theft and Violence in Victorian and Edwardian England," in Gatrell et al., *Crime and the Law*, 303.

39. Malcolm M. Feeley and Jonathan Simon, "The New Penology," *Criminology* 30 (1992) 455, 459; Wacquant, *Punishing the Poor*, 145.

40. Jonathan Simon, *Poor Discipline: Parole and the Social Control of the Underclass, 1890–1990* (Chicago 1993) 33–34.

41. O'Brien, "Prison on the Continent," 209–212, 220; Morris, "Contemporary Prison," 256.

42. Ruff, *Violence in Early Modern Europe*, 111–112.

43. An overview on the decline of violence is in Eisner, "Long-Term Historical Trends in Violent Crime."

44. Tyler, *Why People Obey the Law*, 22–30.

45. Durkheim, "Two Laws of Penal Evolution," 80.

46. Susan Trevaskes, *Policing Serious Crime in China* (New York 2010) 17.

47. Dressler, "Reassessing the Theoretical Underpinnings," 95–96.

48. William Rann Kennedy, "The State Punishment of Crime," *The Brief* 2 (1899–1900) 25.

49. Green, *Verdict according to Conscience*, 32.

50. Beattie, *Crime and the Courts*, 336, 411, 420; F. W. M. McElrea, "The Legal Enforcement of Non-utilitarian Morality," *Otago Law Review* 1 (1965–1968) 206.

51. Guyora Binder, "Punishment Theory: Moral or Political?" *Buffalo Criminal Law Review* 5 (2002) 330–331; Alan Scheflin and Jon Van Dyke, "Jury Nullification: The Contours of a Controversy," *Law and Contemporary Problems* 43, 4 (1980) 71; Paul Butler, "Racially Based Jury Nullification: Black Power in the Criminal Justice System," *Yale Law Journal* 105 (1995) 701.

52. Beattie, *Crime and the Courts*, 490–491, 336; Spierenburg, *History of Murder*, 185.

53. Randall McGowen, "Managing the Gallows: The Bank of England and the Death Penalty, 1797–1821," *Law and History Review* 25, 2 (2007) 251–253.

54. A. Chantemesse and F. Borel, *Hygiène internationale: Frontières et prophylaxie* (Paris 1907) 241. Other examples of self-defeating strict public-health laws are given in Sheldon Amos, *A Comparative Survey of Laws in Force for the Prohibition, Regulation, and Licensing of Vice in England and in Other Countries* (London 1877) 95.

55. Evans, *Rituals of Retribution*, 695.

Chapter 9

1. Henry Ansgar Kelly, "Inquisitorial Due Process and the Status of Secret Crimes," in Stanley Chodorow, ed., *Proceedings of the Eighth International Congress of Medieval Canon Law* (Vatican City 1992) 419–420.

2. Pollock and Maitland, *History of English Law*, 2:474–475.

3. Abbott Gleason, *Totalitarianism: The Inner History of the Cold War* (New York 1995) 89–107.

4. Schneider, "Imprisonment in Pre-classical and Classical Islamic Law," 161; Ames, *Righteous Persecution*, 167.

5. Dale's Laws, 24 May 1610, in J. F. Maclear, ed., *Church and State in the Modern Age* (New York 1995) 35–37.

6. Talal Asad, "Medieval Heresy: An Anthropological View," *Social History* 11, 3 (1986) 355.

7. Mark 14:64.

8. Mommsen, *Römisches Strafrecht*, 572; Assmann, *Price of Monotheism*, chap. 1.

9. Peter Burnell, "The Problem of Service to Unjust Regimes in Augustine's City of God," *Journal of the History of Ideas* 54, 2 (1993) 178; Levy, *Treason against God*, 107–108.

10. Bernard McGinn, "'Evil-Sounding, Rash, and Suspect of Heresy': Tensions between Mysticism and Magisterium in the History of the Church," *Catholic Historical Review* 90, 2 (2004) 200. Hence, the emphasis in much heresy on the annihilation of the self, which let God speak through the heretic.

11. Michael Frassetto, "Reaction and Reform: Reception of Heresy in Arras and Aquitaine in the Early Eleventh Century," *Catholic Historical Review* 83, 3 (1997) 391; David J. Nicholls, "The Nature of Popular Heresy in France, 1520–1542," *Historical Journal* 26, 2 (1983) 271; Shannon McSheffrey, "Heresy, Orthodoxy, and English Vernacular Religion 1480–1525," *Past and Present* 186 (2005) 50, 61.

12. Levy, *Treason against God*, 118–119, 227–230.

13. William Allan, "Divine Justice and Cosmic Order in Early Greek Epic," *Journal of Hellenic Studies* 126 (2006) 8–9.

14. Christoph Riedweg, "The 'Atheistic' Fragment from Euripides' 'Bellerophontes' (286 N 2)," *Illinois Classical Studies* 15, 1 (1990) 52.

15. Judges 6:25–32.

16. Levy, *Treason against God*, 18.

17. Alexander Murray, "Confession before 1215," *Transactions of the Royal Historical Society* 3 (1993) 60.

18. Terence McKenna, "'Treason against God': Some Aspects of the Law Relating to 'Blasphemy,'" *Southern Cross University Law Review* 5 (2001) 29.

19. Nash, "Analyzing the History of Religious Crime," 6; Moore, "Cruel and Unusual Punishment," 735–736.

20. Robert N. Bellah, *Religion in Human Evolution* (Cambridge MA 2011) chap. 6; Wolfgang Reinhard, *Geschichte der Staatsgewalt* (Munich 2000) 260; Durkheim, *Division of Labour*, 227.

21. Gerd Schwerhoff, "Horror Crime or Bad Habit? Blasphemy in Premodern Europe, 1200–1650," *Journal of Religious History* 32, 4 (2008) 407.

22. Elisheva Carlebach, *The Pursuit of Heresy: Rabbi Moses Hagiz and the Sabbatian Controversies* (New York 1990) 11.

23. Mommsen, *Römisches Strafrecht*, 602.

24. Levy, *Treason against God*, 98, 64–65.

25. Peters, *Inquisition*, 29.

26. Levy, *Treason against God*, 92.

27. Claus-Peter Clasen, "Medieval Heresies in the Reformation," *Church History* 32, 4 (1963) 392.

28. Jiang, *Mandate of Heaven*, 25–28.

29. Levy, *Treason against God*, 110; Peters, *Inquisition*, 41; Schwerhoff, "Horror Crime," 403.

30. Peters, *Inquisition*, 48.

31. Pieper, *Concept of Sin*, 50.

32. 1 Samuel 15:23.

33. Isabel Iribarren, "From Black Magic to Heresy: A Doctrinal Leap in the Pontificate of John XXII," *Church History* 76, 1 (2007) 32, 41; von Bar, *History of Continental Criminal Law*, 227–228.

34. Witchcraft Act of 1604, 2 James I, c. 12; Cuttler, *Law of Treason*, 53; Young, *Magic as a Political Crime*, passim.

35. Jiang, *Mandate of Heaven*, 76; Kollmann, *Crime and Punishment*, 28; Walker, *Popular Justice*, 14.

36. John P. Bartkowski, "Claims-Making and Typifications of Voodoo as a Deviant Religion," *Journal for the Scientific Study of Religion* 37, 4 (1998) 567–569; Carolyn Webber and Aaron Wildavsky, *A History of Taxation and Expenditure in the Western World* (New York 1986) 534.

37. Paul Horwitz, "Scientology in Court," *DePaul Law Review* 47 (1997) 103, 109.

38. Whitmarsh, *Battling the Gods*, 117–118; Jones, *Law and Legal Theory of the Greeks*, 95.

39. Plato, *Laws*, 908a–909a.

40. Mommsen, *Römisches Strafrecht*, 36, 567, 569–570.

41. Von Bar, *History of Continental Criminal Law*, 43–44.

42. Mommsen, *Römisches Strafrecht*, 574–575, 295.

43. Schwerhoff, "Horror Crime," 403.

44. Peters, *Inquisition*, 45–48; Levy, *Treason against God*, 162, 169.

45. Quoted in Ethan H. Shagan, "The English Inquisition: Constitutional Conflict and Ecclesiastical Law in the 1590s," *Historical Journal* 47, 3 (September 2004) 549.

46. R. H. Helmholz, "Natural Law and the Trial of Thomas More," in Henry Ansgar Kelly et al., eds., *Thomas More's Trial by Jury* (Woodbridge 2011) 56.

47. Levy, *Treason against God*, 175.

48. Asad, "Medieval Heresy," 356; Ames, *Righteous Persecution*, 201.

49. Peters, *Inquisition*, 93.

50. This remains one of the fundamental distinctions between the millions killed by the Nazis and by the Soviets: Jews or other ethnically identified enemies could do nothing, not even betray themselves, to save their lives, but a coerced outward ideological conversion punished those who submitted only with the pain of inauthenticity. And class identity in the Soviet Union was malleable—the bourgeoisie could become proletarians through hard labor. Christopher R. Browning and Lewis H. Siegelbaum, "Frameworks for Social Engineering: Stalinist Schema of Identification and the Nazi Volksgemeinschaft," in Geyer and Fitzpatrick, *Beyond Totalitarianism*, 243–244.

51. Levy, *Treason against God*, 128–29; Peters, *Inquisition*, 94.

52. Quoted in Radzinowicz, *History of English Criminal Law*, 5:447.

53. Peters, *Torture*, 120.

54. Ingraham, *Political Crime in Europe*, 121–135; Szabo, "Political Crimes," 8.

55. Eric A. Arnold Jr., *Fouché, Napoleon, and the General Police* (Washington DC 1979) 159; Payne, *Police State of Louis Napoleon*, 65–67.

56. F. W. Pethick Lawrence, "The Trial of the Suffragette Leaders," in Jane Marcus, ed., *Suffrage and the Pankhursts* (London 1987) 55–56.

57. Fletcher, "'A Star Chamber,'" 507–508; Brian Harrison, *Peaceable Kingdom* (Oxford 1982) 58–59.

58. Radzinowicz, *History of English Criminal Law*, 5:439.

59. C. J. Bearman, "An Army without Discipline? Suffragette Militancy and the Budget Crisis of 1909," *Historical Journal* 50, 4 (2007) 879–880; Diane Atkinson, *Rise Up, Women! The Remarkable Lives of the Suffragettes* (London 2018) 167–168.

60. Maud Ellmann, *The Hunger Artists: Starving, Writing, and Imprisonment* (Cambridge MA 1993) 12; Padraic Kenney, *Dance in Chains: Political Imprisonment in the Modern World* (New York 2017) chap. 8.

61. Kenney, *Dance in Chains*, 5.

62. Fletcher, "'Star Chamber,'" 511; Radzinowicz, *History of English Criminal Law*, 5:445, 461.

63. Greenberg, *Crime and Law Enforcement*, 76.

64. B. L. Ingraham and Kazuhiko Tokoro, "Political Crime in the United States and Japan," *Issues in Criminology* 4, 2 (1969).

65. Lionel Wee, "The Hunger Strike as a Communicative Act: Intention without Responsibility," *Journal of Linguistic Anthropology* 17, 1 (2007) 68.

66. Anja Shortland, *Kidnap: Inside the Ransom Business* (Oxford 2019) 10, 102, 199.

67. Aogán Mulcahy, "Claims-Making and the Construction of Legitimacy: Press Coverage of the 1981 Northern Irish Hunger Strike," *Social Problems* 42, 4 (1995) 451; Whitman, *Harsh Justice*, 127–128.

68. Roscoe Pound, *Law and Morals*, 2nd ed. (Chapel Hill 1926) 65.

69. John Locke, *A Letter concerning Toleration,* trans. W. Popple (Huddersfield 1796) 33.

70. Immanuel Kant, *Groundwork of the Metaphysics of Morals*, 4:436–441; McElrea, "Legal Enforcement of Non-utilitarian Morality," 210.

71. Malcolm Davies, "Sisyphus and the Invention of Religion," *Bulletin of the Institute of Classical Studies* 36 (1989) 18.

72. Norenzayan, *Big Gods*; Dominic Johnson, *God Is Watching You: How the Fear of God Makes Us Human* (New York 2016) chap 4.

73. Pettazzoni, *All-Knowing God*, 5, 151–152, 164–165.

74. Laurin et al., "Outsourcing Punishment to God," 3272; Plucknett, *Edward I and Criminal Law*, 64.

75. Jane K. Wickersham, *Rituals of Prosecution: The Roman Inquisition and the Prosecution of Philo-Protestants* (Toronto 2012) 6, 65.

76. Jones, *Law and Legal Theory of the Greeks*, 141; Allen, *World of Prometheus*, 104.

77. Ullmann, "Medieval Torture," 134; Esmein, *History of Continental Criminal Procedure*, 114.

78. Perry, *Crime and Society in Early Modern Seville*, 88; Levy, *Treason against God*, 142, 185–186.

79. Jonathan Michael Gray, *Oaths and the English Reformation* (Cambridge 2013) 176; Susan Banfield, *Joan of Arc* (London 1988) 88–98.

80. Levy, *Treason against God*, 148; Ames, *Righteous Persecution*, 211.

81. Drapkin, *Crime and Punishment*, 96.

82. Page DuBois, *Torture and Truth* (New York, 1991) 50–56.

83. Peters, *Torture*, 13–15; MacDowell, *Law in Classical Athens*, 245–246.

84. McAuley, "Canon Law and the End of the Ordeal," 498–499; Fraher, "Theoretical Justification," 586.

85. Langbein, *Torture*, 4–8; Bartlett, *Trial by Fire and Water*, 141. Chinese codes of the Han and T'ang Empires similarly required confession for conviction, and thus they tortured until they got it. Finer, *History of Government*, 778.

86. Richard M. Fraher, "Preventing Crime in the High Middle Ages: The Medieval Lawyers' Search for Deterrence," in James Ross Sweeney and Stanley Chodorow, eds., *Popes, Teachers, and Canon Law in the Middle Ages* (Ithaca 1989) 216.

87. Langbein, *Torture*, 55–56. The Chinese use of torture was similar. Dutton, *Policing and Punishment in China*, 114–115.

88. Langbein, *Torture*, 137–138; Williams, *Tudor Regime*, 397; Bellamy, *Tudor Law of Treason*, 109–112, 120.

89. Langbein, *Torture*, 47–48; McAuley, "Canon Law and the End of the Ordeal," 490–491; Peters, *Torture*, 44.

90. Vittorio Bufacchi and Jean Maria Arrigo, "Torture, Terrorism, and the State: A Refutation of the Ticking-Bomb Argument," *Journal of Applied Philosophy* 23, 3 (2006) 360.

91. Rejali, *Torture and Democracy*, chap. 20. On the compatibility of torture with democracy, see W. Fitzhugh Brundage, *Civilizing Torture: An American Tradition* (Cambridge MA 2018); Bernard E. Harcourt, *The Counterrevolution: How Our Government Went to War against Its Own Citizens* (New York 2018) 66–69.

92. Jim Dwyer et al., *Actual Innocence* (New York 2000) 115; Rejali, *Torture and Democracy*, passim; Walker, *Popular Justice*, 174–175; Peters, *Torture*, 124, 172, 177, 119–121 104–105; Martin, *Crime and Criminal Justice under the Third Republic*, 78.

93. Henry Shue, "Torture in Dreamland: Disposing of the Ticking Bomb," *Case Western Reserve Journal of International Law* 37 (2006) 234, 237.

94. Ames, "Does Inquisition Belong to Religious History?," 21; Peters, *Torture*, 46; Bartlett, *Trial by Fire and Water*, 79.

95. Charles D. Hackett, "Entrance Rites, Confessions of Sin, and Identity In the Sixteenth Century," *Anglican and Episcopal History* 73, 1 (2004) 18–19, 22–23.

96. John Bossy, "The Social History of Confession in the Age of the Reformation," *Transactions of the Royal Historical Society* 25 (1975) 22.

97. Only in the latter half of the twentieth century did confession become more frequent than once a year. Bill Cosgrave, "The Decline of Confessions: Disaster or Return to Normal?" *The Furrow* 45, 3 (1994) 159.

98. Bossy, "Social History of Confession," 22; Ames, *Righteous Persecution*, 144; Murray, "Confession before 1215," 51.

99. Theodore A. McConnell, "Confession in Cross-Disciplinary Perspective," *Journal of Religion and Health* 8, 1 (1969) 77–78.

100. Bossy, "Social History of Confession," 30–33, 36.

101. Murray, "Confession before 1215," 62.

102. R. F. Clarke, "The Practice of Confession in the Catholic Church," *North American Review* 169, 517 (1899) 829; Murray, "Confession before 1215," 52.

103. Bossy, "Social History of Confession," 26; Ronald K. Rittgers, "Private Confession and the Lutheranization of Sixteenth-Century Nördlingen," *Sixteenth Century Journal* 36, 4 (2005) 1066–1068.

104. Rittersporn, "Terror and Soviet Legality," 186.

105. Owen Gingerich, "The Galileo Affair," *Scientific American* 247, 2 (1982) 143.

106. Iain Lauchlan, "Chekist *Mentalité* and the Origins of the Great Terror," in Harris, *Anatomy of Terror*, 20.

107. Gleason, *Totalitarianism*, 95–98. Aryeh Neier sees such confessions as more patently transactional. "Confining Dissent," in Morris and Rothman, *Oxford History of the Prison*, 413.

108. Robert Conquest, *The Great Terror* (London 1968) 146–147, 550; Robert Sharlet and Piers Beirne, "In Search of Vyshinsky: The Paradox of Law and Terror," *International Journal of the Sociology of Law* 12 (1984) 166; Harald J. Berman, ed., *Soviet Criminal Law and Procedure: The RSFSR Codes,* 2nd ed. (Cambridge MA 1972) 66.

109. The modern version of using certain acts as indicators of forbidden attitudes came with the Chinese crackdown on Uighurs and the Karakax list of suspicious activities that prompted detainment, including using Virtual Private Networks and clicking on foreign internet links. *Financial Times*, 18 February 2020.

110. Peters, *Inquisition*, 50; Wickersham, *Rituals of Prosecution*, 85.

111. Wickersham, *Rituals of Prosecution*, 13–14; R. Po-Chia Hsia, *Social Discipline in the Reformation* (London 1989) 68.

112. David Shearer, "Stalinist Repression, Modernity, and the Social Engineering Argument," in Harris, *Anatomy of Terror*, 113.

113. Ning, "Public Opinion and the Death Penalty," 87–88. More than a quarter of all death sentences in China were for such crimes.

Chapter 10

1. Leon Shaskolsky Sheleff, "Morality, Criminal Law, and Politics," *Tel Aviv University Studies in Law* 2 (1976) 217.

2. Ames, *Righteous Persecution*, 45, 183.

3. Grey, *Legal Enforcement of Morality*, 29.

4. Lobban, "From Seditious Libel to Unlawful Assembly," 307–309.

5. Pringle, "Are We Capable of Offending God?," 35.

6. Norenzayan, *Big Gods*, 131.

7. Solomon Bloom, "The 'Withering Away' of the State," *Journal of the History of Ideas* 7, 1 (1946) 114.

8. Eugene Kamenka and Alice Erh-Soon Tay, "Beyond the French Revolution: Communist Socialism and the Concept of Law," *University of Toronto Law Journal* 21 (1971) 118; Evgeny B. Pashukanis, *Law and Marxism* (London 1978) 61, 160, 175–176.

9. Sidney Monas, *The Third Section: Police and Society in Russia under Nicholas I* (Cambridge MA 1961) 22.

10. Thaman, "Marxist and Soviet Law," 302.

11. V. I. Lenin, *The State and Revolution*, in *Collected Works* (Moscow 1974) 25:417.

12. Gretason, "Crime, Guilt, and Punishment," 143.

13. Von Bar, *History of Continental Criminal Law*, 81.

14. Trigger, *Understanding Early Civilizations*, 437; Strathern, *Unearthly Powers*, 38–39.

15. Svend Ranulf, *The Jealousy of the Gods and Criminal Law at Athens* (London 1933) 1:66.

16. Ingolf Dalferth, "How Is the Concept of Sin Related to the Concept of Moral Wrongdoing?" *Religious Studies* 20, 2 (1984) 176–178.

17. Riedweg, "The 'Atheistic' Fragment from Euripides' 'Bellerophontes,'" 42.

18. David G. Attfield, "The Morality of Sins," *Religious Studies* 20, 2 (1984) 230.

19. The Scholastic philosophers debated whether some of the Commandments, such as observing the Sabbath, were ceremonial rather than moral. Jean Porter, "Christian Ethics and the Concept of Morality: A Historical Inquiry," *Journal of the Society of Christian Ethics* 26, 2 (2006) 13.

20. Clasen, "Medieval Heresies," 393, 404.

21. Levy, *Treason against God*, 245.

22. Gershom Scholem, *Sabbatai Ṣevi: The Mystical Messiah: 1626–1676*, 2nd ed. (Princeton 1975) 628; Carlebach, *Pursuit of Heresy*, 9, 184.

23. Alan Watson, *The State, Law, and Religion: Pagan Rome* (Athens GA 1992) 4–5; Mary Beard, "The Sexual Status of Vestal Virgins," *Journal of Roman Studies* 70 (1980) 13.

24. Porter, "Christian Ethics," 3–4.

25. Hobbes, *Leviathan*, chap. 27; R. J. Spjut, "Hobbes' Definition of Crime," *Anglo-American Law Review* 13 (1984) 6.

26. Von Bar, *History of Continental Criminal Law*, 399; Beattie, *Policing and Punishment*, 82.

27. Locke, *Letter concerning Toleration*, 43.

28. Beccaria, *On Crimes and Punishment*, chap. 2.

29. Kelly, *Short History of Western Legal Theory*, 295.

30. *Anmerkungen zum Strafgesezbuche für das Königreich Baiern* (Munich 1813) 2:59–60.

31. Strafgesetzbuch, Bavaria, 1813, art. 400–401.

32. Montesquieu, *Spirit of the Laws*, 12:4.

33. Charles Donahue Jr., "The Ecclesiastical Courts," in Wilfried Hartmann and Kenneth Pennington, eds., *The History of Courts and Procedure in Medieval Canon Law* (Washington DC 2016) 249.

34. McKenna, "Treason against God," 33.

35. Ames, *Righteous Persecution*, 183.

36. Blasphemy Act 1697, 9 William III, c. 35.

37. Levy, *Treason against God*, 245, 252, 302–306, 313.

38. Quoted in Devlin, *Enforcement of Morals*, 10.

39. Devlin, *Enforcement of Morals*, 25.

40. "Laws Penalizing Blasphemy, Apostasy, and Defamation of Religion Are Widespread," Pew Research Center, 21 November 2012, http://www.pewforum.org/2012/11/21/laws-penalizing-blasphemy-apostasy-and-defamation-of-religion-are-widespread/.

41. James R. Moore, "Blasphemy Laws and Hate Speech Codes: Threats to Freedom of Expression, Dissent, and Democracy," *International Journal of Humanities and Social Science* 3, 18 (2013) 13.

42. Thomas J. Curry, "Church and State in Seventeenth and Eighteenth Century America," *Journal of Law and Religion* 7, 2 (1989) 262; Kathryn Preyer, "Penal Measures in the American Colonies," *American Journal of Legal History* 26, 4 (1982) 342.

43. Nash, "Analyzing the History of Religious Crime," 14; Samuel G. Freedman, "A Man's Existentialism, Construed as Blasphemy," *New York Times*, 20 March 2009.

44. McKenna, "Treason against God," 35–37.

45. H. L. A. Hart, *Law, Liberty, and Morality* (Stanford 1963) 44; Nash, "Analyzing the History of Religious Crime," 13; Pringle, "Are We Capable of Offending God?," 37.

46. Some examples of recent Australian legislation are in McKenna, "Treason against God," 45.

47. Nash, "Analyzing the History of Religious Crime," 14; Gauri Viswanathan, "Blasphemy and Heresy: The Modernist Challenge," *Comparative Studies in Society and History* 37, 2 (1995) 406–407, 410.

48. McKenna, "Treason against God," 40; Levy, *Treason against God*, x; Viswanathan, "Blasphemy and Heresy," 400.

49. Jytte Klausen, *The Cartoons That Shook the World* (New Haven 2009); Langer, *Religious Offence and Human Rights*, chap. 1.

50. The musical also harbored a surprisingly uncommented-upon denigrating view of Africans. The premise is that all it took to improve the lives of Africans was a bit of mumbo-jumbo improvised by some adolescent Mormons who were paying too little attention in Sunday school to recall the dogma they were sent abroad to preach.

51. Lucien Febvre, *The Problem of Unbelief in the Sixteenth Century* (Cambridge MA 1985) 462–464.

52. Hobbes, *Leviathan*, chap. 39, 248; Locke, *Letter concerning Toleration*, 56.

53. Peter Jimack, "The French Enlightenment II: Deism, Morality, and Politics," in Stuart Brown, ed., *Routledge History of Philosophy* (London 1996) 5:255–256; Adriano Sofri and Lydia Cochrane, "On Optimism," *Critical Inquiry* 30, 4 (2004) 754.

54. Alex Schulman, "The Twilight of Probability: Locke, Bayle, and the Toleration of Atheism," *Journal of Religion* 89, 3 (2009) 346; Pierre Bayle, *Various Thoughts on the Occasion of a Comet* (Albany 2000) 180.

55. Ryan McKay and Harvey Whitehouse, "Religion and Morality," *Psychological Bulletin* 141, 2 (2015) 448.

56. Former French president François Hollande is among the few leaders of major nations to openly acknowledge their atheism, joined by Alexis Tsipras, once prime minister of Greece, and Zoran Milanović, the current president of Croatia. Alison Lesley, "Current European Leaders Are Leaning towards Atheism," *World Religion News*, 3 February 2015; Charlie Campbell, "China's Leader Xi Jinping Reminds Party Members to Be 'Unyielding Marxist Atheists,'" *Time*, 25 April 2016.

57. Stephen, *History of the Criminal Law of England*, 2:80–81.

58. The Hart–Devlin debate, accounted for in Ronald Dworkin, "Lord Devlin and the Enforcement of Morals," *Yale Law Journal* 75, 6 (1966).

59. Devlin, *Enforcement of Morals*, 8–16.

60. In his *Moral Limits of the Criminal Law* (Oxford 1985) v. 2, Joel Feinberg argued for making offense as actionable as harm. For criticism of this view, see Harcourt, "Collapse of the Harm Principle," 130, and Tatjana Hörnle, "Offensive Behavior and German Penal Law," *Buffalo Criminal Law Review* 5, 1 (2001) 261–262.

61. *Report of the Committee on Homosexual Offences and Prostitution*, Cmnd. 247 (September 1957) 115–116.

62. John Wolfenden, "Crime and Sin," *British Medical Journal* 2, 5192 (1960) 142.

63. Calvin Woodard, "Thoughts on the Interplay between Morality and Law in Modern Legal Thought," *Notre Dame Law Review* 64 (1989) 791–795.

64. Pound, *Law and Morals*, 43, 96–97.

65. John Warwick Montgomery, "Law and Morality," *Law and Justice* 122–123 (1994) 90–91.

66. Hans Kelsen, *The Pure Theory of Law* (Berkeley 1967) 63–64.

67. A. R. Louch, "Sins and Crimes," *Philosophy* 43, 163 (1968) 43–45.

68. Kent Greenawalt, "Legal Enforcement of Morality," *Journal of Criminal Law and Criminology* 85, 3 (1995) 710; Basil Mitchell, *Law, Morality, and Religion in a Secular Society* (Oxford 1967) chap. 2.

69. Not enforcing old statutes was in itself a form of changing the law, however. Gordon, *Controlling the State*, 51.

70. Hart, *Law, Liberty, and Morality*, 26–27; Gabrielle Viator, "The Validity of Criminal Adultery Prohibitions after *Lawrence v. Texas*," *Suffolk University Law Review* 39 (2005–2006) 837; Ethan Bronner, "Adultery, an Ancient Crime That Remains on Many Books," *New York Times*, 14 November 2012.

71. T. A. Roberts, "Law, Morality, and Religion in a Christian Society," *Religious Studies* 20, 1 (1984) 81.

72. Steven Shavell, "Law versus Morality as Regulators of Conduct," *American Law and Economics Review* 4, 2 (2002) 231.

73. The law's expressive function, broached most famously by Durkheim, is surveyed in David Garland, *Punishment and Modern Society* (Chicago 1990) chap. 2.

74. Hans-Dieter Bahr, *Die Sprache des Gastes* (Leipzig 1994); Seyla Benhabib, *The Rights of Others* (Cambridge 2004) chap. 1.

75. Uniform Commercial Code, art. 1-201 (19); Montgomery, "Law and Morality," 95.

76. Steinfeld, *Coercion, Contract, and Free Labor*, 45–47.

77. A. L. Goodhart, *English Law and the Moral Law* (London 1953) 118.

78. Pound, *Law and Morals*, 27, 56; Brague, *Law of God*, 142.

79. French civil code, art. 1131–1133; German civil code, sect. 138, 242.

80. Woodard, "Thoughts on the Interplay between Morality and Law," 788; Miethe and Lu, *Punishment*, 195.

81. W. Bertelsmann, "The Essence of *Mens Rea*," *Acta Juridica* 34 (1974) 44; Nancy Travis Wolfe, "Mala in Se: A Disappearing Doctrine?" *Criminology* 19, 1 (1981) 138.

82. Pieper, *Concept of Sin*, 66–67; Aristotle, *Nicomachean Ethics*, bk. 5, chap. 7.

83. Rollin M. Perkins, "The Civil Offense," *University of Pennsylvania Law Review* 100, 6 (1952) 832; Richard L. Gray, "Eliminating the (Absurd) Distinction between Malum in Se and Malum Prohibitum Crimes," *Washington University Law Quarterly* 73 (1995) 1375.

84. *Morissette v. United States*, 342 US 246 (1952) 260. In appeals courts, the distinction between *mala in se* and *mala prohibita* was made as late as 1980. Erik Luna, "Principled Enforcement of Penal Codes," *Buffalo Criminal Law Review* 4, 1 (2000) 526; Rollin M. Perkins, "Criminal Liability without Fault," *Iowa Law Review* 68 (1983) 1076.

85. Seipp, "Distinction between Crime and Tort," 59–60.

86. Coffee, "Does 'Unlawful' Mean 'Criminal'?," 195, 239; Coffee, "Paradigms Lost," 1876, 1884–1885.

87. New Jersey and Rhode Island no longer ban incestuous relationships, though they do not recognize marriages within forbidden degrees of consanguinity. "Statutory

Compilation regarding Incest Statutes," March 2013, https://ndaa.org/wp-content/uploads/Incest-Statutes-2013.pdf.

88. Joseph Henrich et al., "The Puzzle of Monogamous Marriage," *Philosophical Transactions of the Royal Society: Biological Sciences* 367 (2012) 657.

89. The German Pirate Party demanded the right to polyamorous unions. *Economist,* 22 October 2011, 62; *Economist,* 28 April 2012, 60.

90. Rajeev Ranjan et al., "(De-)Criminalization of Attempted Suicide in India," *Industrial Psychiatry Journal* 23, 1 (2014).

91. Attenborough, *Laws of the English Kings,* Wihtred cap 9–11.

92. Schedule of tariffs, posted in any Swedish taxi.

93. *FT Weekend Magazine,* 5–6 July 2008, 22–23.

94. Rittersporn, "Terror and Soviet Legality," 181; Thaman, "Marxist and Soviet Law," 320–321.

95. Durkheim, *Division of Labour,* 64.

96. Goodhart, *English Law and the Moral Law,* 147.

97. British and American law are among the few that allow testamentary freedom with few restrictions.

98. Sheleff, "Morality, Criminal Law, and Politics," 202–203; Baldwin, *Copyright Wars,* chap. 8.

99. Julian V. Roberts, "Public Opinion, Crime, and Criminal Justice," *Crime and Justice* 16 (1992) 135.

100. Coffee, "Does 'Unlawful' Mean 'Criminal'?," 235–237.

101. Nasser Arshadi and Thomas Eyssell, *Law and Finance of Corporate Insider Trading* (New York 1993) 43–45; Harry V. Ball and Lawrence M. Friedman, "The Use of Criminal Sanctions in the Enforcement of Economic Legislation," *Stanford Law Review* 17, 2 (1965) 197–198.

102. Buell, *Capital Offenses,* chap. 7.

103. Bertelsmann, "Essence of *Mens Rea,*" 48.

104. Green, "Why It's a Crime to Tear the Tag off a Mattress," 1565.

105. J. T. Morgan, "The Mythical Erosion of Mens Rea," *Natural Resources and Environment* 23, 3 (2009) 29; Bill Devall, "Deep Ecology and Radical Environmentalism," *Society and Natural Resources* 4 (1991) 248.

106. "Perjury: The Forgotten Offense," *Journal of Criminal Law and Criminology* 65, 3 (1974) 363.

107. Statute of Winchester, 1285, 13 Edw. I, c. 4.

108. Greenawalt, "Legal Enforcement of Morality," 713–715. Four US states have weak Good Samaritan statutes.

109. T. B. Macaulay et al., *The Indian Penal Code as Originally Framed in 1837* (Madras 1888) 140–141.

110. The contrast is narrowed insofar as Anglo-American common law punishes commission by omission more than civil law does. Thus, a parent or guardian who stands by while someone over whom they have a duty of care drowns would be liable for murder or manslaughter. French law recognizes no such commission by omission. Edward A. Tomlinson, "The French Experience with Duty to Rescue," *New York Law School Journal of International and Comparative Law* 20 (2000) 463.

111. Strafgesetzbuch, §323c; French penal code, art. 223–226; Swiss penal code, art. 128.

112. Sheleff, "Morality, Criminal Law, and Politics," 214.

113. Grey, *Legal Enforcement of Morality*, 168–169, 174.

114. Tomlinson, "French Experience," 462, 470–472; Peter M. Agulnick and Heidi V. Rivkin, "Criminal Liability for Failure to Rescue: A Brief Survey of French and American Law," *Touro International Law Review* 8 (1998) 107–109.

115. Ronald P. Sokol, "The Kindness of Strangers," *International Herald Tribune*, 3–4 June 2006.

116. Tomlinson, "French Experience," 497.

117. The UN Convention of the Law of the Sea (art. 98) requires all signatories to have legislation making it a duty to render assistance to ships and persons in distress.

118. Roberts, "Public Opinion," 128; Robinson and Darley, "Utility of Desert," 457.

119. Sharpe, *Crime in Early Modern England*, 182–183; Spierenburg, "Body and the State," 58; Winslow, "Sussex Smugglers," 149.

120. Spierenburg, *Spectacle of Suffering*, 126; Ruff, *Violence in Early Modern Europe*, 239.

121. Sanford H. Kadish, "Some Observations on the Use of Criminal Sanctions in Enforcing Economic Regulations," *University of Chicago Law Review* 30, 3 (1963) 439–440.

122. Coffee, "Does 'Unlawful' Mean 'Criminal'?," 237.

123. Roberts et al., *Penal Populism*, 100; Friedman and Havemann, "Rise and Fall of the Unwritten Law," 1054.

Chapter 11

1. Wallace-Hadrill, "Bloodfeuds of the Franks," 141; Treston, *Poine*, 227.

2. Specific deterrence of the individual offender could be done privately, of course, but not general deterrence of other potential offenders.

3. "Capitulary of Charlemagne," 199.

4. Fraher, "Preventing Crime," 231.

5. Moran, "Origin of Insanity," 512; Kennedy, "State Punishment of Crime," 20.

6. Meranze, *Laboratories of Virtue*, 27; Philips, "New Engine of Power," 158–159; Douglas Hay, "Property, Authority, and the Criminal Law," in Hay et al., eds., *Albion's Fatal Tree*, 50.

7. Bodde and Morris, *Law in Imperial China*, 24.

8. "Capitulary of Charlemagne," 198–199.

9. Fraher, "Preventing Crime," 220, 231–232; McAuley, "Canon Law and the End of the Ordeal," 494–495.

10. Schneider, "Imprisonment in Pre-classical and Classical Islamic Law," 166; Given, *Inquisition and Medieval Society*, 84–85; Ames, *Righteous Persecution*, 171.

11. Stephen J. Davies, "The Courts and the Scottish Legal System 1600–1747," in Gatrell et al., *Crime and the Law*, 128; Banner, *Death Penalty*, 65; Claire Duchen,

"Crime and Punishment in Liberated France: The Case of the *les femmes tondues*," in Claire Duchen and Irene Bandhauer-Schöffmann, eds., *When the War Was Over: Women, War, and Peace in Europe 1945–1956* (London 2000).

12. Most dramatically in the registries put online as of 2018 in Poland: Nina Apin, "Populismus statt Opferschutz," *taz.de*, 3 January 2018.

13. Trevaskes, *Policing Serious Crime in China*, 71.

14. Workhouse Test Act 1723; Paul Slack, *The English Poor Law 1531–1782* (Houndmills 1990) 40.

15. *Poor Law Commissioners' Report of 1834*, Cd. 2728 (1834) 44.

16. Émile Durkheim, *Moral Education* (New York 1961) 198–199.

17. Bailey, "Shadow of the Gallows," 312.

18. Beccaria, *On Crimes and Punishment*, chap. 28; Wright, *Between the Guillotine and Liberty*, 167, 172; Clive Emsley, *Crime, Police, and Penal Policy* (Oxford 2007) 33.

19. Davis, *Conflict and Control*, 128.

20. Liang, "Sources of Variation," 123.

21. Drapkin, *Crime and Punishment*, 75; Peters, "Prison before the Prison," 17; E. N. Gladden, *A History of Public Administration* (London 1972) 1:134.

22. Finer, *History of Government*, 1117; Moore, "Cruel and Unusual Punishment," 731, 752; Miethe and Lu, *Punishment*, 124–125. In China, the coup de grace was usually given early in the process, and the aim was less physical cruelty than to prevent the offender's spirit from regaining its wholeness in a future life. Bodde and Morris, *Law in Imperial China*, 93.

23. "Historical Concept of Treason," 74; Harrington, *Faithful Executioner*, 48; Spierenburg, "Body and the State," 52–54; Evans, *Rituals of Retribution*, 122.

24. Gatrell, *Hanging Tree*, 70.

25. Friedland, *Seeing Justice Done*, 56–65.

26. Foucault, *Discipline and Punish*, 3–5. The Chinese, however, seem not to have turned their executions into spectacles. Mühlhahn, *Criminal Justice in China*, 40–41.

27. Kollmann, *Crime and Punishment*, 406; Beattie, *Crime and the Courts*, 489, 524–525.

28. Plato, *Laws*, bk. 9, chap. 12.

29. Peter Linebaugh, "The Tyburn Riot against the Surgeons," in Hay et al., eds., *Albion's Fatal Tree*, 76. As late as 1904, a Massachusetts statute reaffirmed dissection of murderers. Banner, *Death Penalty*, 78. And in China, dissections of the corpses of poor prisoners continued into the twentieth century. Dikötter, *Crime, Punishment, and the Prison in Modern China*, 90.

30. Criminal Justice (Scotland)Act 1949, s. 14.

31. Gatrell, "Decline of Theft and Violence," 266–267; Banner, *Death Penalty*, 12.

32. Langbein, *Torture*, 40; Weisser, *Crime and Punishment*, 138; Radzinowicz, *History of English Criminal Law*, 1:76; Gatrell, *Hanging Tree*, 8–9; Patrick Joyce, *The State of Freedom: A Social History of the British State since 1800* (Cambridge 2013) 126.

33. Clive Emsley, *Policing and Its Context, 1750–1870* (London 1983) 59; Evans, *Rituals of Retribution*, 228; Radzinowicz, *History of English Criminal Law*, 1:288.

34. Gatrell, *Hanging Tree*, 91–92; Wiener, *Reconstructing the Criminal*, 93; Evans, *Rituals of Retribution*, 257–258; Meranze, *Laboratories of Virtue*, chap. 3.

35. Friedland, *Seeing Justice Done*, chaps. 5–7; Banner, *Death Penalty*, chap 6.

36. Beccaria, *On Crimes and Punishment*, chap. 27.

37. Beccaria, *On Crimes and Punishment*, chap. 12; Binder, "Punishment Theory," 335; Bentham, *Introduction to the Principles of Morals*, 170.

38. Fraher, "Preventing Crime," 231; Adam Smith, *Lectures on Jurisprudence*, Glasgow ed., ed. R. L. Meek et al. (Oxford 1978) 331.

39. Packer, *Limits of Criminal Sanction*, 44–45; Robinson and Darley, "Utility of Desert," 454.

40. Beattie, *Crime and the Courts*, 523; Friedland, *Seeing Justice Done*, 212; Beccaria, *On Crimes and Punishment*, chap. 28.

41. Spierenburg, "Body and the State," 58; Wiener, *Reconstructing the Criminal*, 97.

42. Friedland, *Seeing Justice Done*, chaps. 8–10; French penal code of 6 October 1791, art. 2–5.

43. Evans, *Rituals of Retribution*, 305, 315; Gatrell, *Hanging Tree*, 10; Banner, *Death Penalty*, 156; Friedland, *Seeing Justice Done*, 270, 275.

44. Beattie, *Crime and the Courts*, 614; Wright, *Between the Guillotine and Liberty*, 70.

45. Bakken, "Moral Panics," 80; Susan Trevaskes, "Severe and Swift Justice in China," *British Journal of Criminology* 47 (2007) 39.

46. Pfeifer, *Rough Justice*, 136.

47. Foucault, *Discipline and Punish*, 9.

48. Vaale, *Dommen til Døden*, 66.

49. Trevaskes, *Policing Serious Crime in China*, 5.

50. Lucia Zedner, "Policing before and after the Police: The Historical Antecedents of Contemporary Crime Control," *British Journal of Criminology* 46, 1 (2006) 84.

51. Von Bar, *History of Continental Criminal Law*, 245.

52. Ethan Shagan, *The Rule of Moderation: Violence, Religion, and the Politics of Restraint in Early Modern England* (Cambridge 2011) 76.

53. Quoted in Nicholas Davidson, "Theology, Nature, and the Law: Sexual Sin and Sexual Crime in Italy from the Fourteenth to the Seventeenth Century," in Dean and Lowe, *Crime, Society, and the Law in Renaissance Italy*, 78.

54. Pollock and Maitland, *History of English Law*, 2:475.

55. Sayre, "Criminal Responsibility," 720.

56. Kelly, *Short History of Western Legal Theory*, 296; Dubber, *Police Power*, 31.

57. Mommsen, *Römisches Strafrecht*, 77.

58. Francis Bowes Sayre, "Mens Rea," *Harvard Law Review* 45 (1931–1932) 985, 1005; Moran, "Origin of Insanity," 487–488; Beattie, *Crime and the Courts*, 85.

59. Criminal Lunatics Act 1800, 39 & 40 George III, c. 94, detailed in Moran, "Origin of Insanity."

60. Aitken and Aitken, "M'Naghten Case," 54–56.

61. Aristotle, *Politics*, 1274b; Mommsen, *Römisches Strafrecht*, 1043.

62. David McCord, "The English and American History of Voluntary Intoxication to Negate Mens Rea," *Journal of Legal History* 11 (1990) 373–776, 381.

63. Oliver Wendell Holmes Jr., *The Common Law* (Boston 1881) 3.

64. Perkins, "Civil Offense," 833.

65. Michel Foucault, "About the Concept of the 'Dangerous Individual' in 19th Century Legal Psychiatry," *International Journal of Law and Psychiatry* 1 (1978) 1–2, 9.

66. David Bashevkin, *Sin*a*gogue: Sin and Failure in Jewish Thought* (Boston 2019) chap. 5; Ruth Kara-Ivanov Kaniel, "'Gedolah Aveirah Lishmah': Mothers of the Davidic Dynasty, Feminine Seduction, and the Development of Messianic Thought, from Rabbinic Literature to R. Moshe Haim Luzzatto," *Nashim: A Journal of Jewish Women's Studies & Gender Issues* 24 (2013) 28.

67. Sanford H. Kadish, "The Decline of Innocence," *Cambridge Law Journal* 26, 2 (1968) 274; Broughton, "Snowden Affair," 11.

68. Larson, "Forgotten Constitutional Law," 901–902.

69. *Regina v. Thurborn*, 169 Eng. Rep. 293 (1848); Fletcher, "Metamorphosis of Larceny," 514.

70. Sayre, "Mens Rea," 999–1000.

71. Benjamin A. Mains, "Virtual Child Pornography, Pandering, and the First Amendment," *Hastings Constitutional Law Quarterly* 37, 4 (2010) 833.

72. Fletcher, "Case for Treason," 206; Meli, "Hate Crime," 926.

73. It remains unclear whether this applies also to primitive law. Mueller, "Tort, Crime, and the Primitive," 304, 327, 331.

74. Gagarin, *Drakon*, 11–13; qualified in Saunders, *Plato's Penal Code*, 14–15.

75. Jones, *Law and Legal Theory of the Greeks*, 262; Drapkin, *Crime and Punishment*, 239–241.

76. Von Bar, *History of Continental Criminal Law*, 68.

77. Quoted in Sayre, "Mens Rea," 977–978; Peter H. Karlen, "Mens Rea: A New Analysis," *University of Toledo Law Review* 9, 2 (1978) 205; Pollock and Maitland, *History of English Law*, 1:54.

78. *Hales v. Petit*, Plowd. 253, 259a (1563), quoted in Sayre, "Mens Rea," 992.

79. Mueller, "Tort, Crime, and the Primitive," 319; Drapkin, *Crime and Punishment*, 96; Genesis 9:5–6.

80. Plato, *Laws*, bk. 9, chap. 12.

81. Lenman and Parker, "The State, the Community, and the Criminal Law," 31; Teresa Sutton, "The Nature of the Early Law of Deodand," *Cambrian Law Review* 30 (1999) 14.

82. Mommsen, *Römisches Strafrecht*, 835; Helmholz, *Natural Law in Court*, 63; Perry, *Crime and Society in Early Modern Seville*, 72.

83. Exodus 21:12–14; Deuteronomy 19:4–13.

84. Deuteronomy 22:23–26; Cohen, *Law, Sexuality, and Society*, 126.

85. Bodde and Morris, *Law in Imperial China*, 30; Li, *Early China*, 291.

86. Plato, *Laws*, bk. 9, chap. 8; Drapkin, *Crime and Punishment*, 211; Parker, *Miasma*, 112; Jerome Hall, "Criminal Attempt: A Study of Foundations of Criminal Liability," *Yale Law Journal* 49, 5 (1940) 790.

87. Von Bar, *History of Continental Criminal Law*, 8; Treston, *Poine*, 53, 199; MacDowell, *Law in Classical Athens*, 113–114.

88. Albert Levitt, "The Origin of the Doctrine of Mens Rea," *Illinois Law Review* 17 (1922–1923) 118; von Bar, *History of Continental Criminal Law*, 20.

89. Twelve Tables, Table VIII, §12; Fletcher, "Metamorphosis of Larceny," 477; Drapkin, *Crime and Punishment*, 233.

90. King, *Law and Society in the Visigothic Kingdom*, 86, 259–260; Attenborough, *Laws of the English Kings*, Alfred cap 36; Levitt, "Origin of Mens Rea," 121; Drapkin,

Crime and Punishment, 283; Treston, *Poine*, 53; Mueller, "Tort, Crime, and the Primitive," 324.

91. Ullmann, *Medieval Idea of Law*, 144, 147. De Penna went so far as to argue that if the delinquent was not motivated by evil intent, there was no reason to punish.

92. Sayre, "Mens Rea," 980–981, 985.

93. Von Bar, *History of Continental Criminal Law*, 126.

94. Green, "Societal Concepts of Criminal Liability for Homicide," 669; Green, "Jury and the English Law of Homicide," 419–420.

95. Kaye, "Early History of Murder," 366; Gray, "Eliminating the (Absurd) Distinction," 1374.

96. Sayre, "Mens Rea," 993; Green, *Verdict according to Conscience*, 30; Kaye, "Early History of Murder," 365–366; Beattie, *Crime and the Courts*, 91.

97. Karlen, "Mens Rea," 238; Robbins, "Double Inchoate Crimes," 16.

98. Model Penal Code, 240.1.

99. Davis, *Conflict and Control*, 257; Andrew Ashworth and Lucia Zedner, "Prevention and Criminalization: Justification and Limits," *New Criminal Law Review* 15, 4 (2012) 545.

100. Stuntz, "Pathological Politics," 516.

101. Dubber, "Policing Possession," 835; Dubber, *Dual Penal State*, 221.

102. Bernadette McSherry, "Expanding the Boundaries of Inchoate Crimes: The Growing Reliance on Preparatory Offenses," in Bernadette McSherry et al., eds., *Regulating Deviance: The Redirection of Criminalization and the Futures of Criminal Law* (Oxford 2009) 157.

103. Sexual Offences Act 2003 (England and Wales) s. 15.

104. Frederick Schauer and Richard Zeckhauser, "Regulation by Generalization," *Regulation and Governance* 1 (2007) 69–74; Fletcher, "Case for Treason," 203.

105. Larry Alexander and Kimberley D. Kessler, "Mens Rea and Inchoate Crimes," *Journal of Criminal Law and Criminology* 87, 4 (1997) 1138–1139.

106. Herbert Wechsler et al., "The Treatment of Inchoate Crimes in the Model Penal Code of the American Law Institute," *Columbia Law Review* 61 (1961) 958; Francis B. Sayre, "Criminal Conspiracy," *Harvard Law Review* 35, 4 (1922) 399.

107. Robbins, "Double Inchoate Crimes," 30–33.

108. Alexander and Kessler, "Mens Rea," 1169–1170.

109. Dworkin and Blumfeld, "Punishment for Intentions," 400–401; Larry Alexander and Kimberly Kessler Ferzan, "Risk and Inchoate Crimes: Retribution or Prevention?," in G. R. Sullivan and Ian Dennis, eds., *Seeking Security: Pre-empting the Commission of Criminal Harms* (Oxford 2012) 111.

110. Michael T. Cahill, "Defining Inchoate Crime: An Incomplete Attempt," *Ohio State Journal of Criminal Law* 9 (2011–2012) 753. In ancient China, however, offenders who confessed before the authorities discovered their crime could receive reduced punishments. Bodde and Morris, *Law in Imperial China*, 42. And in the United States, perjury can be recanted in the same proceeding where it was committed. 18 US Code §1623(d).

111. Swedish penal code, chap. 23, sect. 3. In many US states, the accomplice hoping to withdraw must also seek to prevent the crime. Carol A. Schwab,

"Accomplice Liability under the 1979 Missouri Criminal Code," *Missouri Law Review* 44, 2 (1979) 234, 265–266.

112. Kimberly Kessler Ferzan, "Inchoate Crimes at the Punishment/Prevention Divide," *San Diego Law Review* 48 (2011) 1278–1280.

113. Alexander and Kessler, "Mens Rea," 1142.

114. Ferzan, "Inchoate Crimes," 1280; Fletcher, "Metamorphosis of Larceny," 523.

115. Fletcher, "Case for Treason," 198; Robbins, "Double Inchoate Crimes," 9.

116. Wechsler et al., "Treatment of Inchoate Crimes," 1001–1002; Richard J. Hoskins, "A Comparative Analysis of the Crime of Conspiracy in Germany, France, and the United States," *NYU Journal of International Law and Politics* 6 (1973) 256, 265.

117. Calker et al., *Verbrechen und Vergehen*, 39–44; Ingraham, *Political Crime in Europe*, 126–127.

118. Matthew 5:28.

119. Ullmann, *Medieval Idea of Law*, 144.

120. Pound, *Law and Morals*, 67.

121. Aquinas, *Summa Theologica*, first part of the second part, question 91, art. 4.

122. *Leviathan*, chap. 27.

123. Attenborough, *Laws of the English Kings*, Wihtred cap 28; Harrington, *Faithful Executioner*, 97; An Act for the Better Prevention of Offences 1851, 14 & 15 Vict., c. 19, §1, quoted in Dubber, "Policing Possession," 924.

124. Kaye, "Early History of Murder," 382; *R. v. Taylor* (1859) 1 F & F 511, 175 *Eng. Rep.* 831–32.

125. Hall, "Criminal Attempt," 794.

126. Levitt, "Origin of Mens Rea," 122, 128; Ingraham, *Political Crime in Europe*, 66.

127. Plutarch, *Lives of the Noble Greeks and Romans*, "Dion," 9.

128. Lear, *Treason*, 128; Bellamy, *Tudor Law of Treason*, 8.

129. Fletcher, "Case for Treason," 198; "Historical Concept of Treason," 72–73; Elton, *Law of Treason*, 222, 231–232; Orr, *Treason and the State*, 18.

130. 21 Richard II (1397); Hall, "Criminal Attempt," 795; Young, *Magic as a Political Crime*, 32; Bellamy, *Tudor Law of Treason*, 32.

131. Alexander and Ferzan, *Crime and Culpability*, 192–196; Vormbaum, *Modern History of German Criminal Law*, 195; Paul H. Robinson and Markus D. Dubber, "The American Model Penal Code," *New Criminal Law Review* 10, 3 (2007) 320.

132. McKnight, *Quality of Mercy*, 60.

133. Lorton, "Treatment of Criminals," 13–14.

134. Treston, *Poine*, 223–224; MacDowell, *Law in Classical Athens*, 115–116; Mommsen, *Römisches Strafrecht*, 95, 742.

135. Mueller, "Tort, Crime, and the Primitive," 326; von Bar, *History of Continental Criminal Law*, 68, 102–103.

136. Von Bar, *History of Continental Criminal Law*, 157; Xavier Rousseaux, "From Case to Crime: Homicide Regulation in Medieval and Modern Europe," in Dietmar Willoweit, ed., *Die Entstehung des öffentlichen Strafrechts* (Cologne 1999) 150.

137. Hall, "Criminal Attempt," 791, 805; Langbein, *Prosecuting Crime*, 170.

138. *Rex v. Scofield*, Cald. 397 (1784) (1786 ed.); Francis Bowes Sayre, "Criminal Attempts," *Harvard Law Review* 41 (1927–1928) 821–827, 834; Wiener, *Reconstructing the Criminal*, 68.

139. *King v. Higgins,* 2 East 5, 102 *Eng. Rep.* 269 (1801); Hall, "Criminal Attempt," 809.

140. *Regina v. Eagleton,* 169 *Eng. Rep.* 826 (Crim. App. 1855); Robbins, "Double Inchoate Crimes," 13; *R. v. Taylor* (1859) 1 F & F 511, 175 *Eng. Rep.* 831–832.

141. Robbins, "Double Inchoate Crimes," 12–14.

142. *Regina v. Collins,* 9 Cox C. C. 497, 498, 169, *Eng. Rep.* 1477, 1478 (1865); Hall, "Criminal Attempt," 833.

143. Wechsler et al., "Treatment of Inchoate Crimes," 578; G. L. Peiris, "Liability for Inchoate Crime in Commonwealth Law," *Legal Studies* 4 (1984) 56.

144. This started with the Model Penal Code in the United States and the Criminal Attempts Act 1981 in Britain. Wechsler et al., "Treatment of Inchoate Crimes," 573. But in Japan impossible crimes remain unpunished. Peiris, "Liability for Inchoate Crime," 63.

145. *People v. Dlugash,* 41 N.Y.2d 725, 363 N.E.2d 1155, 395 N.Y.S.2d 419 (1977); Ira P. Robbins, "Attempting the Impossible," *Harvard Journal on Legislation* 23 (1986) 422–423, 432–434.

146. Sayre, "Criminal Conspiracy," 396, 401; Hall, "Criminal Attempt," 793.

147. Attenborough, *Laws of the English Kings,* Ine cap 13; Harcourt, "Collapse of the Harm Principle," 153.

148. Pennington, "'Pro peccatis patrum puniri,'" 138.

149. Sayre, "Criminal Conspiracy," 407, 413; Hoskins, "A Comparative Analysis of the Crime of Conspiracy," 267–268.

150. Hoskins, "A Comparative Analysis of the Crime of Conspiracy," 246, 250.

151. Robbins, "Double Inchoate Crimes," 64, 38–40, 45–46.

152. Dubber, "Policing Possession," 907.

153. Fletcher, "Metamorphosis of Larceny," 523; Ferzan, "Inchoate Crimes," 1283.

154. Ashworth and Zedner, "Just Prevention," 284.

155. Bernard Lewis, *The Assassins* (New York 1967).

156. Ashworth and Zedner, *Preventive Justice,* 179–180, 184–189.

157. Terrorism Act 2006, s. 5(1).

158. McSherry, "Expanding the Boundaries of Inchoate Crimes," 142, 152–153; Ashworth and Zedner, "Just Prevention," 285.

159. Terrorism Act 2006; Lucia Zedner, "Fixing the Future? The Pre-emptive Turn in Criminal Justice," in McSherry et al., *Regulating Deviance,* 49; Ashworth and Zedner, "Prevention and Criminalization," 545.

160. Terrorism Act 2000, s. 16(2); McSherry, "Expanding the Boundaries of Inchoate Crimes," 142.

161. Serious Crime Act 2007, s. 2(1)(b); Zedner, "Fixing the Future?," 51.

162. Michael T. Cahill, "Attempt by Omission," *Iowa Law Review* 94 (2008–2009) 1209, 1236, and passim.

163. Pound quoted in Dubber, *Police Power,* 127.

164. Jean Floud and Warren Young, *Dangerousness and Criminal Justice* (Totowa 1981) 155–157.

165. Robinson, "Punishing Dangerousness," 1445–1446.

166. Saunders, *Plato's Penal Code,* 111; Mommsen, *Römisches Strafrecht,* 299; Goebel, *Felony and Misdemeanor,* 70.

167. Attenborough, *Laws of the English Kings*, Ine cap 18, 37; Pollock and Maitland, *History of English Law*, 1:49; Bodde and Morris, *Law in Imperial China*, 95; Harrington, *Faithful Executioner*, 31; Walker, *Popular Justice*, 14.

168. Simon A. Cole, *Suspect Identities: A History of Fingerprinting and Criminal Identification* (Cambridge MA 2001) 13–14.

169. Kelling and Coles, *Fixing Broken Windows*, 244; Lawrence W. Sherman, "Attacking Crime: Police and Crime Control," in Michael Tonry and Norval Morris, eds., *Modern Policing* (Chicago 1992) 176–179.

170. David H. Bayley, *Police for the Future* (New York 1994) 103.

171. Emsley, *English Police*, 152; Anthony A. Braga and David L. Weisburd, *Policing Problem Places: Crime Hot Spots and Effective Prevention* (New York 2010).

172. Fraher, "IV Lateran's Revolution," 103.

173. Goebel, *Felony and Misdemeanor*, 69–75; Peters, *Inquisition*, 34; Langbein, *Prosecuting Crime*, 146; Esmein, *History of Continental Criminal Procedure*, 302.

174. Bartlett, *Trial by Fire and Water*, 31; Wormald, "Charters," 160; Peters, *Inquisition*, 34; Ames, *Righteous Persecution*, 149.

175. Ullmann, "Some Medieval Principles," 23–24; Ullmann, "Medieval Torture," 130; Mike Macnair, "Vicinage and the Antecedents of the Jury," *Law and History Review* 17 (1999) 574.

176. Peters, *Torture*, 44–45; Langbein, *Prosecuting Crime*, 146.

177. Fraher, "Preventing Crime," 224–226; Soman, "Deviance and Criminal Justice," 11.

178. Blackstone, *Commentaries on the Laws of England*, 4:248.

179. Uberto Gatti and Alfredo Verde, "Cesare Lombroso: Methodological Ambiguities and Brilliant Intuitions," *International Journal of Law and Psychiatry* 35 (2012) 23–24.

180. Floud and Young, *Dangerousness*, 23–24; Zedner, "Fixing the Future," 39–40; Leon Radzinowicz and Roger Hood, "Dangerousness and Criminal Justice," *Criminal Law Review* (1981) 758; Henry J. Steadman and Joseph J. Cocozza, *Careers of the Criminally Insane: Excessive Social Control of Deviance* (Lexington 1974) chaps. 5 and 8.

181. Only one out of three predictions were accurate. Phil Woods and Gerri C. Lasiuk, "Risk Prediction: A Review of the Literature," *Journal of Forensic Nursing* 4, 1 (2008) 3.

182. Michael A. Norko and Madelon V. Baranoski, "The State of Contemporary Risk Assessment Research," *Canadian Journal of Psychiatry* 50 (2005) 19–20.

183. "Advances in AI Are Used to Spot Signs of Sexuality," *Economist*, 9 September 2017; R. Karl Hanson and Monique T. Bussière, "Predicting Relapse: A Meta-analysis of Sexual Offender Recidivism Studies," *Journal of Consulting and Clinical Psychology* 66, 2 (1998) 349, 351, 356; Gilles Launay, "The Phallometric Assessment of Sex Offenders," *Criminal Behaviour and Mental Health* 4 (1994) 56.

184. Martha J. Farah et al., "Functional MRI-Based Lie Detection: Scientific and Societal Challenges," *Nature Reviews Neuroscience* 15 (2014) 124.

185. Frank Ridgeway, *Blood in the Face: The Ku Klux Klan, Aryan Nations, Nazi Skinheads, and the Rise of a New White Culture*, 2nd ed. (New York 1995) 35, 45. Lombroso thought the same of the criminal type. David G. Horn, "Making Criminologists," in Peter Becker and Richard F. Wetzell, eds., *Criminals and Their Scientists* (Cambridge

2006) 331. Darwin considered blushing uniquely human, found among all *Homo sapiens*. Christopher Boehm, *Moral Origins: The Evolution of Virtue, Altruism, and Shame* (New York 2012) 14.

186. Dikötter, *Crime, Punishment, and the Prison in Modern China*, 208; Ken Alder, *The Lie Detectors* (Lincoln 2007) 108–109.

187. Robin Marantz Henig, "Looking for the Lie," *New York Times*, 5 February 2006; Kelly A. Gates, *Our Biometric Future: Facial Recognition Technology and the Culture of Surveillance* (New York 2011) chap. 5.

188. Henry T. Greely and Judy Illes, "Neuroscience-Based Lie Detection: The Urgent Need for Regulation," *American Journal of Law and Medicine* 33 (2007) 380.

189. Aldert Vrij et al., "Pitfalls and Opportunities in Nonverbal and Verbal Lie Detection," *Psychological Science in the Public Interest* 11, 3 (2010) 94–96.

190. Ian Hacking, *The Taming of Chance* (Cambridge 1990).

191. Harcourt, "Shaping of Chance," 106.

192. Robinson and Darley, "Utility of Desert," 468.

193. Packer, *Limits of Criminal Sanction*, 49–51; Douglas Husak, *Overcriminalization: The Limits of the Criminal Law* (New York 2008) 80.

194. Wechsler et al., "Treatment of Inchoate Crimes," 587; Kadish, "Decline of Innocence," 285–286.

195. Norko and Baranoski, "State of Contemporary Risk Assessment," 23.

196. Michael Gottfredson and Travis Hirschi, "The True Value of Lambda Would Appear to Be Zero: An Essay on Career Criminals, Criminal Careers, Selective Incapacitation, Cohort Studies, and Related Topics," *Criminology* 24, 2 (1986) 217.

197. Steadman and Cocozza, *Careers of the Criminally Insane*, 150–152; Alan M. Dershowitz, "The Law of Dangerousness: Some Fictions about Predictions," *Journal of Legal Education* 23 (1970) 25.

198. Garnot, "La législation et la répression des crimes," 79; Syed Ahmad Huda, "Legal Remedies for the Gypsies: Can the European Legal Frameworks Hold France Liable for the Expulsion of the Roma?" *University of Pennsylvania Journal of International Law* 33, 4 (2012) 1083.

199. Judith Walkowitz, *Prostitution and Victorian Society* (Cambridge 1980) 109; Dubber, "Policing Possession," 912–913.

200. *Papachristou v. City of Jacksonville*, 405 US 156 (1972) 164, quoted in Peter W. Poulos, "Chicago's Ban on Gang Loitering: Making Sense of Vagueness and Overbreadth in Loitering," *California Law Review* 83 (1995) 387.

201. Baumgartner et al., *Suspect Citizens*, 8–11.

202. Kim Strosnider, "Anti-gang Ordinances after *City of Chicago v. Morales*: The Intersection of Race, Vagueness Doctrine, and Equal Protection in the Criminal Law," *American Criminal Law Review* 39 (2002) 101–103; Lawrence Rosenthal, "Gang Loitering and Race," *Journal of Criminal Law and Criminology* 99 (2000) 101–102; Kelling and Coles, *Fixing Broken Windows*, 55–64.

203. R. A. Duff, "Dangerousness and Citizenship," in Andrew Ashworth and Martin Wasik, eds., *Fundamentals of Sentencing Theory* (Oxford 1998) 153–156.

204. Harcourt, "Shaping of Chance," 117; Nora V. Demleitner, "Abusing State Power or Controlling Risk? Sex Offender Commitment and *Sicherung[s]verwahrung*," *Fordham Urban Law Journal* 30 (2003) 1651.

205. Ingraham, *Political Crime in Europe*, 264; Hsi-Huey Liang, *The Rise of Modern Police and the European State System from Metternich to the Second World War* (Cambridge 1992) 251.

206. Garland, *Punishment and Modern Society*, 136.

207. Alexis de Tocqueville, *Democracy in America*, chap. 15, pt. 2.

208. Mühlhahn, *Criminal Justice in China*, 26–27, 33, 54; Plato, *Laws*, bk. 10, chap. 15.

209. Peters, *Inquisition*, 30; Levy, *Treason against God*, 107–108.

210. Karen Sullivan, "Disputations, Literary and Inquisitorial: The Conversion of the Heretic Sicart of Figueiras," *Medium Ævum* 78, 1 (2009) 58.

211. Asad, "Medieval Heresy," 356–357; Ames, *Righteous Persecution*, chap. 4.

212. Gorski, "Protestant Ethic Revisited," 282; Beattie, *Crime and the Courts*, 473.

213. Beattie, *Crime and the Courts*, 492, 497–499; Beattie, *Policing and Punishment*, 54.

214. Radzinowicz, *History of English Criminal Law*, 1:14, 376.

215. Walker, *Popular Justice*, 85.

216. Richard F. Wetzell, *Inventing the Criminal: A History of German Criminology, 1880–1945* (Chapel Hill 2000) 33–35; Packer, *Limits of Criminal Sanction*, 54–55.

217. Bernard E. Harcourt, *Against Prediction: Profiling, Policing, and Punishing in an Actuarial Age* (Chicago 2007) 52; Rotman, "Failure of Reform," 174.

218. Walker, *Popular Justice*, 92–95; Miethe and Lu, *Punishment*, 95; Harcourt, *Against Prediction*, 39–40; Whitman, *Harsh Justice*, 149.

219. David Garland, *The Culture of Control: Crime and Social Order in Contemporary Society* (Chicago 2001) 3–9; Wacquant, *Punishing the Poor*, chap. 4; Marie Gottschalk, *The Prison and the Gallows: The Politics of Mass Incarceration in America* (Cambridge 2006) chaps. 5 and 6.

220. Garland, *Culture of Control*, chap. 3; Feeley and Simon, "New Penology," 467–468.

221. Walker, *Popular Justice*, 246–249; Harcourt, "Shaping of Chance," 107–109.

222. Hanns von Hofer and Henrik Tham, "Punishment in Sweden," in Vincenzo Ruggiero and Mick Ryan, eds., *Punishment in Europe* (Basingstoke 2013) 34.

223. Susan R. Klein, "The Return of Federal Judicial Discretion in Criminal Sentencing," *Valparaiso University Law Review* 39 (2005) 693; Harcourt, *Against Prediction*, 93; Roberts et al., *Penal Populism*, 35; Howard, *Unusually Cruel*, 53–57.

224. Howard, *Unusually Cruel*, chap. 5; Nicola Lacey, *The Prisoners' Dilemma: Political Economy and Punishment in Contemporary Democracies* (Cambridge 2008) 26–27.

225. Demleitner, "Abusing State Power," 1623; Cavadino and Dignan, *Penal Systems*, 141; Markus Dirk Dubber, "Theories of Crime and Punishment in German Criminal Law," *American Journal of Comparative Law* 53, 3 (2005) 698.

226. Floud and Young, *Dangerousness*, 72–76; Eric S. Janus, *Failure to Protect: America's Sexual Predator Laws and the Rise of the Preventive State* (Ithaca 2006) 17.

227. Garland, *Culture of Control*, 36.

228. O'Brien, "Prison on the Continent," 219. But the French penal code of 1810 also used nonfixed terms with maximums and minimums. Von Bar, *History of Continental Criminal Law*, 338.

229. Roberts et al., *Penal Populism*, 36.

230. John Stuart Mill, *On Liberty* (Boston 1863) 114.

231. Miethe and Lu, *Punishment*, 140; Giacomo Bono, "Commonplace Forgiveness: From Healthy Relationships to Healthy Society," *Humboldt Journal of Social Relations* 29, 2 (2005) 94.

232. Pound, *Law and Morals*, 65–66; Vernon Palmer, "A General Theory of the Inner Structure of Strict Liability," *Tulane Law Review* 62 (1988) 1313.

233. Steven Shavell, "Strict Liability versus Negligence," *Journal of Legal Studies* 9 (1980) 2–3.

234. David A. Moss, *When All Else Fails: Government as the Ultimate Risk Manager* (Cambridge MA 2002) 233.

235. Jed Handelsman Shugerman, "The Floodgates of Strict Liability: Bursting Reservoirs and the Adoption of *Fletcher v. Rylands* in the Gilded Age," *Yale Law Journal* 110, 2 (2000) 336–337.

236. Copyright violation is also strict liability: see Dane S. Ciolino and Erin A. Donelon, "Questioning Strict Liability in Copyright," *Rutgers Law Review* 54 (2002), and Francisco Bonet Ramón, "Strict Liability," *Louisiana Law Review* 42 (1981–1982) 1699–1701.

237. John L. Diamond, "The Myth of Morality and Fault in Criminal Law Doctrine," *American Criminal Law Review* 34 (1996) 117–118; Francis Bowes Sayre, "Public Welfare Offenses," *Columbia Law Review* 33 (1933) 58.

238. Coffee, "Does 'Unlawful' Mean 'Criminal'?," 210–215; Robinson and Darley, "Utility of Desert," 480.

239. James E. Starrs, "The Regulatory Offense in Historical Perspective," in Gerhard O. W. Mueller, ed., *Essays in Criminal Science* (South Hackensack 1961) 237–238, 242; Karlen, "Mens Rea," 233–234; Feeley and Simon, "New Penology," 452; Sayre, "Public Welfare Offenses," 58; Sayre, "Criminal Responsibility," 719.

240. Coffee, "Does 'Unlawful' Mean 'Criminal'?," 216; Coffee, "Paradigms Lost," 1880; Heyman, "Losing All Sense of Just Proportion," 142.

241. Richard A. Epstein, "A Theory of Strict Liability," *Journal of Legal Studies* 2 (1973) 152–153.

242. John Austin, *Lectures on Jurisprudence*, 3rd ed. (London 1869) 1:441–443; Richard A. Epstein, "Crime and Tort: Old Wine in Old Bottles," in Randy E. Barnett and John Hagel III, eds., *Assessing the Criminal* (Cambridge MA 1977) 235–236.

243. Dan W. Morkel, "On the Distinction between Recklessness and Conscious Negligence," *American Journal of Comparative Law* 30, 2 (1982) 326–327; George P. Fletcher, "The Theory of Criminal Negligence," *University of Pennsylvania Law Review* 119, 3 (1971) 427.

244. Kyron Huigens, "Virtue and Criminal Negligence," *Buffalo Criminal Law Review* 1, 2 (1998) 431; James B. Brady, "Punishment for Negligence: A Reply to Professor Hall," *Buffalo Law Review* 22 (1972) 108–109.

245. Exodus 21:29; King, *Law and Society in the Visigothic Kingdom*, 261.

246. Attenborough, *Laws of the English Kings*, Ine cap 42, Alfred cap 23; King, *Law and Society in the Visigothic Kingdom*, 220.

247. Friedland, *Seeing Justice Done*, 41; Harriet Ritvo, *The Animal Estate: The English and Other Creatures in the Victorian Age* (Cambridge MA 1987) 2.

248. Kimmo Nuotio, "Normative and Epistemological Aspects Concerning Legal Liability for Risk-Taking," *Retfærd* 18, 71 (1995) 64.

249. R. D. L., "Crimes: Negligence and Criminal Negligence," *Michigan Law Review* 24, 3 (1926) 286–287; James B. Brady, "Conscious Negligence," *American Philosophical Quarterly* 33, 3 (1996) 326.

250. Duff, "Criminalizing Endangerment," 944.

251. Model Penal Code, 2.02(2); Dubber, "Theories of Crime and Punishment," 692.

252. Ashworth and Zedner, *Preventive Justice*, 101–102; Duff, "Criminalizing Endangerment," 942.

253. Duff, "Dangerousness and Citizenship," 152–153.

254. Claire Finkelstein, "Is Risk a Harm?," *University of Pennsylvania Law Review* 151 (2003) 963–966.

255. Jerome Hall, "Negligent Behavior Should Be Excluded from Penal Liability," *Columbia Law Review* 63 (1963) 635–636.

Chapter 12

1. Issa Kohler-Hausmann, *Misdemeanorland: Criminal Courts and Social Control in an Age of Broken Windows Policing* (Princeton 2018) 1.

2. Robert Estienne, *Dictionnaire François–Latin*, 1539, quoted in Williams, *Police of Paris*, 8.

3. Markus Dubber, however, argues in *Dual Penal State* that police law continues a powerful and underacknowledged force in American penality.

4. That the English did not give broad regulatory powers to their police leads historians of Britain to odd conclusions, such as interpreting the Victorian spread of behavioral legislation (regarding vagrancy, public drunkenness, prostitution) as a new eruption of policing into conduct formerly controlled only by informal prohibitions, but from a continental perspective this approach was nothing particularly new. See Wiener, *Reconstructing the Criminal*, 260, for an example.

5. Chapman, *Police State*, 51; Gerstle, *Liberty and Coercion*, chap. 2; William J. Novak, *The People's Welfare: Law and Regulation in Nineteenth Century America* (Chapel Hill 1996) chap. 5.

6. David H. Bayley, *Patterns of Policing* (New Brunswick 1985) 39; J. J. Tobias, "Police and Public in the United Kingdom," *Journal of Contemporary History* 7 (1972) 202; Beattie, *Policing and Punishment*, 77; Chapman, *Police State*, 38–39. Patrick Colquhoun's *Treatise on the Police of the Metropolis* stood in the *Polizei* tradition, but, published in 1797, was late and derivative.

7. Chapman, *Police State*, 13; Franz-Ludwig Knemeyer, "Polizei," *Economy and Society* 9 (1980) 174–175; Liang, *Rise of Modern Police*, 1.

8. Beattie, *Policing and Punishment*, 124; Joel F. Harrington, *Reordering Marriage and Society in Reformation Germany* (Cambridge 1995) 123, 210–212.

9. Friedland, *Seeing Justice Done*, 76–77; Williams, *Police of Paris*, 26, 30–35, 41, 101; Knemeyer, "Polizei," 177; Axtmann, "'Police' and Formation of the Modern State," 42, 57; Charles Tilly, "Food Supply and Public Order in Modern Europe," in Charles Tilly, ed., *The Formation of National States in Western Europe* (Princeton 1975) 441–442.

10. John Merriman, *Police Stories: Building the French State, 1815–1851* (New York 2006) 24; Clive Emsley, *Gendarmes and the State in Nineteenth-Century Europe* (Oxford 1999) 82.

11. Monkkonen, *Police in Urban America*, 34, chap. 3; Neil Weissman, "Regular Police in Tsarist Russia, 1900–1914," *Russian Review* 44, 1 (1985) 56–57.

12. James F. Richardson, *The New York Police: Colonial Times to 1901* (New York 1970) 150, 226–228.

13. Robert Reiner, *The Politics of the Police*, 2nd ed. (Toronto 1992) 69.

14. Raymond B. Fosdick, *European Police Systems* (New York 1915) 20–21, 113, 128.

15. David H. Bayley, "The Police and Political Development in Europe," in Tilly, *Formation of National States*, 336; Mawby, *Comparative Policing Issues*, 46.

16. John Brewer et al., *The Police, Public Order, and the State*, 2nd ed. (New York 1996) 209.

17. Fosdick, *European Police Systems*, 147; Reiner, *Politics of the Police*, 69; Wilbur R. Miller, *Cops and Bobbies: Police Authority in New York and London, 1830–1870* (Chicago 1977) 128.

18. Rainer, *Politics of the Police*, 142, 212.

19. According to some studies, only one-third of police radio calls involved criminal matters that might lead to arrest. Wilson, *Varieties of Police Behavior*, 4.

20. Mark Harrison Moore, "Problem-Solving and Community Policing," in Tonry and Morris, *Modern Policing*, 114; Reiner, *Politics of the Police*, 139, 97, 141.

21. Bayley, *Patterns of Policing*, 149; Bayley, *Police for the Future*, 20.

22. Wilson, *Varieties of Police Behavior*, 6.

23. Knemeyer, "Polizei," 185–86; Axtmann, "'Police' and the Formation of the Modern State," 46–47.

24. Allgemeines Landrecht, part 2, title 17, §10.

25. Bayley, *Patterns of Policing*, 110–111.

26. Gatrell, "Decline of Theft and Violence," 271–272.

27. Liang, *Rise of Modern Police*, 19.

28. David H. Bayley, "Comparative Organization of the Police in English-Speaking Countries," in Tonry and Morris, *Modern Policing*, 535.

29. Emsley, *Gendarmes*, 134.

30. Bayley, *Patterns of Policing*, 204; Roger Lane, "Urban Police and Crime in Nineteenth-Century America," in Tonry and Morris, *Modern Policing*, 18.

31. Bayley, "Police and Political Development," 373; Reiner, *Politics of the Police*, 63–68.

32. Richardson, *New York Police*, 70–71.

33. Liang, *Rise of Modern Police*, 4.

34. Dorothy H. Bracey, "Policing the People's Republic," in Ronald J. Troyer et al., eds., *Social Control in the People's Republic of China* (New York 1989) 130.

35. Sherman, "Attacking Crime," 208; Kelling and Coles, *Fixing Broken Windows*, 86; Bayley, *Police for the Future*, 8; Rejali, *Torture and Democracy*, 458–459.

36. Julie Ayling et al., *Lengthening the Arm of the Law: Enhancing Police Resources in the Twenty-First Century* (Cambridge 2009) 190–206; Treitel, *Science for the Soul*, 146.

37. Daniel Jütte, *The Strait Gate: Thresholds and Power in Western History* (New Haven 2015) 92; Williams, *Police of Paris*, 73, 232; Funk, *Polizei und Rechtsstaat*, 279; Emsley, *English Police*, 225.

38. Janus, *Failure to Protect*, 66.

39. Bellamy, *Tudor Law of Treason*, 83; Wickersham, *Rituals of Prosecution*, 97.

40. Karina M. Tehusijarana, "Fears Grow over App to Police Minorities," *Jakarta Post*, 26 November 2018.

41. "Violence against Women: Government Bill 1997/98:55," Swedish Government Offices, Fact Sheet, 1999.

42. Strafgesetzbuch, §§138–139. A few exceptions to the criminalization of knowing of a crime but not reporting it are now carved out for professional secrecy.

43. Sandra Guerra Thompson, "The White-Collar Police Force: 'Duty to Report' Statutes in Criminal Law Theory," *William and Mary Bill of Rights Journal* 11, 3 (2002) 36; Ayling et al., *Lengthening the Arm of the Law*, 52–55.

44. Robert D. Storch, "The Policeman as Domestic Missionary: Urban Discipline and Popular Culture in Northern England, 1850–1880," *Journal of Social History* 9, 4 (1976) 482; Ashworth and Zedner, *Preventive Justice*, 41; Emsley, *English Police*, 74–75.

45. Richardson, *New York Police*, 110, 181.

46. Eric Luna, "Race, Crime, and Institutional Design," *Law and Contemporary Problems* 66 (2003) 185–187.

47. Hindle, "Keeping of the Public Peace," 237 and passim; Hay, "Property, Authority, and the Criminal Law," 36–37; Emsley, *Gendarmes*, 3.

48. Funk, *Polizei und Rechtsstaat*, 82.

49. Miller, *Cops and Bobbies*, 107–108; Gatrell, "Decline of Theft and Violence," 276.

50. Miller, *Cops and Bobbies*, 64–66; David Philips, *Crime and Authority in Victorian England* (London 1977) 124–126; Braithwaite, *Crime, Shame, and Reintegration*, 40.

51. Moore, "Problem-Solving and Community Policing," 149; Kelling and Coles, *Fixing Broken Windows*, 26.

52. Rosenthal, "Gang Loitering," 113; Butler, "Racially Based Jury Nullification," 697; Tracy L. Meares and Dan M. Kahan, "The Wages of Antiquated Procedural Thinking: A Critique of *Chicago v. Morales*," *University of Chicago Legal Forum* 197 (1998) 199; James Forman Jr., *Locking Up Our Own: Crime and Punishment in Black America* (New York 2017).

53. Hunter, *Policing Athens*, 3, 145–149; Lintott, *Violence in Republican Rome*, 94; Ikram, *Ancient Egypt*, 231; Mommsen, *Römisches Strafrecht*, 298.

54. Susan Trevaskes, "The Private/Public Security Nexus in China," *Social Justice* 34, 3–4 (2007–2008) 39; Lena Y. Zhong and Peter N. Grabosky, "The Pluralization of Policing and the Rise of Private Policing in China," *Crime, Law, and Social Change* 52 (2009) 437.

55. Sharpe, *Crime in Early Modern England*, 106–107; Goebel, *Felony and Misdemeanor*, 67–68.

56. Statute of Winchester, 1285, 13 Edw. I, c. 4; Henry Summerson, "The Enforcement of the Statute of Winchester, 1285–1327," *Journal of Legal History* 13, 3 (1992) 233.

57. Weisser, *Crime and Punishment*, 56; Philips, "New Engine of Power," 160; Beattie, *Policing and Punishment*, 114, 147.

58. Beattie, *Crime and the Courts*, 68–69; Beattie, *Policing and Punishment*, 173, 157.

59. Dale, *Criminal Justice in the United States,* 9; Emsley, *Policing,* 37; Merriman, *Police Stories,* 24; Weissman, "Regular Police in Tsarist Russia," 49–50.

60. Bayley, *Police for the Future,* 11; Ohlin and Stauber, "Applicability of Citizen's Arrest Powers," 342; Ayling et al., *Lengthening the Arm of the Law,* 106.

61. Gary S. Becker and George J. Stigler, "Law Enforcement, Malfeasance, and Compensation of Enforcers," *Journal of Legal Studies* 3 (1974) 13.

62. Goebel, *Felony and Misdemeanor,* 68; Brackett, *Criminal Justice and Crime in Late Renaissance Florence,* 30–31; Bayley, *Patterns of Policing,* 25.

63. Ruff, *Violence in Early Modern Europe,* 90.

64. Beattie, *Policing and Punishment,* chap. 5; Emsley, *Gendarmes,* 149; Weisser, *Crime and Punishment,* 160.

65. Martin, *Crime and Criminal Justice under the Third Republic,* 43; Brown, *No Duty to Retreat,* 55–60.

66. Emsley, *Crime, Police, and Penal Policy,* 204; Clifford Shearing, "The Relation between Public and Private Policing," in Tonry and Morris, *Modern Policing,* 404; David A. Sklansky, "The Private Police," *UCLA Law Review* 46 (1999) 1212.

67. John A. Chamberlin, "Bounty Hunters: Can the Criminal Justice System Live without Them?" *University of Illinois Law Review* 1998, 4 (1998) 1195; Andrew DeForest Patrick, "Running from the Law: Should Bounty Hunters Be Considered State Actors and Thus Subject to Constitutional Restraints?" *Vanderbilt Law Review* 52 (1999) 175.

68. Zedner, "Policing before and after the Police," 90; Bayley, *Patterns of Policing,* 8–9. On Blackwater, now Academi, in the United States and their Russian equivalents, Wagner, see "How 'Wagner' Came to Syria," *Economist,* 2 November 2017.

69. William C. Cunningham et al., *The Hallcrest Report II: Private Security Trends (1970 to 2000)* (July 1990) 229, https://www.ncjrs.gov/pdffiles1/Digitization/126681NCJRS.pdf; Creveld, *Rise and Decline of the State,* 404; Malcolm Anderson, *In Thrall to Political Change: Police and Gendarmerie in France* (Oxford 2011) 415.

70. Sklansky, "Private Police," 1175; Joh, "Paradox of Private Policing," 55; Trevaskes, "Private/Public Security Nexus," 40; Dutton, *Policing Chinese Politics,* 294.

71. Sklansky, "Private Police," 1183–1184; Joh, "Paradox of Private Policing," 65.

72. Clive Emsley, "A Typology of Nineteenth-Century Police," *Crime, histoire et sociétés* 3, 1 (1999) 34.

73. Emsley, *Gendarmes,* 17–20, 42; Arnold, *Fouché, Napoleon, and the General Police,* 13, 24; Payne, *Police State,* 4.

74. Ruff, *Violence in Early Modern Europe,* 91; Emsley, *Crime, Police, and Penal Policy,* 65.

75. Philips, "New Engine of Power," 168–169; Spierenburg, *History of Murder,* 169.

76. Williams, *Police of Paris,* 92–93; Liang, *Rise of Modern Police,* 27; Emsley, *Gendarmes,* 202.

77. Creveld, *Rise and Decline of the State,* 165.

78. Weissman, "Regular Police in Tsarist Russia," 59; Miller, *Cops and Bobbies,* 25–32.

79. Emsley, *Gendarmes,* 58.

80. Garland, *Culture of Control,* 114; Albert J. Reiss Jr., "Police Organization in the Twentieth Century," in Tonry and Morris, *Modern Policing,* 51–53; Kelling and Coles, *Fixing Broken Windows,* chap. 5.

81. John Brewer, *The Sinews of Power: War, Money, and the English State, 1688–1783* (New York 1988) 51.

82. Weisser, *Crime and Punishment*, 158; Pat Thane, "Government and Society in England and Wales, 1750–1914," in F. M. L. Thompson, ed., *Cambridge Social History of Britain, 1750–1950* (Cambridge 1990) 34; Richardson, *New York Police*, 142.

83. V. A. C. Gatrell, "Crime, Authority, and the Policeman-State," in Thompson, *Cambridge Social History of Britain*, 266; Emsley, *English Police*, 115–118.

84. Abigail R. Hall and Christopher J. Coyne, "The Militarization of U.S. Domestic Policing," *Independent Review* 17, 4 (2013) 491.

85. Robert W. Thurston, "Police and People in Moscow, 1906–1914," *Russian Review* 39, 3 (1980) 322.

86. Fosdick, *European Police Systems*, 126, 93; Mawby, *Comparative Policing Issues*, 46.

87. Jens Meierhenrich, *The Remnants of the Rechtsstaat: An Ethnography of Nazi Law* (Oxford 2018) 144.

88. Derek Lutterbeck, "Between Police and Military: The New Security Agenda and the Rise of Gendarmeries," *Cooperation and Conflict* 39, 1 (2006) 46–49.

89. Monkkonnen, *Police in Urban America*, 36.

90. Gatrell, "Crime, Authority, and the Policeman-State," 298; Emsley, *English Police*, 57–58; Emsley, *Crime and Society in England*, 133.

91. Nicolas Boring, "Comparative Summary," in *Police Weapons in Selected Jurisdictions*, Law Library of Congress, Global Legal Research Center (September 2014) 1, https://www.loc.gov/law/help/police-weapons/police-weapons.pdf; Clare Feikert-Ahalt, "United Kingdom," in *Police Weapons in Selected Jurisdictions*, 91; Nicolas Boring, "France," in *Police Weapons in Selected Jurisdictions*, 40.

92. P. A. J. Waddington et al., "Singing the Same Tune? International Continuities and Discontinuities in How Police Talk about Using Force," *Crime, Law, and Social Change* 52, 2 (2009) 116.

93. Eighty-nine percent of US police departments had such units by 1995. On this issue, see Hall and Coyne, "Militarization of Domestic Policing," 486; Yung, "Emerging Criminal War," 446; Peter B. Kraska and Victor E. Kappeler, "Militarizing American Police: The Rise and Normalization of Paramilitary Units," *Social Problems* 44, 1 (1997) 7.

94. Karena Rahall, "The Green to Blue Pipeline: Defense Contractors and the Police Industrial Complex," *Cardozo Law Review* 36 (2015) 1789, 1818; John Paul and Michael L. Birzer, "The Militarization of the American Police Force," *Critical Issues in Justice and Politics* 1, 1 (2008) 18.

95. Bayley, *Police for the Future*, 137; Boring, "France," 40–41.

96. Rahall, "Green to Blue Pipeline," 1791, 1786–1787; Reiner, *Politics of the Police*, 85–89.

97. Peter K. Manning, "Information Technologies and the Police," in Tonry and Morris, *Modern Policing*, 351.

98. Green, "Jury and the English Law of Homicide," 431; Given, *Society and Homicide*, 92.

99. Herrup, *Common Peace*, 144; Sharpe, *Crime in Early Modern England*, 93; Janelle R. Greenberg and Martin S. Greenberg, "Crime and Justice in Tudor–Stuart England and the Modern United States," *Law and Human Behavior* 6, 3–4 (1982) 269;

John H. Langbein, "Shaping the Eighteenth-Century Criminal Trial: A View from the Ryder Sources," *University of Chicago Law Review* 50, 1 (1983) 43.

100. Emsley, *Crime, Police, and Penal Policy*, 124; Benjamin Carter Hett, "The 'Captain of Köpenick' and the Transformation of German Criminal Justice, 1891–1914," *Central European History* 36, 1 (2003) 12–13.

101. James M. Donovan, "Justice Unblind: The Juries and the Criminal Classes in France, 1825–1914," *Journal of Social History* 15, 1 (1981) 93; Martin, *Crime and Criminal Justice under the Third Republic*, 184.

102. Cavadino and Dignan, *Penal Systems*, 178.

103. Percentages of prosecution leading to conviction for 2015: 97.9 percent, France; 91.6 percent, United States; 83.8 percent, United Kingdom; 81.1 percent, Germany. The number of people prosecuted taken from United Nations Office on Drugs and Crime (UNODC) Statistics, https://data.unodc.org/, search string: Crime and Criminal Justice; Criminal Justice; Persons Prosecuted; Total Persons; Total Persons Prosecuted, All Crimes; Count; 2015, relevant country. The number of people convicted taken from UNODC Statistics, https://data.unodc.org/, search string: Crime and Criminal Justice; Criminal Justice; Persons Convicted; Total Persons Convicted; Total Persons Convicted, All Crimes; Count; 2015.

104. McKnight, *Quality of Mercy*, x; William B. Taylor, *Drinking, Homicide, and Rebellion in Colonial Mexican Villages* (Stanford 1979) 101; Jeroen Duindam, *Dynasties: A Global History of Power, 1300–1800* (Cambridge 2016) 25.

105. Annie Kensey and Pierre Tournier, "French Prison Numbers Stable since 1988, but Populations Changing," in Michael Tonry, ed., *Penal Reform in Overcrowded Times* (New York 2001) 146; McKnight, *Quality of Mercy*, 20.

106. Beccaria, *On Crimes and Punishment*, chap. 46.

107. The number of police employees is multiplying faster than officers. See Angela K. Dills et al., "What Do Economists Know about Crime?," in Rafael Di Tella et al., eds., *The Economics of Crime: Lessons for and from Latin America* (Chicago 2010) 276–277; Lutterbeck, "Between Police and Military," 52–53; Kraska and Kappeler, "Militarizing American Police."

108. P. S. Squire, *The Third Department: The Establishment and Practices of the Political Police in the Russia of Nicholas I* (Cambridge 1968) 47.

109. Wilson, *Varieties of Police Behavior*, 19; Bayley, *Police for the Future*, 17.

110. Richard V. Ericson and Kevin D. Haggerty, *Policing the Risk Society* (Toronto 1997) 19–20.

111. Arnold, *Fouché, Napoleon, and the General Police*, 13.

112. Herrup, *Common Peace*, 70; Beattie, *Policing and Punishment*, 82, 120, 131–132.

113. Quoted in Kelling and Coles, *Fixing Broken Windows*, 106.

114. Greenberg, *Crime and Law Enforcement*, 159–161; Miller, *Cops and Bobbies*, 146; Jerome Hall, "Legal and Social Aspects of Arrest without a Warrant," *Harvard Law Review* 49 (1936) 579.

115. Miller, *Cops and Bobbies*, 16; Sklansky, "Private Police," 1184–1185; Ohlin and Stauber, "Applicability of Citizen's Arrest Powers," 347–350.

116. Joh, "Paradox of Private Policing," 64; Roberta Mary Fay, "Citizen's Arrest: International Environmental Law and Global Climate Change," *Glendale Law Review* 14 (1995) 88–89.

117. Howard E. Wallin, "Citizens' Arrests and the Fourth Amendment," *Touro Law Review* 4 (1987) 17–18, 28–30.

118. Samuels, "Non-Crown Prosecution," 33–35.

119. Robbins, "Vilifying the Vigilante," 583; V. F. Nourse, "Self-Defense and Subjectivity," *University of Chicago Law Review* 68, 4 (2001) 1271–1274; Boaz Sangero, "Heller's Self-Defense," *New Criminal Law Review* 13, 3 (2010) 454.

120. Beattie, *Crime and the Courts*, 71–72; Beattie, *Policing and Punishment*, 121–122, 197; Williams, *Police of Paris*, 232.

121. Yair Mintzker, *The Defortification of the German City, 1689–1866* (Cambridge 2012) 21.

122. Sklansky, "Private Police," 1187; Maitland, *Constitutional History of England*, 236, 488–489.

123. Miller, *Cops and Bobbies*, 54, 7, 63–64; Richardson, *New York Police*, 190; Gatrell, "Crime, Authority, and the Policeman-State," 266–267.

124. Sally Bedell Smith, "Billionaire with a Cause," *Vanity Fair*, 2 January 2008, https://www.vanityfair.com/magazine/1997/05/goldsmith199705?currentPage=5.

125. Sklansky, "Private Police," 1213.

126. Saunders, *Plato's Penal Code*, 39; Christopher Andrew, *The Secret World: A History of Intelligence* (New Haven 2018) 37.

127. Peters, *Inquisition*, 54; Ames, *Righteous Persecution*, passim.

128. Given, *Inquisition*, 42–45. In fourteenth-century England, possession of works in English, especially Bibles, was prima facie evidence of heresy. John Baker, "Magna Carta and Personal Liberty," in Robin Griffith-Jones and Mark Hillin, eds., *Magna Carta, Religion, and the Rule of Law* (Cambridge 2015) 89.

129. Thornley, "Treason Legislation of Henry VIII," 91; Elton, *Policy and Police*, chap. 8; Bellamy, *Tudor Law of Treason*, 84–85.

130. Brackett, *Criminal Justice and Crime in Late Renaissance Florence*, 30; Squire, *Third Department*, 63.

131. Chapman, *Police State*, 24; Axtmann, "'Police' and the Formation of the Modern State," 59.

132. Simon Burrows, "Despotism without Bounds: The French Secret Police and the Silencing of Dissent in London, 1760–1790," *History* 89, 4 (2004) 526–527; Williams, *Police of Paris*, 104–106.

133. Mathieu Deflem, "International Policing in Nineteenth-Century Europe: The Police Union of German States, 1851–1866," *International Criminal Justice Review* 6 (1996) 44.

134. Liang, *Rise of Modern Police*, 10.

135. Gatrell, "Crime, Authority, and the Policeman-State," 261; Bayley, *Patterns of Policing*, 195–196; Emsley, *English Police*, 104–105, 259–261.

136. Deflem, "International Policing," 42–43.

137. Peter Holquist, "'Information Is the Alpha and Omega of Our Work': Bolshevik Surveillance in Its Pan-European Context," *Journal of Modern History* 69, 3 (1997) 422, 439.

138. Liang, *Rise of Modern Police*, 51; Merriman, *Police Stories*, 15.

139. Arnold, *Fouché, Napoleon, and the General Police*, 16; Anderson, *In Thrall to Political Change*, 270.

140. Payne, *Police State*, 267–268; Howard C. Payne, "An Early Concept of the Modern Police State in Nineteenth Century France," *Journal of Criminal Law, Criminology, and Police Science* 43, 3 (1952) 379–380.

141. Lane, "Urban Police and Crime," 10–11.

142. Andrew Pepper, *Unwilling Executioner: Crime Fiction and the State* (Oxford 2016); Matthew Levay, *Violent Minds: Modernism and the Criminal* (Cambridge 2019).

143. Frank Smyth, *Cause of Death: The History of Murder under the Microscope* (London 1982) 9.

144. Elizabeth A. Wood, *Performing Justice: Agitation Trials in Early Soviet Russia* (Ithaca 2005) 16.

145. Reiner, *Politics of the Police*, 183.

146. Lawrence Frank, "'The Murders in the Rue Morgue': Edgar Allan Poe's Evolutionary Reverie," *Nineteenth-Century Literature* 50, 2 (1995) 171.

147. "The Science of Deduction," in Arthur Conan Doyle, *The Sign of Four.*

148. Arthur Conan Doyle, "The Adventure of the Copper Breeches," in *The Adventures of Sherlock Holmes*. And, indeed, it is argued that Peircean abduction is Holmes's method, where, unlike deduction, the conclusion is not logically implied by the rule and premise but requires empirical verification. See Marcello Truzzi, "Sherlock Holmes, Applied Social Psychologist," in Umberto Eco and Thomas A. Sebeok, eds., *The Sign of Three: Dupin, Holmes, Peirce* (Bloomington 1983) 69–70.

149. Squire, *Third Department*, 205–207.

150. Eric Monkkonen, "History of Urban Police," in Tonry and Morris, *Modern Policing*, 550.

151. Weissman, "Regular Police in Tsarist Russia," 48; Thurston, "Police and People in Moscow," 326; Richardson, *New York Police*, 68.

152. Moss, *When All Else Fails*, 8, 257–276.

153. Tomlinson, "French Experience," 494–497.

154. Goebel, *Felony and Misdemeanor*, 64.

155. Bartlett, *Trial by Fire and Water*, 16–20, 29.

156. Cavadino and Dignan, *Penal Systems*, 165, 178; Hans-Heinrich Jescheck, "Principles of German Criminal Procedure in Comparison with American Law," *Virginia Law Review* 56 (1970) 245.

157. Conviction rates in 2015 were 98 percent for France and 84 percent for Britain. The number of people prosecuted is taken from UNODC Statistics, https://data.unodc.org/, search string: Crime and Criminal Justice; Criminal Justice; Persons Prosecuted; Total Persons; Total Persons Prosecuted, All Crimes; Count; 2015, relevant country. The number of people convicted is taken from UNODC Statistics, https://data.unodc.org/, search string: Crime and Criminal Justice; Criminal Justice; Persons Convicted; Total Persons Convicted; Total Persons Convicted, All Crimes; Count; 2015.

158. Esmein, *History of Continental Criminal Procedure*, 328–329.

159. George Fisher, "The Jury's Rise as Lie Detector," *Yale Law Journal* 107, 3 (1997) 583. Ancient Greek courts faced similar problems once oaths were allowed on both sides. Jones, *Law and Legal Theory of the Greeks*, 137–138.

160. Barbara J. Shapiro, "'To a Moral Certainty': Theories of Knowledge and Anglo-American Juries 1600–1850," *Hastings Law Journal* 38 (1986–1987) passim.

161. Hasegawa, *Crime and Punishment*, 35.

162. Saunders, *Plato's Penal Code*, 316.

163. William and Mary, 1692, "An Act for encourageing the apprehending of Highway Men," chap. 8, Rot. Parl., pt. 3, no. 3, v; Hunt, *Governing Morals*, 34, 44, 47–49; Hsia, *Social Discipline in the Reformation*, 19.

164. Michael Braddick, *State Formation in Early Modern England, c. 1550–1700* (Cambridge 2000) 41; Mark Finnane, *Police and Government: Histories of Policing in Australia* (Melbourne 1994) 77–78.

165. Williams, *Police of Paris*, 231; Martin, *Crime and Criminal Justice under the Third Republic*, 77, 44; Dutton, *Policing Chinese Politics*, 152.

166. Weissman, "Regular Police in Tsarist Russia," 49; Thurston, "Police in Moscow," 326.

167. Sheila Fitzpatrick and Robert Gellately, "Introduction to the Practices of Denunciation in Modern European History," *Journal of Modern History* 68 (1996) 150–151; Catherine Epstein, "The Stasi: New Research on the East German Ministry of State Security," *Kritika* 5, 2 (2004) 322; Sheila Fitzpatrick and Alf Lüdtke, "Energizing the Everyday: On the Breaking and Making of Social Bonds in Nazism and Stalinism," in Geyer and Fitzpatrick, *Beyond Totalitarianism*, 284–285; Michael Dutton, "Toward a Government of Contract: Policing in the Era of Reform," in Børge Bakken, ed., *Crime, Punishment, and Policing in China* (Lanham 2005) 211.

168. Ayling et al., *Lengthening the Arm of the Law*, chap. 4; Marc Santora and Stephanie Clifford, "Three Brooklyn Men Accused of Plot to Aid ISIS' Fight," *New York Times*, 25 February 2015.

169. Kaytal, "Conspiracy Theory," 1312.

170. Gary Lease, "Denunciation as a Tool of Ecclesiastical Control: The Case of Roman Catholic Modernism," *Journal of Modern History* 68, 4 (1996) 819–820.

171. MacDowell, *Law in Classical Athens*, 63; Esmein, *History of Continental Criminal Procedure*, 122.

172. Lawrence Stone, "Interpersonal Violence in English Society 1300–1980," *Past and Present* 101 (1983) 31.

173. Andrea Zorzi, "The Judicial System in Florence in the Fourteenth and Fifteenth Centuries," in Dean and Lowe, *Crime, Society, and the Law in Renaissance Italy*, 44; Monas, *Third Section*, 35.

174. Colin Lucas, "The Theory and Practice of Denunciation in the French Revolution," *Jounal of Modern History* 68, 4 (1996) 774–775.

175. Brackett, *Criminal Justice and Crime in Late Renaissance Florence*, 30–31, 26, 36.

176. Beattie, *Crime and the Courts*, 50–51, 134; Bellamy, *Tudor Law of Treason*, 125; Hughes, *Governmental Habit Redux*, 42.

177. Williams, *Tudor Regime*, 150; Beattie, *Policing and Punishment*, 147, 231, 379.

178. Beattie, *Crime and the Courts*, 369; Wacquant, *Punishing the Poor*, 22; Ayling et al., *Lengthening the Arm of the Law*, 105–106.

179. Karen Freifeld and Edward Krudy, "BNP's Monstrous $9 Billion Fine Is Going toward ... New Office Carpets," *Business Insider*, 24 July 2014; David Benjamin Ross, "Civil Forfeiture: A Fiction That Offends Due Process," *Regent University Law Review* 13 (2000) 272–273.

180. Kraska and Kappeler, "Militarizing American Police," 9; Bayley, *Police for the Future*, 82; Kim, "Asset Forfeiture," 529; Barnet, "Legal Fiction and Forfeiture," 100.

181. Insider Trading and Securities Fraud Enforcement Act of 1988, Pub. L. 100-704, 19 November 1988, 102 Stat. 4679; Ayling et al., *Lengthening the Arm of the Law*, 112.

182. Jütte, *Strait Gate*, 64.

183. Dwyer et al., *Actual Innocence*, chap. 3.

184. Noah Clements, "Flipping a Coin: A Solution for the Inherent Unreliability of Eyewitness Identification Testimony," *Indiana Law Review* 40 (2007) 271; Henry F. Fradella, "Why Judges Should Admit Expert Testimony on the Unreliability of Eyewitness Testimony," *Federal Courts Law Review* 2 (2007) 3.

185. Smyth, *Cause of Death*, 19–20; Sung Tz'u, *The Washing Away of Wrongs*, trans. Brian E. McKnight (Ann Arbor 1981) 4, 62–63, 71, 132.

186. Mark Jackson, "Suspicious Infant Deaths: The Statute of 1624 and Medical Evidence at Coroners' Inquests," in Clark and Crawford, *Legal Medicine in History*, 75–81.

187. Frank, "Popular Justice," 259. Further evidence also dispelled the idea of floating lungs. Roth, "Homicide in Early Modern England," 39.

188. Spierenburg, *History of Murder*, 170. The first such case was in Paris in 1902. Martin, *Crime and Criminal Justice under the Third Republic*, 81.

189. Söderman and O'Connell, *Modern Criminal Investigation*, 122–123.

190. Smyth, *Cause of Death*, 18.

191. Cole, *Suspect Identities*, 88–90.

192. Footprints were used as evidence as early as the seventeenth century. Herrup, *Common Peace*, 74.

193. Söderman and O'Connell, *Modern Criminal Investigation*, 256; Dwyer et al., *Actual Innocence*, 45.

194. Emsley, *Crime, Police, and Penal Policy*, 182; Smyth, *Cause of Death*, 75.

195. Dwyer et al., *Actual Innocence*, 208–214.

196. D. H. Kaye, "Revisiting Dreyfus: A More Complete Account of a Trial by Mathematics," *Minnesota Law Review* 91 (2007) 829–830; Henry T. F. Rhodes, *Alphonse Bertillon* (London 1956) 174–175.

197. Dana Dryzal, "Blood Stain Pattern Analysis: Applications and Challenges," *D.U.Quark* 2, 2 (2018); Giovanni Acampora et al., "Bloodstain Pattern Analysis: A New Challenge for Computational Intelligence Community," in *Proceedings of the International Conference on Fuzzy Computation Theory and Applications* (2014); Vincent Denault et al., "The Analysis of Non-verbal Communication: The Dangers of Pseudoscience in Security and Justice Contexts," *Anuario de psicología jurídica* (2019); Vincent Denault and Louise Marie Jupe, "Justice at Risk! An Evaluation of a Pseudoscientific Analysis of a Witness' Nonverbal Behavior in the Courtroom," *Journal of Forensic Psychiatry & Psychology* 29, 2 (2017); Sophie J. Nightingale and Hany Farid, "Assessing the Reliability of Clothing-Based Forensic Identification," *Proceedings of the National Academy of Sciences* 117, 10 (2020) 5176.

198. Quoted in Dwyer et al., *Actual Innocence*, xviii.

199. William C. Thompson, "The Myth of Infallibility," in Sheldon Krimsky and Jeremy Gruber, eds., *Genetic Explanations: Sense and Nonsense* (Cambridge MA 2013) 230; Kimberly Cogdell Boies, "Misuse of DNA Evidence Is Not Always a Harmless Error: DNA Evidence, Prosecutorial Misconduct, and Wrongful Conviction," *Wesleyan Law Review* 17 (2011); Heather Murphy, "When a DNA Test Says

You're a Younger Man, Who Lives 5000 Miles Away," *New York Times*, 7 December 2019. Planting false evidence was a problem also with fingerprints. Cole, *Suspect Identities*, 278.

200. Tal Golan, *Laws of Men and Laws of Nature: The History of Scientific Expert Testimony in England and America* (Cambridge MA 2007) chap. 3.

201. Branding ended in France in 1832 or possibly, by some accounts, not until the 1930s; in Holland in 1854; and in China in 1905. Martin, *Crime and Criminal Justice under the Third Republic,* 80; Söderman and O'Connell, *Modern Criminal Investigation*, 68; Smyth, *Cause of Death,* 111.

202. Cole, *Suspect Identities*, 27–29.

203. Smyth, *Cause of Death,* 112–117; Emsley, *Crime, Police, and Penal Policy*, 187; Cole, *Suspect Identities*, chap. 2.

204. Pa̋ge Hinners et al., "Determining Fingerprint Age with Mass Spectrometry Imaging via Ozonolysis of Triacylglycerols," *Analytical Chemistry*, 3 January 2020.

205. Finnane, *Police and Government*, 80–82.

206. Michael Kirkpatrick, assistant director in charge, Criminal Justice Information Services Division, FBI, testimony before the US House of Representatives, Judiciary Committee, 30 March 2004, https://archives.fbi.gov/archives/news/testimony/fbi-fingerprint-program; Cole, *Suspect Identities*, 198. The claim that the FBI had 160 million fingerprints by the early 1970s seems fanciful. It is made in Walker, *Popular Justice*, 187, which takes it from Samuel Walker, *A Critical History of Police Reform: The Emergence of Professionalism* (Lexington 1977) 157–159, which gives no verifiable source. Smyth mentions 140 million in 1956 in *Cause of Death*, 143.

207. Miller, *Cops and Bobbies*, 119.

208. Laurent Lopez, "Policiers, gendarmes et signalement descriptif," *Crime, histoire et sociétés* 10, 1 (2006) 53–54, 65; Merriman, *Police Stories*, 120. The ancient Egyptians had developed something similar. Söderman and O'Connell, *Modern Criminal Investigation*, 68.

209. Wacquant, *Punishing the Poor*, 272; Anderson, *In Thrall to Political Change*, 401.

210. Edwin Chadwick, "Preventive Police," *London Review* 1 (1829) 252, 304–308.

211. Kelling and Coles, *Fixing Broken Windows*, 50–51.

212. Registration at hotels, strictly enforced in Europe, is more laxly regulated and often only at the local level in the United States, though the use of a credit card to ensure payment has largely erased the difference. Söderman and O'Connell, *Modern Criminal Investigation*, 13.

213. Davis, *Conflict and Control*, 107; John Torpey, *The Invention of the Passport: Surveillance, Citizenship, and the State*, 2nd ed. (Cambridge 2018).

214. Kevin D. Haggerty and Richard V. Ericson, "The Militarization of Policing in the Information Age," *Journal of Political and Military Sociology* 27 (1999) 240, 242.

215. Emsley, "Mother, What Did Policemen Do," 369–371; Reiss, "Police Organization," 84; Finnane, *Police and Government*, 101.

216. Thompson, "Myth of Infallibility," 248; Gates, *Our Biometric Future*, passim.

217. Patrick Radden Keefe, "Total Recall," *New Yorker*, 22 August 2016, 56; Paul Mozur, "Inside China's Dystopian Dreams," *New York Times*, 8 July 2018; https://www.bbc.com/news/world-asia-china-43751276?ref=gazelle.popsugar.com.

218. Durkheim, *Division of Labour*, 234; Gates, *Our Biometric Future*, 83–85.

219. Zedner, "Fixing the Future," 54.

220. "Advances in AI Are Used to Spot Signs of Sexuality," *Economist*, 9 September 2017; "Are Programs Better Than People at Predicting Reoffending?" *Economist*, 17 January 2018.

221. Alec Wilkinson, "Annals of Crime: The Serial-Killer Detector," *New Yorker*, 27 November 2017.

222. Jessica Saunders et al., "Predictions Put into Practice: A Quasi-experimental Evaluation of Chicago's Predictive Policing Pilot," *Journal of Experimental Criminology* 12 (2016) 350–352; Darwin Bond-Graham and Ali Winston, "All Tomorrow's Crimes," *SF Weekly*, 30 October 2013; Ali Winston, "Palantir Has Secretly Been Using New Orleans to Test Its Predictive Policing Technology," *Verge*, 27 February 2018.

223. Miller, *Bloodtaking*, 183.

224. Ruff, *Violence in Early Modern Europe*, 221.

225. Chadwick, "Preventive Police," 273.

226. *The Odyssey*, 21.5–7, 46–50; Matthew 16:19; Angela Cervi, "Keys and Locks," in *Encyclopedia of Ancient History*.

227. Liang, *Rise of Modern Police*, 119, 251.

228. Summerson, "Enforcement of the Statute of Winchester," 233.

229. Beattie, *Policing and Punishment*, 84, 215; Chadwick, "Preventive Police," 274, 285.

230. Quoted in Adler, "Perverse Law of Child Pornography," 271. Texas governor Rick Perry more recently got into hot water by suggesting that electric lights powered by fossil fuels helped cut sexual assault in Africa. "Rick Perry under Fire for Suggestion Fossil Fuels Can Reduce Sexual Assault," *Guardian*, 2 November 2017.

231. French penal code, 1810, art. 385; Eloise Moss, *Night Raiders: Burglary and the Making of Modern Urban Life in London, 1860–1968* (Oxford 2019) 5.

232. Moore, "Problem-Solving and Community Policing," 122, but see also Sherman "Attacking Crime," 190.

233. Ericson and Haggerty, *Policing the Risk Society*, 144–145; Nicolai Ouroussoff, "Uncle Sam, Visionary Builder?" *New York Times*, 19 September 2004. More generally, see Neal Kumar Kaytal, "Architecture as Crime Control," *Yale Law Journal* 111 (2002); Samia Henni, *Architecture of Counterrevolution: The French Army in Northern Algeria* (Zurich 2017).

234. Edwin Chadwick calls for the latter in "Preventive Police," 272.

235. Josh Barro, "Here's Why Stealing Cars Went Out of Fashion," *New York Times*, 12 August 2014.

236. Clifford D. Shearing and Phillip C. Stenning, "From the Panopticon to Disney World: The Development of Discipline," in Anthony N. Doob and Edward L. Greenspan, eds., *Perspectives in Criminal Law: Essays in Honour of John Ll. J. Edwards* (Aurora 1997).

237. Bodde and Morris, *Law in Imperial China*, 24; Dutton, *Policing and Punishment in China*, 24, 73, 123; Lewis, *Sanctioned Violence*, 61; Dutton, *Policing Chinese Politics*, 165–168.

238. Jonathan Drimmer, "When Man Hunts Man: The Rights and Duties of Bounty Hunters in the American Criminal Justice System," *Houston Law Review* 33 (1996) 744; Duker, "Right to Bail," 37; Wendy Davies, "People and Places in Dispute

in Ninth-Century Britanny," in Davies and Fouracre, *Settlement of Disputes in Early Medieval Europe*, 77.

239. Statute of Winchester, 1285, 13 Edw. I, c. 2; Weisser, *Crime and Punishment*, 92; Given, *Society and Homicide*, 9–10.

240. Donald V. Kurtz, "The Legitimation of the Aztec State," in Henri J. M. Claessen and Peter Skalnik, eds., *The Early State* (The Hague 1978) 184; Kollmann, *Crime and Punishment*, 71, 124.

241. Décret sur la police intérieure des communes de la République, 10 Vendémiaire an IV (2 October 1795), https://www.1789-1815.com/loi_10_vend_an4.htm; Frank Biess, *Homecomings: Returning POWs and the Legacies of Defeat in Postwar Germany* (Princeton 2006) 35; Hazard and Stern, "'Exterior Treason,'" 90.

242. Ingraham, *Political Crime in Europe*, 304; Dershowitz, "Law of Dangerousness," 28.

243. Criminal Code of Canada, sect. 810; Jian Ghomeshi, "Reflections from a Hashtag," *New York Review of Books*, 11 October 2018.

244. Allan Y. Jiao, "Crime Control through Saturated Community Policing," *International Journal of Comparative and Applied Criminal Justice* 21, 1 (1997) 80.

245. Chamberlin, "Bounty Hunters," 1181; Emily Michael Stout, "Bounty Hunters as Evidence Gatherers," *University of Cincinnati Law Review* 65 (1997) 670.

246. Lorton, "Treatment of Criminals," 40–45; Bartlett, *Trial by Fire and Water*, 50; Hindle, "Keeping of the Public Peace," 218.

247. Blackstone, *Commentaries on the Laws of England*, 4:250–253.

248. French penal code, 1810, art. 44; O'Brien, *Promise of Punishment*, 229.

249. Code des délits et des peines, 25 October 1795, art. 19.

250. Adam Smith, *An Inquiry into the Nature and Causes of the Wealth of Nations* (Edinburgh 1814) bk. 3, 213; Durkheim, *Division of Labour*, 233.

251. Manning, "Information Technologies," 355; Bayley, *Police for the Future*, 26; Cohen, *Visions of Social Control*, 67–68.

252. Beattie, *Policing and Punishment*, 120–121.

253. This is the very limited concept meant when it is said that establishing the London Police in 1829 was the triumph of the preventive idea in policing. Emsley, *Policing*, 119; Miller, *Cops and Bobbies*, 2.

254. Quoted in Philips, "New Engine of Power," 188.

255. Ashworth and Zedner, *Preventive Justice*, 34; Emsley, *Policing*, 94.

256. Monkkonen, *Police in Urban America*, 40; Lane, "Urban Police and Crime," 12; Sheryl Gay Stolberg, "Does a Uniform Keep Officers in Line? The Baltimore Chief Thinks So," *New York Times*, 14 April 2017.

257. Reiner, *Politics of the Police*, 70; Monkkonen, *Police in Urban America*, 39; Miller, *Cops and Bobbies*, 33.

258. Williams, *Police of Paris*, 221; Emsley, *Policing*, 58; Fosdick, *European Police Systems*, 239.

259. Richardson, *New York Police*, 64–66.

260. Carol S. Steiker, "The Limits of the Preventive State," *Journal of Criminal Law and Criminology* 88, 3 (1998) 774.

261. Kelling and Coles, *Fixing Broken Windows*, chap. 3, 5, 162–163; Bayley, *Patterns of Policing*, 108–109.

262. Mawby, *Comparative Policing Issues*, 115; David H. Bayley, *Forces of Order: Policing Modern Japan* (Berkeley 1991) chap. 2.

263. Bracey, "Policing the People's Republic," 132; Dutton, *Policing Chinese Politics*, 259; "China Wants Eyes and Ears on Every Street," *Economist*, 28 June 2018.

264. Steiker, "Limits of the Preventive State," 803.

265. This future without personal biological secrets is anticipated in the film *Gattica* (1997). See also "People Leave Molecular Wakes That May Give Away Their Secrets," *Economist*, 13 February 2020.

266. Moore, "Problem-Solving and Community Policing," 112.

267. Sherman, "Attacking Crime," 184, 172.

268. Langbein, *Prosecuting Crime*, 145; Hall, "Criminal Attempt," 793; Ashworth and Zedner, *Preventive Justice*, 30; Blackstone, *Commentaries on the Laws of England*, 4: chap. 13; Graeme Newman, *The Punishment Response*, 2nd ed. (New Brunswick 2008) 98.

269. Williams, *Tudor Regime*, 278, 398; Braddick, *State Formation*, 150, 164; Wiener, *Reconstructing the Criminal*, 150; Philips, "New Engine of Power," 168; French penal code, 1810, art. 269–271; Davis, *Conflict and Control*, 219.

270. Vagrancy Act 1824, 5 George IV, c. 83; Metropolitan Police Act 1829, 10 George IV, c. 44, s. 7.

271. Gatrell, "Crime, Authority and the Policeman-State," 277–278; Liang, *Rise of Modern Police*, 251.

272. Dubber, "Policing Possession," 894; Luna, "Principled Enforcement," 328–329; Poulos, "Chicago's Ban on Gang Loitering," 398.

273. Street Terrorism Enforcement and Prevention Act, 1988, California; Strosnider, "Anti-gang Ordinances," 109.

274. *Illinois v. Wardlow*, 528 US 119 (2000); Dubber, "Policing Possession," 882; Ashworth and Zedner, *Preventive Justice*, 52–54.

275. Harcourt, *Against Prediction*, 9; Creegan, "National Security Crime," 403; McSherry, "Expanding the Boundaries of Inchoate Crimes," 158; Ashworth and Zedner, *Preventive Justice*, 100.

276. Harcourt, *Against Prediction*, 2, 103; Baumgartner et al., *Suspect Citizens*, 8.

277. Stephen A. Toth, *Beyond Papillon: The French Overseas Penal Colonies, 1854–1952* (Lincoln 2006) 23–24; Harcourt, "Shaping of Chance," 117; Demleitner, "Abusing State Power," 1651.

278. Weiner, *Reconstructing the Criminal*, 342; O'Brien, *Promise of Punishment*, 289.

279. Habitual Criminals Act, 1869, 32 & 33 Vict., c.. 99.

280. O'Brien, *Promise of Punishment*, 265; Davis, *Conflict and Control*, 223.

281. Walker, *Popular Justice*, 99; McConville, "Victorian Prison," 156; Ashworth and Zedner, *Preventive Justice*, 45; Cole, *Suspect Identities*, 217.

282. Robinson, "Punishing Dangerousness," 1435–1436; Harcourt, *Against Prediction*, 92. Similar legislation passed in Australia. Roberts et al., *Penal Populism*, 55–56.

283. Gottfredson and Hirschi, "True Value of Lambda," 217.

284. *Robinson v. California*, 370 US 660, 667.

285. Benno Weisberg, "When Punishing Innocent Conduct Violates the Eighth Amendment: Applying the 'Robinson' Doctrine to Homelessness and Other Contextual 'Crimes,'" *Journal of Criminal Law and Criminology* 96, 1 (1973) 332–344. Yet

most courts have not held that homelessness is a status—that is, an involuntary state—but rather that it is a condition and therefore not protected. Kelling and Coles, *Fixing Broken Windows*, 54–55.

286. Andrew Guthrie Ferguson, *The Rise of Big Data Policing: Surveillance, Race, and the Future of Law Enforcement* (New York 2017) chap 3; John Eligon and Timothy Williams, "Police Program Aims to Pinpoint Those Most Likely to Commit Crimes," *New York Times*, 24 September 2015.

287. Garen J. Wintemute et al., "Extreme Risk Protection Orders Intended to Prevent Mass Shootings," *Annals of Internal Medicine* 171, 9 (2019) 655; Hannah S. Szlyk et al., "Firearm Suicide as a Human Rights Priority for Prevention," *Washington University Journal of Law and Policy* 60 (2019) 143; Kraska and Kappeler, "Militarizing American Police," 7.

288. Ashworth and Zedner, *Preventive Justice*, 15–16; Dubber, "Policing Possession," passim.

289. Every other thing involved in the production or sale of illegal drugs is also confiscated. 21 U.S. Code §881(a).

290. Susan R. Klein, "Redrawing the Criminal–Civil Boundary," *Buffalo Criminal Law Review* 2 (1999) 699, 701; Kim, "Asset Forfeiture," 529; Ross, "Civil Forfeiture," 260–262.

291. Edward P. Richards, "The Jurisprudence of Prevention: The Right of Societal Self-Defense against Dangerous Individuals," *Hastings Constitutional Law Quarterly* 16 (1989) 330–331, 339.

292. Leviticus 15:1–14.

293. Baldwin, *Contagion and the State*, chap. 5; Peter Baldwin, *Disease and Democracy: The Industrialized World Faces AIDS* (Berkeley 2005) 53–58.

294. Wendy E. Parmet, "Legal Power and Legal Rights: Isolation and Quarantine in the Case of Drug-Resistant Tuberculosis," *New England Journal of Medicine* 357 (2007) 434; Lawrence O. Gostin, "Tuberculosis and the Power of the State," *University of Chicago Law School Roundtable* 219 (1995) 270; Nigel Walker, "Dangerous People," *International Journal of Law and Psychiatry* 1 (1978) 39.

295. Marie Nissen, "Her er de otte hovedpunkter i den hastelov, regeringen vil have vedtaget i dag," *Politiken*, 12 March 2020; Sofie Bak Thorup, "Ny hastelov giver mulighed for at tvangsbehandle: Lægeforeningen bakker op," *Politiken*, 12 March 2020.

296. Malcolm M. Feeley, "Actuarial Justice and the Modern State," in Gerben Bruinsma et al., eds., *Punishment, Places, and Perpetrators* (Uffculme 2004) 62.

297. Janus, *Failure to Protect*, 97–103; Harcourt, "Shaping of Chance," 106; Vitale, *End of Policing*, 92–93.

298. John N. Mitchell, "Bail Reform and the Constitutionality of Pretrial Detention," *Virginia Law Review* 55, 7 (1969) 1231; George W. Pugh, "Administration of Criminal Justice in France," *Louisiana Law Review* 23, 1 (1962) 21; Cavadino and Dignan, *Penal Systems*, 178; Foote, "Coming Constitutional Crisis," 963.

299. Cavadino and Dignan, *Penal Systems*, 145; Bayley, *Forces of Order*, 144.

300. Ashworth and Zedner, *Preventive Justice*, 65–66; Shadd Maruna et al., "Putting a Price on Prisoner Release: The History of Bail and a Possible Future of Parole," *Punishment and Society* 14, 3 (2012) 330; Hans Zeisel, "Bail Revisited," *American Bar Foundation Research Journal* 4 (1979) 774; Thomas H. Cohen and Brian A. Reaves, *Pretrial Release*

of Felony Defendants in State Courts, Bureau of Justice Statistics, Special Report, NCJ 214994 (November 2007), https://www.bjs.gov/content/pub/pdf/prfdsc.pdf.

301. Dershowitz, "Law of Dangerousness," 30; Barbara Gottlieb, "The Pretrial Processing of 'Dangerous' Defendants," National Institute of Justice, January 1984, reprinted in *Report on Bail Reform Act of 1984*, H.R. Rep. No. 98-1121 (1984); Anthea Hucklesby, "Police Bail and the Use of Conditions," *Criminal Justice* 1, 4 (2001) 442.

302. Floud and Young, *Dangerousness*, 103–105, 107–109; Demleitner, "Abusing State Power," passim; Ashworth and Zedner, *Preventive Justice*, 16; Andrew von Hirsch, "Prediction of Criminal Conduct and Preventive Confinement of Convicted Persons," *Buffalo Law Review* 21 (1971–1972) 718. India, too, has preventive detention: Indian Constitution, art. 22.

303. Ashworth, "Social Control," 264.

304. Richards, "Jurisprudence of Prevention," 352–356; Jeslyn A. Miller, "Sex Offender Civil Commitment: The Treatment Paradox," *California Law Review* 98, 6 (2010) 2101. Civil commitment of the potentially dangerous without due-process protection was then reined back in the 1990s, however, requiring mental illness for detention. Tamara Rice Lave, "Controlling Sexually Violent Predators: Continued Incarceration at What Cost?," *New Criminal Law Review* 14, 2 (2011) 255–256.

305. Ashworth and Zedner, *Preventive Justice*, 3, 75, 79–81; Ashworth and Zedner, "Just Prevention," 299. There are even more of such preventive orders: Nonmolestation Orders, Exclusion from Licensed Premises Orders, Football Spectator Banning Orders, Travel Restriction Orders, Sexual Offences Prevention Orders, Foreign Travel Restriction Orders, Risk of Sexual Harm Orders, Drinking Banning Orders, Serious Crime Prevention Orders, Violent Offender Orders, Terrorism Prevention and Investigation Measures.

306. Ashworth, "Social Control," 266.

307. Stuart Macdonald, "A Suicidal Woman, Roaming Pigs, and a Noisy Trampolinist: Refining the ASBO's Definition of 'Anti-social Behaviour,'" *Modern Law Review* 69 (2006) 185–189, 197–198; Elizabeth Burney, "The ASBO and the Shift to Punishment," in Peter Squires, ed., *ASBO Nation* (Bristol 2008) 137; Kenan Malik, "Since When Was It a Police Job to Impose Sanctions on Drill Musicians?" *Guardian*, 9 February 2019.

308. Vrij et al., "Pitfalls and Opportunities," 110.

309. Janus, *Failure to Protect*, 5–6.

310. Hirsch, "Prediction of Criminal Conduct," 733–738; Saunders et al., "Prediction Put into Practice," 351.

311. Floud and Young, *Dangerousness*, 40–42.

312. Given, *Inquisition*, 84.

313. Finnane, *Police and Government*, 75; Allgemeines Landrecht für die Preußischen Staaten, pt. 2, title 20, §5; French penal code, 1810, art. 44–50.

314. Walker, *Popular Justice*, 95–96. On recent developments in parole, see Howard, *Unusually Cruel*, chap. 6.

315. Kohler-Hausmann, *Misdemeanorland*, 80; Ashworth and Zedner, *Preventive Justice*, 156–157.

316. Deuteronomy 22:23–26.

317. Brackett, *Criminal Justice and Crime in Late Renaissance Florence*, 67–68.

318. Gottschalk, *Caught*, 198–200; Yung, "Emerging Criminal War," 449.

319. Gottschalk, *Caught*, 201; Corey Rayburn Yung, "Sex Offender Exceptionalism and Preventive Detention," *Journal of Criminal Law and Criminology* 101, 3 (2011) passim; Miller, "Sex Offender Civil Commitment," 2101; Demleitner, "Abusing State Power," 1640.

320. *Kansas v. Hendricks*, 521 US 346 (1997); Harcourt, *Against Prediction*, 14.

321. Title III, §302, of the Adam Walsh Child Protection and Safety Act of 2006, Pub. L. 109-248, 120 Stat. 587, codified at 18 USC §4248; Yung, "Sex Offender Exceptionalism," 978–979; Klein, "Redrawing the Criminal–Civil Boundary," 685, 702–703.

322. Michaela Pobořilová, "Virtual Child Pornography," *Masaryk University Journal of Law and Technology* 5, 2 (2011) 252.

323. *Our Sexual Future with Robots* (2017) 27–28, https://responsible-robotics-myxf6pn3xr.netdna-ssl.com/wp-content/uploads/2017/11/FRR-Consultation-Report-Our-Sexual-Future-with-robots-1-1.pdf. The literature on automaton sex is growing: see, for example, Kate Devlin, *Turned On: Science, Sex, and Robots* (London 2018); David Levy, *Love and Sex with Robots: The Evolution of Human–Robot Relationships* (New York 2008); John Danaher and Neil McArthur, eds., *Robot Sex: Social and Ethical Implications* (Cambridge MA 2018); Kathleen Richardson, *Sex Robots: The End of Love* (Cambridge 2019).

324. Gabrielle Russell, "Pedophiles in Wonderland: Censoring the Sinful in Cyberspace," *Journal of Criminal Law and Criminology* 98, 4 (2008) 1468–1469, 1488.

325. PROTECT Act of 2003, Pub. L. 108-21 (30 April 2003), 117 Stat. 678, §501 Findings, 9–15; Mains, "Virtual Child Pornography," 811–812; Paula Bird, "Virtual Child Pornography Laws and the Constraints Imposed by the First Amendment," *Barry Law Review* 16 (2011) 165–166; Sofya Peysakhovich, "Virtual Child Pornography: Why American and British Laws Are at Odds with Each Other," *Albany Law Journal of Science and Technology* 14 (2004) 815.

326. Adler, "Perverse Law of Child Pornography," 216.

327. On whether possessing child pornography is preventive of or precipitating toward greater harm, the literature is ambivalent. See Drew A. Kingston et al., "The Importance of Individual Differences in Pornography Use," *Journal of Sex Research* 46 (2009).

328. Peysakhovich, "Virtual Child Pornography," 805–806, 819; Mains, "Virtual Child Pornography," 814.

329. Adler, "Perverse Law of Child Pornography," 254–256, 259–260, 262–263.

330. Criminal Justice and Public Order Act 1994, c. 33, sect. 84; Richard Stone, "Extending the Labyrinth: Part VII of the Criminal Justice and Public Order Act 1994," *Modern Law Review* 58, 3 (1995) 391–392.

331. Peysakhovich, "Virtual Child Pornography," 821. Dutch law prosecutes virtual child porn. Pobořilová, "Virtual Child Pornography," 251. Even in Japan, where laws on child pornography are lax, Tokyo sought to pass a municipal law that covers "nonexistent minors" as well. *Economist*, 20 March 2010.

332. Child Pornography Prevention Act, 1996; Mains, "Virtual Child Pornography," 821.

333. PROTECT Act, 2003, 18 USC §1466A.

334. 18 USC §1466A(c).

335. 18 USC §2256(8)(B).

336. 18 USC §2256(11).

337. 18 USC §2252(c)(1)(2).

338. *US v. Kutzner*, Case No. CR-10–0252-S-EJL, Sentencing Memorandum, 2010; Sean Michael Robinson, "Criminal Contexts: *The Simpsons* 'Child' Pornography Case and Its Implications," *Comics Journal*, 28 January 2011, http://classic.tcj.com/news/sean-michael-robinson-criminal-contexts-the-simpsons-child-pornography-case-and-its-implications/; Keisha April, "Cartoons Aren't Real People Too: Does the Regulation of Virtual Child Pornography Violate the First Amendment and Criminalize Subversive Thought?," *Cardozo Journal of Law and Gender* 19 (2012) 259–262.

339. *United States v. Whorley*, 550 F.3d 326, 331 (4th Cir. 2008), discussed in April, "Cartoons Aren't Real People," 253–256.

Conclusion

1. These are the themes masterfully identified and analyzed by Garland, Wacquant, and Gottschalk, among others.

2. Patrick Sharkey, *Uneasy Peace: The Great Crime Decline, the Renewal of City Life, and the Next War on Crime* (New York 2018); John J. Donohue, "Understanding the Time Path of Crime," *Journal of Criminal Law and Criminology* 88, 4 (1998) 1427; Brian Levin and Sara-Ellen Amster, "Making Hate History: Hate Crime and Policing in America's Most Diverse City," *American Behavioral Scientist* 51, 2 (2007) 320.

3. Dubber, "Theories of Crime," 699–700; Michael Tonry, "Why Aren't German Penal Policies Harsher and Imprisonment Rates Higher?" *German Law Journal* 5, 10 (2004) 1187–1188. Dubber, however, also sees neoretributionism as common to all liberal democracies. *Dual Penal State*, 3–4.

4. Cavadino and Dignan, *Penal Systems*, 33–34; Joachim T. Savelsberg, "Knowledge, Domination, and Criminal Punishment," *American Journal of Sociology* 99, 4 (1994) 916. Total years of imprisonment sentenced increased fourfold for some crimes in Sweden in the late twentieth century, however. Von Hofer and Tham, "Punishment in Sweden," 35–36.

5. This is a leitmotif of Didier Fassin, *Prison Worlds: An Ethnography of the Carceral Condition* (Cambridge 2017) 21 and passim.

6. Miethe and Lu, *Punishment*, 204.

7. Simon, *Poor Discipline*, 57; William Alfred Morris, *The Frankpledge System* (London 1910) 2.

8. Egon Bittner, *The Functions of the Police in Modern Society* (Chevy Chase 1970) 15.

9. Friedrich Nietzsche, *On the Genealogy of Morality*, ed. Keith Ansell-Pearson, trans. Carol Diethe (Cambridge 2006) 47.

10. Langbein, *Torture*, 45–49.

11. Carlo Cattaneo (1840), quoted in Davis, *Conflict and Control*, 153; Charles Dickens, quoted in Ignatieff, *Just Measure of Pain*, 197.

12. Herbert Marcuse, "Repressive Tolerance," in Robert Paul Wolff et al., *A Critique of Pure Tolerance* (Boston 1965) 84–85.

13. *Pace* Dennis Smith, "The Civilizing Process and The History of Sexuality: Comparing Norbert Elias and Michel Foucault," *Theory and Society* 28 (1999) 79–80. And see also Spierenburg, *Violence and Punishment,* 86–90.

14. Michel Foucault, "Technologies of the Self," in *Technologies of the Self: A Seminar with Michel Foucault,* ed. Luther H. Martin et al. (Amherst 1988) 19, 27.

15. Michel Foucault, "The Concern for Truth," in *Foucault Live (Interviews, 1966–84),* ed. Sylvère Lotringer (New York 1989) 296.

16. Bob Jessop, *The State* (Cambridge 2016) 166–167.

17. Peter L. Bernstein, *Against the Gods: The Remarkable Story of Risk* (New York 1996).

18. Abram de Swaan, *In Care of the State* (New York 1988) 164; François Ewald, "Insurance and Risk," in Graham Burchell et al., eds., *The Foucault Effect* (Chicago 1991) 207.

19. James C. Scott, *Seeing Like a State: How Certain Schemes to Improve the Human Condition Have Failed* (New Haven 1998); David L. Hoffmann, *Cultivating the Masses: Modern State Practices and Soviet Socialism, 1914–1939* (Ithaca 2011); David L. Hoffmann, *Stalinist Values: The Cultural Norms of Soviet Modernity, 1917–1941* (Ithaca 2003); Rainer Zitelmann, *Hitler: The Policies of Seduction* (London 2000).

20. Nikolas Rose, "Governing 'Advanced' Liberal Democracies," in Andrew Barry et al., eds., *Foucault and Political Reason: Liberalism, Neo-liberalism, and Rationalities of Government* (Chicago 1996) 58.

21. This is the theme of Nathan Stoltzfus, *Hitler's Compromises: Coercion and Consensus in Nazi Germany* (New Haven 2016).

22. Christian Gerlach and Nicolas Werth, "State Violence—Violent Societies," in Geyer and Fitzpatrick, *Beyond Totalitarianism,* 139–151.

23. Dubber, *Dual Penal State,* 108–109.

24. Thomas Lemke, "An Indigestible Meal? Foucault, Governmentality, and State Theory," *Distinktion* 15 (2007).

25. This is a theme of Joseph Henrich, *The Secret of Our Success: How Culture Is Driving Human Evolution, Domesticating Our Species, and Making Us Smarter* (Princeton 2017).

26. Elman R. Service, *Origins of the State and Civilization* (New York 1975) chap. 3.

27. Maine, *Ancient Law,* 75–78; Henry Sumner Maine, *Lectures on the Early History of Institutions,* 7th ed. (London 1914) 70.

28. Lowie, *Origin of the State,* 5; Henrich, *Secret of Our Success,* 155–156.

29. Norman Yoffee, *Myths of the Archaic State* (Cambridge 2005) 23–27; Timothy Earle, *How Chiefs Come to Power: The Political Economy in Prehistory* (Stanford 1997) 14; Robert L. Carneiro, "The Chiefdom: Precursor of the State," in Jones and Kautz, *Transition to Statehood in the New World,* 37–38.

30. Kirk Endicott, "Peaceful Foragers: The Significance of the Batek and Moriori for the Question of Innate Human Violence," in Douglas P. Fry, ed., *War, Peace, and Human Nature* (Oxford 2013) 246–247; Peter M. Gardner, "South Indian Foragers' Conflict Management in Comparative Perspective," in Fry, *War, Peace, and Human Nature,* 301–303.

31. Jean Briggs, *Never in Anger: Portrait of an Eskimo Family* (Cambridge MA 1970) 256–261; Morten H. Fried, *The Evolution of Political Society* (New York 1967) 12–13; Christopher Boehm, "The Biocultural Evolution of Conflict Resolution between Groups," in Fry, *War, Peace, and Human Nature,* 321; Boehm, *Moral Origins,* 85–86.

32. Patricia Crone, *Pre-industrial Societies: Anatomy of the Pre-modern World* (Oxford 2003) 51.

33. William Seagle, "Primitive Law and Professor Malinowski," *American Anthropologist* 39 (1937) 282–285.

34. Bronislaw Malinowski, *Custom and Crime in Savage Society* (London 1926) 14, 30–31, 54.

35. Steven J. Garfinkle, "Was the Ur III State Bureaucratic?," in Steven J. Garfinkle and J. Cale Johnson, eds., *The Growth of an Early State in Mesopotamia: Studies in Ur III Administration* (Madrid 2008) 56–58. But even this is challenged for the Assyrian state. See Nicholas Postgate, *Bronze Age Bureaucracy: Writing and the Practice of Government in Assyria* (Cambridge 2013) 2, 331–332.

36. Li Feng, *Bureaucracy and the State in Early China: Governing the Western Zhou* (Cambridge 2008) chap. 5; Li, *Early China*, 147–149.

37. Karl A. Wittfogel, *Oriental Despotism* (New Haven 1957); James C. Scott, *Against the Grain: A Deep History of the Earliest States* (New Haven 2017).

38. The willingness of civil society to play along with what the regime wanted has been a theme of recent histories of both Nazi Germany and the Soviet Union, as has been its opposing pendant, the mounting of resistance. For similar themes in China, see Børge Bakken, *The Exemplary Society: Human Improvement, Social Control, and the Dangers of Modernity in China* (Oxford 2000) 2.

39. Roland H. Bainton, "The Left Wing of the Reformation," *Journal of Religion* 21, 2 (1941) 133. On Kiryas Joel, see David Myers and Nomi Stolzenberg, *American Shtetl* (Princeton forthcoming).

40. Rudyard Kipling's story "Thrown Away" in *Plain Tales from the Hills* has an example.

41. William A. Robson, *Civilization and the Growth of Law* (London 1935) 75.

42. Malinowski, *Custom and Crime*, 117.

43. Richard Wrangham, *The Goodness Paradox: The Strange Relationship between Virtue and Violence in Human Evolution* (New York 2019) 20 and passim; Henrich, *Secret of Our Success*, chap. 11.

44. Johan Grolle, "Those Who Obeyed the Rules Were Favored by Evolution," *Spiegel*, 22 March 2019.

45. John M. Hobson, *The Wealth of States: A Comparative Sociology of International Economic and Political Change* (Cambridge 1997) 10–15; Margaret Levi, *Of Rule and Revenue* (Berkeley 1988) 124; Kotsonis, "Taxes and the Two Faces of the State," 233; Bittner, *Functions of the Police*, 18.

46. Elias's belief that the process took place only in early modern Europe has been one of the most serious criticisms leveled against him, though still sparing his basic insight: see Hans Peter Duerr, *Der Mythos vom Zivilisationsprozeß*, 5 vols. (Frankfurt 1988–2002); Jon Ploug Jørgensen, "Taming of the Aristoi: An Ancient Greek Civilizing Process?" *History of the Human Sciences* 27, 3 (2014).

47. Bernal Díaz, *The Conquest of New Spain*, trans. J. M. Cohen (London 1963) 233. However, during ritual dances the Aztecs simply parted the feathers of their loincloths to urinate in place. Miguel Leon-Portilla, ed., *The Broken Spears: The Aztec Account of the Conquest of Mexico*, exp. ed. (Boston 1992) 73.

48. Peter N. Stearns, *Battleground of Desire: The Struggle for Self-Control in Modern America* (New York 1999) 14; Anderson, *In Thrall to Political Change*, 152.

49. Marc Linder and Ingrid Nygaard, *Void Where Prohibited: Rest Breaks and the Right to Urinate on Company Time* (Ithaca 1998).

50. Kerstin Decker, "Das Töpfchen und der Hass," *Tagesspiegel*, 5 May 1999; Kerstin Decker, "Das Töpfchen und das Fremde," in Lothar Probst, ed., *Differenz in der Einheit* (Berlin 1999).

51. Katie Engelhart, "The Powerful History of Potty Training," *Atlantic*, 20 June 2014.

52. M. V. Hughes, *A London Family, 1870–1900* (Oxford 1991) 438–439.

53. Allan Mitchell, *The Divided Path: The German Influence on Social Reform in France after 1870* (Chapel Hill 1991) 270–271; Allan Mitchell, "Obsessive Questions and Faint Answers: The French Response to Tuberculosis in the Belle Epoque," *Bulletin of the History of Medicine* 62, 2 (1988) 223–225; Samuel K. Cohn Jr., *Epidemics: Hate and Compassion from the Plague of Athens to AIDS* (Oxford 2018) 435.

54. Peter Ward, *The Clean Body* (Montreal 2019); Jean-Pierre Goubert, *The Conquest of Water: The Advent of Health in the Industrial Age* (Cambridge 1989) chaps. 2–4 and 9; Georges Vigarello, *Concepts of Cleanliness: Changing Attitudes in France since the Middle Ages* (Cambridge 1988) 173–174, 224.

55. Spierenburg, *Violence and Punishment*, 134–135; Corinne Treitel, *Eating Nature in Modern Germany: Food, Agriculture, and Environment c. 1870 to 2000* (Cambridge 2017) 75; Marketline Industry Profile, *Global Oral Hygiene* (February 2019) 7.

56. Anne Glenconner, *Lady in Waiting: My Extraordinary Life in the Shadow of the Crown* (London 2019) 162.

57. Kinya Tsuruta, "Japanese Perceptions of Westerners in Modern Fiction," in Keizo Nagatani and David W. Edgington, eds., *Japan and the West: The Perception Gap* (Aldershot 1998) 51–52; George A. DeVos and Hiroshi Wagatsuma, "Cultural Identity and Minority Status in Japan," in Lola Romanucci-Ross et al., eds., *Ethnic Identity*, 4th ed. (Lanham 2006) 123. More generally, see B. R. Myers, *The Cleanest Race: How North Koreans See Themselves and Why It Matters* (Brooklyn 2010).

58. Bruno Bettelheim, *Children of the Dream: Communal Child-Rearing and Its Implications for Society* (London 1971) 36–37, 141–143.

59. Sandra Kahn and Paul R. Ehrlich, *Jaws: The Story of a Hidden Epidemic* (Stanford 2018). And this from the savant who alerted us to the perils of overpopulation!

60. Reginald G. Smart, "Is the Post-war Drinking Binge Ending? Cross-National Trends in per Capita Alcohol Consumption," *British Journal of Addiction* (1989) 746; Jussi Simpura and Thomas Karlsson, "Trends in Drinking Patterns among Adult Population in 15 European Countries, 1950 to 2000," *Nordisk Akohol- & Narkotikatidskrift* 18 (2001) 33, 37.

61. OECD, International Transport Forum, *Road Safety Annual Report 2018*, 54.

62. James Miller, *The Passion of Michel Foucault* (New York 1993) 259–262.

63. John Rechy, *The Sexual Outlaw* (New York 1977) 31.

64. Baldwin, *Disease and Democracy*, chap. 8; Peter Baldwin, "Can There Be a Democratic Public Health? Fighting AIDS in the Industrialized World," in Susan Gross Solomon et al. eds., *Shifting Boundaries of Public Health* (Rochester 2008) 39–40.

65. Roland Piana, "Dying without Morphine," *New York Times*, 30 September 2014. In Senegal, the average patient who needs morphine gets 13 milligrams of it a year, compared with 55,704 milligrams in America. "Of Puritans and Pain," *Economist*, 31 January 2019.

66. Surveying the literature to disagree, see R. Brian Ferguson, "Pinker's List: Exaggerating Prehistoric War Mortality," in Fry, *War, Peace, and Human Nature,* 113–114.

67. Curtis W. Marean, "An Evolutionary Anthropological Perspective on Modern Human Origins," *Annual Review of Anthropology* 44 (2015) 538–539; Azar Gat, "Social Organization, Group Conflict, and the Demise of the Neanderthals," *Mankind Quarterly* 39, 4 (1999) 443.

68. Jonathan Haas and Matthew Piscitelli, "The Prehistory of Warfare," in Fry, *War, Peace, and Human Nature,* 176–178.

69. Robert L. Kelly, "From the Peaceful to the Warlike: Ethnographic and Archaeological Insights into Hunter–Gatherer Warfare and Homicide," in Fry, *War, Peace, and Human Nature,* 156; Mark N. Cohen, "The Ecological Basis of New World State Formation," in Jones and Kautz, *Transition to Statehood in the New World,* 111.

70. Ferguson, "Pinker's List," 121–122; R. Brian Ferguson, "The Prehistory of War and Peace in Europe and the Near East," in Fry, *War, Peace, and Human Nature,* 201–202.

71. Scott, *Against the Grain,* 46, 117.

72. Robert L. Carneiro, "Political Expansion as an Expression of the Principle of Competitive Exclusion," in Ronald Cohen and Elman R. Service, eds., *Origins of the State* (Philadelphia 1978) 205–210.

73. Pinker, *Better Angels of Our Nature,* 47–56.

74. John G. Rule, "Wrecking and Coastal Plunder," in Hay et al., eds., *Albion's Fatal Tree,* 174–175; Sharpe, *Fiery and Furious People,* 14, 34; Allan Silver, "The Demand for Order in Civil Society," in David J. Bordua, ed., *The Police* (New York 1967) 17–19.

75. Gordon, *Controlling the State,* 198; Tabatha Abu El-Haj, "All Assemble: Order and Disorder in Law, Politics, and Culture," *University of Pennsylvania Journal of Constitutional Law* 16 (2014) 952, 961.

76. Miller, *Cops and Bobbies,* 109.

77. Robert W. Malcolmson, *Popular Recreations in English Society 1700–1850* (Cambridge 1973) 95–96; Robert D. Storch, "The Problem of Working-Class Leisure: Some Roots of Middle-Class Moral Reform in the Industrial North, 1823–50," in A. P. Donajgrodzki, ed., *Social Control in Nineteenth Century Britain* (London 1977) 146–149.

78. Schneider, "Imprisonment in Pre-classical and Classical Islamic Law," 164; Philip S. Gorski, *The Disciplinary Revolution: Calvinism and the Rise of the State in Early Modern Europe* (Chicago 2003) 79–113; Michel Foucault, "Governmentality," in Burchell et al., *Foucault Effect,* 91–92; Gerhard Oestreich, *Neo-Stoicism and the Early Modern State* (Cambridge 1982) 155–165.

79. Gregory Clark, *The Son Also Rises: Surnames and the History of Social Mobility* (Princeton 2015).

80. Giovanna Procacci, "Social Economy and the Government of Poverty," in Burchell et al., *Foucault Effect,* 160–162.

81. Alison Wolf, *The XX Factor: How the Rise of Working Women Has Created a Far Less Equal World* (New York 2013).

82. Nikolas Rose, *Powers of Freedom* (Cambridge 1999) 61–78.

83. Morris Janowitz, "Sociological Theory and Social Control," *American Journal of Sociology* 81, 1 (1975) 83–85; David J. Rothman, "Social Control: The Uses and Abuses of the Concept in the History of Incarceration," in Cohen and Scull, *Social Control and the State,* 107–108.

84. Roscoe Pound, *Social Control through Law* (New Haven 1942) 18.

85. Marcuse, "Repressive Tolerance," 90, 110.

86. John A. Mayer, "Notes towards a Working Definition of Social Control in Historical Analysis," in Cohen and Scull, *Social Control and the State*, 19.

87. Margaret E. DeLacy, "Grinding Men Good? Lancashire's Prisons at Mid-century," in Victor Bailey, ed., *Policing and Punishment in Nineteenth Century Britain* (London 1981) 184–189.

88. David E. Rothman, *The Discovery of the Asylum: Social Order and Disorder in the New Republic* (Boston 1971); Erving Goffman, *Asylums: Essays on the Social Situation of Mental Patients and Other Inmates* (New York 1961).

89. Bernard E. Harcourt, "Should We Aggregate Mental Hospitalization and Prison Population Rates in Empirical Research on the Relationship between Incarceration and Crime, Unemployment, Poverty, and Other Social Indicators?" *Chicago Unbound* (2006). Similar figures for France are given in Fassin, *Prison Worlds*, 289–290.

90. Michel Foucault, *Power/Knowledge* (New York 1980) 156.

91. Donald Black, *The Behavior of Law* (New York 1976) 107.

92. Braithwaite, *Crime, Shame, and Reintegration*, 86, 171.

93. Michael Shalev, "Israel's Domestic Policy Regime," in Francis G. Castles, ed., *The Comparative History of Public Policy* (Cambridge 2002) 100–116, 139–140; Jill Quadagno, *The Color of Welfare: How Racism Undermined the War on Poverty* (New York 1994) 3–31, 61–87; Will Kymlicka, "The Multicultural Welfare State?" in Peter A. Hall and Michele Lamont, eds., *Successful Societies* (Cambridge 2009) 226–253; Robert Putnam, "E Pluribus Unum: Diversity and Community in the 21C," *Scandinavian Political Studies* 30, 2 (2007) 137–166.

94. This is the logic of the argument in Baldwin, "Return of the Coercive State," and David Garland, "Penal Controls and Social Controls: Toward a Theory of American Penal Exceptionalism," *Punishment and Society* 21, 1 (2019). However, Garland's supposition that welfare policies bolster the traditional institutions of socialization, such as the family, is debatable, and precisely the opposite is often claimed for them—with daycare undermining family control, old age homes hollowing out family solidarity, and the like.

95. Peter Baldwin, "State and Citizenship in the Age of Globalisation," in Peter Koslowski and Andreas Føllesdal, eds., *Restructuring the Welfare State* (Berlin 1997) 113–117; Peter Baldwin, "Riding the Subways of *Gemeinschaft*," *Acta Sociologica* 41, 4 (1998) 378–379.

96. Italy now has measles vaccination rates lower than Ghana. "The Campaign against Vaccination," *Economist* 19 January 2019; "How to Inoculate against Anti-vaxxers," *New York Times*, 19 January 2019.

97. Garland, *Culture of Control*, passim; Thomas Mathiesen, "The Future of Control Systems: The Case of Norway," in David Garland and Peter Young, eds., *The Power to Punish* (London 1983) 137.

98. Stuntz, "Pathological Politics," 519–520.

99. Most of the literature on overcriminalization cited elsewhere here takes a moderately Leftist approach, but see also ACLU Pennsylvania, *More Law, Less Justice* (October 2019), https://www.aclupa.org/sites/default/files/field_documents/more_law_less_justice_10.16.2019_read_this_version.pdf. From the Right, see Paul J. Larkin Jr., *The Extent*

of America's Overcriminalization Problem, Heritage Foundation (9 May 2014), https://www.heritage.org/report/the-extent-americas-overcriminalization-problem; Copland and Mangual, *Overcriminalizing America*; Paul Rosenzweig and Brian W. Walsh, *One Nation under Arrest: How Crazy Laws, Rogue Prosecutors, and Activist Judges Threaten Your Liberty* (Washington DC 2010); Paul Craig Roberts and Lawrence M. Stratton, *The Tyranny of Good Intentions: How Prosecutors and Law Enforcement Are Trampling the Constitution in the Name of Justice* (New York 2008).

100. Gary Fields and John R. Emshwiller, "Federal Offenses: As Criminal Laws Proliferate, More Ensnared," *Wall Street Journal*, 23 July 2011.

101. Fields and Emshwiller, "Federal Offenses"; Dubber, "Criminalizing Complicity," 997.

102. William Seagle, *There Ought to Be a Law: A Collection of Lunatic Legislation* (New York 1933) 7.

103. James Bryce, "Laissez Faire," in his *The American Commonwealth* (London 1888).

104. S. J. Barrows, "New Crimes and Penalties," *Forum* (January 1900) 539.

105. Katharine K. Baker, "Sex, Rape, and Shame," *Boston University Law Review* 79 (1999) 687.

106. Sexual Offences Act 2003; Reiner, *Politics of the Police*, 143; Jeannie Suk, "Criminal Law Comes Home," *Yale Law Journal* 116 (2006) 8, 58–59; Simon, *Governing through Crime*, chap. 6.

107. Garland, *Culture of Control*, 132; John Conyers Jr., "The Incarceration Explosion," *Yale Law and Policy Review* 31 (2013) 379.

108. Mary Fulbrook, *The People's State: East German Society from Hitler to Honecker* (New Haven 2005) 70–71; Amy Qin, "Chinese City Uses Facial Recognition Technology to Shame Pajama Wearers," *New York Times*, 21 January 2020; James E. Starrs, "The Regulatory Offense in Historical Perspective," in Gerhard O. W. Mueller, ed., *Essays in Criminal Science* (South Hackensack 1961) 254; Strosnider, "Anti-gang Ordinances," 110, 133; Danielle Demetriou, "Japanese School Pupils Told: Dye Your Hair Black to Fit in," *Telegraph*, 22 May 2019; Benhabib, *Rights of Others*, 183–185.

109. Bouke de Vries, "The Right to Be Publicly Naked: A Defence of Nudism," *Res Publica* 25 (2019) 408–409.

110. Ken Jennings, *Planet Funny: How Comedy Took Over Our Culture* (New York 2018) 252.

111. Samuel Brenner, "'Negro Blood in His Veins': The Development and Disappearance of the Doctrine of Defamation *per se* by Racial Misidentification in the American South," *Santa Clara Law Review* 50 (2010) 338–341.

112. Jonathan Petropoulos, *Artists under Hitler* (New Haven 2014) 160; Dietz Bering, *The Stigma of Names: Antisemitism in German Daily Life, 1812–1933* (Ann Arbor 1992) 249; Roger Karoutchi and Olivier Babeu, *Jean Zay* (Paris 2006) 85–86.

113. Baker, "Revisiting the Explosive Growth of Federal Crimes," 1; Copland and Mangual, *Overcriminalizing America*, 7.

114. James A. Strazella, *The Federalization of Criminal Law*, American Bar Association, Task Force on Federalization of Criminal Law (Chicago 1998) 7. This growth of federal criminal provisions was due in part to the federal government's

encroachment on what had been largely a local state matter. See Susan A. Ehrlich, "The Increasing Federalization of Crime," *Arizona State Law Journal* 32 (2000).

115. Lucia Zedner, "Is the Criminal Law Only for Citizens? A Problem at the Borders of Punishment," in Katia Franko Aas and Mary Bosworth, eds., *The Borders of Punishment: Migration, Citizenship, and Social Exclusion* (Oxford 2013) 41; Dutton, "Toward a Government of Contract," 191.

116. Smith, "Overcoming Overcriminalization," 544.

117. Creveld, *Rise and Decline of the State*, 166.

118. 2016: 1.3 million active military personnel, 933,000 law enforcement employees, 650,000 officers, 810,000 private-security employees. Office of the Under Secretary of Defense, Personnel and Readiness, *Population Representation in the Military Services: Fiscal Year 2016 Summary Report*, 2, https://www.cna.org/pop-rep/2016/summary/summary.pdf; Federal Bureau of Investigation, *2016 Crime in the United States*, table 25, https://ucr.fbi.gov/crime-in-the-u.s/2016/crime-in-the-u.s.-2016/tables/table-25; Statista, *Security Services in the U.S.* (2018) 26.

119. UK Ministry of Defence, *UK Armed Forces Quarterly Service Personnel Statistics, 1 July 2018* (23 August 2018) 1, https://assets.publishing.service.gov.uk/government/uploads/system/uploads/attachment_data/file/735105/20180701-_SPS.pdf; House of Commons Library, "Police Service Strength," 19 April 2018, https://researchbriefings.parliament.uk/ResearchBriefing/Summary/SN00634; CoESS, "Facts and Figures, Private Security in Europe 2015," 1 July 2017, http://www.coess.org/newsroom.php?page=facts-and-figures.

120. Quoted in Baumgartner et al., *Suspect Citizens*, 8.

121. The class disparities of justice are the subject of countless justifiably angry exposés, of which Tony Platt's *Beyond These Walls: Rethinking Crime and Punishment in the United States* (New York 2018) serves as a good example.

122. Arthur Cleveland Hall, *Crime in Its Relations to Social Progress* (New York 1902) 274–276, 326–329.

123. Some comparative figures for the last two decades of the twentieth century are given in US Bureau of Justice Statistics, *Cross-National Studies in Crime and Justice*, NCJ 200988 (September 2004) ix, xi.

124. 2.7 percent of adults had ever served time in state or federal prisons in 2001 compared to 1.3 percent in 1974. This average varied widely, of course, by sex and ethnicity, from 0.3 percent of white women to almost 17 percent of Black men in 2001. Thomas P. Bonczar, *Prevalence of Imprisonment in the U.S. Population, 1974–2001*, Bureau of Justice Statistics Special Report, NCJ 197976 (August 2003).

125. Georgina Sturge, *UK Prison Population Statistics*, House of Commons Library, Briefing Paper CBP-04334, 23 July 2019, 5, https://researchbriefings.parliament.uk/ResearchBriefing/Summary/SN04334.

126. Alex Kozinski and Misha Tseytlin, "You're (Probably) a Federal Criminal," in Timothy Lynch, ed., *In the Name of Justice* (Washington DC 2009) 44; Luna, "Overcriminalization Phenomenon," 726.

127. Amy Lerman and Vesla Weaver, *Arresting Citizenship: The Democratic Consequences of American Crime Control* (Chicago 2014) 30–36; Kohler-Hausmann, *Misdemeanorland*, passim.

128. Matthew R. Durose et al., *Recidivism of Prisoners Released in 30 States in 2005: Patterns from 2005 to 2010*, Bureau of Justice Statistics, Special Report, NCJ 244205 (April 2014).

129. Thomas P. Bonczar and Allen J. Beck, *Lifetime Likelihood of Going to State or Federal Prison*, Bureau of Justice Statistics, Special Report, NCJ 160092 (March 1997).

130. Kohler-Hausmann, *Misdemeanorland*, 77–78; Daniel Ohana, "Günther Jakob's *Feindstrafrecht*," in Markus D. Dubber, ed., *Foundational Texts in Modern Criminal Law* (Oxford 2014) 355; Zedner, "Is the Criminal Law Only for Citizens?" 42; Vormbaum, *Modern History of German Criminal Law*, 253.

131. Michael Tonry, "Ethnicity, Crime, and Immigration," in Michael Tonry, ed., *Ethnicity, Crime, and Immigration* (Chicago 1997) 6. In a misguided spirit of equality, the French do not collect data on ethnic minorities, thus blinding themselves statistically to the problem. According to informal tallies, the overrepresentation of minorities in prison is even worse in France than in the United States (Fassin, *Prison Worlds*, 61–63).

132. Lacey, *Prisoners' Dilemma*, 144–146; OECD, *Society at a Glance 2006*, chart C02.2, 105.

133. Tonry, "Ethnicity, Crime, and Immigration," 12; Loïc Wacquant, "'Suitable Enemies': Foreigners and Immigrants in the Prisons of Europe," *Punishment and Society* 1, 2 (1999) 216–217.

134. Brian Bell and Stephen Machin, "Immigration and Crime: Evidence for the UK and Other Countries," Migration Observatory, 13 November 2013, 6, http://www.migrationobservatory.ox.ac.uk/wp-content/uploads/2016/04/Briefing-Immigration_and_Crime.pdf.

135. Barker, *Nordic Nationalism*, 91–92.

136. Mühlhahn, *Criminal Justice in China*, 21.

137. Paul Weithman, "Augustine's Political Philosophy," in Norman Kretzmann and Elenore Stump, eds., *Cambridge Companion to Augustine* (Cambridge 2001) 238.

138. Frank E. Manuel and Fritzie P. Manuel, *Utopian Thought in the Western World* (Cambridge MA 1979) 56–58, 419, 423, 544, 546, 735–736; Krishan Kumar, *Utopianism* (Milton Keynes 1990) 56–57.

139. P. J. Proudhon, *Idée générale de la révolution au dix-neuvieme siècle*, 2nd ed. (Paris 1851) 339; Bernard E. Harcourt, *The Illusion of Free Markets: Punishment and the Myth of Natural Order* (Cambridge MA 2011) chap. 1.

140. Robert Sharlet, "Stalinism and Soviet Legal Culture," in Robert C. Tucker, ed., *Stalinism* (New Brunswick 1999) 168–178; Kamenka and Tay, "Beyond the French Revolution," 125.

141. Alan Hunt, "Foucault's Expulsion of Law," *Law and Social Inquiry* 17, 1 (1992). Though others argue that this is due largely to Foucault's only late interest in other forms that law has taken in the era of governmentality. Pat O'Malley and Mariana Valverde, "Foucault, Criminal Law, and the Governmentalization of the State," in Dubber, *Foundational Texts*, 323.

142. Durkheim, *Division of Labour*, 59–64, 79–80, 83.

143. Axel Hannerz, *Cultural Complexity: Studies in the Social Organization of Meaning* (New York 1993).

144. Robinson and Darley, "Utility of Desert," 474.

145. Steven Lukes and Devyani Prabhat, "Durkheim on Law and Morality: The Disintegration Thesis," *Journal of Classical Sociology* 12, 3–4 (2012) 370–371, 378–380.

146. Durkheim, "Two Laws of Penal Evolution," 98.

147. I share some of the view of the state's omnicompetence, although when it is argued in a purely theoretical way, with little historical backing, it suffers from unfalsifiability. See Peter J. Steinberger, *The Idea of the State* (Cambridge 2004) 176–187.

Index